To
Deanna
With best wishes
Srini
Nov 15, 2005.

To my mother, Mythili;
my wife, Kanchan;
and my daughters, Tanu and Madhu

TABLE OF CONTENTS

14 PRINCIPLES FOR
BUILDING & MANAGING THE LEAN SUPPLY CHAIN

LEAN SUPPLY CHAIN PRINCIPLE 1

Improving the performance of every subsystem does not necessarily improve system performance. Improvements in subsystem performance must be gauged only through their impact on the whole system.

LEAN SUPPLY CHAIN PRINCIPLE 2

Focus on improving the performance of the lean supply chain—but do not ignore the supply chain's business ecosystem.

LEAN SUPPLY CHAIN PRINCIPLE 3

Focus on customer needs and process considerations when designing a product. Enterprises can gain tremendous competitive advantage through best-in-class practices that cut across industries.

LEAN SUPPLY CHAIN PRINCIPLE 4

Maximize external variety while minimizing internal variety. Maintain inventories in an undifferentiated form for as long as it is economically feasible to do so.

LEAN SUPPLY CHAIN PRINCIPLE 5

Buffer variation in demand with capacity, not inventory.

LEAN SUPPLY CHAIN PRINCIPLE 6

Use forecasts to plan and pull to execute. A system that reacts to pull signals will have less variation than a comparable system that adopts a push mode of operation.

LEAN SUPPLY CHAIN PRINCIPLE 7

Build partnerships and alliances with members of the supply chain strategically, with the goal of reducing the total cost of providing goods and services.

LEAN SUPPLY CHAIN PRINCIPLE 8

The role of operations strategy is to give the enterprise the ability to cope with changing customer preferences. Products and processes should be designed to promote strategic flexibility.

LEAN SUPPLY CHAIN PRINCIPLE 9

Formulate performance measures that allow the enterprise to better align functions and move from a functional to a process orientation.

LEAN SUPPLY CHAIN PRINCIPLE 10

Time lost at a bottleneck resource results in a loss of productivity for the whole enterprise (entire supply chain). Time saved at a non-bottleneck resource is a mirage.

LEAN SUPPLY CHAIN PRINCIPLE 11

Decisions should promote a growth strategy. While enterprises should attempt to simultaneously increase throughput, decrease inventory, and decrease operating expenses, the focus must be on improving throughput.

LEAN SUPPLY CHAIN PRINCIPLE 12

Focus on bottleneck resources because they control the flow. Synchronize flow by first scheduling the bottleneck resources on the most productive products; then schedule non-bottleneck resources to support the bottleneck resources.

LEAN SUPPLY CHAIN PRINCIPLE 13

Do not focus on balancing capacities. Focus on synchronizing the flow.

LEAN SUPPLY CHAIN PRINCIPLE 14

Reduce variation in the system. Reduced variation allows the supply chain to generate higher throughput with lower inventory and lower operating expense.

FOREWORD

For many executives, the organization's delivered product or service is the absolute focus—its performance, styling and price create the "market-place buzz," customer satisfaction, wealth and future growth. But underlying an organization's ability to provide valued products and to profitably grow is a core competency that is increasing in complexity and importance—specifically, the competency of *supply chain integration and management.*

Dr. Srinivasan's book, *"Streamlined: 14 Principles for Building and Managing the Lean Supply Chain"* could not come at a more appropriate time in this period of industrial change. Srini brings his years of experience as a practitioner, researcher, teacher and editor to the task of clearly identifying the principles for attacking this fundamental challenge that is facing industry today. So many times, business books only address one segment of an audience. Srini uses a holistic approach in addressing the supply chain, and he makes the book very easy to read even for someone without a manufacturing background. Srini's book provides a much-needed coverage of how the theory of constraints, with its "enterprise, or systems, view" of the lean supply chain, combines with lean concepts and practices to provide specific approaches and tools for improvement.

There is no sense of tedium—*"Streamlined"* flows well—its readers are not pushed through the text; rather they experience the benefit of being pulled through the material. His initial chapters develop the basic principles required for building the lean supply chain and enhancing its competitiveness in the marketplace. His subsequent chapters provide principles for managing the lean supply chain and improving its profitability. The flow of the principles presented gives experts and non-experts a real appreciation of the tremendous benefits resultant from the joint application of lean and theory of constraints. Srini provides numerous examples to illustrate the principles that he presents in the book. These examples provide real world issues, best approaches for breaking down large problems to identify root cause, and the ways to most effectively progress in creating a leaner supply chain.

In all for-profit companies, the returns on invested capital are linked directly to operating margins and to the velocity with which products flow through the organization to the paying customers. Both margins and velocity are *directly and critically* linked to an organization's competency in supply chain integration and management. In many companies the supply chain network provides two-thirds or more of the value of their products!

Srini's *"Streamlined"* aligns very well with the direction that industry is heading. For example, to support the current ramp-up for the Air Force's F/A-22 fighter aircraft, Lockheed Martin Aeronautics has had to make major strides in managing and deploying a lean supply chain. The F/A-22 Raptor is being produced using a lean production system. This world-class production capability includes a pulsed assembly line with point-of-use provisioning of tools and parts. The line has been designed ergonomically to enhance productivity and worker safety and health. Major sub-systems and components, such as the engines, transparencies, landing gear and avionics, are secured and staged contiguous with the line to improve the production velocity. To exploit the full potential of this lean production system, the flow of each and every item required in the final F/A-22 Raptor product must be known. Enabling (or conversely, constraining) this lean production line are 1,000 suppliers in 43 states and seven countries. The supply chain business model is network centric and "touches" suppliers at every tier within the chain. The roles for strategic suppliers and preferred suppliers are clearly defined and used to establish the overall supply base for the Raptor Program. Suppliers are involved in the early stages in the design, and continuous focus is placed on ensuring that the suppliers have access to all information and capabilities needed to deliver material on time. The purpose of the network-centric business model is to enhance the effectiveness of the entire supply chain in adding value to the paying customer's product or service and eliminating waste.

The vast majority of industry recognizes that supply chain integration and management must be a core business competency. The industrial base is in a state of significant change, and more change is on the way. *"Streamlined"* is value added in this journey. There are so many ways to approach this topic that we often make things too complicated. This book helps us to see when we are making it difficult for ourselves—once again, a principles-based approach keeps focus on what really matters.

"Streamlined" is focused exactly on the right audience—students, entry-level practitioners and the managers involved directly in supply chain integration and management. This book is a "must read" for the targeted audience since they are on the front line in the quest to effectively integrate and manage the supply chain into the overall realization of products valued by the customers.

Ralph Heath
Executive Vice President of Lockheed Martin Aeronautics Co. and General Manager of the F/A-22 Raptor program.

PREFACE

Managers in the business world hear the words "supply chain" practically every day. They know that to succeed in an increasingly competitive global economy they must manage their businesses more effectively. They also know that the efficiency of the supply chain will affect the profitability of their business, and so they have to manage their business in the context of the supply chain.

Though they may have read many books and heard all the recent buzzwords, most managers still find it difficult to see what must be done in order to really *manage* their business, or how they can go outside the four walls of their enterprise to manage their supply chain more efficiently. This book is written to help those managers. It presents key principles for building and managing the lean supply chain in a systematic manner. At the same time, the book presents specific steps and instructions to help the manager deal with the complexities of running the business from a logistics and operations perspective.

Motivation for the book

I was motivated to write this book in the early 1990s when I began to teach in executive M.B.A. programs and work on a number of projects with participants from the Lean Enterprise Systems Design Institute at the University of Tennessee. Having worked in the automobile industry for many years, I was eager to present in my seminars the developments in lean thinking, the theory of constraints, and factory dynamics.

These topics were cutting edge concepts at that time. Most business schools were still teaching traditional disaggregated topics like location planning, capacity planning and materials requirement planning, topics that were not adequate to equip professionals to manage enterprises in an increasingly competitive environment. I was unable to find one single book that covered all the topics I was interested in teaching.

Moving into the 21st century, it became increasingly apparent that the battleground was shifting—from competition between enterprises to competition between supply chains. The need to integrate supply chain concepts into the curriculum made it all the more necessary to write a comprehensive book that would cover all the topics of interest.

What is unique about this book?

Many books address lean thinking or the theory of constraints. Many other books address the supply chain. Most of these books present concepts at a high level, without detailing just how to translate the concepts into practice, or showing how lean thinking and the theory of constraints can work together to provide a significant competitive advantage for the enterprises in a supply chain. This is the first book to explain what a lean supply chain is in depth. It presents 14 guiding principles for building and managing the lean supply chain; principles that are both meaningful *and* practical. At the same time, the book offers a good understanding of how to implement lean thinking and the theory of constraints, offering *specific tools* to integrate the supply chain, especially in the chapters that discuss how to create flow through the supply chain and do rate-based planning.

Rate-based planning is an example of an area that has been discussed in the past, but only from a conceptual perspective. To my knowledge, this is the first time the reader is shown *how to actually implement* rate-based planning and scheduling. I thank Ken Gilbert for his contribution in moving this topic beyond the concept stage so that the reader can understand how rate-based planning can help the enterprise become more flexible and responsive to customer needs.

Flow of material

Supply chains can be addressed from many functional perspectives—financial, marketing, operations, logistics, etc. This book is concerned with operations and logistics. The flow of material is organized in four parts.

Part I, "Envisioning the Lean Supply Chain," points out that every enterprise is part not just of a supply chain but also of a larger business ecosystem that includes the supply chain itself and other entities, such as the stakeholders, regulatory agencies, and competing supply chains. This awareness is essential for managers who want to manage the supply chain more effectively.

Part II, "Building the Lean Supply Chain," walks through the steps required to build lean supply chains. The presentation in Part II progresses in a top-down manner; it moves from a discussion of general principles for building lean supply chains to partnering in the supply chain, then down to the enterprise level on operations strategies and on integrating the different functions within the enterprise.

In Parts III and IV, the presentation moves from the enterprise back to the supply chain. Part III, "Achieving Exceptional Performance," is mainly concerned with two key tools for achieving exceptional performance: the Theory of Constraints and Lean Thinking. These two tools have typically been applied only for managing operations within the enterprise. In Part IV, "Managing the Lean Supply Chain," we show how these tools can be applied in conjunction with information technology to significantly leverage the performance of the lean supply chain. Part IV also presents rate-based planning, a powerful technique that allows enterprises in a supply chain to plan their operations at the same rate that the *end-customer* is demanding products.

The glossary contains definitions of the acronyms used in the book. The figure below presents the flow of the material in the book graphically.

Figure PI: The Progression of Topics in the Book

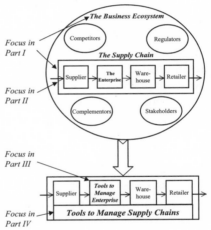

Part I: Envisioning the Lean Supply Chain
Lean Supply Chains and Business Ecosystems

Focus in Part I

Part II: Building Lean Supply Chains
Lean Supply Chains: The Foundation
Partnering in the Supply Chain
Operations Strategies: How to Compete

Focus in Part II

Part III: Achieving Exceptional Performance
Lean Thinking
Systems Thinking and the Theory of Constraints
Success Stories in Applying Lean Thinking and
Theory of Constraints

Focus in Part III

Part IV: Managing the Lean Supply Chain
Creating Flow through the Supply Chain
Rate-Based Planning: Planning and Scheduling
the Drumbeat
Effective Deployment of Information Technology

Focus in Part IV

Who should read this book

Although the original intent was to write a book for M.B.A. students, both entering and executive, the book evolved rapidly to one a professional could readily use. It can be a guide for logistics and operations professionals to better manage their activities within the broader context of the supply chain they have to deal with. At the same time, the book should still be valuable to students in an executive M.B.A. or similar professional program that offers courses in operations, logistics, and supply chain management. It is also a useful reference book for educators, consultants and practitioners who interact with any element in the supply chain.

ACKNOWLEDGMENTS

This book is the product of my interactions with industry professionals, colleagues and graduate students over the past decade. These individuals have generously shared their knowledge and enriched my understanding of the supply chain.

Special thanks are due to Ken Gilbert and "Shri" Srikanth for their contributions to this book. I have learned a great deal from Ken Gilbert over these years. He has helped frame my thoughts in a number of chapters; in particular, Chapter 9 is entirely his contribution. Shri was a catalyst for this book project and we have had several stimulating discussions on the future of information technology in supply chain management; Chapter 10 is mostly his contribution. I owe a lot to Tom Greenwood who inspired me with his knowledge and understanding of the lean enterprise. The following individuals provided specific data and support for preparing Chapter 7 in this book: K. Mahesh, N. Kirithivasan, R. Ramasubramanian, V. R. Janardhanam, and Tom Nied of Sundaram Brake Linings, Ltd.; Darren Jones and Mike Wilson of the Marine Corps Logistics Base, Albany, Georgia.

I want to acknowledge the support of Chad Toney and Amanda Baugous for carefully and patiently reading through practically the entire manuscript and for their many helpful comments. My colleagues, Bruce Behn, Alex Miller and Mahender Singh provided insightful comments on a number of chapters. I also wish to acknowledge valuable input from some of the participants in our executive MBA programs: Angelia Epps, Bob Russell, Ron Dresen, Bob Hochwarth, Eric Daggett, Rob Whittaker, Terry Sutton, Wayne Grachek and Cathy Johnson. Elizabeth Lowry provided valuable support, expediting the publication of this book. Thanks are due to Steve Momper, Senior Acquisitions Editor of Thomson/South-Western, for his support through the entire project.

Finally, I would like to thank my wife, Kanchan, who showed a great deal of patience and understanding during the past two years that I have worked on this project. She has been a constant source of support and encouragement.

Envisioning the Lean Supply Chain

1

Lean Supply Chains and Business Ecosystems

"Our imagination is the only limit to what we can hope to have in the future."

Charles F. Kettering, Inventor

I magine, for a moment, a supply chain[1] that operates as follows: The consumer demands a product from its supplier (the retailer). The retailer fills this order immediately and places an order with *its supplier* (the factory) to replenish the inventory. The factory processes a unit of raw material to fill the retailer's order right away, places an order with its raw material supplier to replenish the material just consumed—and so on all the way up and down the supply chain.

This is a vision of a supply chain that every enterprise would like to be part of. Every member of the chain works with short cycle times and a level production schedule, responds very quickly to a demand from a customer, and delivers just what the customer wants, on time. In this supply chain, enterprises are able to fill orders at relatively low cost, without having to carry a lot of inventory.

Such a vision was unattainable for many businesses in the past. Has anything changed in recent years to bring reality closer to the vision?

Yes—the whole business landscape has changed:

- The Internet and advances in information technology now make it possible for supply chain members to observe the end user's actual demand.

---

1. A supply chain is a network of the enterprises involved in delivering specific products to the consumer. It includes the enterprise itself, its upstream suppliers, any downstream enterprises that may further process the products, and possibly a distribution system consisting of distributors, wholesalers, and retailers.

- A revolution in manufacturing methods has led to a quantum reduction in the time it takes a manufacturer to fulfill customer demand.
- Advances in logistics have achieved similar quantum reductions in the time products spend in storage and in transit.
- There is a perceptible change among members of many supply chains to set aside their traditional arms-length relationships and build long-term partnership arrangements in industries as diverse as automobile manufacturing, aerospace, healthcare, grocery retailing, and apparel manufacturing.

Yes, we are in a better position to realize this vision of a *lean supply chain*.

THE LEAN SUPPLY CHAIN

A lean supply chain integrates all the key processes and partners necessary to deliver the final product to the user. Lean supply chains adapt to changing customer needs and still deliver products quickly. As a result, enterprises that are part of a lean supply chain have lower costs than their competitors. A survey by the Supply Chain Council found that, on average, enterprises spent about 11 percent of revenue on supply chain management, yet best-in-class enterprises got the cost down to between 3 and 6 percent.[2]

To understand the impact of these numbers, note that logistics-driven costs alone accounted for $970 billion in the United States in 2001.[3] Those costs translate into approximately 9.5 percent of gross domestic product (GDP). Reducing these costs by 5 percent would save about *$50 billion*. That is not small change. And logistics is only one of the many cost components in the supply chain. If other costs—order processing, materials acquisition and inventory, supply chain planning, supply chain financing, and information management—are considered, the potential savings from effective supply chain management would be much higher.

Moreover, these figures do not take into account a multitude of costs that are either hidden or, in Dr. Deming's terms, "unknown and unknowable."[4] Nor do they consider the less quantifiable

---

2. OpMg. 2001. "Optimizing Costs along the Supply Chain." *Operations Management Roundtable,* April 2001, *www.omr.executiveboard.com.*

3. R. Wilson and R.V. Delaney (2002), "Understanding Inventory—Stay Curious!" 13th Annual 'State of Logistics Report,' *http://www.mi-clm.org/downloads/13th%20Annual%20state%20of%20the%20Logistics.pdf.*

4. Deming, W. E. 1982. *Out of the Crisis.* Cambridge, MA: MIT Center for Advanced Engineering Study.

benefits. They do not, for example, consider the potential for increased market share for supply chains that respond faster to customer needs.

A recent study that analyzed the link between supply chain and financial performance[5] revealed that virtually all winning business strategies have, at their core, supply chain strategies that provide a competitive advantage. Zara is a Spanish clothing manufacturer/retailer whose supply chain strategy is to set the industry standards for time to market, costs, order fulfillment, and customer satisfaction. At the heart of this enterprise's success is a vertically integrated business model that spans design, just-in-time production, marketing, and sales. This model gives Zara more flexibility than its rivals to respond to fickle fashion trends.

Unlike other international clothing chains, Zara makes more than half its clothes in-house instead of relying on a network of disparate and often slow-moving suppliers. To do so, Zara has adopted a number of lean management techniques: It acquires fabrics in only four colors and delays committing these fabrics to the dyeing and printing operations until the last stage of production. By delaying commitment to special colors, Zara substantially reduces buildup of unwanted inventory that might otherwise have to be cleared through huge markdown sales—a chronic problem for enterprises in the clothing industry.

Zara keeps designers attuned to changing customer preferences. Sales managers send timely customer feedback from its 450 retail stores to inhouse designers. Because of better-managed inventories, reduced obsolescence, and tight linkages between demand and supply, Zara is clearly well positioned to gain market share. It's no wonder that in May 2001 *The Economist* identified Zara as the "world's fastest growing retailer."[6]

CHALLENGES TO THE LEAN SUPPLY CHAIN

Although the potential benefits are huge, building and managing a lean supply chain poses a challenge because supply chain activities are so highly interconnected. The present business environment is also significantly more challenging than the business environment of the production-centric era that prevailed for the

---

5. D'Avanzo, R., H. von Lewinski, and L. N. Van Wassenhove. "The Link Between Supply Chain and Financial Performance." *Supply Chain Management Review,* November/December 2003, pp. 40–47
6. "Spain's Zara: Floating on Air." *The Economist,* May 17, 2001, pg. 68

greater part of the 20th century. In that era, demand for goods and services often outstripped production capacity. The producers held the most clout in the supply chain, charged what the market would bear, and operated businesses to maximize utilization of their own scarce capacity. In many industries, lack of global competition created, in effect, domestic cartels that dictated the price consumers paid for the product. Enterprises were able to run their business in relative isolation, formulating strategies that optimized their own operations with little regard for how these decisions affected the other enterprises in their supply chain.

Today, we are in the era of the consumer. In a customer-centric world, production capacity exceeds customer demand in many industries. Prices are now determined by more competitive market forces than existed when capacity constrained sales volume. Insightful managers in today's business world are well aware of the fierce competitive environment in which they must manage their enterprises. Consumers are demanding better products, and they want them cheaper and faster. To stay competitive, enterprises are compelled to respond to these customer demands even as product life cycles are getting smaller and smaller. Still, a number of model enterprises are rising to the challenge and are establishing their dominance in this new era. For instance, as a result of its superior supply chain management, Zara, the Spanish clothing giant can introduce a new line of garments in three weeks—the industry standard for introducing a new line is between five to nine months.

The consumer-centric era requires businesses to manage their supply chains in a radically different manner. To respond to increasingly demanding consumers, enterprises not only have to excel at *producing* the goods or service they sell; they must also excel at *delivering* products quickly and efficiently to the consumer. As the business environment becomes more challenging, enterprises must continuously search for ways to deal with these challenges. Fortunately, such tools are already available. Philosophies and concepts formulated in the 1980s and 1990s can be applied to the management of lean supply chains. Two of these philosophies are treated extensively in this book: (1) lean thinking and (2) the theory of constraints (TOC).

THE PHILOSOPHICAL BASIS FOR LEAN SUPPLY CHAINS

Lean thinking and TOC have typically been applied to manage operations *within* an enterprise, and most enterprises that endorse either of these philosophies apply them in isolation, drawing little synergy from them. In parts III and IV of this book, these concepts are analyzed in detail followed by a discussion on how lean thinking and TOC can work together to significantly facilitate the management of the lean supply chain. Here, only a broad overview of these philosophies and a suggestion of how they work in concert is presented.

Lean Thinking

Lean thinking is founded on the just-in-time (JIT) principles conceived by Japanese automobile manufacturers in the 1930s and perfected in the 1970s. In 1990, Womack, Jones, and Roos wrote the book, *The Machine That Changed the World*[7], that kindled interest in JIT and lean thinking in America. Not long after, in 1996, Womack and Jones elaborated on the concept in *Lean Thinking*,[8] explaining that the goal of lean thinking is to eliminate *muda* (a Japanese word for wastefulness) and prescribing a specific course of action to implement lean concepts within an enterprise.

In the United States, the principles in lean thinking were first applied in the automobile industry—a natural consequence of the fact that JIT principles had originally been tested in the automobile industry in Japan. However, lean thinking is now being successfully applied in industries as diverse as paints, furniture, electrical switchgears, aerospace, aircraft maintenance, electrical appliances, and office products.

As U.S. enterprises began to understand and embrace lean principles, the body of knowledge also started to grow. It was observed that lean principles, in particular the concept of flow, could be extrapolated beyond internal operations to entire supply chains. The lean enterprise became a new model for making, distributing, and selling products that evolved from a union of new capabilities in manufacturing, information technology, and logistics.

---

7. Womack, J. P., D. T. Jones, and D. Roos. 1991. *The Machine That Changed the World*. New York: Harper-Collins.
8. Womack, J. P., and D. T. Jones. 1996. *Lean Thinking*. New York: Simon & Schuster.

Lean thinking is directed at eliminating wasteful activity at all levels in the enterprise (and the supply chain). Eliminating wasteful activity achieves two goals:

1. It reduces lead times[9] and makes the enterprise more flexible and responsive. In a supply chain, each enterprise is more responsive to downstream customers and provides smoother, more predictable demand for upstream suppliers. For example, the Denso starter and alternator plant in Maryville, Tennessee, operates on a product cycle in which every product is made multiple times per shift. The short product cycles makes it possible for both Denso and its upstream suppliers to produce virtually in lockstep with the automobile manufacturers that use Denso's starters and alternators. Only a day or two elapses between the time a casting is made at the Denso facility and the time it becomes part of a starter or an alternator on a completed car. The benefits of this short lead time—short quality feed back loop, responsiveness to the customer, elimination of supply chain costs related to inventory tracking—are primarily realized outside the four walls of Denso's operation. In fact, if all elements of the supply chain in the automobile industry were as responsive as Denso, the automobile industry would be poised to adopt Dell, Inc.'s direct sales model.

2. The elimination of wasteful activities frees up resources for deployment elsewhere in the business. Lean thinking thus facilitates a growth strategy.[10] An enterprise that exemplifies the growth model is Michigan-based Freudenberg NOK, the American partnership of the German Freudenberg and Japan's NOK, the world's largest producers of oil seals and custom-molded rubber products. Created in 1989, this enterprise has relentlessly applied lean concepts to squeeze out waste in its processes, freeing up capacity for further growth while at the same time becoming more flexible and responsive. In barely 12 years, Freudenberg NOK quadrupled its revenues by 2001 to nearly $1 billion, and estimates revenue growth to $1.5 billion by 2005.

Enterprises that successfully implement lean concepts can respond to customer demands faster and more reliably than their competition. In turn, that encourages customers to place orders with the enterprise that better reflect the actual demand rather

---

9. The lead time is defined as the elapsed time from the moment an order is received until the time the order is executed and delivered correctly to the customer.

10. *See also* Sprovieri, J. 2001. "Want to Grow? Think Lean First." Interview of T. Greenwood, *Assembly,* August; *http://www.assemblymag.com/* and Reeve, J. "The Financial Advantages of the Lean Supply Chain." *Supply Chain Management Review,* March/April 2002, pp. 42–52

than a demand the customer has deliberately inflated to build a safety cushion, or deflated to reduce excess inventories. The enterprise can thus work with a smoother production schedule and in turn set up a smoother schedule with its materials suppliers. This facilitates strong relationships with suppliers, thus providing lean enterprises with another competitive advantage. Lean enterprises are thus able to build custom products for individual customers much more easily without having to carry large amounts of inventory.

The Theory of Constraints

The theory of constraints (TOC) states that the goal of an enterprise is to make money and it is constraints in the system that prevent it from making more money.[11] Since system constraints determine how much money the enterprise can make, the intent is to get the maximum productive use out of the constraints. TOC attacks the assumptions of the *cost world* perspective that prevails in traditionally managed enterprises. In the cost world, cost control is the key factor that drives decision-making.

The cost world perspective, for instance, could result in a decision to outsource a product currently produced in-house, moving production to an offshore location, simply because the sum of the labor and the transportation costs is less when it is produced outside the U.S. This is an example of *local optimization,* in which a decision is made based solely on product cost considerations. That decision may generate at least three negative repercussions that need to be carefully considered:

1. The decision process cannot ignore the impact of outsourcing on production costs for all the products still manufactured in-house, because these products will now bear the overhead costs that were previously absorbed by the outsourced product.
2. Even if the enterprise is willing to carry some inventory of the outsourced product, there is a possible loss of responsiveness because of the additional delays in transportation, not to mention possible delays in clearing customs. Offshoring makes the company more dependent on long-term forecasts and more vulnerable to the inevitable demand cycles.

---

11. Goldratt, E. M., and J. Cox. 1992. *The Goal: A Process of Ongoing Improvement.* Great Barrington, MA, North River Press Publishing Company.

3. Since it is no longer intimately involved in manufacturing the product, there is a real danger that the enterprise will be unable to manufacture it in-house at a later date if the situation requires it. The analogy here is that if some muscles in a body are not used, they could atrophy.

TOC avoids the pitfalls of such local thinking by adopting a global perspective, one with an objective of maximizing the profit of the enterprises rather than the profit of individual products. TOC refers to this perspective as the *throughput world* perspective. To promote a throughput world perspective, TOC looks at three measures: (1) throughput (T), (2) inventory (I), and (3) operating expense (OE). TOC defines throughput as sales revenue, less direct expenses, expressed in dollars per unit time—the rate at which the enterprise generates money through products sold per unit time. Inventory is defined as the sum of all the money invested in purchasing things needed by the enterprise to sell its products. Inventory in the TOC definition includes fixed assets. Operating expense is all the money the system spends turning inventory into throughput; OE covers all fixed costs that would be incurred by the enterprise regardless of how much it produces.

Since the goal of an enterprise is to make money, *T* is the measure that gets the most attention in TOC. Costs that are relatively fixed (measured by *OE*) are considered a secondary measure that should be subordinated to the goal of maximizing throughput. In the throughput world, there are no product costs or product profits—only an enterprise-wide profit, calculated *T − OE*. Intuitively, thinking in terms of enterprise profit rather than individual product profits leads to a more global perspective. TOC therefore promotes *systems thinking*. The three measures prescribed by TOC provide a framework for decision-making. When arriving at a decision, the manager needs to consider the following questions[12]:

1. Will the decision help sell more products profitably?
2. Will the decision help reduce investment in resources?
3. Will the decision help reduce payments or other expenses?

The prescription by TOC to focus on systems constraints to leverage T is intuitive, and a large number of enterprises have

---

12. These are questions that Jonah, the TOC guru, poses to Alex Rogo in Goldratt, E.M. and J. Cox. 1992. *The Goal: A Process of Ongoing Improvement.* Great Barrington, MA, North River Press Publishing Company.

benefited from this perspective. Valmont Industries[13] is one of them. Valmont was an $800 million enterprise that had used materials requirement planning (MRP) until 1997 to schedule its shops. It had a lot of problems with MRP, was constantly expediting deliveries, and was facing a growing number of past due orders. After Valmont implemented TOC in 1987, it soon found that its process time was significantly shorter than the lead times quoted to customers, eliminating a need for finished goods inventory. Some of the other significant benefits it reported from using TOC were:

- An immediate reduction in work-in-process (WIP)
- The disappearance of the end-of-the-month spike in production often seen in traditional enterprises, and its replacement by a more level production schedule
- Significant increase in throughput, in one of its plants, from $6.5 million in 1986 to $46.5 million in 1996.

Valmont's success story has been widely replicated. Mabin and Balderstone[14] analyzed reports by some of these enterprises. Based on a sample of 32 enterprises that reported reductions in lead times, they found that the average lead-time reduction was an impressive 69 percent, with similar improvement numbers observed in inventory levels and due-date performance. Based on a sample of 18 enterprises, the average increase in revenue (T) was 68 percent. Five of these enterprises reported increases of over 100 percent within one year. One of these enterprises, Lucent Technologies, reported a 600 percent increase in T in one year.

Synergies Between Lean Thinking and TOC

Lean thinking and TOC are philosophies that combine to support organizational growth by addressing different aspects of strategic planning. TOC, with its systems perspective, can identify the process steps that offer the greatest leverage. Then the tools provided by lean thinking remove wasteful activities at these key process steps. The result is reduced lead times and increased *throughput velocity*—the speed with which products are delivered to the customer.

---

13. *See http://www.goldratt.com/valmont.htm.*
14. Mabin, V. J., and S. J. Balderstone. 1999. *The World of the Theory of Constraints: A Review of the International Literature.* Boca Raton, FL: St. Lucie Press.

Shorter lead times result in lower inventory, and when lead times are reduced there is a corresponding reduction in supply chain inventories. The reduction in inventories facilitates the smooth flow of products along the supply chain. Correspondingly, product costs are also reduced, making the products more profitable to the enterprises in the supply chain or, alternately, more attractive to consumers if cost savings are passed on to them. Increased customer satisfaction in turn enhances the growth strategy by generating additional demand and improving market share.

The discussion so far underscores some key themes that are emphasized throughout the book—*systems thinking, lead time reduction, flexible response,* and the concept of *flow.* Information technology (IT) is a crucial enabler in this context because it provides visibility throughout the lean supply chain, further reducing any wasteful activity because actual customer demand is propagated up the supply chain, allowing its members to operate with lower inventory levels. The use of IT can also highlight any constraints that may hinder the smooth flow of the product through the supply chain.

The following quote by Fred Smith, the founder of Federal Express, effectively sums up the preceding discussion:

> *"Find the essence of each situation, like a logger clearing a log jam. The pro climbs a tall tree, locates the key log, blows it, and lets the stream do the rest. An amateur would start at the edge of the jam and move all the logs, eventually moving the key log. Both approaches work, but the essence concept saves time and effort. Almost all problems have a key log if we learn to find it."*

The quote underscores the importance of systems thinking. From a local perspective, it would have been more "intuitive" to try to move the logs, one at a time, from the outside in. The global perspective allowed the pro to rise above the situation to identify the bottleneck.

Lack of systems thinking has a number of undesirable consequences. Optimizing the separate links of the supply chain independently does not optimize the supply chain. In other words, it is no longer sufficient for an enterprise to be the best at what it does inside its own walls. It must also collaborate and communicate with partners throughout the supply chain.

SYSTEMS THINKING AND THE BUSINESS ECOSYSTEM

The traditional approach to managing a large complex system is to split it up into individual components (processes). Each process is studied in detail with a view to making it run as efficiently as possible. This is often referred to as the *analytic* approach; the root of the word "analysis," in fact, means "to break into constituent parts." The proponents of this approach recognized that it was not ideal, but they had no other means to solve the management problem. When the analytic approach breaks down the enterprise into smaller units, it charges them with meeting or exceeding specific financial goals. It is assumed that if every unit meets its budgeted target, the enterprise as a whole benefits. Each unit also competes for resources to improve its local subsystems.

Systems thinking takes a fundamentally different approach. Whereas the traditional approach studies the different subsystems in relative isolation, systems thinking is concerned with *synthesis:* with how the processes in the system interact with each other. Instead of trying to optimize a process in isolation, systems thinking works by considering all the significant interactions the process has with other processes. This can result in a radically different decision than would be generated by traditional forms of analysis, especially if the processes in the system depend on each other.

The key points to note about systems are these:

- Each system component makes a contribution to the system as a whole, but only the system delivers the end result. As an analogy, the carburetor is essential for the car, as are the engine, the tires, and all the other subsystems. But only the system in its entirety, namely the car, can serve as a means of transportation.
- To improve the performance of a system, it is not enough to improve the performance of each subsystem. Since they work together, the improvement of a subsystem is gauged only through its impact on the whole. Improving subsystem performance in isolation may actually have a negative impact on the system as a whole, or as it has been phrased: "The sum of local optima does not equate to the global optimum."

These key points are summarized by the first supply chain principle:

LEAN SUPPLY CHAIN PRINCIPLE 1

Improving the performance of every subsystem does not necessarily improve system performance. Improvements in subsystem performance must be gauged only through their impact on the whole system.

From a systems perspective, because the term *supply chain* suggests a linear relationship among the various elements in the supply chain, it is a misnomer. This term, which is so ingrained in our vocabulary, is no longer an appropriate metaphor for the integration required to competitively deliver goods and services to consumers.

Consider the characteristics of a chain. It is bidirectional, with a single beginning and end; a fixed sequence connects each link to the next in a prescribed order. Usually, the links are made of steel, never to be broken. These characteristics do not describe the emerging reality. Enterprises today are forming *trading communities* to facilitate the coordination of people, assets, and information so as to deliver the right items, in the right quantities, to the right place, at the right time. Meeting these expectations requires coordination of multiple inputs and outputs among several enterprises. It is not simply a matter of passing orders up the chain, then executing back down; the potential time delays and distortions are too great. Vendors, brokers, OEMs, transportation providers, warehouses, and customers need information to coordinate their activities if delivery of goods and services is to be timely and efficient.

Unlike a chain, the links between enterprises are not made of steel; they are fluid arrangements that can be disconnected, reconnected, or strengthened depending on the needs of the immediate customer. The idea of a *supply web* better reflects this new paradigm, though that is not yet part of the language of management.

Regardless of the term used, the supply chain is actually part of a large system that affects the operation of all the enterprises in the chain. An increasing number of enterprises are realizing that today, more than ever, they are a part of a living, breathing, constantly adapting system of interrelationships and interdependencies. They are elements in a *business ecosystem.*

THE BUSINESS ECOSYSTEM

The business ecosystem incorporates the enterprise, its customers and suppliers, its competitors, the owners/stakeholders, and government agencies and other regulatory bodies whose activity affects the operations of the enterprise. Figure 1.1 illustrates a business ecosystem for an enterprise.

Figure 1-1. The Business Ecosystem for an Enterprise

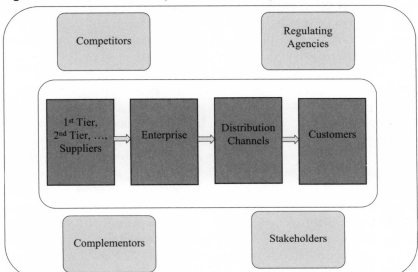

In Figure 1.1, *complementors* are business entities that facilitate the growth of an enterprise's supply chain even though they do not directly participate in it. To give a simple example, Microsoft and Intel are complementors to one another in the PC industry. Each new generation of Microsoft software creates demand for more computing power from Intel. Each new generation of Intel processors creates demand for Microsoft's latest software.

In a larger context, we view complementors not just as business entities but also as industries that nurture one another. If you are in the business of selling golf clubs, suppliers of golf shoes are complementors to your business. Similarly, advances in techniques for manufacturing silicon wafers have considerably abetted recent advances in telecommunications.

Some enterprises deliberately build, acquire, or merge with other enterprises that complement their products. Pepsi-Cola Company and Frito-Lay Company merged to form PepsiCo Inc. in 1965. PepsiCo now tries to leverage sales of products from both divisions by advertising that a bag of Doritos chips taste so much better with a can of Pepsi. The salted snack industry is a complementor in the soft drink ecosystem.

Awareness of the business ecosystem can highlight, more effectively, threats that your enterprise might encounter. To give a simple example, in the 1990s, if you were a supplier of casings to a floppy disk manufacturer and had been aware of what was happening in the ecosystem, you would have quickly pulled out of that business—you would have identified the threat posed by more efficient storage media, such as compact discs.

Understanding the ecosystem can also highlight opportunities, say, for creating synergies among the members of the ecosystem. An enterprise could conceivably team up with a competitor to co-evolve capabilities and launch a product neither could have been able to launch on their own.

To give another example of how a systems perspective and knowledge of the ecosystem can alert you to potential opportunities or threats, consider the impact of airline deregulation on the air transport ecosystem. Airline deregulation, which commenced in 1978, has been a real boon to travelers, giving them more than $19 billion in value from lower fares and more frequent schedules.[15] Within a few years of deregulation, flying went from being a privilege available only to business travelers and the rich to a common mode of transportation. It also led to a number of start-up airlines, most of which failed almost immediately.

Apart from benefiting passengers and generating a few start-up airlines, did airline deregulation affect anyone else? Consider this: If you were in the car rental business at the beginning of 1978 and had anticipated the resulting increase in airline traffic, you could have positioned yourself well for the consequent significant increase in demand for car rentals at airports.

Logistics management was also significantly affected by deregulation. The Airline Deregulations Act of 1977 and 1978, the Staggers Rail Act of 1980, the Motor Carrier Act of 1980, and the Shipping Act of 1984 affected air, rail, road, and ocean transportation in a major way. The customer directly benefited from deregulation because it made carriers more market-oriented and gave them the incentive to build a better infrastructure for their business. For instance, the airline and trucking industries expanded service to smaller cities and to other countries.

At the same time, deregulation resulted in a substantial decrease in transportation rates, especially in the airline and trucking industries. Both shippers and carriers were free to innovate with respect to products, services, routes, and prices and they were able to pass on much of the savings to their customers. Deregulation led to the rise of the air express industry and integrated third-party logistics providers (3PLs).

---

15. Lynch, M. W. 2001. "Fix The Friendly Skies." *ReasonOnline*, March 29, 2001. *http://reason.com.*

As we continue to explore ways and means of building and managing the lean supply chain, we always want to be aware of the extrinsic elements in a supply chain's business ecosystem. The ecosystem perspective can bring tangible and intangible benefits to every member of the ecosystem: An enterprise competing for a contract may win the job partly as a result of the strengths of its partnerships. When it lands that contract, its partners reap benefits as well. For the sales force of the first enterprise, the advantage is being able to sell a more complete package to the customer. Other enterprises in the ecosystem realize increased business even without having to directly promote sales of their products. For instance, an increase in the sale of putters and drivers by Callaway™ Golf Company is very likely to generate a corresponding increase in the sale of Nike™ Air Tour Tiger Woods Men's Golf Shoes. The sneaker industry is a complementor in the golf club ecosystem.

However, in the long-run, the greatest benefits of an ecosystem perspective are likely to be less tangible. Far greater benefits will come from intangibles, such as the freedom to focus on core competencies, the opportunities to connect with other supply networks and the ability to tap into their knowledge base, to help each other improve offerings and create new ones, to share in innovation, and to stay agile in the marketplace.

As you read this, you may be thinking, "I'm having enough trouble just trying to comprehend my own enterprise, let alone the whole supply chain. Why should I have to worry about a business ecosystem?" At the same time, you may also be answering this question for yourself: The ecosystem for your business plays a significant role in supply chain management. The key points to keep in mind are these:

- Too many managers devote their attention to immediate operational issues within their enterprise and ignore the supply chain in which it operates, let alone the extrinsic elements of the business ecosystem. In other words, they fail to visualize the big picture.
- The ecosystem perspective gives real meaning to the term "supply web," rather than "supply chain." In a business ecosystem, a partnership is not a marriage; it is a mesh of interlocking relationships where customers, suppliers, producers, and other supply chain partners are not just linked but interlinked.
- A partnership with an enterprise in one ecosystem could open doors for potential partnerships with other supply chains or ecosystems, enabling the enterprise to make contacts that

otherwise would not have been available. Partnerships also facilitate joint relationships with customers, and the opportunity to pursue new alliances with them.

These key points are summed up in the second lean supply chain principle:

LEAN SUPPLY CHAIN PRINCIPLE 2

Focus on improving the performance of the lean supply chain—but do not ignore the supply chain's business ecosystem.

As an example of a business ecosystem, from among the many possible choices I have picked an ecosystem that has significantly affected the business landscape over the last 25 years and brought the vision of the ideal lean supply chain painted at the start of this chapter one step closer to reality. This is the personal computer (PC) ecosystem. We will follow that up with a case study on Dell Inc., an enterprise that redefined the PC ecosystem. To facilitate the discussion, it is convenient to think of the business ecosystem as consisting of two major parts: (1) intrinsic elements (the supply chain that includes the enterprise and others involved directly in the flow of its products or services), and (2) extrinsic elements (complementors, competitors, regulatory agencies, and stakeholders).

THE PERSONAL COMPUTER ECOSYSTEM

The PC industry presents a fascinating case of business ecosystem development. In the late 1970s, Apple, Tandy Corporation, and others introduced early versions of the PC and began building ecosystems around their individual enterprises.

When IBM entered the PC industry in 1981, it adopted an open-systems approach. IBM's strategy was to depend on suppliers to provide standardized components. It encouraged the suppliers to access its computer architecture by publishing technical literature. IBM stimulated demand for its new machine through clever marketing and distribution.

The approach was a big success by any measure: IBM's PC business grew from $500 million in 1982 to $5.65 billion by 1986[16] and the IBM ecosystem dominated the market. Shortly after IBM

---

16.   Moore, J. F. 1993. "Predators and Prey: A New Ecology of Competition." *Harvard Business Review*, May-June 1993. Volume 71: pp. 75–83

entered the PC industry in 1981, it allowed other enterprises to manufacture PC clones. With IBM's open policy, most PC manufacturers just copied the format of the IBM machine.

IBM soon found that demand outstripped capacity. Perhaps as a consequence, it kept its prices high, which allowed manufacturers like Compaq and others to enter the market. IBM tried to keep up with demand, investing directly in a number of key suppliers to help them grow their businesses so they could supply IBM. Concerned that the regulators in its ecosystem could intervene with antitrust objections, IBM told the suppliers that the assistance came without any strings attached.[17] The key suppliers, like Intel and Microsoft, were thus able to diversify their risk portfolio by supplying other computer makers like Compaq. IBM did not object to its new competitors using the suppliers it had nurtured in its ecosystem because demand was still outstripping supply. By 1986, the combined revenue of sales of IBM PCs and the PC clones was approximately $12 billion. Eventually, manufacturers like Compaq began to threaten IBM's ecosystem.

On the other hand, Apple, the other market leader at that time, decided to adopt its own standards, standards that were not compatible with IBM's; it used an operating system architecture best described as closed. It refused to license its Macintosh software to the rest of the industry and policed its patents very strictly even as IBM adopted an open policy.

In July 1980, IBM asked Bill Gates of Microsoft to write the operating system for its upcoming PC. In July 1981, Microsoft bought all rights to an operating system called DOS from its developer, Seattle Computer Products, and renamed it MS-DOS. When Gates tried to get Apple to license its operating system, Apple refused. Microsoft set to work creating its own copy of an operating system for the PC market. The system went through several evolutions before it finally was fit to market as Windows 3.1. Windows 3.1 evolved to Windows 95, Windows 98 and, eventually, Windows XP.

Apple's closed-system architecture discouraged software developers from creating applications and games for it, so they concentrated on writing programs for IBM PCs and their clones. Despite an admittedly superior architecture, Apple began losing market share. Its 1986, revenues of $2 billion were completely dwarfed by the $12 billion generated by the PC makers.

---

17. Ibid.

Despite the entry of PC clone manufacturers like Compaq, IBM was still secure in its position. It had built the PC ecosystem practically from the ground up, and, in 1986, it still had about 50 percent of the market share for PCs. However, IBM's leadership role would soon be challenged. Like all PC manufacturers, IBM relied on a long supply chain with a distribution channel for pushing products out to retail outlets. The stage was ripe for a new entrant into the PC business—an entrant that would redefine the PC ecosystem.

CASE STUDY: THE BUSINESS ECOSYSTEM FOR DELL, INC.

An enterprise that exemplifies the benefits gained from lean supply chains is Dell, Inc., which has been growing its business primarily by increasing its market share in the PC world. That growth in market share has generated tremendous value for Dell shareholders. Figure 1.2 shows that as of April 2003 Dell enjoyed a *30,000 percent* increase in share price since the initial public offering in 1988.

Dell's percentage increase in share price is all the more impressive considering that the share price dropped nearly 50 percent as a result of the downturn in the industry and the dot-com meltdown that started in March, 2000. Figure 1.2 also shows the share price for Compaq Computers (now a part of Hewlett-Packard), which at one time was the market leader among PC manufacturers.

Figure 1-2. Growth in the Share Price of Dell, Inc.

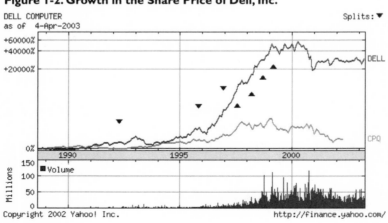

Dell continued to prosper even during the worldwide economic recession of the first few years of the 21st century. Dell's outstanding performance during this bleak period is amazing because the PC industry as a whole has been beset with plummeting prices on weakening sales. Even as other PC manufacturers continued to slash prices to sell computers in a weak market, Dell's revenues increased as it continued to grab market share. For the 52 weeks that ended January 30, 2004, Dell's revenues increased 17 percent over the previous year, to $41.44 billion and net income rose 24.6 percent, to $2.65 billion. At the start of 2003, Dell was selling $49 million online each day, which accounted for about 50 percent of its revenues, and was turning inventory 60 times per year.

How does Dell manage to deliver while its competitors are languishing? Its ecosystem has played a significant role. Consider the roles played by the intrinsic and extrinsic elements in Dell's ecosystem. Figure 1.3 illustrates Dell's business ecosystem.

Figure 1-3. Dell's Business Ecosystem

Other industries such as airline, automobile, energy, ...

Competitors: Compaq, IBM, HP, Gateway, Toshiba, ...

Regulating agencies: US Government, state governments, Malaysian government, Chinese government, local governments.........

Telephone service companies, financial institutes, third-party technical supporters, AD companies, ...

Suppliers:
o Phillips, Nokia, Samsung, Sony, Acer
o SCI, Celestica
o Seagate, Maxtor, Western Digital, IBM
o Barcelona, HP
o Hon Hai/Foxteq
o Quanta, Compal, Acer
o ....

Close proximity to suppliers

DELL:
o Enterprise systems (servers)
o Notebook computers
o Desktop computers
o ....

Direct sale

Customers:
o Home & Home Office
o Small Business (up to 400 employees)
o Medium & Large Business (over 400 employees)
o State & Local Government
o Federal Government
o Education
o Healthcare
o ....

Third-party logistics providers such as UPS, Caliber, transportation companies, ...

Stakeholders: NASDAQ, Investors

Complementors: Microsoft, digital device makers, Internet service providers, computer skills trainers, PC game developers ....

Technology development   Status of the Economy   Culture ....

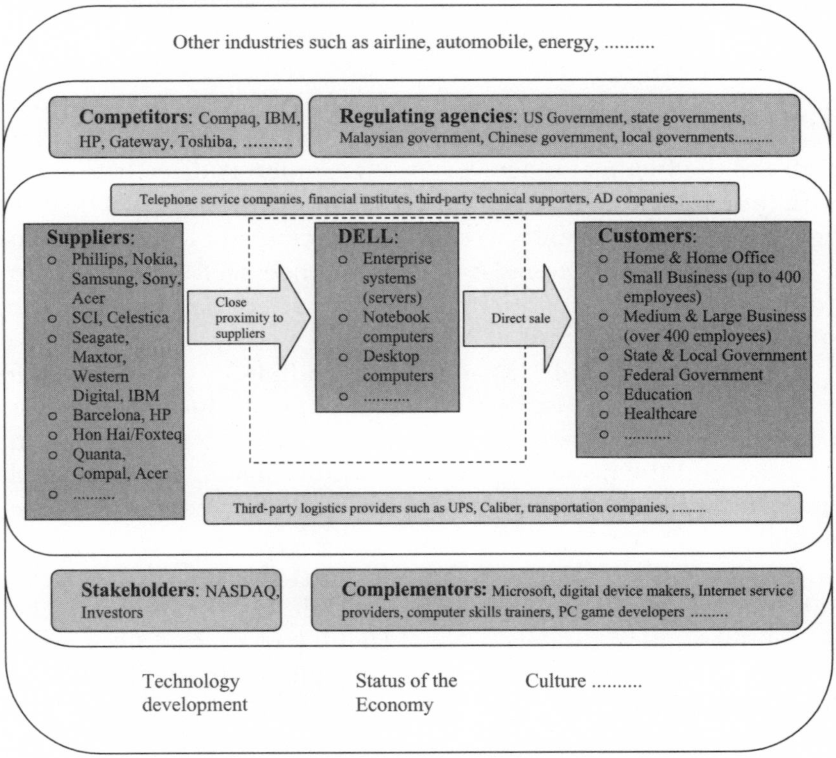

When Michael Dell started operations in 1984, under the name PCs Ltd., the business ecosystem was perfectly positioned to enable his vision of becoming the market leader in PC manufacture and assembly. The market leader at the time, IBM, had made large-scale investments in production, research and development, marketing, and distribution to exploit the PC market and had organized a PC business ecosystem centered on itself that included outside suppliers for IBM PC components, and software and distribution partners.

Capitalizing on IBM's open policy, Michael Dell began operations in Austin, Texas. The ecosystem he built was small at first, with a start-up capital of $1,000. That made Dell a fairly small player in the game, compared to IBM and Apple. However, he was assisted by the fact that the PC industry was poised for a huge growth as customers realized that the IBM PC and the Apple Macintosh could bring computing power into their homes.

THE INTRINSIC ELEMENTS

Among the intrinsic elements in Dell's business ecosystem, we will discuss the distribution and supply channels.

The Distribution Channel

Dell was the first manufacturer to sell computers directly to users with the Dell-Direct model. Dell uses the *build-to-order* (BTO) strategy that allows consumers to configure their own products, within a limited range of options. As a consequence, Dell's supply chain (the intrinsic elements in Dell's ecosystem) is simpler than the supply chain for most other enterprises.

The direct model was almost serendipitous. Michael Dell adopted the direct distribution channel at the inception of his business because it was small and he lacked both distribution partners and the power to negotiate with retailers. So he skipped the distributors and retailers and set up a telephone direct-sale model.

However, the real story of Dell starts with the emergence of the Internet as a viable technology. Since Dell was already using the direct distribution model, Michael Dell seized on the new opportunities the Internet gave him—opportunities that he could not have foreseen.

Dell depends on IT to enhance its build-to-order strategy. It uses the Internet to enhance sales and provide better technical support service. By December 1996, Dell's sales on the web had reached $1 million a day. The dramatic rise in the value of Dell stock, along with the rise in its Internet business is seen in the comparison between Dell and Compaq shown in Figure 1.2.

In addition, Dell fully exploited the capabilities of the Internet to make serious inroads into corporate and governmental agencies by using initiatives like the creation of company-specific portals. Dell has increased customer satisfaction while increasing its sales and profits by capitalizing on its integrated supply channels and technology.

When a customer places an order for a specific computer with a 17-inch monitor, the Dell information system immediately knows whether this unit is available at the Sony plant in Mexico from which the units are shipped. If the 17-inch monitors are out of stock, Dell will offer the customer the option of buying another monitor that is in stock, say, a 19-inch unit, encouraging the customer to do so by offering a discount on the usual price. In all likelihood, the customer will accept and, remarkably, Dell, the monitor supplier, and the customer all walk away with a positive feeling. Dell keeps its reputation of being able to deliver what the customers want and makes more money, as does the monitor supplier, and the customer walks away with the satisfaction of having bought a superior product at a discount. This true win-win-win scenario is referred to as *up-selling*.

At the same time, the Dell information system will also offer the customer the accessory products typically needed for the computer—power supplies, software, etc. In short, Dell has created a situation in which direct orders are handled as if there was a seasoned sales person on hand who had full knowledge about the product, its availability, and how the customer is going to use it.

Dell's Web-based sales continue to grow. In 1999, Dell introduced E-Support Direct from Dell, on-line technical support to enhance its on-line business capability. By February 2000 the company's on-line sales were generating $40 million in daily revenues, almost 50 percent of total sales.

In fact, Michael Dell is credited with creation of the Internet-enabled direct channel model that challenges all the advantages of the multitiered distribution model that Dell's competitors use. As one example of the advantage Dell enjoys, look at lifetime profits for new products in this fast-moving industry. In this industry, product prices are usually quite high, as is the production cost. However, early adopters of technology are not as price-sensitive. In a very short time, often measured in weeks, the steeply declining cost and price curves approach each other as competitors enter the picture. It is not an exaggeration to say that the total lifetime profit on a new product line in this industry is based on sales made during the first two to three months. If this window of opportunity is missed, the chances of making money are very slim.

An overlay of this picture with the Dell and Compaq distribution models shows the monumental advantage Dell enjoys. Compaq had four to six weeks of inventory tied up in the channel; Dell had just a few days. If a new Intel chip were available today, Dell could have products with the new chip to its customers in days. Compaq, on the other hand, would require several weeks before it could offer the new Intel chip to customers and it had the problem of unloading its devalued inventory of computers with older chips. While Compaq dealt with channel inventories, Dell was enjoying profits from new products. In this scenario, the faster new products were introduced, the greater the advantage Dell enjoyed. The significantly higher price-to-sales ratio that Dell enjoyed on its stock reflected the perception by Wall Street that Dell "got the Internet model" and Compaq did not.

While it was investing heavily in technology on the customer and direct model side, Dell remained one of the few companies that did not invest heavily in enterprise resource planning (ERP) systems, as competitors like Compaq did. Dell instead chose to streamline its supply chain and gain real competitive advantage while investing in technology that gave it capabilities to do things it could not have otherwise done. Only at a later and more mature stage did Dell invest in supply chain software systems, again specifically used to design the new processes Dell felt were required to support its business strategies.

The Supply Channel

To get a competitive advantage, Dell first worked with both customers and suppliers to determine the right levels of component inventory to keep in its assembly facilities. Suppliers for Dell include standard PC electronic component manufacturers like Sony (monitors), Western Digital (disc drives), Microsoft (software), and Intel (processor chip). Microsoft's dominance in PC operating systems software and Intel's growing dominance in microchips facilitated Michael Dell's vision, so he formed strategic alliances with them. As its business grew, Michael Dell *lean*-ed out the supply chain by reducing his supply base, using only preferred suppliers with whom it established long-term arrangements and partnership agreements. Dell reduced the number of suppliers from 204 in 1992 to 47 in 1997. In the three years, from 1999 to 2001, only two or three of the top suppliers changed.

Generally, sourcing of major components, such as processor chips and hard disks, is done centrally for suppliers with global capabilities, such as Intel, SCI, IBM, Samsung, and Toshiba. Most components are made in Asia and shipped to distribution centers (hubs) near Dell's assembly facilities. These distribution centers are usually within a 15 to 30 minute drive of Dell facilities. Suppliers with manufacturing facilities in the U.S. also locate their factories or warehouses nearby. For instance, Dell's assembly facility in Lebanon, Tennessee, has key suppliers virtually across the street, ready to supply them with components. When it set up operations in Ireland, Dell asked the suppliers for its Limerick plant to locate facilities within a 30 minute travel time to the plant. Similarly, in Malaysia, suppliers are located within a 15-minute travel time of the Penang plant. In some cases, components are actually kept in trucks backed up to shipping docks and pulled into Dell's plants as needed. Suppliers own the components until they are put onto Dell's assembly line.

When a customer submits an order to Dell, his or her choices are immediately relayed to Dell's suppliers, who respond immediately. Dell helps its suppliers with their own materials planning by sharing its forecasts and production plans with them. Suppliers can also access Dell's manufacturing process information to adjust their production schedules.

Trust is the core of the partnering arrangements. For example, because Dell trusts Sony to provide high-quality monitors, Dell ships PCs from its Round Rock facility without monitors. Similarly, Dell trusts third-party providers like Caliber and UPS Logistics to manage logistics so that the PC and the monitor are properly matched and delivered to the consumer, even though the PC is shipped from Round Rock and the monitor is shipped from Sony's factory in Mexico. Such partnering arrangements mean that there is only a very short time from the moment an order is placed until it is fulfilled. Dell has the additional advantage of being uniquely qualified to attract suppliers willing to do what it takes to do business with Dell because of its purchasing power.

THE EXTRINSIC ELEMENTS

Among the extrinsic elements in Dell's business ecosystem, we will discuss competitors, complementors, and regulators.

Competitors

Dell's major competitors in its core corporate PC market are Compaq, IBM, and Hewlett-Packard. In the consumer and small business market, it faces competition from Gateway, Compaq, Hewlett-Packard, Apple, and eMachines. In the portable PC business, key competitors are Toshiba, IBM, and Compaq. In the critical server and Internet infrastructure markets, Dell competes with Sun, Compaq, HP, and IBM. As Dell moves into new service businesses, such as Internet hosting, it faces new competitors, such as Exodus and Corio—some of whom may also be Dell customers.

Some manufacturers, notably Gateway, imitated Dell's model and entered the PC market, threatening Dell. As the competition in the PC industry intensified, with margins falling from 35-40 percent in the early 1990s and to 15 percent in the late 1990s, Dell fought back. Dell strengthened its supply chain in two ways: (1) it used advanced information technologies and (2) it changed its relationships with suppliers and customers. With these efforts, in 2000, Dell cut firm-wide inventory from an already enviable six days down to five. In contrast, Compaq, Gateway, and IBM averaged 50 to 90 days of inventory.

Dell now holds about two hours of component inventory in its assembly plants. Its customers' problems are usually solved within 24 to 48 hours. The fact that Dell has no more than five days of inventory on hand is a crucial advantage in a business where product life cycles are so small and the value of components in the PC depreciate very fast, sometimes up to 2 percent every week.

Complementors

IT, and in particular the Internet, is a major complementor in Dell's ecosystem. Dell depends on IT to enhance its build-to-order strategy and consolidate its supply chain. It uses the Internet to enhance sales and provide better technical support.

IT is also used widely in its manufacturing process. Dell uses Advanced Planning Systems software (Supply Chain Planner, Demand Planner, Factory Planner) to make its production plans visible to its suppliers. In mid-1999, Dell launched *valuechain.dell.com*, a secure extranet that acts as a portal for Dell suppliers to collaborate in managing the supply chain. Suppliers can log on, submit invoices, check engineering change orders, review negotiated and forecasted cost reports, and track their performance.

In 2001, Dell managed relationships with more than 80 percent of its suppliers through the Internet. At present, 90 percent of Dell's purchases from suppliers are on-line. The Internet enabled Dell to decrease the direct costs of configuration, ordering, tracking, and support for its transactional business by about 15 percent.[18]

Other complementors are telephone service providers, financial institutions, and third-party logistics service providers. Incidentally, Dell had to modify its direct sale model when it began to market its products in China since the infrastructure (and the trust in the direct model) was not in place. In 1989, less than 1 percent of Chinese citizens owned a telephone. China also lacked a mature credit system and an express delivery system until the late 1990s.

Makers of home digital devices are also complementors to Dell and they are becoming more and more important. The increasing number of such devices as digital cameras, printers, and MP3 players helps Dell sell more media-enabled PCs.

Regulators

Regulatory agencies did not affect the PC ecosystem as much as they did the software ecosystem of which Microsoft is a part, but one significant effect that local agencies had on Dell was influence on its choice of locations. In 1994, Dell, then located in Austin, was offered a package of incentives from the neighboring city of Round Rock that Austin did not attempt to match. Round Rock offered to peg taxes on Dell's sales at just 2 percent and offered a further rebate of 31 percent on the tax for the next 60 years. It also provided property tax abatements of 100 percent for five years, then 75 percent for the next five years, and 50 percent for the following 50 years.[19] Dell moved to Round Rock in 1994. The low tax rates and other incentives offered by Limerick in Ireland,

18. H. Mendelson (2000), "Dell Direct." Case No. EC-17, Graduate School of Business, Stanford University, November 2000.

19. Kraemer, K. L., and J. Dedrick. 2002. "Dell Computer: Organization of a Global Production Network." Working paper, Center for Research on Information Technology and Organizations, University of California, Irvine.

Penang in Malaysia, and Nashville in Tennessee also strongly influenced Dell's decision to locate its assembly operations in these cities.

THE FUTURE OF DELL'S BUSINESS ECOSYSTEM

Despite having good products and services produced by well-run processes, Dell will survive the natural selection that takes place in businesses only if its efficient supply chain continues to function superbly. As Moore says:

> *"Even excellent businesses can be destroyed by the conditions around them. They are like species in Hawaii. Through no fault of their own, they find themselves facing extinction because the ecosystem they call home is itself imploding. . . . Incumbency must be continually reinforced and restored. Even Intel and Microsoft, the current sovereigns of the computer chip and the PC operating software ecosystems, must be on guard, for they are constantly being challenged. . . . The major challenge for many companies is to get others to co-evolve with their vision of the future. In a global market, you want to make use of the other players—for capacity, innovation, and capital."*[20]

Being an incumbent in a stable ecosystem and having control of a dominant design, the Dell-Direct model, is certainly a nice advantage, but it is not necessarily a permanent one. In the business world, many factors favor enterprises that compete with the market leader. The dethroning of IBM with the entry of a large number of clone companies into the IBM-created PC ecosystem proves the point.

In general, Moore favors seeking out partners to create something of value, achieve market coverage, and block alternative ecosystems. In later stages of business ecosystems, members must look beyond their community for new ideas and work to prevent partners and customers from defecting. Enterprises must constantly reach out to customers to gather information that will help make possible accurate predictions about how the marketplace will change. In the corporate Galapagos, it is co-evolve, or die.

With the changing environment, Dell has to continually renew and reinforce its ecosystem. Dell is perhaps best known for the personal computers it assembles and sells, but Dell is also in the enterprise computing market with servers, data storage devices, and network switches. One significant new trend is that software

---

20. Moore, J. F. 1996. *The Death of Competition: Leadership and Strategy in the Age of Business Ecosystems.* New York: Harper Business.

developers are producing hardware while hardware makers are selling software. Dell is gearing up to deal with such trends by providing more products and services, such as personal digital assistants, MP3 players, printers, software, network integration, Internet service, financial services, etc. To recognize the company's expansion beyond computers, the stockholders approved changing the company name from Dell Computer Corporation to Dell, Inc. at the annual meeting in 2003.

What are the next steps for Dell? We are not sure. Perhaps a whole new business model and marketing strategy are needed.

SUPPLY CHAINS THROUGH THE AGES

The dependence between supply chains and the extrinsic elements of the business ecosystem will be expanded throughout this book, illustrating this dependence with examples. As background, the evolution of the supply chain through the ages is briefly examined, with a discussion on how the Industrial Revolution, technological advances, and advances in methods of transportation shaped its evolution. The discussion will reveal how extrinsic elements in the business ecosystem, in particular complementors and regulators, influenced the development of a supply chain perspective. The evolution of supply chains, leading up to the theory and practice of modern supply chain management, is framed in four distinct phases:

- **Phase 1: The Trading Supply Chain.** This phase extended from the Phoenicians of 4,500 years ago to about 1750. Most production was local, with individuals or very small groups producing products from local materials. At first products were sold only locally, but with improvements in transportation trade with 'distant' places emerged. All dominant enterprises were trading enterprises, though some were quasigovernmental, such as the East India Trading Company that flourished during the 17th and 18th centuries.

  Manufacturing supply chains began to emerge with the 18th century. The growth of the textile industry in Manchester, England in the 17th century triggered the Industrial Revolution in England, which in turn played a key role in the evolution of manufacturing supply chains. Until the Industrial Revolution, goods were often produced simply, by hand or basic machine, and were usually made within individual homes in rural areas from local raw materials. An individual or a group of individuals typically worked on any item until it was complete and ready for shipment to the customer. This was the *craft method* of production. A few craftsmen worked in shops or towns as part of associations called *guilds*.

- **Phase 2: The First Industrial Revolution.** The application of power-driven machinery to manufacturing from 1750 through 1880 defined the first Industrial Revolution. It was enabled by the steam engine and its application in new machines as well as by rapid advances in transportation. Now for the first time there was organization of production into factories. Advances in telecommunication—the telegraph and the telephone—facilitated rapid commercial transactions across the globe.

  A number of enterprises, and in a larger context, industries, played the role of complementors during this period, collaborating to leverage a better standard of living and increased productivity. Considerable synergies were established between the manufacturing and transportation industries. Steam-power generation attracted much more attention when people found that it could be used to drive machinery. Because these machines produced products so much faster, they provided the impetus for the development of manufacturing supply chains. These in turn drove innovations in transportation, such as railroads and efficient steamships. Improved communication facilitated the allocation of more resources to the development of the transportation and the manufacturing industries, creating a virtuous circle.

- **Phase 3: Mass Production, or The Second Industrial Revolution.** This period lasted about 100 years, from around 1880 to 1980. The evolution of supply chains accelerated during the mass production age, catalyzed by a number of developments. For instance, the use of electric power to drive machinery was a major step in the evolution. This development alone was responsible for most of the advances during this period. Other key catalysts were airplanes, automobiles, and telecommunication. Advances in transportation, particularly the automobile and aircraft, greatly facilitated the creation of manufacturing supply chains and also linked them with trading supply chains. The 1900s witnessed the pioneering efforts of Henry Ford that paved the way for lean thinking.

  The aftermath of World War II saw the emergence of strong financial controls to manage large industrial corporations. The mass production age covered the heyday of U.S. manufacturing in the 1950s and the 1960s—followed in the 1970s by the emergence of Japanese methods of manufacturing that undermined the preeminent position that U.S. automakers had established.

Complementors played a significant role during the mass production age. An obvious complementor to the supply chain was the digital computer, which automated many routine functions, such as the maintenance of inventory control records and the clerical functions involved in procuring components. Other obvious candidates for automation were payroll and some accounting functions. Computers also significantly facilitated the task of scheduling manufacturing activities. In turn, the digital computing industry had a complementor: the telecommunications industry.

Regulatory agencies, which had a limited role in the evolution of supply chains during the First Industrial Revolution, became prominent during the Second. First, the U.S. Congress enacted a law regulating railroads in 1887, the Interstate Commerce Act. Another law preventing large enterprises from controlling a single industry, the Sherman Antitrust Act, was enacted in 1890. Because at first these laws were not rigorously enforced, they had little or no impact on what was happening through the 19th century, but they began to be applied more stringently early in the 20th century when those sympathetic to the views of the progressives came to power.

This was the era of regulation during which many of today's regulatory agencies were created, including the Interstate Commerce Commission, the Food and Drug Administration, and the Federal Trade Commission. One agency that had a considerable impact on the ecosystem was the Federal Communications Commission (FCC), which, among other things, was responsible for the break up of AT&T into the regional Bell operating companies.

- **Phase 4: The Consumer Age, or the Customer Information Revolution.** In the 1980s, the customer came to the fore. The 1980s saw the emergence of Japanese techniques like JIT manufacturing that significantly raised the quality of mass-produced consumer goods, and that also focused the attention of managers on inventory and its impact on organizational efficiency.

  The Consumer Age is characterized by the global reach of suppliers and customers at all levels within the supply chain. It is also characterized by the extensive use of IT to "customize" goods for the consumer while optimizing processes for the producer. Dell and Wal-Mart are two enterprises that exemplify this age. The Consumer Age is covered in more detail throughout the rest of the book.

CONCLUSIONS

We live in a customer-centric era. Customer-centrism means you must take a fresh look at how you manage your enterprise. No manager can afford to manage a business in isolation; all managers need to adopt a systems perspective. The systems perspective can result in a radically different decision than would be generated by a traditional form of analysis. Improving subsystem performance in isolation could, in fact, adversely impact the performance of the system as a whole. Again, "The sum of local optima often does not add up to the global optimum."

The battleground has now shifted from competition between enterprises to competition between supply chains. It is no longer simply a case of, say, Home Depot competing against Lowe's; it is Home Depot's supply chain competing against Lowe's supply chain. Furthermore, as new products are introduced at an increasingly faster rate, managers need to look even further outwards and carefully examine the ecosystem in which their enterprise operates. Awareness of the ecosystem can alert managers both to potential threats and to potential opportunities that the enterprise can exploit.

As you work your way through this book, keep in mind the following questions:

- Does the success of your enterprise depend on partnerships and collaborative relationships within the supply chain? How aggressively is your enterprise pursuing collaborative relationships across its supply chain?
- How can your enterprise become indispensable to the supply chain?
- What types of technology are you acquiring to advance your supply chain competencies? Are you a leader or a follower? If you are a follower, what are the leaders doing?
- What techniques are you using to manage your enterprise and the supply chain? Are you applying systems thinking? Reducing lead time? Building flexible response capabilities? Are you employing concepts and philosophies like lean thinking and TOC to reduce waste and adapt to changing customer preferences?
- Are you living in the throughput world? Or are you stuck in the cost world? If you are in the cost world, how can you move to the throughput world?

PART 2

Building Lean Supply Chains

Lean Supply Chains: The Foundation

"May you build a ladder to the stars, and climb on every rung, . . . May you have a strong foundation, when the winds of changes shift."
Bob Dylan

In his path-breaking work on systems dynamics, Jay Forrester stated that:

"There will come general recognition of the advantage enjoyed by the pioneering management who . . . improve their understanding of the interrelationships between separate company functions and between the company and its markets, its industry, and the national economy."[1]

Forrester, in effect, was stressing the need for managers to understand supply chain dynamics and adopt a holistic view, a *systems perspective,* to run their business. Although he did not say so in as many words, he was urging managers to consider the business ecosystem in which their enterprise was operating. Forrester had essentially identified the key management issues associated with supply chain management.

Forrester illustrated supply chain dynamics and their effect on supply chain performance using a computer simulation created in the early 1960s as part of his research on industrial dynamics. It clearly illustrated the challenges faced in managing supply chains. The simulation, since refined, is now played as the popular Beer Game simulation.[2] The game underscores the importance of understanding supply chain dynamics and applying systems thinking to coordinate activities within and between enterprises, the crucial role lead times play in enhancing or inhibiting

---

1. Forrester, J.W. 1958, "Industrial Dynamics: A Major Breakthrough for Decision Makers." *Harvard Business Review,* 36: pp. 37-66, No. 4.
2. Forrester, J. W. 1961. *Industrial Dynamics.* Cambridge, MA: M.I.T. Press; Senge, P. M. 1994. *The Fifth Discipline: The Art and Practice of the Learning Organization.* New York: Doubleday.

competitiveness, and the role of information systems in the lean supply chain.

This chapter lays the groundwork for building lean supply chains. We first discuss supply chain dynamics so that the causes of inventory buildups, long lead times, poor flow, etc. can be identified. Following this discussion, we present seven steps enterprises can take to build the lean supply chains.

SUPPLY CHAIN DYNAMICS

In the fall of 2000, Solectron, the world's biggest contract electronics manufacturer, knew something was going awry. The major manufacturers of telecommunication equipment, including Cisco, Ericsson, and Lucent, were predicting explosive growth in demand for networking gear and wireless equipment. These telecom giants were asking Solectron and other contractors to supply components and raw materials for their operations as fast as they could, assuring them they would pay for excess materials. Solectron, which supplied each major player, knew that the supplies its customers were demanding implied a demand for telecommunications equipment that was unreasonably high, even under a best-case scenario, but it was forced to produce at maximum throughput to meet customer demands. Relying on forecasting software that projected continued growth, top management at Cisco was blindsided. It did not see the signs of a slowdown that Solectron was seeing.

In 2001, "irrational exuberance" collided with reality. The explosive growth in demand the software had been forecasting did not materialize. Instead, Cisco's sales plunged 30 percent in the third fiscal quarter of 2001. It was forced to write off $2.2 billion in inventory and lay off 8,500 people. Cisco's stock sank to less than $14 from a high of $82 just 13 months earlier.[3] When demand for their equipment shrank dramatically in 2001, all the telecom giants scaled back their operations sharply and that hit their suppliers hard. Many suppliers were left with excessive inventory that had been built in response to their customers' demand forecasts. Solectron alone was stuck with $4.7 billion in inventory.[4]

It is arguable that the problems faced by Cisco and Solectron were precipitated by the dot-com implosion, but their experiences are mirrored by enterprises in almost every industry, although not

---

3. Berinato, S. 2001. "What Went Wrong at Cisco." *CIO Magazine,* August.
4. Engardio, P. 2001. "Why the Supply Chain Broke Down." *Business Week,* March 19, 2001.

often so dramatically. Enterprises experience huge variations in inventory levels, orders, and shipments at each step in the chain, with the variations typically more pronounced the further upstream the enterprise is from the ultimate user. These demand and inventory variations result in large inventory holding costs, lost sales from stock-outs, and, most important, lack of responsiveness to customer demand. And it turns out that much of the demand variation is caused *by the supply chain* itself, not by the customer.

Consider the food industry and the experience of Barilla SpA, the world's largest pasta manufacturer. Barilla sells to a wide range of retailers through a network of wholesalers and distributors. In 1989, an analysis of the demand for dry food pasta at Barilla SpA's distribution centers and factories revealed extremely high variation in demand.[5] The variation in demand was all the more remarkable considering that the demand for pasta in Italy is fairly level.

The fast-moving consumer goods industry displays similar behavior. Consider the production and distribution of diapers. Given the consistency in diaper demand, it would be natural to expect the diaper supply chain to operate efficiently. Indeed, when logistics executives at Proctor & Gamble examined the demand for its diapers at retail stores, it found a relatively level demand. However, the orders Proctor & Gamble was placing with suppliers for this product showed considerable variation.

The Bullwhip Effect

These examples suggest that even minor fluctuations in demand at the end-user or the retail level result in huge variation in demand at upstream enterprises in the supply chain. This phenomenon is known as the *bullwhip* effect.

The term originates from the fact that a slight motion of the handle of a bullwhip can make the tip of the whip thrash wildly at speeds up to 900 miles per hour—about 20 percent faster than the speed of sound. In the context of a supply chain, the bullwhip effect manifests itself through increasing demand variability as one goes upstream in the supply chain: Small shifts in the level of customer demand experienced by the retailer are magnified as the demand information is passed up the supply chain, creating increasingly higher variation in the orders received by upstream

---

5. Hammond, J. H. 1994. "Barilla SpA (A)." Harvard Business School Case 9-694-046.

suppliers. The bullwhip effect causes tremendous inefficiencies in the supply chain. It results in excessive inventory investment, poor customer service, lost revenues, misguided capacity planning, and ineffective transportation and production schedules.

Many enterprises have gained a significant competitive advantage by understanding the causes of the bullwhip effect and working with supply chain partners to reduce it. This, in turn, enables them to reduce inventories and become more responsive to customer demand. A very effective way to demonstrate the causes of the bullwhip effect is through the Beer Game simulation.

The Beer Game

The beer game simulation assumes a serial supply chain consisting of four enterprises engaged in the production and delivery of a single blend of beer: (1) a factory, (2) a distributor, (3) a wholesaler, and (4) a retailer. Figure 2.1 illustrates this linear arrangement. The goal of each enterprise is to manage the demand imposed by its customer. Each enterprise in the supply chain is managed by one or two players. Participants are usually told that the game will run 50 weeks, although the game is determined well before that time to avoid end-gaming strategies by players.

Figure 2-1. The Bullwhip Effect in the Beer Game

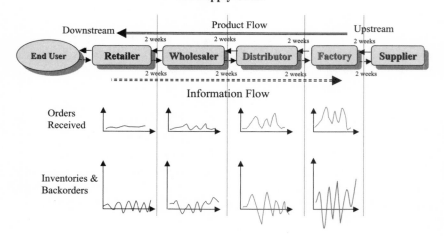

The Supply Chain

Each week, an enterprise in the supply chain receives orders from its downstream customer and places orders with its upstream supplier. At each stage there is a lag between when an order is placed and when it can be filled. Players are not allowed to share any information beyond what is conveyed by orders and shipments. All four enterprises in the supply chain have to decide what to order from their upstream supplier based on the orders they receive from their down-stream customer and their inventory on hand. There is a two-week lead time before an order placed by an enterprise reaches its upstream supplier. Similarly, there is a two-week manufacturing lead time from the time an enterprise receives an order until the shipment of the order reaches the downstream customer—in sum, a four-week lead time from the time an order is placed until it is received (see Figure 2.1).

At the start of the simulation, the system is in steady state with the consumer buying four cases of beer each week, while each enterprise is ordering and receiving four cases of beer each week. Each enterprise is holding an inventory of 12 cases of beer. The retailer's demand is revealed at the start of each week; for the first few weeks this demand is steady at four cases a week. The demand on the other enterprises in the supply chain is determined by the orders working their way upstream, again initially four cases a week. At the end of each week, each position in the supply chain decides how many cases it wishes to order from its upstream supplier.

The steady state is disrupted in week five, when the consumer increases demand to eight cases a week, which holds steady thereafter. Yet, even this one-time step change is enough to cause significant problems upstream. As the change in demand propagates upstream, shortages or surpluses accumulate at each stage in the supply chain. As Figure 2.1 shows, orders and inventories spike wildly, with the spikes magnified as one moves upstream.

Analysis of the Bullwhip Effect[6]

A familiar theme in post-game discussions is that a major cause for the chaos in the supply chain is the lack of visibility. Participants work with limited information because there is no communication permitted between them, so they all act in their own self-interest

---

6. The discussion in this section is based on Gilbert, K. 2003. "The Lean Enterprise," in E. R. Cadotte and H.J. Bruce, eds., *The Management of Strategy in the Marketplace*. Mason, OH: Thomson-South-Western.

and on the basis of their own forecasts. The only certain thing about a forecast is that it's wrong, but no one ever knows just how wrong. If participants could see along the entire supply chain, the chances are they would do much better. Thus, a common belief of participants after the beer game is that the bullwhip effect is mainly due to lack of point-of-sale (POS) data or good forecasts. In fact, obtaining POS data and good forecasts are often cited as the primary reasons why enterprises in the supply chain should collaborate.

On the contrary, it turns out, the primary culprit for the bullwhip effect is *lead time*. Even when there are no breakdowns in communication, the bullwhip effect will still be felt due to procurement and manufacturing delays. This is not to say that POS information and improved forecasting have little impact. In fact, reducing lead time, in combination with improved visibility along the supply chain, can significantly and positively relieve the bull-whip effect, as demonstrated below.

So how exactly does each variable affect the bullwhip effect? It is instructive to analyze the beer game using a quantitative approach in order to identify the impact of the variables a little more precisely. Remember the beer game begins with each enterprise carrying 12 cases of beer, with a demand for four cases of beer each week. The lead-time for each enterprise to receive a shipment against an order is four weeks.

At the start of the simulation, the system is in steady state; then the equilibrium is disrupted when the consumer wants eight cases in week five. The retailer begins this week with 12 cases, receives four cases, but sells eight cases, leaving only eight cases in inventory. The retailer must now decide how many cases to order.

Suppose that each player's ordering policy is based on two very simple but logical rules, one to forecast demand and the other to determine order quantity:

1. **The forecast rule:** The weekly demand for each of the next four weeks is the average of the weekly demand over the four most recent weeks.
2. **The order quantity rule:** Given the forecast, the amount ordered is just enough to replenish the ending inventory (four weeks from now when the order arrives) to a target of 12 cases.

Using rule 1, the retailer forecasts weekly demand to be five cases a week for each of the next four weeks: $(4 + 4 + 4 + 8)/4 = 5$.

Rule 2 requires that the retailer's inventory on hand plus the inventory on order be sufficient to meet forecasted demand for the next four weeks and leave 12 cases in inventory. Therefore, the retailer must order the sum of the inventory target (12) plus the forecasted demand for the next four weeks minus the inventory he already has on hand or on order, so:

Order: Inventory target (12) + Forecasted demand for next four weeks (5 each) – Current inventory (8) – Orders already placed for the next three weeks (4 each) = 12 + (5+5+5+5) – 8 – (4+4+4) = 12 + 20 – 8 – 12 = 12.

The retailer will thus order 12 cases from the wholesaler.

A fundamental insight: The consumer demand increased by 100 percent (from four cases per week to eight cases per week) but the retailer's order to the wholesaler increased by 200 percent (from four cases to 12 for the following week). *The retailer thus doubled the variation in demand.* The increase in variation is due to the four-week lead time required to react to the forecasted increase in demand.

Assume now that the wholesaler behaves the same way as the retailer except that the wholesaler's demand is created by the retailer's orders. The wholesaler, who has been receiving four cases a week, selling four cases a week, and ending each week with 12 cases, is surprised by the retailer's unexpected order for 12 cases. When she fills it, she will be left with an inventory of only four cases. She uses the four-week average forecasting rule and the inventory target of 12 cases to arrive at the following order decision:

Forecast: (4 + 4 + 4+ 12)/4 = 6 cases per week.
Order: Inventory target + Forecasted demand for the next four weeks – Current Inventory – Orders already placed for the next three weeks = 12 + (6+6+6+6) – 4 – (4+4+4) = 20.

The wholesaler's order on the distributor has thus increased from four cases a week to 20, an increase of 400 percent.

Using the same forecasting and order quantity rules, the distributor reacts to the wholesaler's order of 20 cases by ordering 36 cases, an increase of 800 percent. The factory responds to this by ordering enough raw material from its supplier to make 68 cases, an increase of 1,600 percent.

The variation has doubled at each stage. However, of the 64-case increase in the factory's orders, only four cases were directly attributable to a change in consumer demand. *The lead times present in this value stream created 94 percent of the variation pobserved in the factory's orders.*

The implications of this are:

- Lead times significantly exacerbate the bullwhip effect. For the beer game analysis, with a four-week lead-time and all orders placed using the same forecasting rule, the variation in orders grows by a factor of 2 at each stage, so the increase in variation at each stage is multiplicative.

We thus observe that a moving average forecast does not reduce the bullwhip effect. The effect is present even when there is perfect information about the present and the future, instantaneously available to all enterprises in the supply chain.

The Impact of Information on the Bullwhip Effect

Assume the same beer game scenario except that each stage is instantly made aware of the consumer's orders. Assume, too, that the consumer orders four cases in weeks one through four, and eight cases in week five, as before. To enable a proper comparison with the previous analysis, it is also assumed that the perfect information scenario reveals that the consumer demand for week six onwards is five cases of beer. This assumption allows a fair comparison, because the forecasting method used in the preceding section predicts a steady demand on the retailer for five cases of beer in the following weeks. Assume, too, that the demand information is conveyed instantaneously upstream. To keep the comparison fair, assume that the lead-time to react to an order remains four weeks at each stage.

Following exactly the same approach as before, the retailer will order 12 cases of beer from the wholesaler in week five to bring inventory back to the target level of 12 cases. As before, the 100 percent increase in demand on the retailer translates to a 200 percent increase in demand on the wholesaler over the previous week. Since the retailer sees the demand for the following weeks to be five cases of beer each week, the retailer tells the wholesaler to expect a demand of five cases for each of the following weeks. The wholesaler, to bring up the target inventory to 12 cases, orders 16 cases of beer from the distributor. This time, a 100 percent increase in the demand on the retailer translates to a 300 percent increase in demand on the distributor. Similarly, the factory will receive an order for 12 cases, a 400 percent increase over the previous week, while the raw material supplier will receive an order for 24 cases, a 500 percent increase over the previous week.

This example, which assumes perfect information about the present and the future, would require POS data to be available at all stages in the supply chain *and* a perfect forecasting mechanism. This is not a very likely scenario. The point of the example is to show that the bullwhip effect is still present even with perfect information, although it is smaller. With perfect information the variation in the orders generated at successive stages does not grow multiplicatively but additively (by 100 percent at each successive stage).

A variant on the beer game, *the near-beer game*, demonstrates that POS data and good forecasting tools do not eliminate the bullwhip effect. In the near-beer game, the supply chain consists of three enterprises: (1) supplier, (2) brewery, and (3) customer. Participants manage the brewery, which brews only one type of beer. It takes one week to receive raw material ordered from the supplier, one week to brew the beer, and one week to deliver it to the customer.

The near-beer system is initially in steady state with the customer ordering 10 cases of beer each week. The brewery has 10 cases in inventory, 10 cases brewing, and 10 cases of raw materials arriving from the supplier. In week two, the customer increases demand to 15 cases a week and it remains at 15 thereafter. The game ends when the supply chain is back in equilibrium with 15 cases of beer. In the near-beer game, the brewery has perfect information about the demand for beer but the bullwhip effect does not go away.

The near-beer game reinforces all the lessons conveyed by the beer game and teaches one additional lesson: *The bullwhip effect is present even if there is perfect information about the future that is shared among all channel partners.* Though having perfect information about the future is even better than having POS data and excellent forecasting tools, the near-beer game demonstrates that the bullwhip effect is best addressed by reducing manufacturing and order lead times.

The Impact of Lead Times on the Bullwhip Effect

As our analysis suggests, lead times can multiply the variation in demand and so everyone in the supply chain should be working to reduce lead times. With shorter lead times, operating costs decline because less capacity is needed to handle demand fluctuations. Reducing lead time also lowers inventory costs. The well-known Little's Law states that average inventory in the system is equal to average system lead time multiplied by system throughput,[7] or, as more commonly stated:

> *"The lead time in the system is directly proportional to the inventory in the system. In particular, average system lead time is equal to the average inventory in the system divided by system throughput."*

The implications of Little's Law are that when inventory in the supply chain is high, lead times increase, and, conversely, longer lead times result in more inventories in the pipeline. This problematic and cyclical relationship between lead times and inventory is a powerful reason for reducing lead times.

How does all this apply to the ideal scenario visualized at the start of Chapter 1? Ideally, if lead times were small and every enterprise in the supply chain could react to a pure pull signal, it would be possible to run the supply chain with near zero inventory. Each enterprise in the chain would wait for its customer to place an order before it ordered parts from its suppliers, and would begin production on the order only when the parts arrive. Thus, none would need to carry any raw material, WIP, or finished goods in inventory. In turn, the lower inventories would result in lower lead times, generating a virtuous cycle. Needless to say, the ideal is unlikely to be realized in practice for most supply chains unless lead times are reduced first.

Reducing lead times has an added benefit. Suppose the manufacturer in a supply chain operates in a build-to-stock environment. If the manufacturer requires, say, four weeks to build products, then the entire supply chain must maintain at least four weeks of inventory. The implication is that the manufacturer is building to a forecast four weeks out into the future.

However, if the lead time is two weeks, the manufacturer only needs to build to a forecast for two weeks out.

---

7. Little's Law is an exact formula. An intuitive, though slightly flawed, explanation of Little's Law is this: Suppose each job takes t (time units) to process. The throughput rate, TH (the number of jobs processed per unit time) is thus $TH = 1/t$. Suppose that work-in-process is W units. If a new order is placed, the lead time, LT, for this order will be the time it takes to clear W units of WIP: $LT = W\ t$. This gives $W = TH \times LT$.

Consider the implications. As Figure 2.2 shows, the longer the time horizon for a forecast, the less reliable it is. So, a forecast made for a demand that is two weeks out into the future is clearly more reliable than one made for a demand four weeks out into the future.

Figure 2-2. Forecast Accuracy Decreases as Forecast Horizon Increases

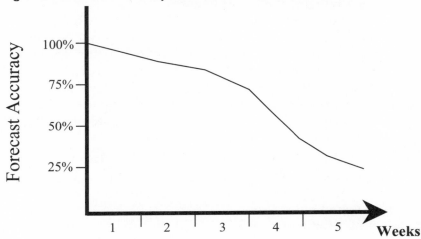

Building to a forecast always carries an element of speculation. The enterprise that builds products based on forecasts typically pads the forecast to buffer against the uncertainty in the forecast. Padding further distances the amount produced from true customer demand, adding to the variation in the supply chain; the longer the lead time, the more padding there is. Hence, as lead times decrease, the demands of elements in the supply chain converge more closely to a pure pull strategy with no variation added at any point in the chain.

Lessons from the Beer Game

The analysis of the bullwhip effect shows that long lead times and the lack of POS data exacerbate the bullwhip effect. A direct consequence of this observation is that since lead times increase with each stage and handoffs in the supply chain, reducing the number of stages reduces the bullwhip effect. The analysis also shows how the variation at each stage is either additive or multiplicative depending on whether the system had perfect information about the future.

The use of POS data can also help reduce the bullwhip effect from a behavioral perspective. Managers of lean supply chains realize that end-user demand is more predictable than the demand experienced by factories, so they tend to ignore signal distortions sent through the supply chain and instead look at the end-user demand. This means they do not react to day-to-day fluctuations but instead run a level production schedule each day, which helps mitigate the bullwhip effect.

It must be noted, though, that without perfect information about the future, sharing POS information does not give much leverage to enterprises when lead times are high. Future consumer orders need to be anticipated. Unless consumer orders are steady, the bullwhip effect will be multiplicative. *In sum:* Point-of-sale data can reduce the bullwhip effect. However, without perfect information about the future, POS data does not eliminate the bullwhip effect. It is also necessary to reduce lead time.

Here are other ways to mitigate the bullwhip effect:

- Smaller orders result in smaller fluctuations. The solution is to work with suppliers on more frequent deliveries of smaller order increments.
- Keeping product prices stable reduces the temptation to the customer to buy more than necessary when prices are low and cut back on orders when prices are high. It levels out customer demand.
- Allocating products among customers based on past orders rather than solely on their present orders will reduce hoarding behavior when there are shortages. Unrestricted ordering can be controlled by lowering the maximum order size and implementing capacity reservations. One option is to allow a customer to reserve a fixed quantity for a given year and specify how much should be sent in each order shortly before it is needed, as long as the sum of the order quantities equals to the reserved quantity. Leading enterprises like Barilla SpA adopt this distribution strategy.

A key learning point from the beer game is that *structure drives behavior.* How the supply chain is constructed largely determines how it will perform. The structural framework for the beer game has the following components, all of which play a role in enhancing the bullwhip effect:

- Lack of visibility along the supply chain: No POS data and a lack of coordination or communication up and down the chain
- Long lead times for material and information flow

- Many stages in the supply chain
- Lack of pull signals
- Order batching
- Price discounts and promotions.

The observation that structure determines behavior is not a novel concept. Deming alluded to it when he said that management must take the responsibility for poor performance and take steps to reduce process variation instead of blaming workers for poor quality. However, certain behavioral phenomena, not necessarily driven by the structure, also contribute to the bullwhip effect:

- Over-reaction to backlogs
- Withholding orders in an attempt to reduce inventory
- Hoarding; where customers order more than they need because they are anticipating a price increase or because the supplier has a promotional sale
- Shortage gaming where customers order more than they need because they lack faith in the supplier's ability to deliver quality products or because they think the supplier cannot deliver the entire order
- Demand forecast inaccuracies where a customer adds a certain percentage to the demand estimate, reducing the visibility of true customer demand
- Attempts to meet end-of-month, quarterly, or yearly metrics.

In the beer game, the bullwhip effect is observed even though the supply chain deals with a single product and there is just a one-time spike in demand. In the real world, enterprises usually deal with multiple products with demands that vary from period to period. Furthermore, in the real world there are many other factors to deal with. Quality problems and unplanned events, such as strikes and accidents, induce additional variation in the supply chain, exacerbating the bullwhip effect. It is easy to see why the bullwhip effect is present in almost every industry.

Since structure drives behavior, many enterprises have gained a significant competitive advantage by delving into the underlying causes of the bullwhip effect and redesigning the structural framework within their own enterprise, as well as working with upstream and downstream partners to mitigate the bullwhip effect. In the following section, we present seven steps managers can use to build the necessary structural framework.

SEVEN STEPS FOR BUILDING LEAN SUPPLY CHAINS

Working through these steps to erect the structural framework is obviously easier for supply chains that include a dominant enterprise, like Wal-Mart or Dell. Those companies have the power and authority to ensure that other members in the supply chain cooperate with them on slimming down the supply chain. However, even when there is no clearly dominant authority in the supply chain, it will benefit members if they are at least aware of the steps that can be taken to make their supply chain more competitive. The true competitive edge is realized only when all members in the supply chain work jointly on these seven steps:

1. Adopt a systems perspective.
2. Understand the customers and their expectations.
3. Map the supply chain.
4. Benchmark best practices.
5. Design products and processes to manage demand volatility.
6. Create flow across the supply chain.
7. Formulate metrics based on a systems perspective.

Adopt a Systems Perspective

The beer game demonstrates the importance of systems thinking and how it can affect a supply chain. It shows that a locally managed supply chain is inherently unstable. The systems perspective recognizes that if each element in the supply chain tries to optimize its own operations in isolation, everyone suffers over time. In the beer game, each enterprise in the supply chain makes decisions in isolation without input from its immediate upstream and downstream supply chain partners. Moving from a local to a global optimization framework poses a tremendous challenge for managers, because it is a radical shift away from the traditional approach to managing enterprises.

Systems thinking has been cited many times as strategically important but it is still not sufficiently understood. For instance, an important step in building lean supply chains is to establish long-term partnerships with key suppliers. Suppose management institutes a measurement system that rewards the purchasing department for obtaining products at low cost. Though reduced materials costs directly affect the profitability of the enterprise, that policy could drive the purchasing department into an adversarial position with its suppliers, encouraging the department to play off potential suppliers against each other in an attempt to drive them to lower prices. The lack of a systems perspective thus brings about a situation where the enterprise will find it very difficult to establish long-term partnerships with its suppliers.

Or, assume a supply chain with just two enterprises, A and B, with A as the supplier to B. A receives a management mandate to reduce its finished goods inventory and responds accordingly, and from a local perspective, the performance of A is enhanced. But if the inventory reduction at A is done in isolation, without any change in the pattern of B's demands on its supplier, A might be putting itself in jeopardy because it will be unable to react promptly to unforeseen changes in demand from B. From B's perspective, A will be perceived as less flexible, so B may either decide to carry some inventory of its own or find another supplier. The lack of supply chain metrics has led the manager of A to make local improvements that did not improve the performance of the supply chain as a whole.

In hindsight, systems thinking is so intuitive that it is curious that it was not applied to supply chains earlier. One reason is that advocated by Senge,[8] who claims that enterprises do not practice systems thinking because they are more absorbed with "detail complexity," rather than "dynamic complexity." A manager who deals only with detail complexity is obstructed from seeing how different types of interactions reach beyond the immediate enterprise, and how they change over time.

Another reason systems thinking was not applied in the past was that, until a few years ago, requiring members of the supply chain to work to unify the supply chain would have at best seemed a dream. Now that the Internet and technology can make end-user demand visible to all supply chain partners, there has been a perceptible change. Supply chains where customer demand is visible to all members are in a better position to ensure that small fluctuations in that demand do not amplify into huge swings in the demands placed on the manufacturer.

That is why members in many supply chains are more willing now to set aside their traditional arms-length relationships and build long-term partnering arrangements that achieve the competitive benefits that can be derived from an integrated supply chain. The increased visibility of end-user demand also allows managers in supply chains to better understand customer expectations.

---

8. P.M. Senge (1994): "The Fifth Discipline: The Art and Practices of the Learning Organization," Doubleday, NY 1994.

Understand the Customers and Their Expectations

If you were traveling from Knoxville, Tennessee to Washington, D.C., would you catch a flight or would you drive? After reading a report by Dr. Bruce J. Holmes[9] of the NASA Langley Research Center, you might conclude that you would be better off driving. He reports that for trips of less than 500 miles, the average speed from doorstep to destination with state of-the-art airplanes in the hub-and-spoke system is between 35 to 80 miles per hour.[10]

More than 95 percent of today's air travelers use the hub-and-spoke system, going through one of 29 hub airports to one of about 600 spoke airports. Though the system may help keep ticket prices low, it results in frustrated and fatigued travelers who are forced to go out of their way and waste valuable time getting to their destination. In fact, it would not be an overstatement to claim that most passengers dislike the current system. This is an industry that does not appear to deliver customer value.

What *does* the customer value? This is a crucial question that must be addressed first. As the supply chain is built, or rebuilt, customer needs and values must be analyzed. This is an opportunity for the supply chain partners to challenge the way the product is traditionally delivered. For instance, in the airline industry, the direct point-to-point method used by airlines like Southwest and JetBlue Airways may soon be the choice for a large majority of passengers who travel 500 miles or less. That may put the classic hub-and-spoke airline companies out of business in this customer segment, with a corresponding growth in the production of smaller aircraft.

Understanding customer value means that, at minimum, the attributes a product *must* have need to be identified—the order qualifiers and order winners for a product. *Order qualifiers*[11] are attributes that the product must have before the customer will even consider buying it. *Order winners* are the attributes that will get the actual order. Order qualifiers and order winners determine the competitive priorities for a supply chain. Should it be speed to market? product design? product quality? on-time delivery? a combination of these? something else? The answer lies in what is important to a customer base.

---

9. Holmes, B. J. 2001. "Small Aircraft Transportation System: A Vision for 21st Century Transportation Alternatives." Technical Report, NASA Langley Research Center.

10. *See also* Fallows, J. 2002. *Free Flight: From Airline Hell to a New Age of Travel.* New York: Public Affairs Press.

11. Hill, T. 2000. *Manufacturing Strategy.* Boston: Irwin McGraw-Hill.

Order qualifiers and order winners will be different for different customer segments. For an airline that wants to attract family vacationers traveling relatively short distances, low price tickets could be order winners. Business travelers traveling coast to coast in the U.S. might be more interested in traveling on wide-body jets; for them comfort and on-time travel would be order winners.

Not only must customer order qualifiers and order winners be understood, current performance relative to the competition and in the eyes of customers also needs to be evaluated. Order qualifiers and order winners are dynamic; changes in the market place and in technology can change them. Over the past few years, many perennial order winners have become mere order qualifiers because of the tremendous advances in manufacturing technology, planning systems, and IT. The combination of quality and low cost that packed a winning punch only a short time ago is no longer a differentiator. A key function of marketing is to stay abreast of changes so an enterprise can remain proactive in meeting customer expectations, and growing revenues.

Different product delivery strategies are necessary for different customer segments and markets. As far as possible, it would be best to wait for the customer's order and build the product to customer specifications—but if the customer is not prepared to wait and will go elsewhere if the product is not available when ordered, a small inventory of finished goods needs to be maintained. The delivery strategy may thus be a combination of several models: Build-to-stock (BTS), build-to-order (BTO), engineer-to-order (ETO), etc. At a macro level, the supply chain structure should delineate which segments will operate in a BTS mode and which in a BTO mode. For instance, a BTS mode of operation is required if the response time for the supply chain or a segment of it is longer than the time the customer is willing to wait for the product.

Map the Supply Chain

Because a supply chain map illustrates the physical flow of goods and the information flow, it highlights areas in the chain that need more attention. There is a considerable literature on supply chain mapping (also known as *value stream mapping*).[12] A typical practice

---

12. *See, for instance,* Rother, M., and R. Harris. 2001. *Creating Continuous Flow.* Brookline, MA: Lean Enterprise Institute, Inc.; Rother, M., and J. Shook. 1999. *Learning to See.* Brookline, MA: Lean Enterprise Institute, Inc.; and Womack, J. P., and D. T. Jones. 2002. *Seeing the Whole: Mapping the Extended Value Stream.* Brookline, MA: Lean Enterprise Institute, Inc.

is to first select the product family for which the value stream should be mapped. The choice is often based simply on the biggest customer for the enterprise. The next step is to draw a map of the existing supply chain (an "as-is" map). Non-value-added work and constraints are then minimized to design a map of the desired end-state supply chain (a "to-be" map).

It is usually hard to determine the degree of detail that is useful for a supply chain map. The manager is mainly interested in the immediate linkages the enterprise has with its upstream and downstream partners, so broadening the map to include enterprises beyond them can result in loss of detail. Still, if the flow can be mapped to second-tier suppliers and the customer's customer, it may be easier to visualize the kind of systems that must be in place if customer service is to be improved.

Advances in IT have significantly facilitated supply chain mapping. It is now possible to capture what is happening, and what could happen, in much greater detail than was previously possible. Executives at Franciscan Estates in St. Helena, California, the winemaking division of Constellation Brands Inc., use a software program from E.piphany Inc. to delve into the raw information supplied by distributors through a central information-clearing house. Franciscan knows not only which products are selling well through the distributors, it can also track sales down to the retail level. According to McDougall,[13] if a premium product like Franciscan's Cuvee Sauvage chardonnay is not selling in a well-to-do area of Silicon Valley where it should be a natural success, the Franciscan sales staff can directly target individual stores in those zip codes with a sales campaign for that product.

Once the as-is map is complete, key structural elements should be examined to identify how they should be managed to best enhance the performance of the entire supply chain. From an operational point of view, there are several key areas of concern in any product/work flow, among them:

- Segments of the supply chain where processing times are large. Time is a key element in gaining a competitive edge in the consumer era. Segments that have difficulty in responding quickly to changes should be managed carefully.
- Any segment or path that contains physical constraints, whether they are material or capacity constraints: Effective

---

13. McDougall, P. 2001. "Collaborative Business: Companies that Dare to Share Information Are Cashing in on New Opportunities." *Information Week*, May, *http://www. informationweek.com.*

management of the supply chain is impossible without knowing where the constraints are and how they influence the performance of the supply chain as a whole.

- Points where there is a high degree of resource sharing. When the same resource is used in a variety of products, contention for priorities will arise; any mismanagement of these priorities can cause delivery problems.
- Points where common materials are transformed into different product streams. In an integrated steel mill, the basic pig iron can be converted into a variety of different alloy steels. Once the transformation is complete, the processes cannot be reversed. If the wrong product is produced, the inventory of that product rises even as there is an urgent shortage of the product that should have been produced.
- Points where multiple materials must come together. These are assembly points. Since the assembly process requires all necessary materials to be available, the logistical challenge of making sure that all the different materials required arrive on time is significant.
- Points of excessive variation.

A comprehensive supply chain map can thus highlight the weakest links, the points in the chain that have high lead times, etc. It can identify where resources are insufficient to manage supplier relationships, whether there is a proliferation of suppliers at some points, or whether the size of the supply chain allows to create sound supplier development strategies.

Benchmark Best Practices

Benchmarking is a continuous, systematic procedure aimed at measuring the enterprise's products, services, and processes against best-in-class practices. Benchmarking is not aimed at imitation. Instead, it studies and learns from others and adapts the practices that best suit the enterprise. Enterprises can choose to perform either *competitive* or *functional* benchmarking.

In competitive benchmarking, enterprises compare themselves with others in the same industry, usually the leader in that industry. This type of benchmarking allows the enterprise to avoid making the mistakes the leader may have already made in its journey to the top in the industry. The obvious disadvantage of this type of benchmarking is that the enterprise becomes a follower. Typically, the leader will stay one step ahead of the competition.

Functional benchmarking, on the other hand, compares processes and activities like customer service, the design process, and the product delivery system against the outstanding practices of best-in-class enterprises in any industry. This is a more ambitious form of benchmarking because it attempts to match up with selected enterprises that are recognized as world leaders in some processes. Enterprises might, for example, choose to benchmark against Disney for customer service, Dell for rapid customization, Toyota for process execution, and American Express for its ability to get customers to pay quickly.

The advantage of functional benchmarking is twofold: First, the enterprise doing the benchmarking does not need to worry about staying behind the leader in its own industry. Second, and more important, it offers opportunities for the enterprise to identify innovative ways of fulfilling customer demand. Taiichi Ohno, widely acknowledged as the person responsible for the Toyota production system, credits his contributions to this system to two concepts: (1) the moving assembly line pioneered by Henry Ford and (2) the supermarket.[14]

In a visit to the United States in 1956, Ohno observed how supermarket operations provided their stores with a continuous supply of merchandise. This gave Ohno the idea of setting up a pull system in which each production process became a "supermarket" for the succeeding process. Each process would produce to replenish only the items that the downstream process had used. When Ohno adopted the supermarket concept for Toyota, he gave the company a competitive edge since no other car manufacturer was then taking this approach. The third lean supply chain principle makes this point concisely.

LEAN SUPPLY CHAIN PRINCIPLE 3

Focus on customer needs and process considerations when designing a product. Enterprises can gain tremendous competitive advantage through best-in-class practices that cut across industries.

---

14. Ohno, T. 1988. *Toyota Production System: Beyond Large-Scale Production.* Cambridge, MA: Productivity Press.

Design Products and Processes to Manage Demand Volatility

The beer game showed us how even a small change in demand can lead to large inventories upstream, especially when lead times are large. This makes a clear case for the supply chain to design products and processes that mitigate demand volatility.

Demand volatility is an accepted fact of life in business that has become even more challenging as consumers have grown more demanding. The first challenge is to structure the supply chain and support it with policies that reduce demand volatility as far as possible. Having mitigated demand volatility, the next challenge is to manage the remaining demand volatility with processes and equipment that achieve high customer satisfaction and operational effectiveness.

It is a remarkable fact that demand volatility is often self-induced. A classic example is the instability created by sales promotions or rebates, which usually generates a sharp surge in end-user demand that causes the inevitable bullwhip effect. Managers generally fail to recognize that often volatility of demand is significantly influenced by the enterprise's sales or marketing activities. Conversely, the sales and marketing group often fail to use tools and techniques that mitigate demand volatility.

One simple approach to eliminating self-induced volatility is to adopt an every-day-low-price policy, as Wal-Mart does. The end-of-quarter or end-of-year "channel-stuffing" that is carried out to show higher operating efficiencies and margins increases demand volatility. It typically results in inventory elsewhere in the pipeline that will have to be disposed of through a sale, exacerbating the bullwhip effect. Ignoring noisy data from promotional activity or end-of-the-quarter channel-stuffing will help prevent the bullwhip effect from propagating upstream.

Batching is another example of self-induced volatility. While end-user demand for a product may be fairly level, enterprises often deliver the product in large lots to achieve economies of scale. The manufacturer who chooses to wait until cumulative demand reaches an "economic" lot size before beginning production is doing batching. From the beer game we observed that a single spike in demand created large ripple effects upstream. Batching a steady end-user demand immediately generates a bullwhip effect on upstream suppliers. The solution here is to work with small batches and level production schedules.

Improving the responsiveness and reliability of the supply chain is yet another way to reduce demand volatility. The responsiveness of the supply chain is itself a major determinant of demand volatility. First, as we observed earlier, the further out into the future the forecast, the more unreliable the forecast is. A supply chain that is less responsive—requires more time to deliver products to the consumer—has to contend with a demand forecast that is further out and correspondingly less reliable, so the variation in the actual demand observed is higher.

Second, if customers sense that the supplier is unable to deliver what they want, on time, they will understandably hedge their requirements. They may demand more product than they actually need. Or they may ask for it to be delivered sooner than it is really needed. In either case, demand volatility is increased. On the flip side, if the enterprise responds quickly to customer demands, customers will have more faith in the delivery process and are therefore less likely to pad their requirements or desired due dates.

A very useful approach to manage demand volatility is to "maximize external variety while minimizing internal variety." This captures the basic principle that should be followed especially in designing supply chains that deal with high product variety and demand volatility. The way to execute this is to structure product offerings so that a commitment of material and resources can be postponed for as long as possible. In other words, it is best to work with a relatively small number of standard products ("modules") internally in semi-finished or finished form that can be configured as a large variety of end products. Another way to refer to this is as the RAP principle: Keep in-process inventory as "raw as possible." Figure 2.3 illustrates the RAP principle.[15]

The RAP principle should drive the design of new products and services. It is a very convenient way to meet customer demand quickly without carrying a lot of finished goods inventory. At the same time, it delays committing raw material, labor, and fixed assets to products based on fore-casts in anticipation of future demand. As shown in the "After" portion of Figure 2.3, differentiation of the product is postponed to the final assembly stage, which makes it possible to maintain an inventory of the products in an undifferentiated "sub-assembly" form, ready for conversion relatively quickly into one of three possible finished products. The fourth lean supply chain principle captures this idea.

---

15. This principle is often referred to in the literature as the *principle of postponement.*

Figure 2-3. The RAP Principle

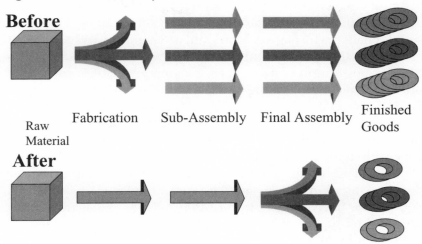

LEAN SUPPLY CHAIN PRINCIPLE 4

Maximize external variety while minimizing internal variety. Maintain inventories in an undifferentiated form for as long as it is economically feasible to do so.

The RAP principle is particularly valuable for managing products that have a short life span. It increases service levels while reducing costs and order fulfillment risk, so it is especially useful when there are many derivative products and forecast error is high.

The RAP principle has an added benefit. When a number of independent demands are aggregated, the aggregate demand has significantly less variation than the individual demands. When the RAP principle is adopted, the same standard modules go into a wide variety of end products. If modules rather than end products are stored, then demand volatility can be managed with much less inventory because the variation in the demand for modules is much less than the variation in the demand for end products.

Despite our best efforts to manage demand volatility using one or a combination of the approaches discussed, suppose demand variation is still present in the supply chain. What should be done to cope with this variation? The classical, traditional, approach is to resort to inventorying finished goods to buffer the variation. But that approach has its drawbacks, because high inventory results in slower responsiveness and longer lead times. In fact, Taiichi Ohno, Toyota's production guru, is reputed to have said that "Inventory is the root of all evil."[16] Little's Law shows us that lead times and inventory go hand in hand, creating a problematic and cyclical relationship; the beer game showed us the effect of lead times on supply chain performance. Moreover, when enterprises are forced to commit their scarce and inflexible resources to produce finished goods inventory in the face of demand volatility, they quite often end up misallocating the resources to produce the wrong kind of products.

Clearly, there are powerful incentives to reduce inventories in the supply chain. So, the question remains: How can enterprises cope with demand variation?

Instead of using inventory, a better approach is to buffer demand variation with a small amount of reserve capacity. This approach is likely to meet with resistance from managers who do not view the supply chain from a systems perspective—those who are driven by metrics that force them to cut costs and run their operations at full tilt. Those managers would be penalized if they did not use up their flex capacity even though the situation might not warrant it. However, as has been repeatedly emphasized, a key factor in building lean supply chains is to maintain flexibility at every stage. That is best achieved with capacity, not inventory. That leads to the fifth lean supply chain principle:

LEAN SUPPLY CHAIN PRINCIPLE 5

Buffer variation in demand with capacity, not inventory.

While buffering variation with capacity is ideal, there are definitely situations where inventory must be used to accommodate variation. In the consumer products industry, the consumer who does not find the goods on the shelf may go elsewhere. If forced to buffer variation with inventory, a related issue is how inventory could be used more strategically. Should finished goods inventory be available or should the RAP principle be applied to have partially processed items, ready to be assembled to customer order, so that flexibility is preserved? The answer, of course, depends on the customer's expectations of lead time. The point is to decide where to *strategically* locate the inventory—how far upstream in the supply chain it could be located in order to still meet customer lead time expectations.

---

16. We would say, instead, that "variation is the root of all evil," because variation is the root cause for the inventory build-up.

In Sum: The ways to mitigate demand volatility are:

- To the extent possible, avoid using sales promotions, rebates, and metrics that promote the end-of-the-quarter syndrome and adopt some variant of the "every-day-low-price" approach.
- Avoid batching; try to work with small batches and a level production schedule.
- Improve the responsiveness and reliability of the delivery system.
- Maximize external variety while minimizing internal variety, using the power of the RAP principle.
- Buffer variation in demand with capacity, not inventory.
- When maintaining inventory is necessary, place it at strategic locations in the supply chain to meet customer lead time expectations.

Create Flow across the Supply Chain

The ability to react quickly to customer demand without carrying large amounts of inventory anywhere in the supply chain is better achieved if every enterprise in the chain works in harmony to produce goods at the rate demanded by the end-user. This concept of *flow* balance essentially means that all the enterprises are rowing the boat at the same pace. If some enterprises in the chain are working faster than others, the imbalance in flow will cause an inventory pile-up in front of the weaker links, those that work at a slower pace.

Balancing flow across the supply chain requires a systems perspective. The idea is to focus on the product and identify all the steps it goes through in the process of moving from the raw material stage to the end-user. Do some process steps introduce unnecessary delays? Are there any non-value-added activities that the product goes through? Where are the bottlenecks that delay the smooth flow of the product? Are any of the bottlenecks due to unnecessary processing steps? Have information-processing delays been eliminated? Questions like these will surface problems with existing work practices that hinder the smooth flow of the product.

A major impediment to flow is caused by enterprises that produce products in anticipation of future demand. When enterprises use forecasts to drive their production schedules, the forecasting methods used obviously will affect schedules. A poor forecast may mean that raw material is not available in time to meet the customer's delivery expectations.

Even when the enterprise uses good forecasting techniques, the forecasting *process* could generate problems. Historically, forecasting has been applied with a silo mentality: Separate departments within the same enterprise independently creating forecasts for the same products, using their own assumptions, measures, and levels of detail. The impact of these localized forecasts on the performance of the supply chain is rarely thought through. Functional silos worsen the situation. For instance, the sales function may envision growing demand but the operations function is left to guess how much the customer really wants.

When enterprises use forecasts to drive production schedules, they in effect *push* products out in the form of finished goods, building a buffer of inventory to accommodate demand variation. To put it another way, *push systems schedule production and let inventory absorb demand variation.* As a result, enterprises commit resources to often-unneeded products and are thus unable to react to a firm customer order when one materializes unexpectedly.

A pull system, on the other hand, would wait for a demand signal before committing resources to production. A pull signal from the customer enhances flow, but the real benefit is it results in lower inventories. More precisely, pull systems place a limit on inventories, using capacity to absorb demand variation.

Although it is desirable to use pull systems wherever possible, enterprises in the supply chain still have to anticipate customer demands. They still must rely on forecasts. The key is to resist the temptation to *execute* the production schedule based on a forecast. Use demand forecasts for *planning* production and use pull signals based on true customer demand to *schedule* production.

A system that responds to pull signals has inherently less variation than a system that pushes products through the supply chain. This important point is one that will be revisited in Chapter 8. Lean supply chain principle six summarizes the preceding discussion.

LEAN SUPPLY CHAIN PRINCIPLE 6

Use forecasts to plan and pull to execute. A system that reacts to pull signals will have less variation than a comparable system that adopts a push mode of operation.

It is desirable for enterprises to use pull signals to trigger supplies from their upstream enterprises as well. Carrying this through logically, the idea is to start with the customer, deliver what is demanded, build what is sold, supply what is consumed, and above all, to balance the flow. Figure 2.4 illustrates this concept.

FIGURE 2-4. Use Pull Signals to Create Flow across the Supply Chain

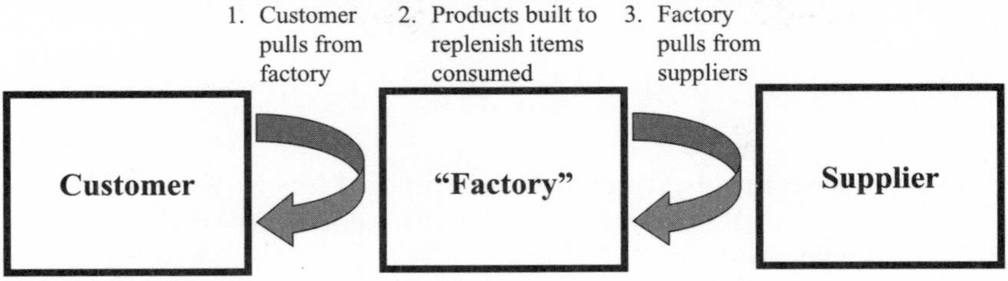

1. Customer pulls from factory
2. Products built to replenish items consumed
3. Factory pulls from suppliers

The discussion so far does not imply that products are built from scratch in response to a customer order. An alternate way of using pull effectively is to maintain a small stock of inventory, preferably in a semifinished rather than a finished state—in other words, follow the RAP principle.

Flow and lead time are closely related. The lack of flow, or any imbalance in flow, results in long lead times; conversely long lead times are a symptom of poor flow. As already learned, if the supply chain is not responsive due to long lead times, that increases volatility in demand. If response to changes in customer demand is quick, fluctuations in production and inventory levels are considerably reduced.

The ability to respond quickly to market changes relies on making only small adjustments in production to meet market demand, which promotes flow. On the other hand, if intervention must be delayed to accommodate an inflexible system, management is forced to make much larger changes in production, which impedes flow. Thus, one way to create flow is to reduce lead times.

Lowering lead times creates more flow in the supply chain, which in turn reduces lead times, again generating a virtuous cycle. Reducing lead times puts the enterprise in a better position to implement pull systems that produce to actual customer demand rather than based on forecasts.

One way the supply chain can reduce lead times and thereby attempt to increase flow is to operate in a build-to-stock (BTS) mode, where the customer can pull from finished goods for an immediate response. However, as stated, this often misallocates capacity and resources, because the enterprise could end up producing, say, light beer when customers are demanding premium lager.

Adopting a mixed-model production schedule will reduce lead times. If every product is produced during every production period, product batch sizes are reduced. As a consequence, the enterprise does not have to store as much inventory. In parts III and IV, a number of others ways to reduce lead times are presented.

To summarize the discussion on creating flow across the supply chain:

- A push system schedules production and lets inventory absorb variation; a pull system holds inventory constant and lets capacity absorb variation.
- Many enterprises incorrectly use forecasts to drive production schedules. The correct approach is to use forecasts only to *plan* production and then to rely on pull signals to trigger production. A pull system has less variation than a push system.
- Flow is enhanced by reducing lead times. Reduced lead times and improved flow go hand in hand, creating a virtuous cycle.

Formulate Metrics Based on a Systems Perspective

When the directors of an enterprise ask the CEO, "How are we doing?" what is the typical response? The CEO will probably talk about the performance of the enterprise in terms of such measures as return on investment, profitability, inventory turns, and material costs. These are important ways to gauge the financial health of the enterprise, but they are all internal measures that may not adequately address the performance of the enterprise in the future.

As discussed at the start, the battle has shifted from rivalry between enterprises to rivalry between supply chains. Outstanding performance at one location in the supply chain is no longer adequate if the rest of the members of the chain are not up to par. The financial health of each enterprise in the supply chain is directly affected by the overall performance of the supply chain. In the future, enterprises must analyze not only internal performance but also performance across the supply chain. That requires a radical shift from a local to a global optimization mindset.

Goldratt says, "Tell me how you will measure me and I will tell you how I'll behave."[17] The statement emphasizes the importance of an effective measurement system. The objective of supply chain metrics is to provide a basis for evaluating the performance of the whole supply chain as one system. That performance is the result

---

17. Goldratt, E. M. 1989. *The Haystack Syndrome: Sifting Information out of the Data Ocean.* Barrington, MA: North River Press Publishing Company.

of policies and procedures that drive critical segments of the supply chain.

In all probability, the current strategy and its resulting structure are a consequence of the individual segments (member enterprises) of the supply chain making isolated decisions that make sense to them from their local perspective. This results is an unsynchronized supply chain characterized by long lead times and many pockets of inventory. Traditional, locally focused, measures of cost and other performance measures are incomplete; they lead to suboptimal decisions.

The challenge in formulating metrics for the supply chain is to find ones that truly measure supply chain performance, instead of ones that measure enterprise performance only. Lambert and Pohlen remark that many of the measures currently identified as supply chain metrics are simply measures of internal logistics operations.[18] This is typically due to the lack of a systems perspective. Typical metrics used to measure delivery performance, such as fill rate or on-time performance, are applied in a different context if a systems perspective is adopted. To give a simple example, an improvement in inventory turns by a retailer is likely to have a more significant impact on supply chain performance than a corresponding improvement in inventory turns by a supplier, because as inventory moves closer to the point of consumption, it increases in value.

The question to really address is this: How can a process be designed for managing enterprises that is consistent with the fact that these enterprises are components of complex and highly interconnected systems? It warrants repeating: Optimizing the separate links independently does not optimize the supply chain.

Consider an enterprise that produces and ships products in large batches. This enterprise has minimized its production and transportation costs, but it has increased inventory, and inventory costs, for the buyer. In fact, viewed from the perspective of the supply chain, the long lead times created by big batches and shipping quantities are very costly. They force large amounts of WIP in the supply chain, reducing its flexibility and responsiveness.

The next question might be: Is there a way to optimize inventory costs across the entire supply chain? In the past, the question would have been dismissed as a theoretical exercise, but today it is

18. Lambert, D. M., and T. L. Pohlen. 2001. "Supply Chain Metrics." *International Journal of Logistics Management,* 12 (1): pp. 1-19.

rapidly changing from a theoretical to a practical one as managers of supply chains face increasing pressures for customer service and asset performance. Because Sony, for instance, is acutely aware of the fact that any inventory of its products at Best Buy and Circuit City affects its profitability if it stays on the shelf for more than a few days, it has changed its delivery metric from "sell-in" to "sell-through." The former metric allowed the Sony sales department to chalk up a sale when the product was shipped to Best Buy or Circuit City; the latter chalks up a sale only when the product is paid for by the consumer. Similarly, Procter & Gamble uses its Vendor Managed Inventory (VMI) process to routinely measure both its own inventory and downstream inventories of its products.

An important set of supply chain metrics relates to speed—timeliness, responsiveness, and flexibility. About a decade ago, the emphasis was on time-based competition. That emphasis was, and still is, very important. The metric of interest today, though, is *supply chain lead time,* not the lead time for an enterprise. It is measured simply by adding up the lead times at each stage in the supply chain. Hausman[19] reports that when one high-tech enterprise began to measure supply chain lead time, once it was made aware of the benefits of the metric, it was able to reduce supply chain lead time from 250 days to less than 190 days by some obvious, simple improvements.

Another important metric related to speed is adherence to quoted delivery time. Enterprises like Dell go to extremes to meet this metric. In fact, Dell's motto is "Under-Promise, Over-Deliver." Dell quotes five-day delivery for a BTO product and typically ships the product in four days or less. Its suppliers are well aware of Dell's emphasis on on-time delivery and are prepared to act accordingly.

A well-designed measurement system can significantly align processes across the supply chain, targeting the most profitable market segments. Some of the key dimensions used to measure supply chain performance are speed, quality, service, and asset management. *Speed,* as mentioned earlier, refers to timeliness, responsiveness, and flexibility. *Quality* can refer to a variety of measures, such as defect rate, reliability, and appearance. *Service* refers to the ability to anticipate, capture, and fulfill customer demand on time. *Asset management* refers to the efficiency with which the supply chain provides return on its assets.

---

19. Hausman, W. H. 2002. "Supply Chain Performance Metrics," in Billington, C., T. Harrison, H. Lee, and J. Neale, eds., *The Practice of Supply Chain Management.* Boston, MA: Kluwer Publishers.

Properly designed supply chain metrics help clarify the relationships between enterprise and supply chain performance. These metrics should encourage cooperation between functions within the enterprise (functional integration) and across enterprises (partnering in the supply chain). Supply chain metrics help align activities and share joint performance measurement information to implement strategies that achieve supply chain objectives.

The vision of supply chain performance metrics is no longer a distant dream. The Internet can be a key enabler for monitoring supply chain performance because it facilitates collaborative and timely sharing of information.

One of the obstacles to formulating supply chain metrics is that members in the chain have to set aside concerns about sharing what is deemed to be confidential information. Many enterprises are reluctant to even share their key performance indicators, much less divulge the values of the indicators. One way to work around such local thinking is to educate the supply chain partners and let them recognize that performance is measured ultimately by the end customer, but that is easier said than done. Unless the partners can see tangible benefits, they may not be willing to give up local thinking.

A more practical way to address this problem is to build trust so that those sharing information do not have to be concerned about the data being used against them. Trust is nourished by working with fewer suppliers on longer-term contracts and partnering with one or at most a select few logistics providers (see Chapter 3).

CONCLUSIONS

The bullwhip effect underscores the need for enterprises to understand the dynamics of the supply chain and how the bullwhip effect works. The primary causes for the bullwhip effect are:

- Lack of visibility along the supply chain
- Long lead times for material and information flow
- Actions undertaken within an enterprise, such as order batching and price discounts and promotions, which exacerbate the bullwhip effect.

In particular, lead times significantly affect the performance of the supply chain:

- Longer lead times lead to increased inventory in the system, which in turn causes lead times to increase, resulting in a vicious cycle.
- Flow, on the other hand, is enhanced by reducing lead times, which in turn improve flow, creating a virtuous cycle.
- Lead times are considerably influenced by variation in the system, so there should be a concentrated management effort to reduce variation.
- In particular, it is important to design products and processes so that they mitigate demand volatility.

The true competitive edge is realized only when all members in the supply chain understand and agree to work with the following basic principles:

- It is not enough to benchmark against the competition; that will result in the enterprise adopting the same practices (good and bad) as the lead competitor and promote a follower mentality. Instead, there is tremendous competitive advantage in adopting best-in-class practices that cut across industries.
- The phrase "maximize external variety while minimizing internal variety" captures the best approach to designing production processes. The RAP principle ("keep the material as Raw As Possible") is a convenient way to respond quickly to customer demand without accumulating a large finished goods inventory. Adopting the RAP principle also reduces variation in the system because aggregated demand has significantly less variation than individual demands.
- Buffer variation in demand with capacity, not inventory. While finished goods may allow the enterprise to serve customers faster, too often the enterprise ends up carrying the wrong kinds of products.
- If you have to hold inventory, it should be located strategically in the supply chain. Use the RAP principle to determine how far upstream it can be located and still meet customer lead time expectations.
- Use forecasts to plan and pull to execute. A system that reacts to pull signals will have less variation than a system that adopts a push mode of operation.

Putting metrics in place is of utmost importance because they will drive the behavior of the enterprises in the supply chain. These metrics must be formulated from a systems perspective; as the beer game demonstrates, a locally managed supply chain is inherently unstable. In deciding to adopt a metric, ask:

- Does the metric help sell more products?
- Does it help reduce payments or other expenses?
- Does it help reduce investments in resources?

3

Partnering in the Supply Chain

"A great marriage is not when the "perfect couple" comes together. It is when an imperfect couple learns to enjoy their differences. "
Dave Meurer, *Daze of our Wives*

In the small town of Canton, Mississippi, employees in the Lextron-Visteon facility assemble front-end and cockpit modules for the interior of the Nissan Quest minivan in 42 minutes. In a matter of hours, these modules are assembled into a minivan in one of Nissan's four assembly lines at its two-million-square-foot plant in Canton. Located within 100 yards of Nissan's trim plant, the Lextron-Visteon facility builds and delivers the modules in a mixed-model sequence, the same sequence in which Nissan builds the minivans.

Nissan uses modular assembly at this plant to build the Quest; the Pathfinder, Armada, and Infiniti sport utility vehicles; the Titan King Cab and Crew Cab trucks; and the Altima sedan. Seven other key suppliers are clustered near the plant, six of them within a two-mile radius. As with Lextron-Visteon, Nissan relies on these suppliers to deliver modules and components in the same sequence as the vehicles are produced on its production lines.

The modular strategy gives Nissan a significant competitive edge. Assembling prebuilt modules frees up valuable space on the production floor and allows Nissan to focus on its core competencies: the design and performance of the automobile. In partnership with suppliers like Lextron-Visteon, it is doing whatever it can to lead automakers in their quest to emulate the successful Dell assembly model. Nissan seems well-positioned to maintain its current status as the most efficient automobile manufacturer in North America,[1] but it may not be able to maintain such a competitive edge unless it can continue to maintain its alliances with key supply chain members.

The Nissan example highlights the important role the purchasing function plays in the lean supply chain. It is the link between the supplier and the enterprise. Equally important is the logistics function. It helps maintain the smooth flow of material into and out of the enterprise. Together, purchasing and logistics help Nissan deal with the multiple, sometimes conflicting, objectives of speed, flexibility, and lower costs.

Consider how the purchase function helps the company meet these objectives. From a strategic perspective, one of the major roles of purchasing is to select suppliers that can support the enterprise mission. In the case of Nissan, an obvious criterion for key suppliers would be their ability to support the mixed-model build sequence flexibly and positively, delivering quality products to the assembly line promptly and cost-effectively.

Cost-effectiveness is a particularly important requirement that must be carefully articulated. In manufacturing enterprises, direct material costs can eat up anywhere between 35 percent and 90 percent of revenues.[2] That means that a reduction in direct material costs of 5 percent can increase the bottom line profitability of a manufacturing company by as much as 45 percent.

While enterprises have recognized the huge potential savings that can result from reducing direct material costs, they have been slow to adopt the right approach: building effective *partnerships* with suppliers and logistics providers to reduce costs across the supply chain. Instead, their purchasing departments typically have an adversarial relationship with the suppliers, and logistics providers. Determined to pay as low a price as possible for materials, purchasing departments in less progressive enterprises either attempt to engage as many suppliers as possible in a bidding war, or they keep the pressure on suppliers to cut costs. Some enterprises in the automobile industry still expect a 5 percent price reduction from suppliers, year upon year.

---

1. Harbour Report North America 2003, Harbour Consulting, Troy, MI.
2. Santos, C., and M. Perogianni. 2001. "E-marketplaces: Challenges for Policymakers." A view by DG Enterprise of the European Commission, Institut für Technikfolgenabschätzung und Systemanalyse (ITAS).

A number of enterprises ask suppliers to deliver products on consignment.[3] There may be good reasons for having products delivered on consignment, but unfortunately, the driving cause for this practice often is simply to comply with a management-imposed mandate to curtail inventory carrying costs. This all-too-typical local thinking has inevitable consequences. In this case, requiring materials to be delivered on consignment can lead to lax procurement practices, because the purchasing department is strongly tempted to order larger quantities than needed in order to save on ordering and transportation costs and because it is not accountable for the additional inventory holding costs.

Building supply chain partnerships and alliances requires a more progressive approach, one based on systems thinking. Enterprises should realize that suppliers' costs are, in effect, their costs. If they ask a supplier to supply three months of consigned material when only a week's supply is needed, the cost of that inventory will ultimately find its way back into the supplier's price. The practice of forcing unconditional price reductions on a supplier may either force the supplier to cut corners to stay in business, make the supplier continue to lose money and eventually fold, or cause the supplier to exit from the relationship altogether. None of these outcomes benefits the enterprise.

While the enterprise should place high demands on suppliers, it should also realize that all parties should share the goal of reducing costs across the supply chain. The philosophy that should drive these partnerships and alliances is summarized in the seventh lean supply chain principle:

LEAN SUPPLY CHAIN PRINCIPLE 7

Build partnerships and alliances with members of the supply chain strategically, with the goal of reducing the total cost of providing goods and services.

This chapter presents guiding principles for building partnerships and alliances to manage the lean supply chain. For clarity, supply chain partners are separated into suppliers and logistics providers and techniques for coordinating the two groups are discussed in separate sections. The discussion first centers on how enterprises form relationships with suppliers, and guidelines for partnering with suppliers are presented. Next, inventory

---

3. That is, even though these products have been delivered to the enterprise, they are deemed to be owned by the supplier until they are consumed by the enterprise. Until they are actually used, the risk of loss, damage, theft, and obsolescence remains with the supplier.

ownership is discussed, followed by a presentation on techniques for partnering with logistics providers. The chapter ends with a discussion on resolving conflicts among supply chain partners.

PARTNERING WITH SUPPLIERS

The success of the supply chain depends heavily on the capabilities of the suppliers that choose to participate in it, collaborating with the enterprise in anticipation of higher profits. In general, enterprises form relationships with suppliers in one of three ways:

1. **Arm's-length relationships:** The enterprise procures parts or raw materials using a number of short-term suppliers and shops for the best prices each time it needs materials.
2. **Vertical integration:** The enterprise produces the materials it needs in-house and controls the buying and sourcing units.
3. **Partnerships or virtual integration:** The stages in the supply chain work together to leverage a competitive advantage.

Arm's-Length Relationships

Arm's-length relationships are formed when the enterprise outsources non-core activities to "specialist" suppliers. This relationship usually does not lead to long-term alliances. Instead, the buyer typically shops for the best prices each time it needs to procure parts or raw materials.

In arm's-length relationships, contracts are awarded to the supplier with the lowest bid, with relatively little attention paid to quality, logistics, or life-cycle costs. Thus, a real challenge with such relationships is how to get a collection of relatively autonomous enterprises to collaborate on complex, customized products. The desire of each enterprise to maximize its own profits (local optimization) often goes counter to the profit objectives of the enterprise next to it in the supply chain, at least for the short term. Thus, enterprises are reluctant to trust each other completely, to share information, or to do anything else that would result in productivity improvements for the entire supply chain.

Low trust and an absence of information characterizes enterprises that have arm's-length relationships, which are often held together by contractual agreements specified on paper but seldom followed. Arm's-length relationships discourage enterprises from investing in dedicated assets—assets mainly linked to a particular customer or supplier. The absence of such investments can hinder the productivity of the supply chain and impair the speed with which the different activities are coordinated.

Vertical Integration

Vertical integration gives enterprises a competitive advantage by building barriers to entry, facilitating investments in specialized assets, protecting product quality, and helping improve scheduling between adjacent stages in the supply chain—at least in theory. The conventional wisdom is that vertical integration makes for better coordination of functions and tasks.

The disadvantages of vertical integration are higher fixed costs, possibly higher variable costs if the enterprise's internal source of supply is high-cost, and a lack of flexibility when technology changes quickly or demand is uncertain. In addition, without measures in place to enforce tight coordination, vertical integration could, in fact, result in worse coordination than if the enterprise outsourced many of its activities. With vertically integrated enterprises, a major challenge is to overcome the "familiarity breeds contempt" syndrome. When two enterprises, one a supplier to the other, report to the same board of directors, there is a real danger that the business relationship could become increasingly casual, leading to problems with cost, quality, and adherence to delivery schedules.

The other extreme of vertical integration is when an enterprise outsources all its activities. In theory, outsourcing noncore activities lowers costs and makes better use of scarce resources, allowing the enterprise to concentrate those resources on its core activities. The enterprise is more flexible and can respond more rapidly to changing market conditions because it does not own the specialized assets needed for the noncore activities. However, outsourcing may have a detrimental effect if important value-creating activities are outsourced, or if the enterprise becomes too dependent on key suppliers.

There is another pitfall to avoid. More than a few enterprises resort to outsourcing to rid themselves of problems they could not solve themselves. The real reason for outsourcing should be to better leverage core competencies by outsourcing noncore activities to suppliers that provide the same product to a number of other customers and are therefore in a better position to exploit economies of scale.

In deciding whether to outsource or to pursue vertical integration, managers face a classic dilemma: Productivity grows with division of labor, which creates an incentive to outsource activities to more specialized enterprises. At the same time, outsourcing increases the costs of communication and coordination of activities, which creates a counterbalancing force to bring activities in-house and manage them under a common hierarchical structure.

Again, vertical integration, at least in theory, makes for effective coordination of functions and tasks, but it is a poor way to achieve the focus and customization necessary for an enterprise to stay at the cutting edge. Partnerships offer an option for resolving the dilemma.

Partnerships or Virtual Integration

Partnerships lie somewhere between vertical integration and arm's-length relationships. Whereas an arm's-length relationship works well if the supplier is providing a commodity, partnerships are preferable with suppliers that produce inputs of high value, requiring a high degree of interdependence between supplier and customer. To address the high levels of coordination and customization needed, enterprises are embracing a new business model aimed at building long-term partnerships and strategic alliances called *virtual integration,* which binds together two very different business models. It offers the tight coordination expected from vertically integrated enterprises yet benefits from the focus and customization derived from outsourcing to a specialist.

One enterprise that has exploited the concept of virtual integration very successfully is Dell. When it started, Dell was small; it could not afford to create every piece of the supply chain. It decided to buck the industry trend favored by Compaq, IBM, and HP to do everything themselves. Instead, Dell dedicated itself solely to the task of assembling and delivering computer systems to its customers. That meant Dell had to outsource a number of its activities, which in turn gave Dell a number of advantages, some of them probably serendipitous. For instance, unlike other major PC makers, Dell did not need a lot of fixed assets for manufacturing and assembling parts, so it did not have to worry about recovering sunk costs in fixed assets—a perceived need still very much in evidence in traditional enterprises that often clouds decision-making.

Dell soon found that building strategic alliances with key suppliers like Sony allowed it to react to customer demands far more quickly than vertically integrated enterprises could. If there were a problem with a new product launch, for instance, engineers from Sony could be at Dell's assembly plants right away.

As it began to forge strategic alliances with its suppliers, Dell found that it was able to adapt much more rapidly to technological advances. For instance, when Intel introduced a new chip, Dell could rely on its specialist suppliers, its strategic partners, to re-design their products to match the new chip design. Since Dell did not have a lot of fixed assets, it could move with the new technology much faster than its competitors could.

In an interview with the editor of *Harvard Business Review,* Michael Dell suggested that virtual integration, with its potential to achieve both coordination and focus, may well become "a new organizational model for the information age."[4] However, not all enterprises are in a position to replicate Dell's success with virtual integration. Many supply chains are rigid; they cannot be easily transformed to take advantage of the demand information available.

Governance Profiles

In a study of practices by original equipment manufacturers (OEMs) in the automobile industry, Dyer[5] found that lean enterprises like Toyota are much more likely to adopt a partnership arrangement whereas less lean competitors like General Motors and Ford are more likely to use a heavy mix of vertical integration and arm's-length relationships. Dyer uses the notion of a *governance profile* to characterize the percentage of inputs by value that are manufactured internally, procured from supply chain partners, and procured from arm's-length suppliers. Figure 3.1 depicts the governance profile for the automobile manufacturers named. In this figure, partnerships are governed by trust and long-term relationships rather than legal contracts, and a supplier is classified to this category if the OEM uses one or at most two suppliers for a product.

---

4. Magretta, J. 1998. "The Power of Virtual Integration: An Interview with Dell Computer's Michael Dell." *Harvard Business Review,* March-April, pp. 72-84
5. Dyer, Jeffrey H. 2000. *Collaborative Advantage: Winning through Extended Enterprise Supplier Networks.* New York: Oxford University Press.

Figure 3-1. Governance Profiles for Toyota, GM, and Ford

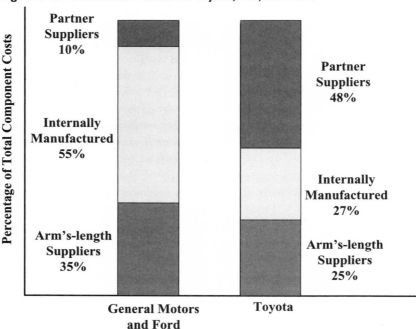

Source: Dyer, Jeffrey H. 2000. *Collaborative Advantage: Winning through Extended Enterprise Supplier Networks.* New York: Oxford University Press.

The governance profile for GM and Ford show clearly that they do considerably less partnering with suppliers than Toyota. GM and Ford are currently attempting to recreate their governance profiles, although the change is not likely to happen quickly in enterprises with such long-established manufacturing cultures.[6]

The optimal governance profile will differ from one industry to another. Industries making complex products may demand greater coordination, resulting in a governance profile with a higher percentage of vertical integration; industries that build simple products are likely to demand a higher percentage of arm's-length relationships. Thus, the fact that automobiles were a highly complex product in the early 1900s may partially explain why General Motors and Ford chose the vertical integration model while they were establishing their dominance in the U.S. automobile industry.

---

6. An article by Austin, R. D. 1999. "Ford Motor Company: Supply Chain Strategy." *Harvard Business School Case* No. 9-699-198, examines challenges faced by Ford as it attempted to move towards a "Dell-direct" model in the late 1990s.

In any event, following Dell's successful business model, enterprises within a lean supply chain are likely to move away from arm's-length relationships. Enterprises trying to build a lean supply chain are also likely to move away from the vertical integration model towards *strategic alliances,* which arguably are just collaborative partnerships carried to the next level.

As Figure 3.2 suggests, strategic alliances involve even more "relational" arrangements than collaborative partnerships (transactional arrangements are common with arm's-length relationships). The nature of these strategic alliances between enterprises will differ depending on whether the enterprise is dealing with a supplier or a logistics provider.

Figure 3-2. Types of Partnering Arrangements

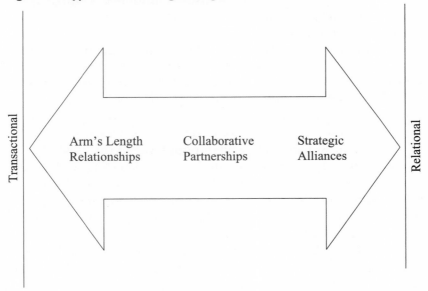

Consider the relationship between a buyer and a supplier. By entering into strategic alliances buyer and supplier gain significant benefits that are both strategic and operational. The strategic benefits include easy entrance into new markets and prompt attraction of new customers. Operational benefits emerge as a result of information transparency, which leads to lower costs, higher reliability, and better quality. What makes partnerships between suppliers and buyers effective are that:

- Suppliers are viewed as partners, not adversaries.
- The buyer's production schedules are increasingly visible to the supplier.

- Supplier and buyer together decide where to hold strategic inventory.
- The buyer enters into long-term contracts, uses blanket purchase-orders,[7] and has single-source suppliers.

Partners, not Adversaries

In general, establishing partnerships requires trust and cooperation. During the heyday of mass production, suppliers were typically treated as adversaries rather than partners. It was not uncommon for the purchasing departments to pit one potential supplier against another and award supply contracts to the lowest bidder without fully understanding the process capabilities of that supplier. Such arm's-length relationships do not evolve into long-term relationships. They do not instill confidence among suppliers, or motivate them to invest in resources for building and delivering a better quality product.

The parties in an adversarial relationship implicitly recognize the potential negative dynamics that accompany such an arrangement. For instance, there is a greater temptation for suppliers to bid low to acquire the contract and then negotiate prices upward based on contingencies. Needless to say, such behavior results in a continual cycle of bidding and contract awards.

The JIT movement that gained popularity in the 1980s on the heels of the success that Japanese automakers enjoyed in the United States changed these dynamics. The Japanese philosophy was that cooperation rather than confrontation maximized the benefits for both parties. The movement took a more systemic view, emphasizing maximization of value rather than local minimization of costs. As a result, instead of working with arm's-length relationships, enterprises formed collaborative partnerships and strategic alliances.

Stable, cooperative relationships have numerous benefits. Cooper and Slagmulder[8] studied 25 innovative Japanese lean enterprises. They found that trust, clear congruence of mutual goals, and a willingness of both parties to invest in specific assets for each other to be the most important benefits from long-term buyer-supplier partnering. Enterprises that have long-term

---

7. A blanket purchase order is an agreement between the enterprise and a supplier for multiple purchases under a single purchase order number.
8. Cooper, R., and R. Slagmulder. 1999. *Supply Chain Development for the Lean Enterprise.* Portland, OR: Productivity, Inc.

relationships also do not have to face the steep learning curve—required to understand and initiate transactions—that results when new contractual relationships are formed.

Once stable and cooperative relationships are established, some of the boundaries between buyer and supplier begin to fade. It is not unusual to find lean enterprises like Toyota or Honda temporarily assigning employees to work with their suppliers as resident engineers. These employees are better positioned to help the suppliers with quality problems because they can communicate the problems more clearly back to their own design and manufacturing departments. It is also not unusual to find lean suppliers sending their design or manufacturing engineers to a buyer's facility to rectify problems at the source and/or develop solutions to prevent further problems at the supplier's facility.

Increased Visibility to Suppliers

While U.S. automakers were quick to emulate the Japanese by introducing JIT operations in their facilities, they did not follow it through by creating partnerships and alliances with suppliers. Instead, their version of JIT was to ask suppliers to supply parts when needed on a "just-in-time" basis, without giving the suppliers clear visibility of assembly schedules. As a consequence, suppliers were typically forced to carry a large finished goods inventory "just-in-case" the buyer's demands changed. The suppliers had to either pass on the cost of carrying inventory to the automakers or, more likely, absorb the cost themselves. In either case, the cost of the inventory in the supply chain was higher.

How did the Japanese automakers leverage JIT across the supply chain so much more effectively than their American counterparts? Not only did they believe in long-term partnerships and alliances with their suppliers, they were willing to grow the joint effort by sharing their production plans with suppliers.

Toyota maintains a long-term contractual agreement to purchase steering gear assemblies from TRW Koyo in Vonore, Tennessee. Toyota gives the TRW Koyo its production schedule for the coming two weeks. In other words, the supplier can see two weeks into the future what it has to supply Toyota. This in turn allows TRW Koyo to communicate its production plans to its raw material suppliers. Because of this visibility of production schedules throughout the supply chain, TRW Koyo can operate with less than two days of raw material inventory, meeting Toyota's demand while supporting a strong relationship with its own supplier.

The Internet and business-to-business (B2B) systems have tremendously increased the ability of enterprises to make their operations visible to suppliers. Wal-Mart uses electronic data interchange (EDI) and POS data to better communicate its requirements to major suppliers like Procter & Gamble (P&G). Wal-Mart's POS system allows its central office in Bentonville, Arkansas, to collect data on tubes of toothpaste sold over an eight-hour period at a specific store in Omaha, Nebraska, so a tube of toothpaste bought at 3:00 p.m. can be restocked in the store by 9:00 p.m. the next day. Suppliers like P&G are happy with this arrangement because it gives them clear visibility on Wal-Mart's *actual* requirements every day. They do not have to rely on a forecast of customer demand.

Dell has about 200 suppliers, but 30 of them account for nearly 80 percent of its total purchases. Dell uses the Internet as a portal through which suppliers have visibility on Dell customer demands. When a customer places an order with Dell, its suppliers see the order immediately and are thus informed about the need to make the appropriate parts. Even medium-sized companies like Woodward Aircraft Engine Systems have harnessed the power of the Internet to give suppliers increased visibility of their production requirements. That goes a long way towards ensuring a stable, mutually rewarding, relationship.

The Internet has benefited customers as well. Because of its B2B systems, General Electric's customers can operate with very little inventory and still provide excellent customer service. Home Depot, for instance, does not carry GE inventory; more than 60 percent of Home Depot's sales of GE appliances are delivered directly from a GE warehouse, after the Home Depot system notifies the GE systems. Home Depot does not need inventory to consummate the transaction. Because GE washers, dryers, and other electric appliances have a high margin, Home Depot wants to partner with GE.

The idea of collaborating by sharing information may sound like one of those business ideas that everyone supports. In reality, though, few enterprises fully embrace the concept because many remain wary of sharing full information. It has been observed, however, that enterprises embracing collaboration find that the more they do it, the more benefits they realize: Forecasting is simpler, actual demand is less erratic and easier to meet, and there is less need for unexpected expediting in the process.

Single Sourcing and Blanket Purchase Orders

Single sourcing implicitly recognizes that buyer/supplier relationships are strengthened through long-term collaboration. In addition to the motivation and commitment to mutual success it generates, single sourcing has other benefits, among them improved quality, innovation sharing, reduced costs, and better coordination of production and delivery schedules.

For a while it seemed that every manufacturer was moving towards single sourcing, but the past decade has seen a significant split in how American enterprises perceive it. A survey by *Purchasing Magazine* found that 81 percent of the enterprises operated with at least one voluntary single-source supply relationship, but the analysis revealed that while the percentage seemed high, the number of enterprises that aggressively pursued a single-sourcing strategy was relatively low.[9] The survey reported that this finding reflects a general attitude toward single sourcing. Those with less enthusiasm for it view the benefits of single sourcing as limited, often seeing it merely as a way to simplify the budgeting processes by obtaining long-term fixed prices.

Establishing single-source suppliers implies that the suppliers are certified as quality suppliers. This trust in the supplier's ability to provide high-quality materials relieves the customer of having to inspect each incoming shipment for quality. It also implies that the suppliers are reliable and will deliver the right quantity at the right time. Unfortunately, this is precisely why a number of purchasers have moved away from the practice of single sourcing. Many suppliers have hurt their cause through the "overpromise, underdeliver" syndrome. Others bid low to secure contracts and then resort to creeping price escalation. Therefore, a large number of enterprises that do believe in the benefits of single sourcing maintain an alternate source of supply in case the primary supplier cannot deliver at the rate and the quality levels specified. Having an alternate supplier also discourages the primary supplier from seeking unsubstantiated price increases.

Another approach to building trust and engaging suppliers in long-term contracts is to use blanket purchase orders. A blanket purchase order is a contract to buy a certain number of items over a specified period. Once the initial contract is executed by the purchasing department, requests for deliveries are typically generated directly by the production department.

---

9.   Porter, A. 1999. "Single Sourcing—Some Love it, Most Fear it." *Purchasing*, *http://www.purchasing.com*, June.

The use of blanket purchase orders is not new. They have been in existence at least since the early 1960s in many countries. However, in the past, when relationships between suppliers and customers were traditionally adversarial, the motivation for using blanket purchase orders was often either to eliminate paperwork or to ensure commitments from suppliers that they would deliver. These days, there is a subtle but perceptible shift in the way blanket purchase orders are viewed. The intent now is to stress long-term relationships with key suppliers.

INVENTORY OWNERSHIP AND CONSIGNMENT INVENTORIES

Many enterprises have consignment inventory arrangements with their suppliers. Under this arrangement, the suppliers place inventory "on consignment" at the customer's site, either directly at point of use or at a warehouse, but the goods are not deemed delivered to the customer until they are actually consumed. This arrangement effectively benefits the customer, who does not have to worry about payment until the product is actually used in production.

At first glance, it may seem that the customer is taking unfair advantage of the supplier. While that may be to some extent true, the supplier benefits as well. When the customer picks up a consignment for production, it is a pull signal to the supplier. It gives better visibility on demand to the supplier, which can now better plan its production. When the partnership operates in this mode, it is more of a win-win situation. In fact, it is the basis for vendor-managed inventory (VMI).

Vendor-Managed Inventory (VMI)

VMI is not a new concept, but there has been renewed interest in it as enterprises analyze core competencies and work on outsourcing non-core activities. With VMI, the supplier is responsible for stocking the customer's shelves. The quantity replenished is typically based on data obtained through EDI, although often the supplier makes regular visits to the customer's facility to determine replenishment quantities. A good example of VMI in action is illustrated by the dispensing machines that now hold tools and tooling equipment in many machine shops. As the operators pull from them, the vendors replenishing them can accurately estimate consumption without having to rely on forecasts.

VMI is referred to by different names, depending on the industry. The apparel industry calls it *efficient consumer response,* the grocery industry uses efficient consumer response and *just-in-time distribution,* and the automobile industry uses VMI and just-in-time distribution.

VMI reduces the number of transactions for the purchasing, inspection, and stores functions. It also gives the supplier clear visibility of the rate at which its products are being consumed. With VMI, suppliers do not have to rely on a customer's purchasing department to give them delivery schedules. Instead, suppliers now control how they replenish their stock at a customer's facility based on shared demand information.

VMI has excellent potential to reduce inventories *and* stock-outs in the supply chain. It lets suppliers prioritize their delivery schedules based on which customer is expected to stock out. And with VMI there is no temptation for the supplier to induce bulk buying by the customer's purchasing department to take advantage of quantity discounts. As we observed in the beer game, discounts produce unpredictable demand surges in the supply chain.

Another compelling reason for enterprises to consider VMI is that it enhances collaboration in the supply chain. Figure 3.3 indicates how implementing VMI has immediate impact on a customer's production. The production department in a traditional enterprise typically transmits a request to the procurement function, which then gives the supplier either a purchase order or a delivery request (sometimes inflated by the purchasing department). This sequence of hand-offs, each with potential for error, is short-circuited by a VMI program.

In summary, the advantages VMI offers to suppliers are:

- A "virtual" shortening of the supply chain—the production function in the downstream enterprise now has direct contact with the supplier.
- Frequent communication of inventory levels, stock-outs, and planned promotions—the supplier now has better visibility. EDI linkages facilitate this communication.
- Reduction in inventories and stock-outs.
- Prioritization of shipments. For example, shipments might be classified from the top down as: (a) items that are expected to stock out; (b) items that are well below targeted stock levels; (c) advance shipments of promotional items (allowed only in the transition phase); and (d) items that are close to targeted stock levels.

Figure 3-3. VMI Enhances Collaboration in the Supply Chain

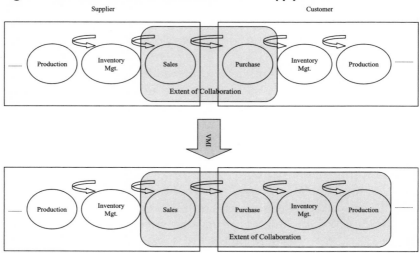

Nevertheless, implementing VMI can be challenging. The problem is not merely one of logistics. When a supplier tries to implement VMI, it can encounter resistance from its sales force. At issue are the roles played by each participant, the skills required, the degree of trust, and the acceptance of power shifts. Sales might view VMI as a threat to incentive bonuses, especially if the bonus depends on how much they are able to "sell" to their customers. There may be skepticism about whether the process will function smoothly and concern that the reduced inventory that usually follows from a VMI program will result in less shelf space and thus the perception of a loss of market share.

If there is an intermediate distribution channel, distributors may also have concerns about VMI, especially if they lose control over what they receive. The distributors may perceive the VMI program as trying to push inventory onto them. Since they do not have any control on what they stock, they may also worry that the supplier could eventually take over the distributor's function, supplying product directly to the customer. When Barilla SpA[10] introduced VMI in the pasta manufacturing industry, the biggest challenges came from distributors who feared that their right to order what they wanted was being denied.

---

10. Hammond, J. H. 1994. "Barilla SpA (A)." *Harvard Business School Case* 9-694-046.

Collaborative Planning, Forecasting, and Replenishment (CPFR)

Collaborative planning, forecasting, and replenishment (CPFR) is a business practice aimed at reducing inventory costs while improving product availability across the supply chain. It is a way to synchronize the demand forecasts that the buyer and the supplier have for the product to arrive at a single consensus forecast.

The basic idea is that enterprises share forecasts and results data over the Internet. Technology, using CPFR, analyzes the data and alerts planners at each enterprise to exceptional situations that could affect deliveries or sales. The enterprises then collaborate to resolve the exceptions by adjusting plans, expediting orders, and correcting data entry errors.

CPFR can be viewed as an outgrowth of VMI, the next step in the supply chain collaboration continuum. In fact, many people believe the movement to CPFR would not have been possible without the foundation laid by VMI and other continuous replenishment strategies.

CPFR was introduced in 1995 when Wal-Mart found that the in-stock averages of pharmaceutical manufacturer Warner-Lambert were not meeting Wal-Mart's vendor performance standards. Wal-Mart partnered with Warner-Lambert, Surgency (formerly Benchmarking Partners), and two software companies, SAP and Manugistics, to define a process that would link customer demand with replenishment needs throughout the supply chain. The pilot project focused on Listerine mouthwash and involved one Warner-Lambert manufacturing plant and three Wal-Mart distribution centers. The results of the study were very encouraging: Warner-Lambert's in-stock averages rose from 87 percent to 98 percent, lead times dropped from 21 to 11 days, and sales increased $8.5 million over the test period.

The CPFR movement gained momentum in 1998 when Voluntary Inter-industry Commerce Standards (VICS) got involved. VICS is a voluntary, nonprofit organization formed by retailers, textile suppliers, and apparel makers in 1986 to develop bar-code and EDI standards for the retail industry. Once VICS got involved, more enterprises were willing to participate in testing and validating CPFR.

One of the more successful pilot projects was between stores in the Wegman's grocery chain and a Nabisco distribution center; Nabisco's sales of 22 Planters nut products grew by 31 percent, while Wegman's dollar sales of nuts increased by 16 percent—yet there was a surprising 18 percent decrease in inventory.

The pilot projects demonstrated that CPFR could deliver such promised benefits as reduced inventory, higher fill rates, and increased sales. The pilot projects also showed that partner enterprises could reduce both fixed assets and drains on working capital.

CPFR success stories continue to make the headlines. More than 100 leading companies including Eastman Kodak, JC Penney, Kimberly-Clark, NCR, Kmart, and Proctor & Gamble are now using CPFR. Still, it is too early to tell whether CPFR is just a passing fad or is here to stay. It has the same problems that VMI faces, and, in addition, requires sophisticated software systems. IT is needed to build, share, and adjust on-line forecasts and plans.

CPFR also requires a cultural shift and investments of human capital. Since not many executives are familiar with CPFR, there is a need for education and better understanding of business impact.

Johnson and Carroll[11] report that the U.S. Department of Commerce estimates that more than $1 trillion in finished goods are routinely held in inventory in U.S.-based stores, distribution centers, and manufacturing plants, and that much of the inventory is 'just-in-case' merchandise "that would not be necessary if trading partners had better visibility to each other's plans."

Quite often, the problem with just-in-case inventory is that, though a customer does need it, it is at the wrong location. CPFR can help determine where to locate the inventory, an added benefit that is often overlooked. Enterprises using CPFR in the supply chain can jointly decide where to locate inventory *strategically* to meet customer lead time expectations. The idea is to determine how far upstream in the supply chain it is possible to locate the inventory.

Properly executed, CPFR has the potential to make a huge impact on delivering the right product, in the right quantity, to the right customer, at the right cost. Kurt Salmon Associates offer a conservative estimate that the benefits of CPFR could total $8.3 billion annually for the apparel industry alone.[12]

---

11. Johnson, M., and T. Carroll. 2002. "The CPFR Value Proposition." Syncra Systems, Inc., *http://www.syncra.com/newsroom/CPFR_ValueProp.pdf.*
12. Ibid.

PARTNERING WITH LOGISTICS PROVIDERS

Logistics is a system of related activities to manage an orderly flow of material within and between firms. Coyle, Bardi, and Langley[13] define the "7 Rs" of logistics: namely, ensuring the availability

1. Of the *right* product
2. In the *right* quantity
3. And the *right* condition
4. At the *right* place
5. At the *right* time
6. For the *right* customer
7. At the *right* cost.

Broadly speaking, logistics is really the management of inventory, whether it is in motion or at rest. The term as understood here covers inventory management, materials handling, warehousing and storage, and transportation from one enterprise to another. Services provided by the logistics function range from activities undertaken in-house by users of the services (e.g., storage or inventory control at a manufacturing plant) to the operations of external service providers. Logistics services comprise physical activities like transport and storage as well as nonphysical activities like choosing contractors and negotiating freight rates.

The importance of logistics integration in the lean supply chain cannot be overstated. It allows logistics providers to deliver quality goods to their customers at the right time. Logistics integration significantly facilitates supply chain decisions about where to position strategic inventory to provide better customer service. It also allows suppliers and customers to work effectively with minimal inventories without having to buffer uncertainties in the logistics process with extra inventory or capacity.

This does not come without cost. Billions of dollars are spent on logistics in the United States. Delaney estimates that logistics costs accounted for $970 billion in 2001, the equivalent of 9.5 percent of the gross domestic product.[14]

It is not possible to treat the logistics function in a single section, or even a chapter. The intent here is to underscore the importance of logistics integration and of partnering with logistics

---

13. Coyle, J. J., E. J. Bardi, and C. J. Langley. 2003. *The Management of Business Logistics,* 7th ed., Mason, OH: South-Western Publishing.
14. R. Wilson and R.V. Delaney (2002). "Understanding Inventory — Stay Curious!" 13th Annual 'State of Logistics Report,' *http://www.mi-clm.org/downloads/13th%20Annual%20State%20of%20the%20Logistics.pdf*

providers. A large number of enterprises are building those kinds of partnerships. For example, Home Depot partners with J.B. Hunt to ensure the delivery of quality products from warehouses to retail stores. The trucking company has installed drop bars in its trucks to secure the different pallet shapes and sizes that it carries for Home Depot.

Logistics providers now ensure timely deliveries of small lot sizes at regular intervals. The concepts of "milk runs" and LTL (less-than-truck-load) quantities have made it possible for enterprises to streamline their operations. Milk runs are delivery routes set up by logistics providers to deliver goods to enterprises at fixed times during the day so that enterprises can rely on timely shipment of goods to their stores. In combination with LTL shipments, they make it possible to deliver small lots at frequent intervals, which considerably enhances the ability to respond quickly and flexibly to changing customer demands. Since the deliveries typically are in small lot sizes from nearby locations, the next delivery can be modified more easily than if full truckload quantities are shipped less often.

Many of the factors that promote effective partnership with suppliers also apply to partnering with logistics providers. Long-term contracts, single-sourcing, and better visibility on shipping and delivery schedules lead to more sustainable relationships between enterprise and logistics provider, though logistics has some unique characteristics not found in buyer-supplier relationships, such as the presence of third-party logistics providers (3PLs).

3PLs/4PLs

When the industrial environment became more competitive in the 1980s and the 1990s, there was tremendous pressure on suppliers to deliver products faster, cheaper, and in smaller lots. Many enterprises were reluctant to cope with these pressures, either because they did not have the resources to invest in a logistics infrastructure or simply because it did not add to their core competencies. After all, their main concern was to manufacture a product. The burden of coordinating the logistics activities thus fell on the willing shoulders of third party logistics providers (3PLs).

A 3PL is an enterprise that provides such logistics services as warehousing, order management, distribution, and transport services to its customer, using its own assets and resources. The rationale is that cost-effective operation can only materialize from an outside party that makes it a core competency. The 3PLs thus provided *integrated logistics management.*

3PLs were embraced by enterprises eager to contract out logistics activities; there has been a tremendous growth in demand for their services throughout the 1990s and into the 21st century. A survey of CEOs of Fortune 500 enterprises conducted in 2002 by Accenture and Northeastern University found that over 90 percent of the respondents were using the services of one or more 3PL providers.[15]

A logistics firm is basically one that provides integrated transport-related or warehousing-related solutions to shippers. The primary services contracted from 3PL providers are inbound and outbound transportation, cross-docking (see below), warehousing, freight bill auditing and payment, and freight consolidation and distribution. A key differentiating factor between a 3PL and a typical transportation or other logistics service provider is that the 3PL can also manage some of the information needs of the enterprises for which they provide logistics support. The use of 3PLs is most widespread among large enterprises, such as Eastman Kodak, Wal-Mart, Home Depot, and Toyota. Examples of the 3PLs they use are Ryder, Transfreight, UPS Logistics, and Fedex Logistics.

Some of the partnerships between manufacturing enterprises and logistics providers have led to solutions beyond the traditional realm of logistics. For instance, Airborne became the air carrier of choice for IBM and Xerox. Then together they identified potential warehouse consolidation opportunities, found or built state-of-the-art facilities, and consolidated pickup and delivery points. By reducing redundant operations and eliminating nonvalue-added activities, the three partners saved $10 million. IBM and Xerox now have colocated parts centers in Seattle and St. Louis.[16]

In the automotive industry, Ford Motor Co., generally viewed as a trendsetter in designing processes for supply chain management, formed a strategic alliance in February 2000 with the UPS Logistics Group, a subsidiary of United Parcel Service, to reduce the time it was taking to deliver vehicles from Ford plants to dealers and customers. The alliance is re-engineering the Ford

---

15. Lieb, R., and M. Hickey. "The Use of Third Party Logistics by Large American Manufacturers, the 2002 Survey," *http://www.accenture.com.*
16. Stock, J. R., and D. M. Lambert. 2001. *Strategic Logistics Management.* Boston: Irwin McGraw-Hill; and Thomas, J. 1998. "Imagination Unlimited." *Logistics Management and Distribution Report,* 37 (9): pp. 71–74

transportation network of rail and road carriers and enhancing quick and reliable deliveries. Not to be outdone, in December 2000, General Motors formed a joint venture with Menlo World-wide called Vector SCM to manage the delivery of more than 8 million vehicles a year from 12,000 points of origin around the world.

The more progressive 3PL providers can constantly update their information technology and equipment to stay current. Thus, the shippers using the 3PLs do not have to be concerned with constantly updating their own technology in this area but can instead focus on their core competencies. In fact, the retailers they ship to may have different, and probably changing, delivery and technology requirements that 3PLs are better positioned to meet in a more cost-effective way.

The 3PLs also give shippers greater flexibility. For instance, suppliers that must provide rapid replenishment may need regional warehouses, but by using 3PLs to handle the warehousing, the supplier does not have to invest time and money in building and maintaining warehouses. 3PLs are also in a better position to consolidate low-volume LTL shipments from different suppliers for delivery.

The services provided by 3PLs inherently depend on long-term relationships oriented towards solving problems for the enterprise, sharing risks and benefits, and recognizing mutual interdependences. The preferred mode of operation is for the enterprise to negotiate with a single 3PL that agrees to provide a broad set of order fulfillment activities from storage to order-picking to transportation to financial management. The 3PL may be given responsibility to design the logistics network and to monitor and control logistics processes.

Such a long-term arrangement demands a long-term commitment of assets on the part of the 3PL. In return, the enterprise, whether shipper or receiver, must be willing to commit to a long-term relationship to make the work of the 3PL economically feasible.

The reality is that the full benefits of 3PLs have not been realized. As 3PLs became more sophisticated at moving goods from one place to another, there was a perception that they were still not offering some activities that could well be outsourced to them. For instance, speedy transfer of and access to information was still missing. Enter the fourth-party logistics providers (4PLs).

4PLs represent further outsourcing. They were the product of consulting enterprises, in particular Andersen Consulting (now Accenture) which trademarked the term in 1996. An example of a 4PL is Vector SCM, a joint venture of General Motors and Menlo Worldwide LLC.

The 4PL is, in theory, a logistics integrator that manages not only the 3PLs but also other supply chain-related activities like IT management. It is an additional service layer between the 3PL and its customer that in effect manages these activities without necessarily carrying any assets. Armbruster[17] notes that:

> *"Their role is like that of a general contractor who manages plumbers, electricians, and carpenters at a construction job site. In logistics, the general contractor is the 4PL; the subcontractors are the 3PLs, truckers, forwarders, customs brokers, and other firms."*

Cross-Docking

Cross-docking is a warehousing strategy that is gaining momentum as major logistics providers recognize the need to become more flexible while staying responsive to upstream and downstream enterprise needs.

Originally envisioned for the retail industry, cross-docking is increasing in popularity in the manufacturing sector as well.

Cross-docking is a process by which products are moved from one enterprise to another enterprise through an intermediate warehouse, where they are not stored for more than a few hours. Basically, cross-docks are an effective alternative to picking orders and delivering in small quantities to each retail outlet using LTL shipments. They enable *economies of scope.*

Cross-docks are essentially marshalling yards in the old railroad sense: Trucks arrive with products that must be sorted, often consolidated with other products, and loaded onto outbound trucks. The incoming trucks typically arrive from an upstream enterprise and the outbound trucks are typically destined for a manufacturing enterprise or a retail outlet. Figure 3.4 shows a cross-dock. Workers place pallets in lanes corresponding to the receiving doors, a second team of workers sorts pallets into shipping lanes, and a third team loads them onto outbound trailers.

---

17. Armbruster, W. 2002. "Third Party Logistics Producers Are Well Established; Now Lean Logistics Providers are Springing Up to Manage Them." *JoC Week,* June, *http://www.joc.com.*

Figure 3-4. A Representation of a Crossdock

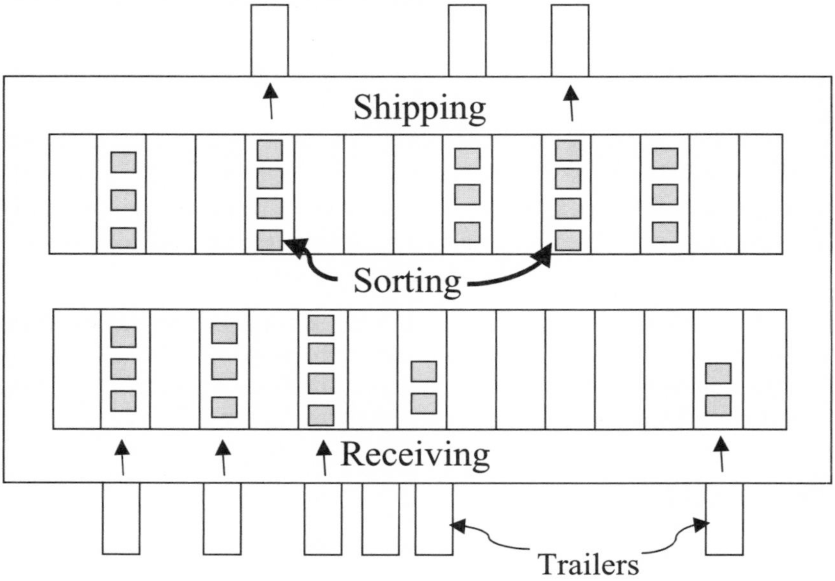

Source: Gue, K. R. 2001. "Cross-docking: Just in Time for Distribution," Report, Naval Postgraduate School, Monterey, CA, May 2001.

In the ideal world, the goal of cross-docking is to transfer products at the warehouse directly from incoming to outgoing trailers without having to store it. Napolitano refers to cross docking as "JIT in the distribution arena."[18] A number of enterprises are now actively using cross-docking as a value-added logistics strategy to slash costs in the supply chain. Cross-docking is practiced by leading logistics providers and 3PL/4PL enterprises, including UPS and FedEx, as well as the United States Postal Service. Gue[19] mentions a number of other enterprises, such as Home Depot, Wal-Mart, and Costco, that use cross-docks.

What are some obvious difference between cross-docking and the traditional warehousing operation? In traditional warehousing, the warehouse receives products, updates its inventory records, and moves the product into a specific location in the warehouse. The product sits there in inventory until it is required by a customer, at which time it is picked, packed, and shipped, and then the inventory records are adjusted.

---

18. Napolitano, M. 2000. *Making the Move to Cross-docking.* Oakbrook, IL: Warehousing Education and Research Council.

19. Gue, K. R. 2001. "Cross-docking: Just in Time for Distribution." Report, Monterey, CA: Naval Postgraduate School, May.

On the other hand, cross-docks typically do not have any inventory records to update because that is unnecessary. Instead, the products are shipped as soon as possible with, at most, a brief waiting time for other trucks to arrive with products bound for the same destination. The product does not go into long-term storage.

To be effective, cross-docking demands advance knowledge of the inbound product and its destination and a system of routing the product to the proper outbound vehicle. A specific system must be in place to ensure efficient exchange of both product and information, and to match and schedule inbound and outbound shipments so that the product flows through the warehouse as quickly as possible.

3PLs operate centralized cross-docks (typically two to four) to cover the North American market. These cross-docks may stock a strategic inventory of high-volume products for urgent delivery. One automaker uses a 3PL to collect parts from suppliers and deliver them to a cross-dock where shipments are consolidated and shipped to 12 different assembly plants throughout North America. The parts are never warehoused or inventoried at the plants.

Napolitano[20] lays out criteria for cross-docking success:

- **The right suppliers:** those with the proven discipline to consistently provide the correct quantity of the correct product at the precise time when it will be needed.
- **The right information flow:** timely, accurate, preferably paperless, information flow among trading partners.
- **The right product flow:** a network of transportation, facilities, equipment, and operations that supports smooth and swift flow of products.
- **Capital,** to sustain a cost-justified cross-docking system.
- **Personnel** who recognize the urgency of moving product and not storing it.

Cross-docking does not come without headaches. It requires extensive coordination between suppliers, distributor, and customers. A cross-docking operation imposes restrictions on suppliers and customers: Supplier may be asked to deliver small shipments more frequently or to attach bar codes to packaging. Customers may be scheduled to receive supplies only on certain days. These restrictions can lead to extra costs and coordination

---

20. Napolitano, M. 2000. *Making the Move to Cross-docking.* Oakbrook, IL: Warehousing Education and Research Council.

for channel partners. If the cross-dock facility needs to know what is on each inbound truck before it arrives, that requires good information systems.

At the same time, cross-docking promises certain benefits over a traditional warehouse. There are the obvious savings in reduced inventories, with a corresponding decrease in the storage space required. Labor costs are reduced because inventory receipts do not have to be recorded; products for inventory do not have to stowed into storage bins; product flow is accelerated so that products reach the customer quicker; and there is reduced opportunity for pilferage.

Improved warehouse management systems, EDI, and radio-frequency identification (RFID) technology have considerably abetted the use of cross-dock programs. Advance ship notices (ASN) also help determine potential cross-dock opportunities and allow for better scheduling of events.

Radio-Frequency Identification Systems (RFID)

Logistics activities, as well as techniques like VMI and CPFR, are enhanced by developments like RFID technology. In its most basic form, the RFID system could be viewed as an inventory-tracking tool, but its potential benefits are so enormous that an entire section is devoted to discussing the technology and how it applies to supply chain management. The benefits of RFID technology range from delivering improved product availability on the retail shelf, substantially improving handling efficiency, to providing full and accurate visibility of inventory all along the supply chain.

The basic component of the technology is the RFID tag, a microprocessor chip that contains data in a machine-readable format. The RFID system has three major components: (1) the tag, (2) the RFID reader, and (3) the data managing/processing system.

In a sense, the RFID tag is like the universal product code (UPC), the familiar bar code now found on almost any package, that has encoded machine-readable alphanumeric data. Historically, bar codes have been the tracking technology of choice because they are cheap and easy to use, but they have limitations: the amount of data they can hold is restricted, scanning them requires a clear line of sight, and once printed they cannot be rewritten. On the other hand, an RFID tag can carry a lot more data that can be rewritten more than 100,000 times; and radio-frequency technology does not require that the tag be visible.

The tag can be "scanned" through materials like plastic, paper, or wood.

While UPC bar codes currently have a cost advantage, the cost of RFID tags is dropping. The cost of RFID tags depends on the application and the features. At the high end are *active* tags that have more features, greater functionality, and more applications than *passive* tags. The cost of a passive tag is currently about 5 cents, and is projected to cost a penny or less by 2010.[21] In contrast, active tags can cost as much as $100 depending on the features built into the tag.

The RFID system, however, has significantly more potential to cut supply chain costs and improve supply chain efficiencies than the symbol. The list of possible supply chain RFID applications is very large, as has been spelled in out in numerous books and articles.[22] This chapter discusses only a few of the ways RFID applications can enhance collaboration among supply chain partners.

Within the factory, RFID can support the assembly process by ensuring that all the items needed for assembly are available in the warehouse. Next, as these items are picked from the warehouse for delivery onto the line, RFID can improve the accuracy of picking, ensuring that the correct parts get to the assembly line. Similarly, when the product is assembled, the technology can ensure that all the right components are incorporated before it is sent to the next downstream location. As the product is dispatched to the customer or the distribution center, assemblies can be counted and automatically denoted as shipped against a customer order. At the same time, the components that went into the assembled product could be automatically *backflushed*[23] from the inventory records at the parts warehouse.

At the distribution center or the warehouse receiving the items, the tag can transmit, through the reader, information that would normally be keyed into an inventory management system by a worker at the warehouse or receiving dock. Eliminating manual labor means products move through the supply chain quicker, yet are tracked more efficiently, while the possibility of human error,

---

21. Rutner, S., M. A. Waller, and J. T. Mentzer. 2004. "A Practical Look at RFID." *Supply Chain Management Review,* January/February: pp. 36–41
22. *See ibid.* for an especially useful recent summary.
23. Backflushing is the automated (computerized) deduction of all the components (sometimes including labor) that goes into an assembled product based on the assembly's bill of material (BOM).

that arises when data is input manually, is eliminated. The RFID system can not only input exact counts of incoming items into the warehouse management system, it can also direct the shipment to the appropriate storage location. For instance, if the material is needed to replenish an out-of-stock item that is badly needed, the system could flag it as one that requires priority handling at the receiving dock.

RFID can support security by preventing pilferage. It can also facilitate bulk storage or temporary storage of pallets that do not have an assigned location. In an industry that uses chemicals, their temporary storage requires caution in order to avoid potential product compatibility problems. With RFID, if the item going into temporary storage is incompatible with the product next door, the system can alert the fork lift operator.

RFID has the potential to significantly improve productivity, accuracy, and reduce costs. For example, GE used RFID tags to reduce the time it took to inventory equipment used in one of its projects. The equipment was spread over 20 acres but the employees tracking the inventory were able to drive around in golf carts using handheld scanners that picked up RFID signals from tags on the equipment at distances of up to 100 feet. Inventory-tracking time was cut from 18 workweeks down to 5.[24]

Properly used, RFID technology can promote better integration between the enterprise, its suppliers, and the logistics providers. While widespread adoption is still perhaps five years away, world-class supply chain enterprises are starting to pilot RFID right now. Wal-Mart has instructed its top 100 suppliers to have RFID tags on all their pallets of products, by January 25, 2005.[25] Procter & Gamble (P&G), one of Wal-Mart's biggest suppliers, expects to have RFID tags on pallets well before that time. Their goal is to use the tags to track goods throughout the supply chain, from the time they are boxed at a P&G manufacturing plant until consumers buy them from retail stores.[26] The decision by the largest U.S. retailer to adopt RFID tags for its supply chain will drive other businesses to use RFID tags as well.

---

24. Bacheldor, B. 2003. "Suppliers Sign On As GE Powers Up RFID." *Information Week,* October 27: *http://www.informationweek.com.*

25. Gonsalves, A. 2003. "Wal-Mart Endorsement Puts Wireless Inventory Tracking Pedal to the Metal." *http://www.informationweek.com,* June 12.

26. Kellam, L. 2003. "P&G Rethinks Supply Chain." *Optimize,* October: *http://www.optimizemag.com.*

Postponement in Logistics

Postponement, the philosophy adopted in lean supply chains, is in direct contrast to *speculation,* where channel members assume risk rather than shifting it. Speculation exploits the economies of large-scale production; its goal is minimizing stockout and order processing costs. Postponement means that a manufacturer begins production or assembly of components or subassembled parts only after receiving a firm order.

Postponement in logistics shifts the risk of owning goods from one channel member to another. Just as a manufacturer may refuse to produce goods until it receives a firm order, an intermediary may postpone owning inventories by buying from sellers who offer faster delivery, or on consignment, or only when a sale has been made. Consumers postpone ownership by buying from retail outlets where products are in stock.

3PLs participate in postponement strategies in a number of ways. They may mix pallets for individual customers as orders are received, repackage products to fit specific customer or country requirements, or perform final assembly or customization in the field.

RESOLVING POWER CONFLICTS

The advantages of partnering have been discussed at length. What about possible drawbacks? For instance, how are conflicts in the supply chain resolved? Which enterprise or enterprises should orchestrate the supply chain and will the other members accept this leadership? Would it make sense to have a truly democratic supply chain that has no designated leader?

The answer to these questions are undoubtedly specific to the dynamics of each unique supply chain, but broadly speaking there are three possibilities:

1. There is a clearly identifiable leader in the supply chain.
2. Several enterprises in the supply chain have clout but there is no single dominant member.
3. There are no dominant enterprises in the supply chain.

When there is a dominant player in the supply chain—a Toyota, a Dell, a Wal-Mart—many issues are resolved easily. The dominant player calls the shots and builds the ecosystem around that enterprise. The other members in the supply chain are usually willing to go with the power. In such a situation, the dominant player sometimes takes steps to ensure continued dominance. For instance, by multisourcing key products to reduce the power of suppliers, or having multiple customers to reduce a customer's dominance.

The drawback to this approach is that having multiple suppliers goes counter to the idea of a lean, collaborative supply chain. Ideally speaking, the dominant player should adopt a systems perspective and orchestrate the supply chain so that all its members benefit. Such a system is more likely to support the growth of the dominant enterprise's ecosystem.

Consider the Wal-Mart ecosystem. Wal-Mart has two lines of business: (1) staple stock items and (2) direct freight items. Staple stock items are products like shampoo and toothpaste that are replenished by suppliers based on consumption signals from Wal-Mart stores. Direct freight items are those that Wal-Mart's procurement department buys and sends to stores on a push basis when products are being sold by suppliers at competitive prices. For instance, in September 2002, Wal-Mart used this strategy to offer Microtel computers for $199.

As far as staple stock items are concerned, every enterprise in Wal-Mart's lean supply chain recognizes Wal-Mart as the undisputed leader of the chain. (Before Wal-Mart attained its current stature, one of its primary suppliers, Procter & Gamble, wielded more clout than Wal-Mart in this supply chain. The roles are now reversed.) For first-tier and upstream suppliers in the supply chain, if Wal-Mart is their key customer, their role is well understood: When Wal-Mart generates more sales, they benefit. The suppliers are usually willing to do whatever it takes to support Wal-Mart's sales. Their job is made easier since Wal-Mart works with POS data to give suppliers clear visibility on its requirements.

If there are a handful of enterprises that have the clout in the supply chain, the ideal scenario is that enterprises work together to enlarge their business. This supply chain is more likely to resemble a supply *web* because many of the enterprises will have suppliers and customers that belong to other supply chains or webs. Here again, the dominant players may take steps to either ensure continued dominance or reduce the dominance of others, by, say, multisourcing or expanding the customer base. In situations like this, techniques like CPFR are likely to benefit all the members of the supply chain. Unless the members are willing to work together, the long-term viability of the supply chain will be uncertain, given today's world. Relationships between the power players are more likely to be arm's-length and transactional here rather than strategic and relational. (See Figures 3.1 and 3.2.)

When there is no obvious dominant player in the supply chain, or web, the situation is like the previous case—unless all members recognize that they have an opportunity to work in a true democracy, which offers a greater chance of collaboration. Techniques like CPFR appear more likely to work in such a situation.

Regardless of the power structure, there are some principles that, if followed, will benefit any supply chain. The issue at hand is: Who should make the decisions? It may depend on which enterprise has the best visibility on the supply chain, but that in turn depends on whether there is trust placed on this enterprise. For instance, in the automotive supply chain, tens of thousands of suppliers have been invited to join Covisint, an electronic exchange established by several international automakers in an effort to connect the entire automotive supply system. However, a lack of confidence in Covisint's ability to deliver has turned off many lower-tier suppliers.

If supply chain partners rely on each other for inventory management, logistics, engineering innovation, and so on, they must realize that these processes and functions cannot be strengthened without mutual trust and cooperation. Today, it is no longer feasible to continue operation without partnering with members of a supply chain. Enterprises that are not willing to play in this new world are likely to fade into oblivion.

CONCLUSIONS

The competitive world we live in today requires that enterprises rethink their strategies. In the 21st century, the spotlight has shifted from competition between enterprises to competition between supply chains. Managers of enterprises have to contend with the fact that some of the biggest challenges they face in the new millennium relate to actions that must be coordinated jointly with their upstream or downstream partners, or both.

To promote effective supply chain partnering, some things need to be kept in mind:

- Enterprises need long-term partnerships with suppliers. That means they must move away from their traditional, adversarial, arms length relationships with suppliers towards more collaborative partnerships and strategic alliances.

- Enterprises will gain from offering suppliers increased visibility on their production plans.
- Trust must be built so that those sharing information do not have to be concerned about their own data being used against them. Trust is nourished by working with fewer suppliers on longer-term contracts.
- Inventory should be maintained at strategic locations so as to minimize the total cost of holding inventory. The 3PLs can use their information and resources so that members in the supply chain can have the right product, in the right quantity, at the right place, when wanted.

4

Operations Strategies: How to Compete

"The good fighters of old first put themselves beyond the possibility of defeat, and then waited for an opportunity to defeat the enemy."
Sun Tzu: *The Art of War*

A 1994 study by Andersen Consulting (now Accenture) compared the management practices and performance of 71 companies that supplied car seats, exhausts, and brakes to automobile assembly plants in nine countries:

(1) Canada, (2) France, (3) Germany, (4) Italy, (5) Japan, (6) Mexico, (7) Spain, (8) UK, and the (9) United States.[1] In its analysis, Accenture identified 13 of the enterprises as "world-class," with regard to their performance on productivity, quality, inventories, deliveries, and schedule variation.

The Accenture study found, on average, a 2:1 difference in performance on these metrics, between world-class enterprises and the rest. The world-class enterprises experienced less variability both in the schedules their customers gave them and in deliveries from their major suppliers. The quality gap was even more significant. For instance, for every defective exhaust system produced by a world-class enterprise, the non-world-class enterprise had 170 defects. The world-class enterprises were also able to *simultaneously* achieve higher quality, higher productivity, lower space requirements, and lower supply chain inventories.

The Accenture study raises these questions: How were the enterprises identified as world-class able to improve performance simultaneously along multiple dimensions? And, what factors

---

1. Andersen Consulting. 1994. "Worldwide Manufacturing Competitiveness Study: The Second Lean Enterprise Benchmarking Project Report." London: Arthur Andersen & Co., SC.

accounted for the observed differences between the world-class and the non-world-class enterprises? After all, the enterprises compared in the study were making the same products.

Before addressing these questions, let's examine the different ways enterprises can compete to leverage positions in the marketplace. In general, enterprises strive to gain a competitive edge because that directly translates to superior financial performance.

GAINING A COMPETITIVE ADVANTAGE

Figure 4.1 presents a framework that enterprises can use to gain competitive advantage. As Figure 4.1 suggests, competitive advantage can result in one of two possible ways: (1) either the enterprise enjoys a strong *structural position* that allows it to dominate the marketplace[2], or (2) it competes on the basis of superior *process execution*. Figure 4.1 also makes it clear that *operational effectiveness* and *strategic flexibility* are vital for superior process execution.

Figure 4-1. A Framework for Gaining Competitive Advantage

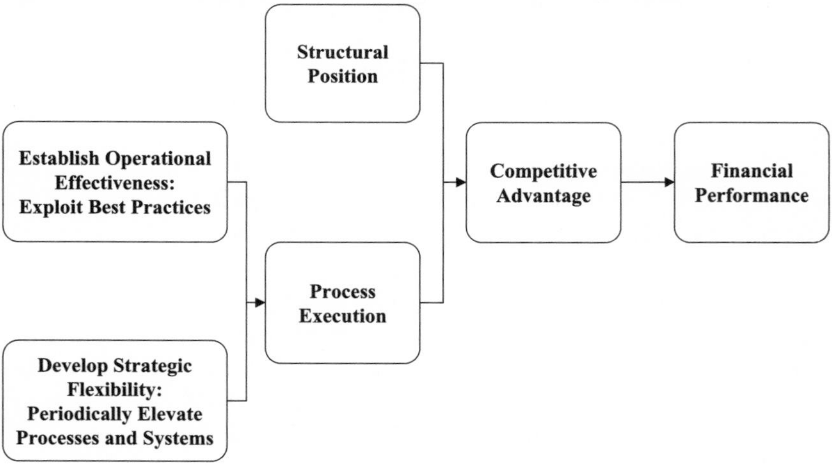

Structural position relates to the position the enterprise occupies within its competitive environment and the structure of that environment. Enterprises that try to improve their structural position work to achieve a favorable competitive advantage by changing and controlling the structure of their industry. They do this

---

2. Miller, A. 1998. *Strategic Management*, 3rd Edition. Boston: Irwin McGraw Hill.

mainly by erecting barriers that dissuade other enterprises from competing with them.

Process execution relates to how well the enterprise executes its core processes. Broadly speaking, core processes are product development, demand management, and order fulfillment. Enterprises compete through process execution by managing these core processes as well as the best-in-class in their industry (*operational effectiveness*), by constantly reevaluating and reinventing these processes and the systems that support them (*strategic flexibility*), or both. Some enterprises successfully exploit their structural position and achieve excellent process execution simultaneously, which places them in an excellent position to dominate their business ecosystem.

BUILDING A STRUCTURAL POSITION

Arguably, most enterprises have some form of structural position, but only a very small percentage of all enterprises have a *dominant* structural position. These enterprises enjoy limited rivalry either because they are a pure monopoly or because they are in a business few enterprises would attempt to enter due to high entry costs. An enterprise that typifies a dominant structural position is Microsoft. Its Windows operating system has a near monopoly in the PC ecosystem. Microsoft also enjoys a very large market share in the office products used in PCs, such as Microsoft Word, Powerpoint, and Excel.

Microsoft maintains its structural position by encouraging independent software developers to create compatible products. In pursuing this strategy, Microsoft, itself a software developer, cooperates with thousands of enterprises that could otherwise be considered its competitors. Thus, it has built its own software eco(sub)system within the PC ecosystem. Thousands of software developers are trying every day to come up with the next operating system and the next Office product that will replace Microsoft's system. However, users of Windows and Microsoft Office will not even consider their software unless these developers can assure full compatibility with Microsoft products. These developers would also have to be able to provide the kind of technical support that Microsoft gives its users, and be able to upgrade their software products like Microsoft often does. The entry barriers are simply too great.

Enterprises like Coca Cola Co. have leveraged structural position through brand identity and by cementing a carefully executed distribution strategy that provides easy access to their products practically any place in the world. Other enterprises, such as utilities and power generators, enjoy structural position because they are in industries that put pressure on potential suppliers of these products *not* to compete. These are industries where customer value is maximized by having a single supplier. Regulations are typically in place to keep such enterprises from abusing their monopoly status, but they nevertheless face very limited competition. The discussion so far makes it clear why it is more common to find enterprises competing through process execution.

COMPETING THROUGH PROCESS EXECUTION

As Figure 4.1 indicates, an enterprise tries to compete through process execution in two ways: It can attempt to gain a competitive edge by (1) exploiting best practices to establish *operational effectiveness*, or (2) building what we call *strategic flexibility*. Let's examine each one of these alternatives.

Operational Effectiveness and the Productivity Frontier

The Accenture study raised two questions:

1. How were the enterprises identified as world-class able to improve performance simultaneously along multiple dimensions?
2. What factors accounted for the observed differences between world-class and non-world-class enterprises, even though the companies compared were making the same products?

If it really is possible for enterprises to improve performance simultaneously along multiple dimensions, that would contradict the findings of a number of researchers who found that trade-offs had to be made between the elements that deliver customer value. The trade-off concept was formally introduced by Skinner,[3] who said:

> *"The variables of cost, time, quality, technological constraints, and customer satisfaction place limits on what management can do, force*

---

3. Skinner, W. 1969. "Manufacturing—Missing Link in Corporate Strategy." *Harvard Business Review,* May-June, vol 47, pp. 136–145

compromises, and demand an explicit recognition of a multitude of trade-offs and choices."

This line of reasoning would decree, for example, that an effort to obtain better quality would decrease productivity because more effort is expected when building a quality product. Similarly, it could be expected that improved service would not be possible without maintaining higher inventory levels.

The notion of trade-offs remained entrenched in the corporate world until concepts and programs like just-in-time and total quality management challenged the notion in the early 1980s. These programs changed the way that activities were performed. They eliminated inefficiencies, improved customer satisfaction, and forced managers to think about best practices. Managers found that improvements in quality also generated improvements in other areas, such as cost and flexibility—findings that were apparently paradoxical, yet in agreement with Accenture's subsequent study. What explains the apparent paradox?

The explanation lies in the notion of a *productivity frontier* that at any given time represents the sum of all existing best practices.[4] It represents the maximum value an enterprise can create in delivering a product or service using the best available technologies, skills, and management techniques. Figure 4.2 illustrates the concept. An enterprise that wants to compete through operational effectiveness would strive to position itself somewhere along the productivity frontier.

Figure 4-2. The Productivity Frontier

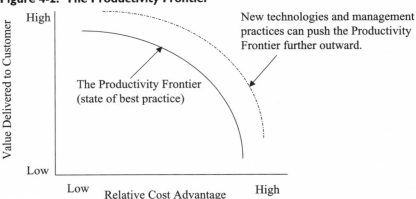

The Productivity Frontier (state of best practice)

New technologies and management practices can push the Productivity Frontier further outward.

---

4.   Porter, M. E. 1996. "What Is Strategy?" *Harvard Business Review,* November-December 1996, vol. 74. pp. 61-78

The productivity frontier as shown in Figure 4.2 thus presents a plausible explanation for both questions raised by the Accenture study. World-class enterprises were positioned above non-world-class enterprises and therefore performed better. Moreover, if a world-class enterprise was positioned below the frontier, improving its operational effectiveness would allow it to move outward towards the frontier, improving simultaneously along multiple dimensions.

Such simultaneity was indeed evidenced by U.S. manufacturers when they adopted Japanese principles in the 1980s to reduce setup times for the dies in their press shops. They were able to both lower costs and better differentiate their products. In doing so, they dispelled notions that trade-offs were *always* necessary—unless the enterprise is already positioned on the frontier.

Once an enterprise is positioned on the frontier, the productivity frontier concept asserts that the enterprise is doing as well as it can along multiple dimensions. At this stage, if the enterprise wishes to improve further on a metric like quality, then it has to find another position along the frontier implying that it has to trade off another metric such as productivity. New technologies and more innovative management practices can, however, push the productivity frontier outward as indicated in Figure 4.2, further improving performance, simultaneously, along a number of dimensions.

Operational Effectiveness and Competitiveness

An enterprise competing by exploiting operational effectiveness in effect raises the bar for every other enterprise in the industry. While enterprises can exploit operational effectiveness in this manner in their attempts to discourage competition, it often does not lead to sustained competitive advantage.

These enterprises may, in fact, begin to suffer from persistently low profits. For instance, time-based competition, which provided a significant competitive edge for many Japanese enterprises in the mid-1980s,[5] revealed a dark side in the early 1990s. It forced Japanese manufacturers to cut prices in an everlasting struggle to maintain market share when there were no breakthrough

---

5. Stalk, G. Jr. 1988. "Time—The Next Source of Competitive Advantage." *Harvard Business Review*, July-August: vol, 66. pp. 41-51

innovations.[6] While the customer ultimately benefited, the competition did not help the profitability and ultimately the commercial viability of the enterprises themselves.

The struggles of the Japanese manufacturers convey another message. Although the goal of many enterprises is to compete by imitating best practices within their industry, this may not be a long-term growth strategy. *It is unwise for an enterprise to expect to achieve any sort of sustained competitive advantage if its only goal is to be as good as its toughest competitors.* For one thing, even as the follower is trying to emulate its toughest competitor, the leader is very likely to be innovating and continuing to increase its lead. In summary,

- When enterprises compete by exploiting operational effectiveness, they tend to benchmark themselves against best-in-class competitors. Unfortunately, the more benchmarking enterprises do with each other, the more they look alike.
- As competitors imitate one another's improvements in quality, cycle times, or supplier partnerships, strategies begin to converge and eventually that results in no enduring winners.

Operational Effectiveness: Necessary but Not Sufficient

The preceding discussion reveals that while operational effectiveness is a necessary condition for competitiveness, it is not sufficient. What else can enterprises do to gain a sustained competitive advantage?

In a customer-centric era that continues to see ever-increasing competition across all industries, mere adoption of better practices and techniques does not create a sustainable competitive advantage. The practices and techniques may be based on breakthrough ideas, but breakthrough practices and techniques rapidly become the industry's standard operating procedure. To draw an analogy from sports, the Fosbury Flop pioneered by Dick Fosbury in the high jump in the 1968 Olympiad was a breakthrough technique, but by the 1972 Olympiad, practically every athlete competing for the high jump was practicing the Fosbury Flop. What was once a competitive advantage soon became just the ante required to play the game. Managers who expect to become competitive simply by emulating successful enterprises have typically abandoned the central concept of a strategy.

---

6. Stalk, G. Jr., and A. M. Webber. 1993. "Japan's Dark Side of Time." *Harvard Business Review*, July-August: vol. 71, pp. 93-102

What is strategy? And what is the role of the Operations function in executing strategy?

A strategy is a description of the manner in which an enterprise intends to gain a competitive advantage. The root cause of the failure of many enterprises in the consumer-centric era lies in failure to distinguish between operational *effectiveness* and *operations strategy*. The Operations function enables an enterprise to *realize* its strategy by providing strategic flexibility: the ability to periodically reinvent its processes and systems in response to changing customer preferences. By building strategic flexibility, enterprises can compete in a customer-centric world. Strategic flexibility also allows the enterprise to reposition itself when the competitive environment changes.

Consider, for instance, the general merchandise retailer, Target Corporation. In the 1980s and early 1990s, Target was considered a deep discount retail store. It had relatively poor store layouts and store environment, and similarly poor customer service.

When Wal-Mart aggressively began to establish itself as the leading low-price discount retailer in the U.S., Target realized it could not compete head-on. Target completely changed its strategy, targeted a specific market, and set expectations for customer experience with regard to store layout, environment, customer service, product selection, and product quality. It deliberately decided to move completely away from its position as a deep-discount retail store. Now its principal strategy is "to provide exceptional value to American consumers through multiple retail formats ranging from upscale discount and moderate-priced to full-scale department stores."[7] Instead of trying to compete by simply imitating Wal-Mart's best practices, Target demonstrated its strategic flexibility by reinventing its processes and systems.

The discussion so far can be summed up as follows:

- Operational effectiveness and operations strategy are both essential to superior performance, but they work in different ways. Operational effectiveness allows the enterprise to perform similar activities better than its rivals; an operations strategy is needed to position the enterprise more effectively in the marketplace.
- An operations strategy should help the enterprise gain a relative advantage through actions that its competitors will find hard to follow, allowing the advantage to be extended even further.

---

7. *See* the Target Web site: *www.targetcorp.com.*

- The goal of operations strategy is to provide strategic flexibility—well-designed concepts and tools that will move the enterprise ahead of the competition and keep it ahead—through periodical reinvention of processes and systems

BUILDING STRATEGIC FLEXIBILITY

For an enterprise that wishes to continue to grow its business, the biggest threat probably stems from inaction. For instance, if an enterprise ignores—or fails to recognize—changing customer preferences, it risks losing market share. If the enterprise is not flexible enough to adapt to changing customer preferences, it faces increased production costs due to the mismatch between production capabilities and market preferences, perhaps leading to loss of market share.

The decline of the U.S. machine tool industry in the early 1980s provides a stark example of the negative consequences of a mismatch between customer preferences and industry capabilities. Because U.S. manufacturers believed that their customers would continue to prefer highly customized machine tools, they continued to organize their manufacturing processes to produce low volumes of specialized machine tools. Since every machine tool was virtually a unique product, this required long lead times and was expensive.

During this period, Japanese machine tool manufacturers entered the U.S. market with more standardized and less elaborate machine tools. Anticipating changing customer preferences for simpler tools, the Japanese were able to offer quality equipment with short lead times that were inexpensive and far superior in quality to those of U.S. manufacturers. The U.S. manufacturers had to spend the next decade scrambling to regain lost ground.

Intel, on the other hand, is an enterprise that exhibits strategic flexibility as it strives to match or even anticipate customer preferences. When we hear the name Intel, the first thought that comes to mind is the phrase, "Intel Inside," the familiar slogan displayed by most PCs. Now probably best known for its Pentium, Centrino, and Celeron chips, Intel has constantly been innovating, staying ahead of the rest of the competition. It has invested heavily in research and development and in capacity, and that has paid off.

Intel's cost advantage over its nearest rival, Advanced Micro Devices (AMD), has been growing, even as its computer chips continue to pull in revenues. A report in *Business Week*[8] shows that between the first quarters of 2003 and 2004, Intel increased its cost advantage over AMD (the difference in the average cost per chip) by around $15 per chip. At the same time, Intel's average selling price per chip was about $100 more than AMD's during the same period.

However, Intel is not content with its dominant position in the PC industry. It is now positioning itself to move into producing chips for flat panel televisions and personal media players and to expand its market in chips for cellular phones. The consumer-electronics, wireless handheld, and communications equipment markets targeted by Intel currently account for $77 billion worth of semiconductors[9] and Intel has less than 6 percent of that market.

Intel has had some missteps with consumer electronics in the past. In 2003, it lost market share for chips in the cell phone business when it tried to put through a 40 percent price increase for flash memory chips that continue to store data after the phone is turned off. When its rivals, Samsung and AMD, held their prices steady, cell-phone makers like Nokia and others bought flash memory chips from rivals instead.

Despite such missteps, Intel is moving with its plans. Its CEO, Craig Barrett, says that Intel has a *demand-pull* strategy, forging closer ties with customers to create products that fit customer needs, instead of a *technology-push* strategy of designing products no one has asked for. Leading executives in the industry believe that the demand-pull strategy, combined with Intel's ability to innovate, could cut the price of some flat panel TVs in half by the end of 2004.[10]

Dell is another enterprise that exhibits strategic flexibility. It recently responded to changing customer preferences by expanding its product range to include mp3 players, personal digital assistants (PDAs), and a variety of other electronic goods. That is one reason it changed its name from Dell Computers to Dell, Inc. However, it has not abandoned its core competency—assembling computers in a build-to-order framework.

---

8. Edwards, C. 2004. "What Is CEO Craig Barrett up to? Hint: It's About much more than Computers." *Business Week*, March 8.

9. Ibid.

10. Ibid.

Neither is Intel abandoning its core competency of making standardized low-cost chips for computers. Even as Intel takes a financial risk by investing in new ventures, its factories making chips for PCs, servers, and other established markets are running full speed, producing cutting-edge chips that continue to uphold Moore's Law.[11]

Enterprises that can rapidly adapt to changing customer preferences and offer effective solutions thus have a better chance of acquiring more customers, increasing their share of the market, and retaining those customers. The primary challenge these enterprises face is to align the Marketing function with the Operations function to evolve integrated marketing and operations strategies that fulfill corporate goals. Strategic flexibility is not achieved simply by *offering* new products to adapt to changing customer preferences. It is achieved by being able to *deliver* the new products to the customer. Enterprises also need to cope with customer demands that often outpace the ability of a business to adapt to the changes customers seek. Finally, there is often no consistent basis for determining how best to respond to, and support, different customer segments each with distinct needs.

One factor that promotes inertia is reluctance to make strategic choices or trade-offs. It is impossible to be all things to all people. Serving one group of customers and excluding others, for instance, places a limit, real or imagined, on a corporate model of flexible response to changing customer preferences. Managers often compromise by taking incremental steps—extending product lines, adding new features, imitating rival's products, and so on. Compromise in the pursuit of growth poses a real danger of eroding any competitive advantage an enterprise has.

What is the right model to follow to promote strategic flexibility? Figure 4.3 presents a model in which enterprises periodically enhance their competitive position by creating new products, processes, and systems. This model, the "S-curve model," consists of a series of S-curves, each depicting incremental improvement in process capabilities over time.

Each S-curve represents a new generation of a process or a technology. The initial part of the S-curve shows a period of slow growth in process capability as the enterprise begins to adapt to the process or technology. This is followed by a period of rapid improvement in process capabilities as the enterprise better

---

11. Moore's Law, attributed to Gordon Moore, the founder and ex-CEO of Intel Corporation, states that computing power should double roughly every 18 months.

Figure 4-3. A Model for Enterprise Growth

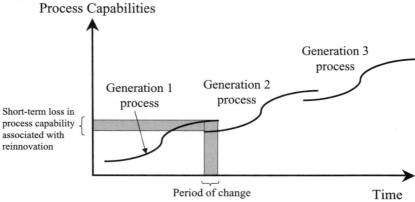

understands the process or technology. At some point, the rate of process improvements begins to slow no matter how much effort is expended in improving the process/technology. At that point, the S-curve flattens out. Once that limit is reached, process capability is improved only through a new generation of process or technology.

Some of these step changes in the period of transition may actually result in a temporary decline in capabilities as the enterprise adjusts to new processes and systems. (See Figure 4.3.) For instance, Intel's attempt to venture beyond the computer chip business into the Web hosting market failed in 2002, resulting in a $100 million charge. Transition periods present the greatest challenge to enterprises; they are a major reason that managers adopt a policy of inaction, especially among risk-averse enterprises. However, if the operations strategy is well executed, such "backward" steps are often followed by periods of robust growth.

The ramification of the S-curve model is that for real continuous improvement, there must be both incremental and innovation improvement. Enterprises must focus on strategic flexibility and be prepared to modify processes and systems as needed. This discussion is summarized with the eighth lean supply chain principle:

LEAN SUPPLY CHAIN PRINCIPLE 8

The role of operations strategy is to give the enterprise the ability to cope with changing customer preferences. Products and processes should be designed to promote strategic flexibility.

Here are factors necessary to maintaining strategic flexibility, periodically adapting processes and systems to continually deliver customer value:

- Maintain a process orientation.
- Bring new products to market faster.
- Co-evolve strategies for marketing and operations.
- Define market segments.
- Identify the order winners and order qualifiers for each market segment.
- Identify processes that will fulfill demand in each market segment.
- Design product delivery strategies for customers in each market segment.
- Provide the necessary infrastructure for Operations to deliver the products.

MAINTAIN A PROCESS ORIENTATION

In Fall 2002, I visited a company that fabricated and assembled display racks for major retail stores. The vast majority of the orders it received were for standard display racks that required modest customization. When the Marketing & Sales department received orders that required even minimal customization, it routed them through the Product Design department to approve the design modifications and then forward the orders to the Production Planning department. Production Planning in turn batched these orders and released them all at once to the Production department when an "economic production quantity" was reached.

The amount of work involved in fabricating and assembling the rack typically required about an hour of labor. However, because of the multiple hand-offs, it took about 15 days from the moment Marketing & Sales received the order until it reached Production, which took another 15 to 20 days to produce the racks. This enterprise at the time had a niche market in the display rack manufacturing industry.

My question was: How could this enterprise exhibit strategic flexibility if it faced significant competition? Its performance was significantly hampered by its *functional* orientation. It needed a *process* orientation that better aligned its internal processes and departments (functions).

Functional Orientation and Functional Silos

Traditional enterprises tend to group similar activities together under functional units like Marketing or Operations. A functional orientation is often easier to manage because the "specialists" are grouped together and supervised by people who have the same skills and experiences. The functional orientation also provides economies of scale. It tends to centralize similar resources and provides mutual support by physical proximity, while clearly defining career paths for employees.

The functional orientation generally works well when the enterprise is small and deals with a steady demand for standard products with no need for much interfunctional coordination. The functional orientation does not, however, easily accommodate changing customer preferences, and it does not facilitate the objectives of the lean supply chain.

The basic tenet with the functional orientation is "just do your task as prescribed"—or alternately, "my boss is the most important customer." That kind of organization promotes the *functional silos* that cause the familiar *over-the-wall syndrome* as shown in Figure 4.4. With the functional silo mentality, communication between functional units is very poor. The seriality of operations shown in Figure 4.4 is very reminiscent of the display rack manufacturing enterprise I visited.

Figure 4-4. Functional Silos: The "Over-The-Wall" Syndrome

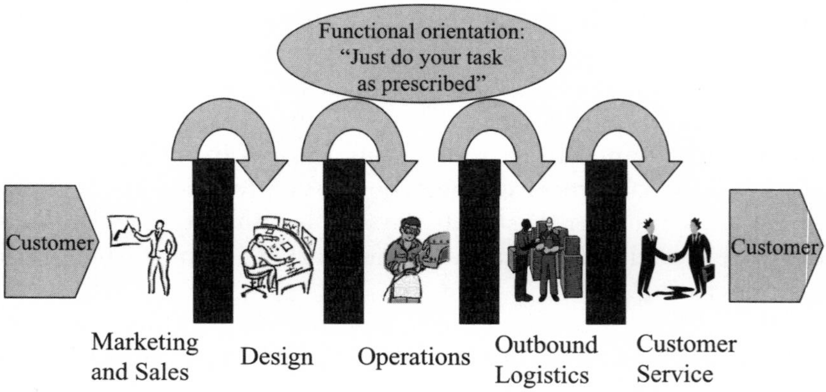

Operating with functional silos can lead to bizarre outcomes. Lee[12] discusses the case of a well-known automobile manufacturer in the mid-90s. Its Marketing and Sales group, faced with an excessive inventory of green cars in the middle of the year, offered the distributors special discounts and rebates on green cars. As the sales of green cars increased rapidly in response to the promotion, the Supply Chain Planning group incorrectly assumed that there was a big demand for green cars and decided to initiate production of even more green cars. As a result of the lack of communication between Marketing & Sales and Supply Chain Planning, the company ended the year with a large inventory of green cars!

Developing a Process Orientation

An increasing number of lean enterprises are embracing a matrix form of organization. They are focusing on the processes that deliver the product to the customer as a key factor in promoting the smooth flow of products through the enterprise. This is a *process orientation*. Figure 4.5 depicts a process-oriented organization structure that contrasts sharply with the functional orientation shown in Figure 4.4. The process-oriented structure is customer-focused, trying to execute orders as quickly as possible.

Figure 4-5. A Process-Oriented Structure

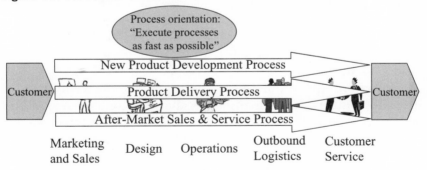

A critical challenge for an enterprise that embraces process orientation is to reconcile the needs of the individual, the function, the enterprise, and the supply chain in a way that realizes full benefits for the supply chain as a whole. For instance, one problem

---

12. Lee, H. L. 2001. "Ultimate Enterprise Value Creation Using Demand-Based Management." Stanford Global Supply Chain Management Forum September 2001, Palo Alto.

with the process orientation is that it may require individuals assigned to a cross-functional team to abandon a customary functional path. Another problem is that such assignments may diminish key functions. When individuals and functions feel threatened by what are officially streamlined processes, the processes may not stay streamlined for long.

Maintaining a process orientation can also be a problem for enterprises whose business is growing. As the business grows, enterprises typically tend to grow in terms of both physical resources and number of employees. During a growth phase, then, there is a natural tendency for enterprises to become more bureaucratic and erect functional boundaries.

Economist John Kenneth Galbraith once wrote, "So complex, indeed, will be the job of organizing specialists that there will be specialists on organization."[13] Galbraith was trying to show that the American economy, which was growing rapidly in the 1970s, was becoming a planned, bureaucratic economy much like the Soviet economy. He postulated that economists would have to study the corporate sector as a form of planned economy using classical economics soon to be seen as anachronistic.

Galbraith charged that an inevitable consequence of bureaucracy was that "an increasing span of time separates the beginning from the completion of any task," using the example of Ford Motor Company, which delivered its first car in 1903, less than five months after the company was formed. The Ford Mustang introduced in 1964, however, took three and a half years from initial planning to delivery to the consumer. Galbraith thus deduced that lead times to deliver products tend to increase as enterprises age and grow in size.

Every enterprise follows a natural pattern of evolution from birth to maturity. The initial stage is characterized by enthusiasm, shared responsibility, and a general desire to respond to customer demands quickly. The emphasis is on learning: to understand the technology, to respond to divergent customer needs, to attract sources of capital, etc. However, as the enterprise matures, it often falls victim to institutionalization: processes are formalized, rigidity sets in, and democratic processes are replaced by hierarchical rankings. The enterprise that begins life as an informal *learning* organization becomes a formal *hierarchical* organization.

---

13. Galbraith, J. K. 1971. *The New Industrial State.* Boston: Houghton Mifflin Co.

Hurst[14] says that "the emergence of hierarchy is probably the most insidious of the aging processes in a maturing organization." He claims that a formalized structure hurts enterprises because it becomes "a major constraint, preventing them from easily changing processes, technologies, goods, and services."

Hurst makes a case that enterprises must be constantly ready for change. Contrary to traditional organizational theory, which emphasizes rationality and control in the management of change, he argues, sometimes managers must deliberately create crises by committing acts of "ethical anarchy" to renew their enterprises.

The discussion so far can be summarized as follows.

- As enterprises grow and mature, they tend to form hierarchical structures.
- Enterprises with formalized hierarchical structures encourage managers to operate in functional silos, promoting and protecting their own functional interests with little concern for the greater good of the enterprise.
- Enterprises with a rigid hierarchical structure are less responsive to changes in customer demand and slower to adapt to changes in processes and technologies.
- Consequently, as enterprises grow and age, they require more time to deliver the product to the customer.

There is thus a strong case to be made for mature enterprises, especially those that have grown in size over the years, to seek ways to rejuvenate themselves. This is precisely what Jack Welch was alluding to when he sought to get the "soul of a small company" into the "large, muscle-bound, big-company body" that GE had become.[15] Even innovative enterprises are not immune to the functional silo trap. Michael Dell found that as his business grew, his information systems group, for instance, gradually began to view its role in the enterprise as just creating information systems, rather than facilitating the flow of information to employees, customers, and shareholders. He once stated,

> *"In the thick of our growth, our team had lost sight of our fundamental values: serving the interests of the customer, the shareholder, and the company as a whole."*[16]

---

14. Hurst, D. K. 1995. *Crisis and Renewal: Meeting the Challenge of Organizational Change.* Cambridge, MA: Harvard Business School Press.
15. Welch, J. 1999. "Letter to Share Owners." *General Electric Annual Report 1999* Fairfield, CT.
16. Dell, M. 1999. *Direct from Dell: Strategies that Revolutionized the Industry.* New York: HarperCollins.

Dell's employees had fallen into the functional silo trap, but Dell recognized it and worked consciously on breaking down the silos.

How can enterprises promote a process orientation? The *balanced scorecard* introduced by Kaplan and Norton[17] is one possible way enterprises can develop metrics to promote a process orientation. The balanced scorecard framework helps align individual, organizational, and departmental initiatives to achieve the same long-term strategic goals.

The Balanced Scorecard

The balanced scorecard is a management tool based on two fundamental principles:

1. You get what you measure.
2. You cannot manage an enterprise with just one kind of performance measure.

The balanced scorecard addresses enterprise performance from four perspectives:

1. How do shareholders view the enterprise (*financial perspective*)?
2. How do customers view the enterprise (*customer perspective*)?
3. What internal processes should the enterprise excel at (*internal business perspective*)?
4. How can the enterprise continue to improve and create value (*innovation and learning perspective*)?

The balanced scorecard framework allows the enterprise to publicize its corporate vision to all levels. It is also an effective way for the enterprise to identify linkages between functions and to develop a process orientation. For instance, a customer perspective goal of responsive supply involves the Marketing and Operations functions, and perhaps other functions, such as Design and Purchasing.

Formulating goals that link the four perspectives is also a way for the enterprise to translate relatively abstract financial goals into effective methods for achieving goals. This puts an enterprise in a better position to specify the processes and technology that must be in place to achieve the financial goals.

---

17. Kaplan, R. S., and D. P. Norton. 1992. "The Balanced Scorecard: Measures that Drive Performance." *Harvard Business Review,* January-February: vol. 70, pp. 71-79.

While the balanced scorecard is a good guide to breaking down functional silos, it is just one of several possible approaches to accomplishing the same objective. The value of the balanced scorecard is that it provides exactly the information and metrics that are essential for managers to set up processes that will align functional units with the corporate strategy.

This discussion is summarized in lean supply chain principle nine:

LEAN SUPPLY CHAIN PRINCIPLE 9

Formulate performance measures that allow the enterprise to better align functions and move from a functional to a process orientation.

While it is desirable to align as many functional units as possible, some alignments are especially critical for the lean supply chain. To determine which are the critical ones, examine some of the attributes that lean enterprises should possess:

- A customer focus
- Quick response to changing market conditions
- Continuous innovation and effective application of new technologies
- Close communication and partnership with customers and suppliers.

These characteristics highlight the need to better align the Operations function with two other functions: (1) Design and (2) Marketing. First, consider the alignment of Design with Marketing and Operations.

BRING NEW PRODUCTS TO MARKET FASTER

For convenience, the term *design process integration* (DPI) will be used to refer to the set of activities and processes that integrate Design with Marketing and Operations. DPI significantly impacts product cost. It also impacts the new product development (NPD) process and the product delivery process for the lean enterprise.

Consider first product cost. Numerous studies[18] have shown that by the time a product design is complete, less than 10 percent of the total product budget is expended, on average. However, in

---

18. *See, for instance,* Anderson, D. M. 1990. *Design for Manufacturability, Optimizing Cost, Quality and Time-to-Market.* Lafayette, California: CIM Press.

that same period of time, *80 percent of the cost of the product, over its lifetime, is committed.* The concept phase of the design process alone typically determines 60 percent of the cost. (See Figure 4.6.)

Figure 4-6. Cost of a Product during its Life

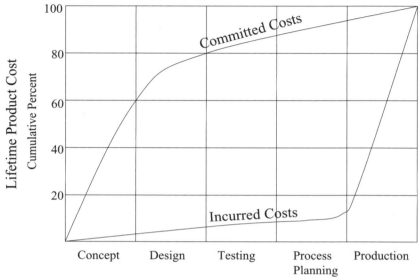

Needless to say, once the design is locked in, it is often very difficult to make substantial changes to it. All too often, the result is an endless stream of engineering change notices that attempt to improve on the design or, worse yet, to rectify errors in design. Typically, these changes are incremental; they offer "patches" to the existing design, very much like the patches made to software programs.

Consider next NPD, one of the major activities the Design function is involved in. NPD projects give enterprises an opportunity to exercise new skills, new knowledge, and new systems—qualities desirable from the balanced scorecard's Innovation and Learning Perspective. NPD projects offer such opportunities because they are sufficiently limited in duration and scope to allow enterprises to experiment without incurring major risk. They also provide a comprehensive, real-time test of the systems, structures, and values of the enterprise.[19] Many enterprises believe

19. Bowen, H. K., K. B. Clark, C. A. Holloway, and S. C. Wheelwright. 1994. "Development Projects: The Engine of Renewal." *Harvard Business Review,* September-October: vol. 72, pp.121–130

that the real source of competitive advantage is innovation. The reasoning is that when an enterprise is no longer on the cutting edge of technological change, its gross margins shrink. That puts pressure on them to cut costs and commit fewer resources to research and development, resulting in a vicious cycle.

Whether or not this belief is universal, it is a fact that we live in a world where product life cycles are continuing to shrink. Enterprises are constantly challenged to bring new products to the market faster and cheaper. To keep up with, or get ahead of, the competition, it is necessary to create, produce, and launch products faster and faster—especially in the electronics industry, where Moore's law still very much applies. Integrating the Design function with Marketing and Operations to bring new products faster to market is a vital necessity for enterprise survival in such an environment.

One industry that has significantly benefited from DPI is the automobile industry. Product development times for automobiles have dropped significantly over the last two decades. Again, for example, in 1964, the Ford Mustang took three and a half years from the initial planning stage until it was available to the customer. In the early 1980s, it took General Motors more than 60 months to bring a new car into the market—after everyone had signed off on the final design. As a result of DPI, however, the auto makers have reduced the time it takes to develop a new vehicle to as little as 14 to 16 months for specialty vehicles like the Ford GT and the Hummer H2. The new goal of automakers now aim at further reducing product development times to as little as 12 months from the time the design is "frozen" until production begins.[20]

Leader versus Follower Strategies in New Product Development

An issue to be resolved is whether the enterprise wishes to be a leader or a follower in bringing new products to the market. The leader tries to be the first-to-market with a product that competitors would find difficult to imitate or improve upon. The follower waits until the competition introduces a new product and imitates it if the product proves successful. Each approach has its advantages and drawbacks.

---

20. Winter, D. 2003. "Shrinking Product Development Time." *Ward's Auto World*, June 1: *http://www.wardsauto.com*.

The proactive approach of the leader has the advantage that the enterprise gains an edge over the competition, from both a market and a technical perspective. From the market perspective, being first-to-market makes it easier to achieve brand recognition. Moreover, the enterprise that is the first-to-market is alerted to problems with the product design and is in a better position to avoid these flaws in the future. On the other hand, enterprises that adopt the proactive approach must devote resources to research and development and be prepared for the possibility of costly mistakes.

The primary advantage of the follower's reactive approach is that the risks and costs of developing and test marketing the product have already been shouldered by the competition. However, enterprises that adopt a reactive approach have to consider the possibility that they may always be one-step behind the competitor who is following a proactive approach.

No matter which approach an enterprise follows today, the fact is that in the face of shrinking product life cycles, almost every industry has been forced to rethink how it develops and launches products. The traditional over-the-wall approach, with its functional orientation, results in significantly long product development times. This is where DPI really assumes importance because, for many enterprises, the design function is confounded by fragmented activities, overspecialization, and delays.

Demand Pull versus Technology Push

As with any other business activity, understanding customer expectations is the first step in DPI. To maintain a competitive edge by bringing innovative products to market faster, enterprises are constantly on the lookout for new processes and technologies. The difficulty comes in deciding if and when to adopt them. It is important to differentiate between a *demand pull* and a *technology push*.

A demand pull occurs when an enterprise identifies a marketplace need and then creates a product to meet that need. Demand pull arises in a variety of ways. It can occur when enterprises seek better technologies to reduce their costs of production or to improve the quality of their existing products. Demand pull can also take place simply in response to the business ecosystem. In the latter case, the enterprises that respond to the demand pull often create their own new technologies or processes to address the demand.

Consider how demand pull influenced the automobile ecosystem. The oil embargo in 1973 caused fuel prices to rise, generating a need, partly mandated by government regulations, for more fuel-efficient vehicles. Among the responses of the big three automakers was an investment in installing microcomputers in automobiles. The microcomputers were initially intended for controlling fuel consumption and improving fuel efficiency, but eventually the automakers found a variety of other ways to use the microcomputers to improve car performance.

Wal-Mart's insistence that its top 100 suppliers have RFID tags on all their pallets of products by January 25, 2005, is a more current example of demand pull. The RFID tag is also an example of a product that is driving new technologies and processes. Chapter 3 noted that the RFID tag does not have to be visible in order to be scanned. However, with the current technology, certain media, such as metal and liquids, can still affect the signal. Metal objects located near the RFID reader can attenuate or distort the signals and thus diminish performance. Certain liquids simply absorb RFID signals. The suppliers of RFID tags are working on new technologies to overcome these challenges.

Demand pull is more likely to be found in market-driven enterprises searching for products that meet the needs of that marketplace. Market-driven enterprises grow market share using available technologies; they aggressively seek new technologies only when forced to do so as in the example of the automobile industry pushed by high fuel prices. Yet, though many manufacturing enterprises concentrate on demand pull activities, they cannot afford to neglect new technologies, whether discovered or created. Otherwise, they run the risk of the competition pulling ahead with a new product line powered by a new technology.

Technology push occurs when enterprises identify an interesting technology, use it to create a product or a new application, and then try to create or find a market for it. On the positive side, a technology push orientation allows the enterprise to look beyond the limitations of current technologies. Its driving assumption is that today's technologies are inadequate for tomorrow's customer needs. The belief is that once the new technologies are created, market opportunities will appear.

Technology push is more likely to be found in technology-driven enterprises. These enterprises tend to be more innovative and entrepreneurial, which has both risks and rewards. There are many instances where technology-driven enterprises produced products for which there were at the time no known uses. Yet these products became outstanding successes. One example is 3M's Scotchgard.

The discovery of Scotchgard in 1953 by a young chemical researcher, Patsy Sherman, was almost serendipitous.[21] In the 1950s, 3M had committed major laboratory resources to research on fluorochemical compounds. While 3M had no particular application in mind, its researchers believed that this class of chemicals would eventually have commercial value.

One day, a technician spilled a dilute solution of the chemical on Patsy Sherman's new tennis shoes. When she tried to rinse it off, she noticed that the color wasn't changed and that the water beaded up. She also noticed that over time the shoe that had the chemical spilled on it remained clean while the other shoe got dirty. This was hard evidence for Patsy Sherman that 3M had the potential to make a commercially useful product from its research, a product many experts had written off as "thermodynamically impossible."

Scotchgard eventually proved to be a tremendous success. An unarticulated need of customers for a versatile fabric and material protector had been articulated—and satisfied.

Needless to say, for every such success story there are a number of failure stories. Technology-driven enterprises risk not finding an application for a truly innovative product. These enterprises typically need large cash reserves and plenty of patience if they are to succeed by limiting themselves to this approach.

CO-EVOLVE STRATEGIES FOR MARKETING AND OPERATIONS

While any two functional units may have conflicting objectives, it has been claimed that there is more disagreement between Marketing and Operations than between any other pair of functions.[22] A major cause for conflict between these functions is that Marketing is charged with generating demand and Operations is charged with satisfying demand.

---

21. *See* the 3M Web site, *http://www.3m.com/about3M/pioneers/sherman.html.*
22. Hayes, R. H., and S. C. Wheelwright. 1984. *Restoring Our Competitive Edge: Competing Through Manufacturing.* New York: John Wiley & Sons.

Consider how the two functions react to a customer order. Marketing is more interested in the order value—how much revenue the order will generate. Operations, on the other hand, is more interested in order make-up— how to produce the order for the customer.

Consider next the issue of product diversity. To satisfy a wide array of consumer preferences, Marketing would like to offer the consumer a wide variety of choices. Furthermore, Marketing's inherent desire to satisfy the customer often leads it to promise individual customers product modifications. Operations, on the other hand, would prefer to work with standard products, because every unique product requires some initial setup or changeover time.

Marketing would like to accept all customer orders that it deems profitable, and that may result in huge swings in the demand for resources that are under the control of Operations. Operations, on the other hand, would prefer to accept orders that balance the load on these resources. With respect to quality control, the conflict is whether to produce a perfect product (arguably, the Marketing perspective) or to compromise on what would be acceptable to the customer (arguably, the Operations perspective).

The conflict between Marketing and Operations is especially severe in enterprises with a functional orientation, where such conflicts are handled typically by working *around* them, rather than *through* them. That is, the existence of the conflict is assumed as given and strategies are formulated to avoid the causes of conflict. In the worst cases, the existence of the conflict is ignored and the Marketing-Operations conflict is typically "resolved" as follows: Corporate objectives are typically communicated in a hierarchical manner to Marketing, which evolves strategies to meet these objectives. These strategies may take the form of increasing the variety of products offered to customers, or offering volume discounts. When corporate objectives are communicated to Operations, it evolves its own strategies in such areas as inventory policies, make-or-buy decisions, or capacity allocation. The corporate goals thus result in functional strategies (a Marketing strategy, an Operations strategy, a Logistics strategy) that are not linked to one another.

In the absence of a real dialog, Marketing-led initiatives usually assume that Operations has the capability to respond positively and flexibly to whatever demands are placed on it, and that should be its role. This often has Operations functioning in a classic, fire-fighting, reactive role, forced to respond to orders as quickly as it can, instead of functioning in a proactive role, determining what levels of demand it can satisfactorily execute.

This is, of course, counter-productive for the enterprise as a whole, since it would be preferable to have Operations functioning proactively. The situation is especially severe because the majority of an enterprise's dollars are usually invested in resources that are directly under the control of the Operations function. *How can an enterprise compete effectively if the functional unit that controls most of its resources operates reactively?*

Any Operations strategy should reflect the intended market position of the enterprise. Some enterprises may choose to compete primarily on cost, others on high levels of customer service, and so on. Whatever the choice, Operations must respond by performing in a manner appropriate for the intended market position. It is not just a matter of selecting the current market position and then asking Operations to adjust its resources and processes to fall in line. Rather, it is necessary to recognize the competencies or capabilities that these resources and processes provide and exploit them accordingly.

So the question is: Should market position dictate how Operations resources are deployed, or should it be the other way around? One way to resolve this impasse is to provide a structure that will allow Operations and Marketing to evolve their strategies in consultation with each other. A framework for integrating Marketing strategies with Operations strategies presented in Figure 4.7 is an adaptation of one set out by Hill.[23]

This framework essentially identifies corporate objectives, such as growth or return on investment, which are translated into Marketing initiatives needed to meet these objectives. Marketing initiatives may involve decisions such as whether to use direct marketing or more conventional distribution channels, whether to be a leader or a follower, whether to be an innovator, and so on.

Order qualifiers and order winners provide an opportunity for engaging Marketing and Operations in a dialog to jointly evolve their strategies. Order qualifiers and order winners were briefly discussed in Chapter 2, but their definitions are reviewed and discussed here in more detail. *Order qualifiers* are the criteria that must be associated with the product before the customer will even consider buying it. Order winners are the criteria that will actually

---

23. Hill, T. 2000. *Manufacturing Strategy: Text and Cases,* 3rd ed. Boston: Irwin McGraw-Hill.

Figure 4-7.A Framework for Co-Evolving Marketing and Operations Strategies

Corporate Objectives	Marketing Strategy	Order Qualifiers & Order Winners	Operations Strategy	
			Structural Elements	Infrastructure
Growth	Advertising	Price	Process Choice	Organizational
Survival	Branding	Quality	Inventory vs.	Structure
Profit	and Positioning	Delivery Speed	Capacity	Workforce Skills
ROI	Single Account	Delivery Reliability	Make or Buy	Planning and
	Penetration	Product Range	Facility	Scheduling
	Direct Marketing	Design	Location	Quality Assurance
	Marketing Channels	Brand image	Choice of	Materials Handling
	Leader vs. Follower	Technical and	Technology	and Logistics
		after Sales Support		

secure the customer's order. By definition, an order winner must also be an order qualifier. The criteria referred to here include cost, quality, availability, brand image, and delivery reliability.

Once these criteria are identified, Operations can work on the processes and systems necessary to deliver products with the desired criteria, adding structural elements and infrastructure as necessary. Once the order winners and order qualifiers have been jointly identified, Marketing can now independently evolve its strategies for increasing customer awareness of the products with the assurance that Operations will be able to deliver products that satisfy these criteria.

Operations strategies involve decisions on structural elements and on infrastructure. Two structural elements are: (1) choice of process and (2) product delivery strategy (inventory versus capacity). Among the decisions on infrastructure, in this chapter workforce skills are specifically addressed.

DEFINE MARKET SEGMENTS

Market segmentation is the division of a market into distinct groups of buyers (customers) who might require different products or marketing mixes. The intent is to classify members of a heterogeneous market, consisting of buyers with different needs, into homogeneous segments of buyers with similar needs and wants. Dividing the market into relatively homogenous subgroups or target markets makes both strategy formulation and tactical decision-making more effective. From the Operations strategy perspective, market segmentation is essential because the order winners and order qualifiers have to be determined for each market segment.

The many variables that could be used to segment the market range from determining demographic factors to variables that describe user behavior or buyer preferences. The segmentation also depends on whether the buyers in question are individual customers or enterprises. Market segmentation factors typically used to classify individual customers are: Geographic (country or region, rural or metropolitan); Demographic (age, sex, marital status, income, education) and Behavioral (intensity of product use, brand loyalty). Figure 4.8 shows an example of market segmentation for three categories of products: (1) those shipped to retail outlets, (2) those sent for further processing to original equipment manufacturers, and (3) those sent to governmental agencies that may have their own pricing, quality, and delivery standards.

FIGURE 4-8. Defining Market Segments

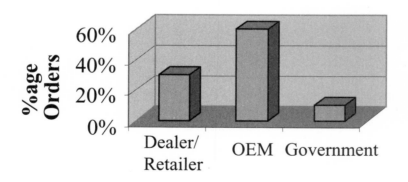

Market Segmentation Graph

Product Type

Enterprises can use other factors for market segmentation. For instance, the distribution centers at Wal-Mart classify customers into two categories: (1) "Staple Stock" and (2) "Direct Freight" customers.[24] Staple stock items are those customers expect to find in the same place every day, such as toothpaste and shampoo—items typically replenished on a *pull* signal from the retail stores. Direct freight items include promotional items— those the buyers in the central office in Bentonville, Arkansas, procure in large quantities, usually at bargain rates, and push out to the retail stores. This is stock the retail customer might find "here today, gone tomorrow."[25] Direct freight also includes items that are somewhat seasonal—those Wal-Mart is probably willing to risk being out of stock.

It is necessary to define market segments because the enterprise can then identify which attributes of its products appeal to which segments. The next step is to define customer values and delivery expectations for each segment. Customer values are determined from a study that identifies the order qualifiers and order winners for the customers in the segment.

IDENTIFY ORDER QUALIFIERS AND ORDER WINNERS

Translating corporate objectives into goals for Marketing and Operations can be very difficult. On the one hand, it is fairly easy for Marketing to arrive at general statements that express a desire to be more responsive, provide better service, be a market leader, or be an innovator. However, such vague expressions of goodwill should be translated into more concrete statements.

Part of the difficulty in arriving at more concrete statements is that Marketing is often not fully conversant with what Operations is capable of doing. Order qualifiers and order winners, however, articulate much more effectively what the goals should be for both Marketing and Operations. These criteria define, clearly and precisely, what customers expect from a product, in a way that Operations can more easily understand. While Marketing will have an important perspective on what these criteria should be, an essential perspective must come from Operations. Order qualifiers and order winners must, therefore, be determined jointly, perhaps iteratively, by Marketing and Operations. This step is the key link between Marketing strategies and Operations strategies.

---

24. Gue, K. R. 2001. "Warehouse Tours," *http://web.nps.navy.mil/~krgue/Teaching/teaching.html.*
25. Ibid.

Order qualifiers and order winners must be established for each market segment, and the enterprise may choose to have different Marketing and Operations strategies for meeting demand within each segment. For Wal-Mart, availability would very likely be an order qualifier for staple stock items like toothpaste, while cost would be an order winner. For direct freight items like a digital camera that Wal-Mart obtains at bargain basement prices because the product is being phased out, product design could be an order qualifier while quality could be an order winner.

Enterprises may decide to further segment the market to arrive at more targeted order qualifiers and order winners. A PC manufacturer/assembler might consider segmenting the market into desktop users, laptop users, and servers. Within the laptop segment, there could be a further segmentation into business and home laptop users. The business laptop user would have a different set of order winners, such as weight and size; for the home laptop user, cost might be the order winner.

Needless-to-say, order qualifiers and order winners must be carefully determined through market analysis, and they can change over time. Consider the laptop computer for business users. While weight and size may currently be order winners, in future they might just be order qualifiers. An order winner in the future might be the ease with which the laptop can synchronize with other electronic devices.

Once the order winners and qualifiers are determined for each market segment, the next step is to translate them into specific product requirements—that is, into tasks for Operations. At issue here, is the question of how the enterprise should respond to customer orders along these different market segments. The decisions involved are structural, such as where to locate the production facilities, which processes to use in making the products, how to design product delivery strategies, and whether to make or buy components of the final product. Discussion on facility location is outside the scope of this book,[26] but the other factors are treated below.

---

26. *For more information on locating facilities, see, for instance,* White, J. A., J. A. White, Jr., and L. F. McGinnis. 1998. *Facility Layout and Location: An Analytical Approach.* Englewood Cliffs, NJ: Prentice Hall; Sule, D. R. 1998. *Manufacturing Facility Location Planning and Design,* 2nd ed. Boston: PWS Publishing Co.

PROCESS CHOICE

Investment in the appropriate processes and infrastructure is fundamental to aligning market needs with enterprise capability to deliver products that match the needs. The order winners and order qualifiers, together with product volumes, influence the choice of the processes used to make the products. If product variety is an order winner, that might suggest the need for a process that is flexible and not capital intensive, especially if production volumes are not as high as would be expected for a standard product. The choice of process dictates and is dictated by other considerations, such as scale of operations and cost. The product-process matrix shown in Figure 4.9 is a simple tool used to determine whether or not proposed strategic choices lie within the enterprise's area of experience. It can also point out what the enterprise needs to change if it decides proactively to pursue a strategy that is not within its current area of expertise.

The lower right-hand corner of the matrix (see Figure 4.9) represents an enterprise operating under the classic *economy of scale* situation, one with a high-volume, low-variety mode of operation. This mode encourages large production batches, often using a continuous-flow type of operation. An enterprise that decides to compete in such a market will typically choose to work with a highly automated system, sacrificing flexibility for output. On the other hand, an enterprise that works with *economies of scope* would favor a more flexible, perhaps more labor-intensive, process (see the upper left-hand corner of the matrix).

Enterprises typically position themselves along the diagonal of the matrix but may deliberately position themselves away from the diagonal to differentiate themselves. For instance, a higher degree of flexibility is characterized by a position anywhere above the diagonal in the matrix. Such a positioning might result in relatively higher costs, because the enterprise is using flexible process capabilities to compete with enterprises using automated, dedicated facilities to make similar products.

Similarly, moving to a position below the diagonal would typically imply lower flexibility. Yet, there too, costs are typically higher because the enterprise is using capital-intensive assets, typically used in flow-shop operations, to produce at low volumes. Marketing pressures tend to push enterprises towards the lower left-hand corner of the product-process matrix. That means there is pressure on Operations to provide increased product variety while at the same time providing the efficiencies of scale afforded by a continuous flow mode of production.

Figure 4-9. The Product-Process Matrix for Manufacturing Enterprises

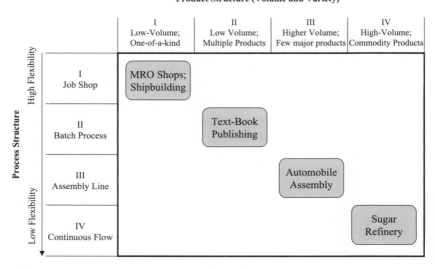

Product Structure (Volume and Variety)

Source: R. H. Hayes and S. C. Wheelwright. 1984. *Restoring Our Competitive Edge: Competing Through Manufacturing.* New York: John Wiley.

Figure 4.9 presents the product-process matrix for enterprises in manufacturing industries, highlighting the trade-offs that typically must be made between volume, variety, and flexibility. Similar trade-offs exist in service industries, where they are typically between the degree of customization (variety) and the amount of flexibility provided by the service. (See Figure 4.10.)

To summarize the discussion so far, enterprises must clearly understand which processes best meet the needs of their markets. Specifically, how effectively they provide the order winners for products in different market segments. The process chosen should reconcile possibly conflicting objectives on product variety and cost. Once this is done, the emphasis shifts to determining how the enterprise should respond to customer orders. More specifically, the enterprise needs to make plans for delivering products based on customer lead-time expectations.

PRODUCT DELIVERY STRATEGIES

Customers have differing delivery expectations. Some customers are prepared to wait for a product that is built exactly according to their specifications. Others are willing to compromise on some product features if they can get the product immediately. For the latter type of customer, unavailability of a product could result in a

Figure 4-10. The Product-Process Matrix for Service Providers

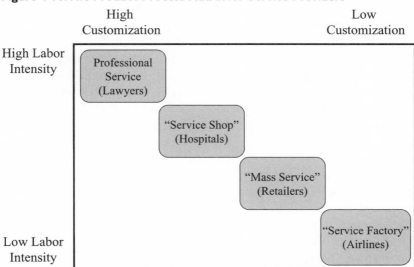

lost sale, so the enterprise may have to carry some finished goods inventory to meet their demand.

However, finished goods inventories do not always solve the problem. Taiichi Ohno is reputed to have said, "The more inventory you have on hand, the less likely you are to have the one item your customer actually wants." The fact that there is a lot of inventory of a certain product can simply mean the wrong kind of finished goods inventory has been built. Deciding on the right kind of finished goods inventory is always a challenge; it is wiser to maintain as little finished goods inventory as possible— especially if you are in an industry like electronics where some products depreciate almost as fast as groceries do.

What is needed is a *customer time-based demand profile* that identifies customer expectations in terms of lead-time, and facilitates the development of finished goods inventory strategies accordingly. To understand how the customer time-based demand profile could be used, consider a product like under-the-counter dishwashers. Customers for this dishwasher are individual homeowners, retail stores, or building contractors. The homeowner is either one who needs a dishwasher right now to replace a dishwasher that is broken and not repairable or is shopping around to replace a functioning dishwasher. For the former, the lead-time expectation on the order is 0. For the latter, shopping around with no sense of urgency, the lead-time could be a month until a really good deal turns up. Meanwhile, the retail store owner can probably wait one day, but the building contractor can probably wait one week.

Clearly, different types of customers have their own lead-time expectations. Clearly, too, the dishwasher manufacturer does not have to carry finished goods inventory for all customer types. If the manufacturer can build dishwashers to order in three days, it only needs to carry finished goods inventory for retail store owners and customers seeking to replace a broken dishwasher. Figure 4.11 shows a customer time-based demand profile.

The profile in Figure 4.11 identifies the percentage of customers who demand products with a lead-time expectation of 0 weeks (they want their order filled right away) and of those that are prepared to wait one week, two weeks, etc. To arrive at the profile, the enterprise gathers data on customer orders received (not filled) and the delivery time expectations associated with each. Ideally, the enterprise should also gather data on customers who decided not to place an order simply because the lead-time was too high. Ideally, too, it creates a time-based demand profile for each product, rather than a generic profile for each market segment.

Figure 4-11. Customer Time-Based Demand Profile

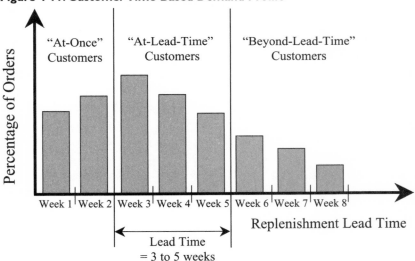

The time-based demand profile is a very useful tool to match customer expectations with Operations capabilities. Suppose the lead-time for the enterprise to fulfill demand is between two to four weeks. All orders requiring delivery in less than two weeks would have to be met with finished goods inventory. Customers placing such orders would be classified as "At-Once" customers.[27] Customers placing orders that fall within the lead-time window are classified as "At-Lead-Time" customers; those prepared to wait for more than four weeks would be "Beyond-Lead-Time" customers. The ideal is to have more At-Lead-Time and Beyond-Lead-Time customers and no At-Once customers, so that all orders could be built to demand; the enterprise can operate in a pure BTO mode. At-Once customers, on the other hand, require a BTS delivery strategy.

The time-based demand profile highlights the importance of reducing lead times, because the At-Once customer base becomes smaller as the lead-time to process an order decreases. To reduce lead-time, the enterprise could pursue strategies such as the RAP postponement strategies discussed in Chapter 2.

The time-based demand profile may also be used as the basis for pricing strategies. At-Once customers might be charged a premium; Beyond-Lead-Time customers might be given a discount. This is a way to influence the demand profile itself so that there are more At-Lead-Time or Beyond-Lead-Time customers.

Once the process choices have been made and delivery strategies established, the next task is to ensure that the infrastructure, particularly for Operations, can meet market needs. This is a critical step in Operations strategy development because infrastructure, like process choice, requires a high investment, which has long-term implications. Infrastructure choices depend on decisions about organizational structure, workforce skills, the type of systems used for planning and scheduling, quality control systems, and material handling/logistics support systems. The planning and scheduling systems relate to popular systems like materials requirement planning (MRP) systems, kanban systems, and drum-buffer-rope (DBR) systems discussed in detail in later chapters. Here, we discuss organizational structure and workforce skills.

---

27.   Greenwood, T. 2003. *The Lean Enterprise Systems Design Institute Workbook.* Knoxville: University of Tennessee.

INSTALLING THE INFRASTRUCTURE NEEDED FOR OPERATIONS

The success of any operations strategy depends on how well it transforms its key business processes into capabilities that consistently provide superior value to the customer. These capabilities are created through strategic investments in infrastructure. Most individual elements of infrastructure do not require as much investment as process choice does, but collectively they can far exceed the investment in processes and technologies.

Organizational structure in the context of functional silos was discussed earlier in this chapter. We observed that the functional orientation typically resulted in increased lead-time to deliver products within the enterprise and stressed the need to replace it with a process orientation. A further problem in many enterprises is the presence of multiple layers of bureaucracy. Typically, the more layers in the organizational structure, the longer it takes for decisions to be made. Hill[28] observes that a typical enterprise in the 1900s had three levels of management; by the 1960s, the number of levels had expanded to 12. The trend today, however, is to reduce this number, and many enterprises have brought the number of layers back down to three.

As enterprises flatten their organizational structure, they increasingly empower the workforce—one of the most important elements of infrastructure. Many of the world's most profitable enterprises have employees who are enthusiastic entrepreneurs, constantly involved in improving productivity. The success of the workforce in improving productivity is not an accident. Productivity is determined by the social structures of the organization, among them measurement systems, incentive systems, job security, freedom to experiment, advancement opportunities—everything that affects the work environment.

Whereas operations strategies that relate to process choice and product delivery strategies can provide enterprises with the competitive edge, ultimately it is the energy and creativity of the workforce that improves productivity. A motivated workforce helps the enterprise build the skill sets and capabilities that provide the ultimate competitive edge.

To enhance workforce skills, the enterprise needs to define and develop generic skill sets. As Hayes and Pisano remark, [29] "Manufacturing strategy is not just about aligning operations to

---

28. Op. cit., n. 22.
29. Hayes, R. H., and G. P. Pisano. 1994. "Beyond World Class: The New Manufacturing Strategy." *Harvard Business Review,* January-February: vol 72, pp. 77–86

current competitive capabilities but also about selecting and creating the operating capabilities a company will need in the future." Slack and Lewis[30] echo this idea, saying "Capabilities are those combinations of organizational resource and process that together underpin sustainable competitive advantage for a specific firm competing in a particular product or market."

While a rival can buy the same technologies and imitate the processes followed by the best-in-class enterprises, it is harder to imitate a combination of activities and processes. Similarly, resources developed in-house through the experience of staff, or interconnected with other resources in the enterprises, cannot be traded easily. As a result, the advantages they create are more likely to be retained over time.

The key is to build generic skill sets so that the enterprise can respond flexibly to changing customer demands. These skill sets give the enterprise core capabilities and competencies that it can use to establish, excel, and protect itself in the marketplace. Maintaining and improving these core capabilities is one of the key tasks of Operations. The next chapters present the two philosophies—lean thinking and the theory of constraints—that present significant opportunities for enterprises to build these generic skill sets.

CONCLUSIONS

"Then said they unto him, 'Say now "Shibboleth"': and he said "Sibboleth": for he could not frame to pronounce it right. Then they took him, and slew him at the passages of Jordan: and there fell at that time of the Ephraimites forty and two thousand."[31]

Failure to distinguish between operational effectiveness and Operations strategy is unlikely to have as serious a consequence as befell the Ephraimites at the hands of the men of Gilead. Yet the consequences can be quite severe. The difference is this:

- *Operational effectiveness* seeks to continually improve every situation where there are no trade-offs, trying to shift the productivity frontier outward in a relentless effort to achieve best practice. While that may produce absolute improvement by raising the bar, it may not lead to relative improvement for the enterprise, because rivals can mimic best-in-class practices.

---

30. Slack, N., and M. Lewis. 2003. *Operations Strategy.* Upper Saddle River, NJ: Prentice Hall.
31. *The Book of Judges*, 12:5-6

Thus, operational effectiveness is a necessary but not sufficient condition for competitiveness.

- *Operations strategy* is about building strategic flexibility and maintaining a competitive advantage by effectively integrating functions and processes. Enterprises must engage in a continuous effort to extend their unique position in the marketplace. Operations strategy should aim at building the competitive edge by developing the ability to respond flexibly to changing customer preferences.

Building strategic flexibility requires:

- A move from a functional to a process orientation. There must also be a concerted effort to maintain the process orientation, especially during periods of growth.
- Metrics should be designed that better align functions and maintain a process orientation. The balanced scorecard framework is one way to help determine the right set of metrics.
- Building a flexible response to changing customer preferences requires a close dialog between Design, Marketing, and Operations to resolve internal inconsistencies and to coevolve strategies. Inconsistencies can arise if, for instance, the enterprise attempts to market too many products, or if Operations tries to perform new tasks with outdated policies and structure, or if the process technology is not suited to the product being produced.
- Order qualifiers and order winners offer a common ground for engaging Marketing and Operations in dialog. Used in conjunction with the customer time-based demand profile, they can help match customer expectations with Operations capabilities.
- It is critical to provide the right infrastructure and build workforce skills and generic skill sets so that the enterprise is able to respond flexibly to changing customer demands. Maintaining and improving these core capabilities is one of the key goals of an Operations strategy.
- Finally, many of the decisions that emanate from an Operations strategy are structural and demand considerable commitments of resources. Because an enterprise rarely has a second chance to correct investment decisions, it must be careful to ensure that those decisions are not approved or rejected based on pure economic hurdles. Decisions should, instead, consider how the investment helps Operations become a competitive weapon.

PART 3

Achieving Exceptional Performance

5

Lean Thinking

"Nothing focuses the mind better than the constant sight of a competitor who wants to wipe you off the map."
Wayne Calloway

In 1980, Japan became the world's leading producer of automobiles, producing just over 11 million units out of a worldwide total of over 38.6 million units. That gave the Japanese automakers 28.5 percent of the world market. Slipping to second place for the first time since taking the lead from France in 1904, the U.S. produced just over 8 million for a market share of about 21 percent.[1] Japanese auto manufacturers had produced only about 69,000 vehicles in 1955, a year in which the U.S. auto industry built 9.2 million vehicles. Who could have predicted that just 25 years later the Japanese auto industry would produce more than 11 million vehicles—3 million more than their U.S. counterparts that year—and remain the world's leading automobile manufacturer for the next 15 years?[2]

Japan's rise to its preeminent position was fueled by its application of lean-thinking principles. It is a widely accepted notion that these principles originated in Japan. What is not widely known is the fact that a number of these principles were created in the United States. It may therefore be instructive to begin this chapter with a brief voyage back in time to discover the origins of the lean

---

1. Antique Automobile Club of America, *Automotive History: A Chronological History, http://www.aaca.org.*
2. Japan maintained its stature as the world's largest automobile manufacturing nation until around 1995. Today, recent mergers and acquisitions by the big three U.S. automakers (Ford has acquired Mazda, Volvo, Aston Martin, Land Rover, and Jaguar; GM has acquired Opel, Saab, and Vauxhall; Chrysler has merged with Daimler Benz) make comparisons less meaningful. Incidentally, the mergers and acquisitions by the U.S. automakers were driven more by the growing cost of developing a new car than by a desire to reestablish world dominance. By entering into such alliances, they could share the fixed costs of new product development and at the same time gain access to new markets and to manufacturing and technological know-how.

approach. The voyage will identify not only the roots of lean concepts but also stumbling blocks an enterprise might encounter as it embarks on its own journey to become lean.

FROM CRAFT TO MASS TO LEAN PRODUCTION

A little known fact is that the first automobile manufacturers in the world were French. In 1889, Rene Panhard and Emil Levassor, partners in a woodworking machinery business, obtained a license from Daimler to build engines for automobiles.[3] Panhard and Levassor built the first car in 1890, but because they saw no future in this business, they granted Armand Peugeot the right to use Daimler engines in self-propelled vehicles.

Peugeot made five cars in 1891 and 29 in 1892. These cars were built using the craft production technique; no two cars were alike. By 1905, less than 15 years after Panhard and Levassor built their first car, hundreds of enterprises in Europe and the U.S. were producing cars in small volumes using craft production techniques,[4] But by then craft production techniques for cars were heading for extinction due to the pioneering efforts of the celebrated "father of mass production," Henry Ford.

Henry Ford and the Origin of Mass Production

Henry Ford was not the first mass producer in the U.S. That title probably belonged to Ransom E. Olds. However, Ford changed the way the world would perceive manufacturing. He introduced the concepts of flow and throughput velocity in automobile manufacturing. His plan was "to keep everything in motion: work to man and not man to work." To create flow, he instituted the well-known moving assembly line in the Highland Park plant that built the Model T automobile.[5] The moving line reduced assembly time for automobiles from 12 worker-hours down to about 1.5 in 1914. For the first time in history, one plant was building 1,000 cars a day.

---

3. Benz in 1885 and Daimler in 1887 produced the first gasoline automobiles. However, they were inventors who had been experimenting with automobile designs simply to test their engines. They licensed patents and sold engines to automobile manufacturers before becoming full-fledged manufacturers themselves.
4. Womack, J. P., D. T. Jones, and D. Roos. 1990. *The Machine that Changed the World*, New York: Rawson Associates.
5. Ford, H. 1926. *Today and Tomorrow*. Garden City, NY: Doubleday; reprinted 1989. Cambridge, MA: Productivity Press; and Ford, H. 1930. *Moving Forward*. New York: Doubleday.

Henry Ford's goal was to reduce waste in any form—not just within the factory walls. He reduced waste and leveraged flow across the entire supply chain. In *Today and Tomorrow,* he claimed: "Our production cycle is about 81 hours from the mine to the finished machine in the freight car, or three days and nine hours instead of the 14 days we used to think was record-breaking."

Ford's relentless attention to removing waste from every step in the process allowed him to slash production costs. As those costs fell, he passed on some savings to customers. His innovations led to a sharp drop in the price of the automobile, from $1,000 to $260. The sharp increases in productivity that accompanied these innovations kept inflationary pressures down and led to periods of "benign deflation."[6] This happened despite the fact that existing supply chains consisted of independent, inflexible enterprises that somehow managed to deliver products to customers.

Not all of Henry Ford's contributions to management were beneficial. He paid excessive attention to manufacturing details, often disregarding important decisions that cost the enterprise thousands of dollars. He equated throughput velocity with product uniformity by insisting on a standard model with a single color.[7] Because of Henry Ford's managerial style, combined with his strategy to produce only a single model, the Ford company lost market share to General Motors between the 1920s and World War II.

Under the leadership of Alfred P. Sloan, GM was taking advantage of a shift it perceived in the buying patterns of the American consumer by introducing a new model every year. While Ford continued to turn out the same model year after year, GM's Chevrolet division introduced the annual model change. In 1921, Ford had 55 percent of the U.S. market; by 1927 its market share was less than 15 percent.

Nevertheless, Henry Ford's contribution to manufacturing cannot be denied. Besides his many contributions to mass production, he was also the inspiration for many of the concepts and tools used in the Toyota Production System. However, it was Sloan who ultimately took mass production techniques to new heights.

---

6. Kerschner, E. M., T. M. Doerflinger, and M. Geraghty. 1999. "The Information Revolution Wars: Fighting for 'Digitizable GDP.'" New York: Paine Webber, Inc.
7. Henry Ford's famous quote, "The customer can have any color so long as it is black," is believed to have a twofold basis: it reduced setups and there was also the notion that black dried faster, which increased throughput velocity.

Sloan succeeded where Ford did not by devising an organization suitable for a mass production system, putting in place a management system for controlling the multiple-enterprise conglomerate that GM had become. By the time Sloan retired in 1946, GM was the biggest enterprise in the world. It is little wonder that when *Fortune* chose the "businessman of the century" in its November 22, 1999 issue, Sloan made it to the final four. (The winner, however, was Henry Ford.)

The three decades after World War II were the glory days of the American automobile industry. The economy in Europe, the only major threat to U.S. industry, was just beginning its long recovery from the devastating effects of the war, so foreign competition was minimal. The domestic economy was flourishing as the U.S. Government poured money into rebuilding infrastructure. Mass production techniques and vertical integration were key factors that established the dominance of the "Big Three" U.S. automakers, as well as U.S. manufacturing in general.

Mass production proved extremely effective. It delivered growth at an extraordinary rate. The U.S. industry flourished well into the 1960s. A time when demand far outstripped supply, this period was perceived as a "golden era" for U.S. industry. However, it was actually a problematic period in a number of ways.

The High Cost of Complacency

The Big Three automakers had effectively become a cartel led by GM. But cartels, like their more integrated cousins, monopolies, tend to become inefficient and ineffective because they can afford to be. Although the U.S. automobile industry had led the world in innovation at the turn of the 20th century, innovation started to take a back seat in the U.S. after the war. The automatic transmission, introduced in the 1940 Oldsmobile models, was the last major U.S. innovation. While an abundance of new popular features was promoted with each new model, there was little to distinguish cars made in the 1960s from those made in the 1950s.

The misapplication of mass production techniques compounded these problems. Conceived in Henry Ford's heyday as a way to deliver products quickly to the customer, the mass production system had over time morphed into a batch production system in which the accepted mode of operation was to use economies of scale. Cars were built in large batches, resulting in large work-in-process (WIP) and finished goods inventories. This did not worry the automakers because demand still exceeded supply in the absence of serious foreign competition. The desire to achieve scale economies drove even low-volume manufacturing enterprises, such as aircraft engine manufacturers, to produce in large batches. Large-lot production soon became the most distinguishing feature of mass production.

Building products in large lots in anticipation of customer demand may have worked satisfactorily in the production-centric era, but it had serious consequences. For instance, with plenty of WIP to buffer any production delays, defects found on the shop floor did not generate a sense of urgency to fix the problem so it did not occur again. Hence, the real impact of the quality problem was marginalized. Worse, quality problems often escaped unnoticed until after the product was sold. Consumers suffered from poor quality because cars were often riddled with defects and needed frequent repairs. In short, the U.S. auto industry was badly in need of a shake-up. It got it in the 1970s when the oil crisis hit.

The Arab-Israeli war in 1973 and the accompanying oil price increases caught U.S. consumers, who favored large cars with large engines, by surprise. Gas guzzlers suddenly lost their appeal and soon the world's largest market was clamoring for smaller, fuel-efficient cars. This opened the door for imports from Japan, which filled the bill, accelerating the decline of U.S. dominance in automobile manufacturing.

The Toyota Production System

The 1960s were pivotal years for Japanese manufacturers. They dedicated themselves as an industry to building compact and subcompact cars with excellent fuel economy. They succeeded in producing those vehicles at low cost by adopting the just-in-time (JIT) production management philosophy and system. The JIT management system, invented by the Toyota Motor Corporation, owes its conception and evolution to two individuals, Kiichiro Toyoda and Taiichi Ohno; the latter is widely acknowledged as the creator of the Toyota Production System (TPS).

Inspired by Henry Ford's book, *Today and Tomorrow,* Kiichiro Toyoda had formulated as early as 1936 a clear mental picture of the production system he wanted. The basic idea was to produce only what was needed on a given day—to initiate a production run only *when it was needed,* rather than in anticipation of a demand. He initiated this idea in the automobile department he had started within his father's enterprise, the Toyoda Automatic Loom Works. Slips were passed around indicating the number of parts to be made or processed that day. This was the origin of the *kan-ban* method of production that became the basis for the JIT system. Toyoda began convincing suppliers to cooperate with his JIT system. He also changed the traditional physical layout of the plant so that machine tools were organized in a flow line. That made the supply line shorter so parts could get into the assembly process sooner.

In 1950, Kiichiro Toyoda's cousin, Eiji Toyoda, toured Ford Motor Company. An important process he learned about during the trip was the Ford suggestion system. Eiji Toyoda instituted the concept and it became to be one of the major building blocks of continuous improvement (*kaizen*). On his return to Japan, he sought the help of Taiichi Ohno to produce cars in small batches more efficiently than the big U.S. enterprises were able to.

Ohno was an ardent admirer of Ford and credits his contributions to TPS to two main concepts.[8] The first concept, the moving assembly line, he had found in Henry Ford's book *Today and Tomorrow*. The second concept was the supermarket operations he saw on a visit to the United States in 1956 that provided stores with a continuous supply of merchandise. Ohno set up a pull system in which each production process became a supermarket for the succeeding process: Each process would produce to replenish only the items that the downstream process had used.

Like Ford, Ohno emphasized waste reduction. Ohno's contention was that waste is so prevalent that we do not eliminate it because we learn to live with or work around it. He modified Ford's ideas to reflect modern market demands. Ford had offered his customers cars in only one color to reduce changeover times between paint colors. Subsequent efforts to introduce product variety into U.S. car industry offerings were hampered by those large changeover times for products as well as paint colors. This apparent inflexibility had become a corporate millstone for U.S. automakers.

The Japanese refused to accept changeover times as a constraint. Instead, they focused relentlessly on reducing changeover times, and they did so. This made it possible for them to provide product variety without having to produce large lots. As Shingo said, "The Toyota production system is the antithesis of

---

8. Ohno, T. 1988. *Toyota Production System: Beyond Large-Scale Production*. Cambridge, MA: Productivity Press.

large-lot production, *not* mass production."[9] Japanese autos were now highly competitive against the U.S. and other foreign cars, both in quality and cost.

Lessons Learned

The brief journey back in time showed that a number of elements in the Toyota Production System—*kaizen,* flow, pull production, and waste elimination—were inspired by Henry Ford. At the same time, the journey also revealed the dangers of complacency and the critical need for enterprises to avoid adopting tools and techniques in a piecemeal manner.

JIT, for instance, emphasizes working with *kanbans* and minimal inventories, but just trying to reduce inventories without considering other factors can have serious consequences because the system is now much more vulnerable to disruptions. Figure 5.1 uses a "river and rocks" analogy that likens the water level to the inventory level in a facility. A higher water level hides potential blemishes in the process, such as unreliable suppliers, scrap loss, and machine breakdowns. As the water (inventory) level is lowered, these problems surface, forcing management to correct the defects. The key is to resist the temptation to reduce the inventory level too quickly. Rather, the idea is to lower the water level a little, break apart the exposed rocks (obstacles), and then lower the water level once again.

Even as attempts are made to reduce inventory levels, other major elements that should be in place are reliable processes, preventive maintenance systems, cross-trained workers, setup reduction programs, and reliable suppliers. If these are not already present in a factory, putting them in place takes time—it cannot happen overnight. The Japanese spent close to 20 years perfecting the system before the U.S. automakers observed TPS in action.

The Japanese management system was also built on partnering arrangements that had mutual benefits for both the automakers and their suppliers. Not only were suppliers given ample visibility on the automakers' assembly schedules but these schedules were adhered to fairly stringently. That made it easier for the suppliers to plan their own production schedules and deliver supplies in a timely manner without having to hold a large finished goods inventory.

---

9. Shingo, S. 1989. *A Study of the Toyota Production System.* Portland, OR: Productivity Press, p. 84.

Figure 5-1. Inventory Hides Defects

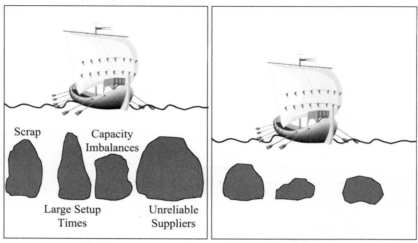

Before:	After:
A high water level hides defects	A low water level exposes hidden problems

In their anxiety to adopt Japanese practices, the U.S. automakers attempted to implement JIT techniques in the 1980s. They studied the Toyota production system and identified a number of TPS tools they believed they could transplant into their factories. In their enthusiasm to catch up with the Japanese competition, they attempted to implement JIT tools too quickly, in a piecemeal fashion. They first tried to drastically reduce their inventory of automobile components. At the same time, they asked suppliers to deliver components just when they were needed.

However, they did not first ensure that their own internal processes were reliable. Because they were not, the automakers were unable to give suppliers clear visibility on their production schedules. Left in the dark about when the next delivery request would come, suppliers built up finished goods inventory so as to better respond to requests from the automakers for JIT supplies. Invariably, the suppliers ended up building the wrong products. Furthermore, relationships with the suppliers at that time were (and in too many cases, still are) adversarial. There were no long-term contracts and components were generally sourced from multiple vendors selected based on price, quality, and delivery, though mainly on price. These factors made the position of suppliers even more tenuous.

U.S. manufacturers probably misunderstood the intended meaning of JIT. The JIT philosophy articulated by Kiichiro Toyoda merely stated that components for an automobile should not be produced before they were needed but should instead be made "just in time." The implication was that every step in the supply chain had to work in harmony to produce when a product was needed, not a single moment before. This philosophy never intended, for instance, to have the supplier maintain a stock of finished goods to supply material just in time.

It bears repeating: Simply adopting tools and techniques piecemeal does not lead to a lasting competitive edge. On the contrary, without a complete understanding of the core concepts and principles of lean thinking, there is considerable potential for doing more harm than good. For instance, lean thinking emphasizes eliminating *muda* or waste[10]—specifically, any activity that absorbs resources but creates no value. If the enterprise has not fully understood the core concepts of lean operations, waste-removal activities could lead it down the wrong path.

Conventional wisdom may suggest that when non-value-adding activities are eliminated, the enterprise has an opportunity to become more efficient through workforce reduction. Nothing could be further from the truth. When lean implementation is viewed as a cost-cutting initiative or an opportunity to reduce the workforce, employees will naturally resist it, leading to eventual migration back to the old way of doing things. On the other hand, if it is made clear that freed-up resources would be productively deployed elsewhere, implementation efforts would have a much better chance of success. Freeing up resources for productive deployment elsewhere is at the very core of lean thinking.

CREATING FLOW: THE TOOLS AND TECHNIQUES OF LEAN

Simply put, lean is a *growth strategy* aimed at uncovering additional capacity that could be deployed for further growth. Put another way, the greatest benefit of lean processes lies in the money that enterprises do *not* have to spend now—by not having to build new plants, not having to invest in a new warehouse, and so on. A lean implementation has the goal of delivering products that the customer values as quickly as possible.

---

10. Womack, J. P., and D. Jones. 1996. *Lean Thinking*. New York: Simon & Schuster.

Enterprises often focus on their own metrics and reduce inventory to save on carrying costs, but there are arguably three other reasons to do so that are more important—more customer-focused:

1. As discussed in Chapter 4, large finished goods inventories of certain products suggest that the enterprise is building the wrong *kind* of products, perhaps because it produces in large batches to exploit scale economies.

2. Reducing inventories reduces lead times,[11] enabling the enterprise to ship the product to the customer faster. For instance, if the enterprise has two weeks of WIP inventory on the shop floor, a new order processed using the first-come-first-served principle will take at least two weeks to complete. The enterprise is also more responsive to changing customer preferences, when inventories are reduced.

3. Finally, reducing inventory exposes problems like poor quality, unreliable suppliers, too much scrap, and large changeover times. (See Figure 5.1.)

Figure 5.1 carries another important message. For the boat to move faster, all the oars should be in the water at the same time. In Chapter 2, we prescribed balancing flow across the supply chain. Similarly, the most effective method of production is to have all processes working at the same rate. There is no point in having some resources working faster than others because that will invariably pile up inventory in front of the slower processes. Making sure all resources respond to *pull* signals ensures a smooth flow of products across the enterprise, or the supply chain. The signal for a resource to produce could be generated simply when the downstream resource draws a unit of WIP from the buffer between the two resources. (See Chapter 8.)

The discussion so far clearly demonstrates the value of containing inventory so as to promote flow. The important tools used by lean thinking to promote flow are:

- 5S
- Flow charts
- *Takt* time
- Average labor content and minimum staffing
- Mixed model scheduling and small batch production

---

11. Little's Law, discussed in Chapter 2, states that Average WIP = Average lead time x Throughput.

- One-piece flow
- Cellular layout
- Standard work
- Pull replenishment
- Point-of-use materials storage
- Mistake proofing and method sheets
- Total productive maintenance
- Continuous improvement and the pursuit of perfection.

Although these lean tools were originally developed for manufacturing enterprises, many service enterprises are finding them very useful. Therefore, as these tools are discussed, think about how they apply in a service setting. For instance, the goal might be a piece of paper that reaches its destination more quickly. How often has one operator sat idle waiting for the next order to present itself? How often has a service delivery been delayed waiting for the paperwork to be completed?

Before applying these tools, the scope of lean implementation must be addressed. Enterprises often create lean cells that put out products at a rapid rate, only to find these products queuing up at a downstream work center. The questions that must first be addressed are:

- Should the enterprise implement lean on all its processes and activities or should it first focus on a subset of processes?
- Should it implement lean on all its products or first on a subset?

The recommendation is that the enterprise choose one product family at a time and implement lean on all the processes and activities that apply to that product family before moving on to the next product family.

5S

The term *5S* is used to denote a systematic process for organizing the workplace based on five simple yet powerful activities, each represented by a Japanese word that begins with an S: (1) *Seiri* (tidiness), (2) *Seiton* (organization), (3) *Seiso* (cleanliness), (4) *Seiketsu* (neatness), and (5) *Shitsuke* (discipline). (See Figure 5.2.) There are five English words that begin with the letter S and convey nearly, though not exactly, the same intended meaning. Some enterprises add a sixth S for Safety.

Figure 5-2. The 5S's and Their Definitions

Japanese	Definition	English	Example
Seiri	Tidiness	Sorting	Throw Away Rubbish
Seiton	Organization	Storing	30-Sec. Doc. Retrieval
Seiso	Cleanliness	Sanitizing	Individual Responsibility
Seiketsu	Neatness	Standardizing	Clear Written Instructions
Shitsuke	Discipline	Sustaining	Do 5S Activities Daily

The first step, *Seiri,* refers to discarding unnecessary items. Literally, it means organizing something that is disorganized. Every item in the work area is classified as either necessary, unnecessary, or "red tag." Items marked as unnecessary are disposed of immediately. Red tag items, which are literally tagged, indicating that it is unclear whether or not the items are needed, are then "auctioned" for anyone to claim as necessary. Red tag items that no one claims are discarded.

The idea behind the second step, *Seiton,* is to arrange the necessary items in order so that they can be picked up easily for use. In Japan, the words *Seiri* and *Seiton* are often used in combination (*Seiri-Seiton*) because there is not a big difference in their meanings as applied. In any case, the second step is intended to create storage systems and provide visual information about what is stored and how much should be stored in a given spot. Convenient locations are created for tools and devices used in the work area. For example, tools are typically hung on boards, with a silhouette ("shadow box") of the tool painted on the board where the tool is to be hung. Drawers are sometimes lined with Styrofoam, with cutouts of the items stored in the drawers.

The third step, *Seiso,* keeping the area clean, implies taking pride in a workplace that is well organized and kept in good condition. This step goes beyond simply making the area more pleasant by sweeping the floor and cleaning up leaks and spills. It includes checks for things like malfunctioning machinery or loose parts on machines. Aside from making the area more conducive to work in, the *Seiso* step provides other practical benefits: If machines are kept clean, for example, oil leaks will be discovered before a catastrophic equipment failure; if aisles are kept clean and free of any oil spills, the chances of accidents are minimized, and so on.

The fourth step, *Seiketsu,* is the basis for standardization. Literally, *Seiketsu* refers to a condition where there is no smear, stain, etc. This step, which covers both personal and environmental cleanliness, defines the standards by which personnel must measure and maintain "cleanliness." It prescribes what the normal condition should be, as well as how an abnormal condition should be corrected. Visual management is an important ingredient of *Seiketsu,* as by color-coding and standardization of colors for easier identification of problems. Personnel are trained to detect such problems using one or more of their five senses and to correct them immediately.

The final step, *Shitsuke,* relates to building the discipline to sustain the first four steps. In Japanese, it refers to making a person keep a rule or order through training. The rationale is that it is often easier to clean up an area than it is to keep it clean. Thus an integral part of a 5S program should be a system for maintaining the first four Ss. The *Shitsuke* step commits to maintaining orderliness and practicing the first four Ss continually; it is vital that this step have full support from top management. Initially, it is very likely that top management has to provide incentives for this step to become habitual. Once the inertia is overcome, however, there is a lasting effect, and the process becomes self-sustaining.

The 5S program improves safety, work efficiency, and productivity and gives employees a sense of ownership. These activities ensure a clean and orderly working environment and help employees become aware of that environment and the condition of the tools and machinery they use.

In many enterprises, the benefits of a 5S program can be so dramatic that there is a real danger that the enterprise may step away from a full-blown lean implementation at this stage, thinking its mission is complete. It is therefore important to note that the 5S program is just the starting point in the lean journey. The 5S program can actually hinder the lean journey if the vital fifth step (*Shitsuke*) is not practiced. A good 5S implementation builds the foundation for continuous improvement.

Flow Charts

In a work environment it is often easy to miss the simple flow of a process from one step to the next. The flow chart is a powerful visual tool that can describe practically any manufacturing or service process. Flow charts enable us to quickly identify the process steps we must eliminate in our drive for simplicity and waste reduction. Identifying and eliminating, or at least reducing, non-value-added activities is key to streamlining a process.

Of the several flow chart methods for capturing value-added and non-value-added activities, a *process flow chart* captures the logical sequence of activities involved in delivering the product and a *spaghetti diagram* depicts the physical movement of products through the plant or office. A process flow chart typically uses standard symbols (see Figure 5.3) to identify different activities, with value-added activities typically color-coded green and non-value-added activities yellow. The process flow chart also captures the time required to complete its activities.

Figure 5-3. Process Flowcharting Symbols

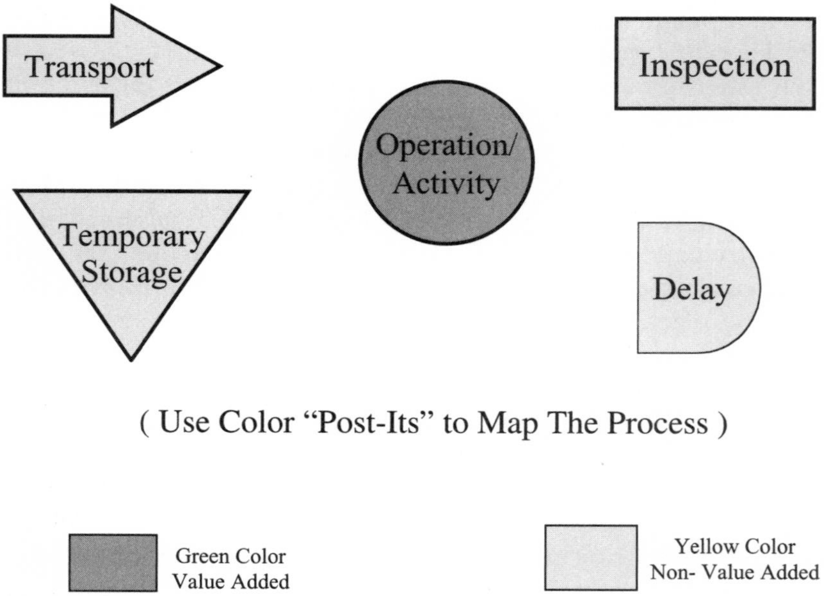

Transport

Inspection

Operation/Activity

Temporary Storage

Delay

(Use Color "Post-Its" to Map The Process)

Green Color
Value Added

Yellow Color
Non- Value Added

Deciding what is a value-added activity and what is not can sometimes be contentious. Does the Marketing function add value? Does the Logistics function add value? If so, which logistics activities are value-added? One way out of the contention is to define a value-adding activity as an activity that either actually transforms the product or one that the customer would be willing to pay for it to happen. *Like Logistics, etc.*

Figure 5.4 presents a process flow chart for a mortgage loan application. In it, the value-added ratio is the ratio of the actual value-added work expressed in time units divided by the time elapsed to complete the process. The summary data in Figure 5.4 presents the value-added ratio as 1.8 percent; a remarkably low number, that is unfortunately all too typical of a majority of processes in the real world. It also indicates the amount of waste that prevails in the system, and the huge opportunities for lean efforts to remove waste. While it is difficult to specify what the value-added ratio should be because it depends on the industry, a ratio of 10 percent has sometimes been suggested.[12]

Figure 5-4. Process Flow Chart for a Mortgage Loan Application

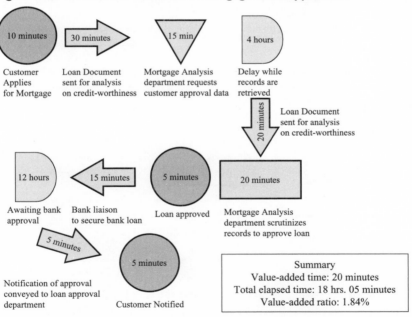

The formula described, however, does not consider the actual effort expended in delivering the product. It is not uncommon for some of the steps, value-added or otherwise, to involve multiple employees. In such situations, a more meaningful formula for the

---

12. *See, for example,* Conner, G. 2001, August. "Jack Sprat Speaks: Tips on Lean Manufacturing," *http://www.thefabricator.com.*

value-added ratio would have the total staff-hours of value-added effort required to produce one unit in the numerator and the total of all the staff-hours employed by the enterprise to produce one unit in the denominator.

A diagram sometimes used to represent the distance a product travels is the spaghetti diagram. Figure 5.5 shows a spaghetti diagram for the same mortgage loan application. A spaghetti diagram, in conjunction with the process flow chart, can give the analyst valuable information for streamlining the process. While the process flow chart will reveal the non-value-added activities, the spaghetti diagram highlights the extent of travel, including any back-tracking the product may undergo. It may suggest how the process could be streamlined through a better process layout.

Figure 5-5. Spaghetti Diagram for a Mortgage Loan Application

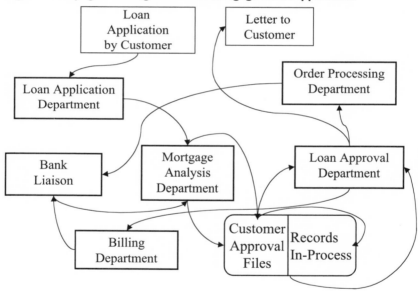

The process flow chart should preferably be drawn *after* the 5S program is in place. If it is drawn before, lack of attention to simple housekeeping activities may obfuscate some of the non-value-added activities the enterprise really needs to focus on. For instance, the operators could be taking more time to change tooling simply because they cannot find the tools, and that may be reflected in the time standards set for tool changeover.

Takt Time

If someone compiled a dictionary of terms used in lean, they would notice the slew of Japanese words in the compilation, but *takt* is a German word for a musical meter, that is used in lean thinking even in Japan. When German aerospace engineers helped Japan build aircrafts during the 1930s, they used the word *takt* to present an analogy to a conductor waving the baton to set the rhythm for the entire orchestra. After World War II, Toyota adopted the word and the accompanying concept as the basis for linking its production capacity to customer demand in TPS: Customer demand became the cadence that dictated the pace of operations on the shop floor.

How do enterprises apply *takt*? First, *takt* time represents customer demand. *Takt* time is calculated as follows:

$$\textit{Takt} \text{ time} = \text{Available time per period} \div \text{Demand per period}$$

The duration of the period may be minutes, hours, days, or even weeks, so long as the same unit of time is used in both numerator and denominator. To illustrate the concept, we start with a simple example of an enterprise working on a single product.

An insurance company, Hungama, Inc., uses four steps in processing applications for property insurance:

1. Data gathering/data entry (*distribution*),
2. Risk analysis (*underwriting*),
3. Computing the premium (*rating*), and
4. Policy writing.

Suppose customer demand for this product is 20 policies per day, and Hungama operates a single shift that is eight hours long.

The first step in calculating *takt* time is to determine the available time per shift. Typically, essential breaks for lunch and bio breaks are deducted from the duration of the shift to arrive at an available time of, say, 6 hours and 40 minutes (400 minutes) each day. *Takt* time is then $400 \div 20 = 20$ minutes per unit. In other words, the enterprise has to process one policy every 20 minutes. (If the enterprise operated two shifts each day, available time per day would be 800 minutes, and *takt* time would be $800 \div 20 = 40$ minutes per unit.)

Since the (external) customer demand is for one unit every 20 minutes, the enterprise should match its (internal) resources to meet this demand. Suppose the average time it takes to process the four steps (the *cycle time*) is 14 minutes for the first, 22 minutes for the second, 6 minutes for the third, and 12 minutes for the fourth. Suppose, too, that there is an individual dedicated to each of the steps. Figure 5.6 shows a load chart depicting the burden on these individuals, before and after the situation is analyzed.

Figure 5-6. Load Chart for Hungama, Inc.

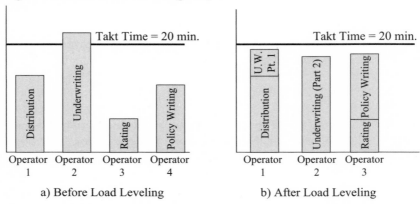

a) Before Load Leveling   b) After Load Leveling

One of the main uses of the *takt* time calculation is to match internal resources to external demand. The load chart helps determine whether the work is assigned equitably and whether anyone is overloaded. In Figure 5.6(a), the Hungama load chart makes it clear that the person in charge of Underwriting is overloaded beyond the *takt* time. This operator is presumably either working overtime or working faster than called for, opening up opportunities for the operator to make errors. At the same time, the load chart helps determine whether there is slack in the system; in Figure 5.6 (a), it is apparent that operators 1, 3, and 4 are underutilized.

What options does Hungama have at this stage? If some of the Underwriting work is reallocated to another operator, operator 2 could now get the work done within *takt* time. Also, the workload for operators 3 and 4 could be combined and assigned to one operator. Figure 5.6 (b) shows the "after load leveling" scenario, where a task that accounts for five minutes of work is moved from operator 2 to operator 1. The loads on the three operators are now 19 minutes, 17 minutes, and 18 minutes.

This discussion assumes that the time to perform each activity is accurate. That issue must be resolved quite early in the decision process and may require some time studies. Once it is resolved, the next question is how the individual operators are loaded. If they are underutilized, there is a likelihood that the work expands to fill the time available, resulting in inefficiencies. On the other hand, loading each operator close to 100 percent may lead to error, particularly if the workload is highly variable with prolonged periods where the operator is loaded beyond capacity. As discussed in Chapter 2, it's best to buffer variation with capacity, not inventory. Loading operators close to 100 percent leaves no room for accommodating increased customer demand without reallocating resources.

Note that *takt* time goes *down* when demand increases. If the demand at Hungama were to increase by 10 percent, to 22 policies per day, *takt* time would go down to 18 minutes per job and operator 1 becomes overloaded. Nevertheless, in some situations it is advisable to keep operators loaded close to 100 percent because that may motivate them to find creative ways of managing the workload so that the resulting cycle time is well within the allotted *takt* time.

The Hungama example used task times that were very discrete. If it were possible to subdivide tasks even more finely, it would be possible to load each operator as close to *takt* time as desired. If such a fine division of tasks were possible, what would be the best way to load each operator?

In the Hungama example, the total workload is $(19 + 17 + 18)$ = 54 minutes, so tasks could be allocated so that each operator had a cycle time of 18 minutes. However, that would uniformly underutilize each operator.

A better alternative may be to have the first two operators loaded with tasks that add up to the *takt* time of 20 minutes, leaving the third operator loaded only up to 14 minutes. This would make the third operator available to help the other operators if they fall behind schedule. In a manufacturing situation, for instance, this operator could also be located at the end of the cell to perform material handling, moving parts into and out of the cell.

Working with a *takt* time has a number of advantages. If each operator is paced to *takt* time, that automatically limits a primary cause of inventory, which is overproduction. Limiting overproduction also stabilizes the system, preventing the frequent stops and starts that inhibit a smooth flow. When a team of operators is asked to pace its work according to *takt* time, there is a heightened awareness of output rates and potential problems that might be barriers to achieving the desired output rate. Operators get immediate feedback if they miss *takt* time on a given cycle and make corrections accordingly. If feedback is only provided after many cycles, the window of opportunity to correct errors may have passed.

At the same time, *takt* time should be applied judiciously. This concept applies better to a flow shop that processes a set of products with relatively predictable demand that does not fluctuate much. *Takt* time may not be very relevant in a job shop environment, but calculating *takt* time is still useful there because it helps determine the number of operators that must be assigned to a process.

How often should *takt* time change? That depends on the industry. If *takt* time decreases for a manufacturing cell, it is not simply a matter of reallocating work to different operators but there may also be equipment-related issues. Adjusting *takt* time daily could well cause chaos. At the same time, if the enterprise is not flexible enough to react quickly, that may result in missed opportunities to fill demand or, conversely, lead to inventory build-ups.

The key is to distinguish between "noisy" data and real trends. For example, a "run" test could be applied to determine when the *takt* time should be changed. Consider the sequence of demands presented in Figure 5.7. The *takt* time (= the desired production rate) could be reevaluated if the demand exceeds the set production rate for, say, five consecutive days.

Consider how *takt* time works for the assembly operations at Dell. Dell assembles its desktop computers in response to customer demand using a number of assembly lines that operate in parallel. Suppose that, based on current customer demand, it has set its assembly *takt* time at 15 seconds per computer. Dell typically allocates one or at most two operators to assemble a computer at each assembly line. Suppose each assembly line has two operators and that each takes two minutes (120 seconds) to do his or her tasks. Since a *takt* time of 15 seconds does not give the assembly operators on a given line enough time to complete all assembly operations, Dell runs a number of assembly lines in parallel. If each assembly line puts out one computer every 120 seconds, then Dell needs eight lines running in parallel to meet a *takt* time goal of 15 seconds (120 ÷ 8 = 15 seconds).

Figure 5-7. Re-Calibrating *Takt* Time

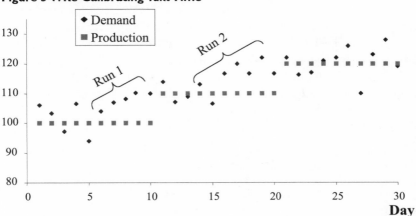

Suppose that on a given day, Dell does not have enough orders on hand to achieve a *takt* time of 15 seconds per computer but instead *takt* time works out to 16 seconds. (Note that that *takt* time goes *up* when demand goes down.) Dell now has several choices. One is to shut down one assembly line. But with seven lines, each assembling one computer every 120 seconds, it will take 17.14 seconds to assemble a computer ($120 \div 7 = 17.14$ seconds), and that would not meet customer demand. Another alternative would be to ask each assembly line to work slower.

A third alternative would be to run all eight lines at full speed, continuing to produce one computer every 15 seconds. This alternative causes minimal disruptions in the assembly process but the overproduction will result in some computers that are built to stock. These computers can either be sold at a discounted price, or it could serve as a buffer for a possible demand increase the following day.

To give another example, Toyota examines its production rate at 10 day intervals and adjusts the *takt* time as needed. Most of the time Toyota may not need to change the production rate or if it does, may decide to do so by changing the length of the workday (overtime), because changing the line rate on an automobile assembly line is a major undertaking. On the other hand, a small manufacturing cell might change its *takt* time weekly or even daily and adjust the number of operators accordingly.

Takt time is one of the most misunderstood concepts in lean manufacturing. I have been to several enterprises where they prominently announce their *takt* time to be, say, "100 pieces per hour." *Takt* time actually is time per piece, not pieces per time. It is also not uncommon for managers to state that their machines have a *takt* time of five minutes. But *takt* time is a measure of external demand; it has nothing to do with machine capacity.

Sometimes *takt* time has also been confused with lead or flow time. Often this is because enterprises simply go through the motions and effect lean piecemeal without fully understanding what they are doing. The primary purpose of *takt* time is to match external demand with internal capacity.

To sum up the discussion on *takt* time:

- *Takt* time is used to represent customer demand. It is expressed in terms of the time available to make one unit to keep pace with customer demand.
- The primary purpose of calculating *takt* time is to match external demand with internal capacity.
- *Takt* time should be adjusted only when it is clear that customer demand has changed. Adjusting *takt* time too often to respond to small fluctuations could result in chaos. The key is to distinguish between "noise" and a trend.

So far, the discussion on *takt* time has been based on a single product. The *takt* time calculation does not change when there are multiple products but the calculations on operator loading become a little more involved. The calculations are demonstrated by expanding on the Hungama, Inc. example.

Hungama Revisited: Hungama, Inc. processes four different types of property insurance applications: RUNS (requests for underwriting), RAPS (requests for price quotes), RAINS (requests for additional insurance on an existing policy), and RERUNS (annual renewal of policies). The daily demand for each type of application is provided in Table 5.1 below.

Table 5-1. Demand Percentages for Hungama, Inc., Tasks

	RUNS	RAPS	RAINS	RERUNS
Jobs/Day	4	12	6	18
% of Total	10%	30%	15%	45%

Each product type requires some or all of the four steps defined earlier: (1) distribution, (2) underwriting, (3) rating, and (4) policy writing. The workload varies by product type. Table 5.2 presents average labor content for each product type.

Table 5-2. Operation Times for Hungama, Inc.

	RUNS	RAPS	RAINS	RERUNS
Distribution	58 min.	50 min.	44 min.	28 min.
Underwriting	43 min.	40 min.	23 min.	19 min.
Rating	72 min.	65 min.	68 min.	75 min.
Policy writing	67 min.	0 min.	55 min.	50 min.
Total labor	240 min.	155 min.	190 min.	172 min.

The *takt* time for this example is determined by simply adding all the demands to obtain a total daily demand of 40 units. Although each product has different time requirements, this is not a matter of concern at this stage because so far only external customer demand is being looked at, not internal resource requirements. Assuming that the enterprise works 400 minutes per day as before, the *takt* time is 400 ÷ 40 = 10 minutes per unit.

Average Labor Content and Minimum Staffing

The next step is to compute the minimum number of operators required to sustain operations. From the data given in Tables 5.1 and 5.2, the average labor content for a job is the weighted average of the labor content for each product type:

$$\text{Average labor content} = 0.10 \times 240 + 0.30 \times 155 + 0.15 \times 190 + 0.45 \times 172 = 176.4 \text{ minutes.}$$

Since the *takt* time is 10 minutes per unit, a minimum of 18 operators (176.4 ÷ 10 = 17.64) are needed to manage customer demand. Clearly, there will be some sharing of tasks, because there will be 18 operators to do the four activities.

There are still workload balancing issues to be resolved. As a starting point, determine how many operators need to be allocated to distribution. The average labor content for this activity is 0.10 x 58 + 0.30 x 50 + 0.15 x 44 + 0.45 x 28 = 40.0 minutes. Since the *takt* time is 10 minutes, the minimum number of operators allocated this task will be 4 (40.0 ÷ 10).

The average labor content for the other activities is computed similarly and works out to be 28.3 minutes for underwriting, 70.65 minutes for rating, and 37.45 minutes for policy writing. A minimum of 3 operators (28.3 ÷ 10 = 2.83) is required for underwriting, 7 for rating (70.65 ÷ 10 = 7.065), and 4 for policy writing

(37.45 ÷ 10 = 3.745). Workload balancing and related issues may mean that more than 18 operators are needed. A load chart can now be constructed to determine how much each operator is loaded.

This exercise demonstrates the importance of scheduling jobs judiciously and avoiding batching to achieve scale economies. Consider the operators doing policy writing: The RUNS, RAINS, and RERUNS demand at least 50 minutes of effort per job, but the RAPS require no time from these operators. If the jobs are scheduled in batches, there will be long periods during which the operators will be overworked because they are working on a RUN, RAIN, or a RERUN, followed by a period when they will be idle because RAPS are being processed by the other Hungama operators. On the other hand, if a *mixed-model* scheduling approach is used, it is possible to level-load the operators and manage them much more effectively.

Mixed-Model Scheduling and Small Batch Production

One characteristic of an efficient production system is that products flow smoothly through the enterprise with no delays. The production schedule is crucial to effecting this smooth flow because it dictates the frequency with which products are scheduled at the various resources. In a perfect world, when the customer pulls a product from the final assembly station, that should generate a signal on each upstream resource to produce exactly what is pulled by the customer. The reality is that often production constraints like changeovers, material availability, or operator availability restrict how products flow through the enterprise. In particular, changeover time significantly influences the extent of batching. Furthermore, plants that make a variety of different products usually tend to produce those products in large batches to exploit economies of scale.

Large-lot production, of course, sends a ripple effect through the enterprise. In the beer game discussed in Chapter 2, a single change in demand at the retailer was enough to cause huge variations in demand four stages upstream at the brewery. Likewise, within the enterprise, a small change in demand at the most downstream operation can cause significant variations in demand at upstream resources; batching only exacerbates this problem.

Typically, these demand variations are absorbed by carrying large amounts of WIP between each stage. In-process buffers are one way to "level" production and work with large batches, but needless to say, larger WIP inventories increase lead time.

There is a better way to level the production schedule. It is simply to produce every product as quickly as possible, at the same rate at which customer demands are made. This in essence is *mixed-model scheduling*, what the Japanese term *heijunka*, which refers to distributing the production of different product types evenly over the course of an hour, day, week, or month.

Suppose an enterprise makes three products, A, B, and C, each of which requires 10 minutes of assembly time. Assume the final assembly shop works 10 hours a day, five days a week. Suppose the customer is demanding these products are a rate of three of A, two of B, and one of C every hour. Though the customer for these products could be demanding them every hour, the enterprise may choose to produce them in large batches for reasons already discussed.

Suppose the final assembly shop decides to produce one week's demand of each product each time. The weekly schedule would then be 150 A, 100 B, and 50 C every week. Instead of receiving products every hour, the customer will receive them once a week. In other words, either the customer or the final assembly shop will carry an average finished goods inventory of 75 As (half the batch, on average), 50 Bs, and 25 Cs. If the final assembly shop had instead produced according to a mixed-model assembly schedule of 3 A, 2 B, 1 C, the finished goods inventory would be negligible because production would exactly match hourly demand. The six units produced in an hour could be even more finely sequenced as follows: A B A C A B.

The example presented above assumes that the assembly time is the same for each product. Mixed-model scheduling does an even better job of smoothing flow when different products have different processing times, as with the Hungama example. No doubt true mixed-model scheduling requires that setup/changeover times be minimal. As changeover times become more significant, it can be argued, batch sizes should correspondingly increase. While there is some truth in this, short-cycle scheduling can still be achieved by producing in small batches in the presence of setup times. (For more discussion of this, see Chapter 9.)

To sum up the discussion so far, producing products in large batches:

- Creates an uneven workload,
- Creates uneven demand for upstream processes, making pull impossible, and
- Causes production to be out of synch with customer demand.

On the other hand, mixed-model production:

- Creates a smooth work-load,
- Creates a smooth demand for upstream processes, and
- Allows production to match customer demand.

While mixed-model scheduling helps level the workload at each work center, its true benefit is realized when it is used in conjunction with another lean concept: one-piece flow.

One-Piece Flow

In the extreme case of mixed-model scheduling, each successive item processed could be a different product type. In other words, products are processed in lots of one. One-piece flow refers to the concept of moving products one unit at a time between workstations, rather than the other extreme of processing an entire batch of parts at a workstation before moving the batch to the next downstream workstation. Mixed-model scheduling in combination with one-piece flow keeps WIP inventories at the lowest possible levels.

The goal of one-piece flow is to reduce the lead time or equivalently reduce WIP inventory. Recall Little's Law, presented in Chapter 2, which states that the average lead time is equal to WIP divided by throughput. If there is a week's worth of WIP sitting at an output queue waiting to be transferred to the next station, one week has been added to the average lead time at that stage.

To elaborate on how one-piece flow affects lead time, consider the example shown in Figure 5.8, which consists of a process with four stages of operation. Suppose the production rate at each stage is 100 per week, and that parts are transferred 60 units at a time, as in part (a) of Figure 5.8. Since the total WIP inventory in the system is 240 units, Little's Law tell us that the average lead time is 2.4 weeks (WIP ÷ throughput = 240 ÷ 100).

Figure 5-8. One-Piece Flow and its Impact on Lead Time

Lead Time = 2.4 weeks

Case a) Transfer batch size = 60 units

Lead Time = 0.04 weeks

Case b) Transfer batch size = 1 unit

On the other hand if the items are transferred one piece at a time, as shown in part (b) of Figure 5.8, the total WIP inventory in the system at any time is four units, and so the average lead time is 0.04 weeks (4 ÷ 100).

One-piece flow also helps improve product quality because it shortens the duration of the feedback loop. When parts are transferred one at a time, the downstream workstation is able to determine if the upstream workstation is producing defective items almost immediately. If a week's worth of WIP is transferred at a time, the entire week's output could be defective without anyone noticing. The feedback delay is thus at least one week.

It must be clarified that one-piece flow does not necessarily mean that just one piece or one part is transferred between two processes each time. The unit of transfer could well be a pallet of parts, although clearly the smaller the number of units transferred, the lower the resulting WIP. One-piece flow is an ideal that the manager should aim for because it minimizes the hand-off time. Products do not have to sit in the output queue of the upstream workstation, waiting for a batch of products to accumulate before being transferred to a downstream workstation.

While one-piece flow is an ideal the manager should aim for, it might be counterproductive when the cell processes a large variety of products with different processing times and routings. There are a number of other situations where one-piece flow is simply not practical. For instance, if the upstream process is a heat-treatment operation that necessarily has to produce a batch at a time, it may not be meaningful to move these parts one at a time because they would come out of the furnace all at once anyway. Similarly, if the downstream operation requires a set up each time it begins work on a new product, one-piece flow may not be the right approach to moving parts to this operation.

Finally, if material transfers are done by the operators themselves rather than through an automated conveyance system, it does not make sense for the operator to be moving parts one piece at a time if the transfer time is close to the processing time per part. In other words, if material handling costs are high, it may be more economical to transfer parts in small batches rather than one piece at a time.

To implement one-piece flow, it is desirable that there be little variability in process times and that the process quality at each of the steps be linked in the one-piece flow. If one step is delayed, it stops the flow of the entire process. The processing steps must also be located next to each other to facilitate moving only one piece at a time.

Cellular Layout

One-piece flow is significantly enhanced when the various processes are organized in a *cellular* layout (also called a *product* layout). A cell consists of the operators and the workstations required for performing the steps in a process segment, with the workstations arranged in the processing sequence. The cellular layout contrasts with a *process* layout, where the workstations are grouped by departments or functions.

When workstations are close together, products moving from one workstation to the next do not have to traverse long distances, which facilitates one-piece flow. Keeping workstations close to one another also allows the operator at the downstream workstation to see what is being produced by the workstation upstream. That helps eliminate the paperwork that might otherwise be necessary to coordinate workstations that are separated from one another by a significant distance.

A common layout used for manufacturing cells is a U-shaped configuration. This layout has a number of advantages. First, it allows for more flexibility in allocating tasks among operators. Consider, for example, the assembly cell shown in Figure 5.9, which has eight assembly tasks each taking 15 seconds. Because the *takt* time is currently 15 seconds, each assembly task requires one operator.

Figure 5-9. A U-Shaped Cell

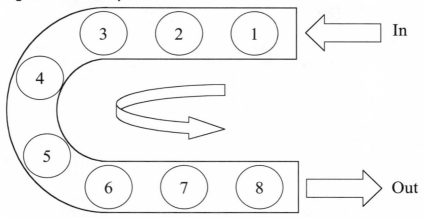

Now, suppose *takt* time increases to 30 seconds. Since each assembly task still requires only 15 seconds, it is possible to operate the cell with four operators, allocating two assembly tasks to each. A U-shaped cell allows more flexibility in allocating tasks. For instance, it is possible to allocate tasks 1 and 8 to one operator, who is now responsible for monitoring parts coming in and going out of the cell. That task allocation would not have been possible with a straight-line layout. The U-shaped layout also makes for easy replenishment of materials from outside the cell and promotes teamwork because the operators are located closer to one another.

Since the U-shaped cell allows for much more flexibility in allocating multiple tasks to operators, there is better employee utilization. This cell shape facilitates reallocation of tasks among operators when an operator is added or removed in response to a change in *takt* time. Other common cell configurations include the T-shaped cell, the L-shaped cell, or a serpentine arrangement (a series of adjoining U-shaped cells).

In summary, some of the benefits associated with one-piece flow and cellular manufacturing are:

- WIP reduction
- Better space utilization
- Reduction in lead time
- Productivity improvement: more flexibility in allocating tasks to operators and rebalancing production to accommodate absenteeism
- Quality improvement: immediate feedback on defects

- Enhanced teamwork and communication, with more support for coworkers who fall behind
- Better visibility of all tasks and operations.

The next step is to identify the best method for performing a particular task and then create a work procedure that anyone doing this task should follow. This is the concept behind *standard* work.

Standard Work

Standard work relates to clear specification of how tasks should be performed. The tasks are first organized in the most effective sequence using the most effective combination of resources. This task sequence and combination of resources is then fully documented and every operator is required to adhere to the sequence and use the same resources. The intent is not to take away from the operator creativity in performing tasks; it is to make every operator follow recognized best practices.

There are a number of reasons why standard work is important. First and foremost, standard work promotes consistency and continuous improvement. If each operator performs tasks in a different way, it is very difficult to improve a process. A documented standard makes it easier to effect continuous improvement and increases the likelihood that the results will be consistent.

Second, standardized work improves safety. Unsafe practices are mitigated when all operators are asked to follow the same routine for specific tasks. Moreover, with standards established, it now becomes easier to measure performance equitably; it is possible to establish a fair output rate and judge everyone by the same standards. Standard work is particularly useful when training new employees.

Standard work recognizes that the best practice may be a moving target. Sometimes the operators performing the tasks may come up with a better way of doing things and the standard work practices would change. Standard work represents a set of tasks allocated to an operator, so standard work will also change when the *takt* time or the model mix changes.

The goals in setting standard work are to give each operator an amount of work less than or equal to the *takt* time while creating a compact footprint for each operator. The operators should be involved in defining standard work. That way, they will be more likely to do their jobs correctly and will help with continuous improvement efforts in the future. Many enterprises have created standard work charts for different *takt* times, requiring various number of operators. These enterprises are able to respond very quickly to *takt* time changes with minimal disruption because the standard work plan is already prepared.

Pull Replenishment

Pull replenishment is a very convenient way to control the flow of products through production. The goal of pull replenishment is to contain inventory. Pull replenishment is achieved in most implementations using *kanbans* (Japanese for *sign* or *signal*), although there are other methods for effecting pull discussed in Chapter 8.

Pull replenishment using *kanbans* is quite simple in concept. The basic idea is to transfer production responsibility to the operators themselves rather than have a production controller decide in advance what each operator should be producing at a given time. Control of operations is decentralized by having each downstream operator signal upstream operators when parts are needed; *kanbans* provide this signaling mechanism. To use *kanbans,* the following conditions must typically be met:

- Demand for the item must be relatively repetitive.
- Lead times must be relatively short.
- Components must be available so an item can be produced on demand when the visual signal is generated.

The first step in designing a *kanban* system is to determine how much inventory will be used to buffer the downstream operator from the upstream operator. Two types of *kanbans* that are often used are: (1) *in-process kanbans* and (2) *material kanbans.* In-process *kanbans* are typically used when the upstream and downstream operations are close enough to each other that the upstream operator can be triggered simply by a visual signal from downstream. They are implemented simply by allocating a physical location between the two operations and specifying the maximum amount of WIP inventory that the upstream operator can place in this location. If the in-process *kanban* is full, the upstream operator must stop production until inventory is drawn from it.

It is common practice to paint a square or a rectangle on the shop floor between the two operations where the part or container of parts should be placed. If there are multiple part types, each might have a different color code. Each location or container has a number allocated to it, indicating the WIP inventory limit.

Material *kanbans* are used in a variety of ways. A production facility may use them to signal a need for replenishment of material from a supermarket or warehouse (a *withdrawal kanban*), another production facility (a *production kanban*), or a supplier (a *supplier kanban*). A production *kan-ban* is used in place of an in-process *kanban* if the upstream and downstream processes are far apart and the upstream operator has no visibility on the needs of the downstream operator.

The replenishment signals are usually transmitted either through a card or an electronic signal. Each card requests that a specific number of items be replenished. At any point in time, the number of *kanban* cards (or, equivalently containers of parts) in circulation is determined using the following formula:

$$\text{Number of } kanban \text{ cards} = \frac{\bar{D} \cdot KCT \cdot (1 + SF)}{Kanban\ size} + 1,$$

where $\bar{D}$ is the average demand per time period, KCT denotes the replenishment lead time (*kanban* cycle time), and SF is a safety factor to buffer the combined variations in demand, replenishment lead time, and quality of the upstream supplier.

The formula assumes that the signal to replenish a container of parts is triggered when the container becomes empty. This formula has two unknown values: (1) the number of *kanban* cards in circulation and (2) the *kanban* size (the term commonly used to denote the number of items in a container). Typically, *kanban* size is determined in consultation with the supplier, or the upstream facility or the supermarket, as the case may be, based on a variety of factors, such as standard container sizes or ergonomic issues. The formula is used to determine the number of cards in circulation.

Some enterprises use a two-bin system of replenishment: they start with two *kanban* cards and use the formula to determine *kanban* size. If the number is unsatisfactory, the number of cards is increased by one and the computation is repeated until a satisfactory *kanban* size is determined. There needs to be a minimum of two cards because there should always be one container at the workstation for the operator to pull parts from.

Withdrawal *kanban* signals are typically generated from a production facility that keeps materials at point of use.

Point-Of-Use Materials Storage

Point-of-use materials storage places the materials in the production process rather than in a central warehouse. The upstream process or external supplier delivers the material direct to the point of use, typically based on *kanban* pull signals. The materials are often stored on flow-through racks just outside the cell. Flow-through racks are storage locations with shelves that can be replenished from the back and consumed from the front, like the beverage coolers in convenience stores. Flow-through racks preserve first-in-first-out material usage and allow material to be replenished from outside the cell.

For material that cannot be stored at point of use, supermarkets (nearby storage locations) are often used in place of centralized storage. A supplier might deliver a large batch of parts used by several cells once a day. Those parts may be stored in the supermarket near the cells and pulled out in hourly quantities. A cell that produces in small batches may have only the materials needed to make one product at the point of use at any given time while the materials for other products are stored at the supermarket.

Total Productive Maintenance

Total productive maintenance (TPM) is a term used to denote the systematic execution of maintenance by all employees. The goal of a TPM program is to significantly increase productive capacity and decrease process variation while at the same time increasing employee morale and job satisfaction. TPM is primarily an equipment management strategy; it was originally developed by Toyota in 1970 to support their Toyota Production System and it evolved from the total quality management (TQM) movement pioneered by Deming and Juran.

When maintenance problems were examined as part of the TQM program, the general concepts did not seem to fit or work well in the maintenance environment, so the original TQM concepts were modified. The modifications elevated maintenance to the status of a separate though integral part of the overall quality program: TPM.

TPM resembles TQM in a number of ways, and the similarities are not coincidental. Traditionally, maintenance can be classified as corrective, preventive, predictive, or proactive:

- *Corrective* maintenance waits until a failure occurs and then remedies it as quickly as possible; an example is a sensor failing in an automobile.
- *Preventive* maintenance aims at maintaining equipment at regular intervals to keep an otherwise troublesome failure mode at bay; an example is changing the oil for an automobile.
- *Predictive* maintenance examines vital signs displayed by equipment, using instruments like vibration analyzers, to determine the health of the equipment; for a car, predictive maintenance would analyze engine wear.
- Finally, *proactive* maintenance analyzes why defects occur in, say, a machining operation, and then designs the problem out of the machine.

TPM is a manufacturing-led initiative that emphasizes the importance of people, a continuous improvement philosophy, and joint effort by production and maintenance staff. The focus is on maintaining the equipment *and* the processes that support manufacturing. It is a vital part of any lean implementation. Because there is a natural tendency for people to follow the "if it ain't broke don't fix it" philosophy, TPM requires that top management commit to sustaining the initiative.

Mistake Proofing and Method Sheets

Mistake proofing and method sheets are tools used to prevent quality problems. Mistake proofing (*poka yoke* in Japanese) is directed at finding techniques to prevent defects from being passed on to the next process. Mistake proofing requires that quality checks be built into both operations and equipment, using sensors to detect errors and stop the process as needed. Combined with other lean tools, mistake proofing works to ensure that 100 percent quality is built into both process and product. An example of mistake proofing is the three-prong electrical plug: There is only one way you can plug it into a socket.

Method sheets are visual instructions located at a workstation that show how a job must be done, the quality checks necessary, and the tools to be used. The instructions show pictures of each step as it is to be performed. The goal is to make instructions so clear and unambiguous that a new operator can understand them immediately.

Continuous Improvement and the Pursuit of Perfection

Complacency can be the toughest challenge in any lean transformation process. Lean is not a one-time effort; nor is it a quality program of the month. It is an ongoing journey that requires a sustained effort at continuous improvement. Transformation to lean is not accomplished by simply applying a few techniques; it is a whole new way of looking at the operations of the enterprise.

Because lean tools and techniques are often quite different from traditional tools, there must be a sustained effort to operate with these tools. Enterprises that do not aim to continue their upward momentum will fall behind their competitors. It is essential to continuously reexamine processes and look for ways to take out waste and non-value-added activities if enterprises are to see significant improvement in financial performance.

To sustain lean implementations, it is therefore necessary that enterprises constantly initiate *kaizen* events that promote continuous improvements. At the same time, there is a need to promote *kaikaku*, [13] the radical redesign of processes and methods geared for achieving breakthroughs in performance and growth. Once a *kaikaku* step is applied, *kaizen* becomes a powerful followup drive to perfect the processes and methods and to continue to adapt to stay relevant. The sequential application of a *kaikaku* step followed by a series of *kaizen* events results in performance improvements that effectively match the S-curve model presented in Chapter 4.

As Womack and Jones suggest, "Dreaming about perfection is fun."[14] Lean thinking offers ways to make such dreams a reality. Applying lean thinking and implementing tools to create flow result in a fundamental change in the way the enterprise thinks about its operations. Employees soon realize there is no end to the pursuit of perfection—to reducing effort, time, space, cost, and mistakes in the process of producing and delivering a product. When products flow faster through the enterprise, they expose hidden waste in the value stream. The harder the pull, the more obstacles are revealed and the more easily they can be removed.

While lean implementations must have commitment and support from top management, shop floor personnel are also critical to their success. Many enterprises have initiated their lean efforts

---

13. This step is often referred to as *kaizen blitz*.
14. Op. cit., note 10.

from the bottom up. Continuous improvement (*kaizen*) events play a vital role in getting employees engaged in the lean journey, and that pays dividends. Managers at all levels became lean thinkers and change agents.

A truly lean enterprise makes it much easier for everyone—shop floor employees, supervisors, lean champions, subcontractors, and first-tier suppliers—to discover better ways to create value. Because feedback loops are significantly shortened, there is faster feedback to employees, providing a more conducive environment for them to pursue perfection.

CONCLUSIONS

Thomas J. Watson, Jr., once said, "Whenever an individual or a business decides that success has been attained, progress stops." Lean is a journey—a continuous journey that requires sustained effort to maintain momentum.

At the same time, once initial resistance is overcome, it becomes much easier to maintain the tools and techniques of lean. Once there is a sharpened awareness among employees of the waste present in the system, there will be a concerted effort to maintain the momentum to reduce it if the right incentives are provided.

All types of enterprises can benefit from lean thinking, regardless of whether they are engaged in manufacturing, process, distribution, software development, or financial services. Important points that enterprises should keep in mind when embarking on a lean journey are these:

- While the goal of lean has often been identified as the removal of *muda* (waste), removing *muda* is just a means to an end.
- The real goal of lean is to reduce lead time: Lean is all about lead-time reduction and creating flow.
- Some of the more important steps that enterprises can take to create flow are *takt* time, standard work, pull replenishment, and 5S. All of them readily apply in a service setting as well.
- Steps like 5S and *takt* time are often misunderstood or misused. For instance, the fifth step in the 5S program, *Sustain,* is vital for maintaining momentum. Once a 5S program is put in place, some enterprises neglect this step. Again, lean is a *journey*—one that really never ends.
- Enterprises that embark on the lean journey typically start by identifying a product family they can apply lean principles to.

- Lean thinking must be applied to all the processes in the enterprise that work on the selected product family. The idea is not to simply lean out some of the process steps and create a few islands of excellence. While some waste may be removed in creating such islands, the products flowing out of them will end up waiting elsewhere in the enterprise, usually queuing up in front of the constraint resources. (This points up the need to apply lean thinking in conjunction with TOC, which is discussed in Chapter 6.)
- Finally, the lean *supply chain* is the ultimate goal. It is the responsibility of the lean enterprise to collaborate with upstream and downstream supply chain members to successfully streamline the supply chain.

6

Systems Thinking and the Theory of Constraints

"Complex solutions do not work, the more complex the problem the simpler the solution must be."
Eli Goldratt

Unlike lean thinking, which evolved from the collective effort of a number of individuals, the Theory of Constraints (TOC) owes its origin to one individual, Eli Goldratt, an Israeli physicist. TOC traces its origins to the 1970s, when Goldratt responded to a friend's request for help scheduling his chicken coop business.[1] Adopting a commonsense, intuitive approach, Goldratt developed a scheduling algorithm that realistically considered the bottlenecks in the system. He followed this with a computer software package in 1979, using mathematical programming and simulation to schedule more complex manufacturing systems. The software was marketed in the early 1980s under the name Optimized Production Technology (OPT).

The idea behind OPT was that in any process, there is one or, at most, a few bottlenecks. The output of a process is constrained by the bottleneck. If you can focus on maximizing the productive use of the bottleneck and schedule it accordingly, then you will maximize your productive output. The other non-bottleneck resources can be scheduled subsequently since they have available capacity by definition, and therefore, we have some latitude with regard to scheduling them. While the scheduling principle was simple, customers did not know precisely how it worked. So, although a large number of copies of OPT were sold initially, the software was not a resounding success, probably because potential users were uncomfortable working with a product they did not understand well.

---

1. R. S. Russell and B. W. Taylor (2003), *Operations Management*, 4th Edition, Prentice Hall., Englewood Cliffs, NJ.

To advertise his ideas more effectively, Goldratt worked with Jeff Cox to publish *The Goal*[2] in 1984. This was a book that conveyed the general logic embedded in OPT software through a fictional account of a plant manager, Alex Rogo, who uses these ideas to save his plant from closure. The immense success of *The Goal* led Goldratt to expand his ideas and develop a more generic suite of tools and techniques that is now known as the Theory of Constraints.

TOC is a philosophy based on systems thinking and what its developer, Goldratt, calls *uncommon sense.* From a systems perspective, the operation of an enterprise (or a supply chain for that matter) can be viewed as a set of interdependent processes that transforms inputs into saleable outputs. To describe TOC, an analogy is often drawn between such a set of processes and a chain. Just like the links of a chain work together to pull or lift objects, the processes within the enterprise work together to generate profit for the shareholders. However, the ability of the chain to pull or lift objects is limited because the chain is only as strong as its weakest link. TOC maintains that:

- The goal of an enterprise is to make more money, now and in the future.
- Every system of interdependent processes is subject to at least one constraint that limits system performance. That is, the money-making potential of the enterprise is limited by the enterprise's weakest link or constraint.

Carrying the chain analogy a little further, to improve the strength of a chain, you would first identify the weakest link and focus on strengthening it. Strengthening other links will have no impact on the strength of the entire chain. Similarly, for an enterprise, you would focus on strengthening the constraint that prevents the enterprise from making more money. Any loss of output at the constraint resource(s) results in a loss of revenue for the enterprise. At the same time, any local optimization efforts aimed at improving the performance of resources other than the constraint resource is unlikely to increase the throughput of the enterprise. These key points are summarized by the next lean supply chain principle.

---

2. E. M. Goldratt and J. Cox (1992), *The Goal*, North River Press, Great Barrington, MA.

LEAN SUPPLY CHAIN PRINCIPLE 10

Time lost at a bottleneck resource results in a loss of productivity for the whole enterprise (entire supply chain). Time saved at a non-bottleneck resource is a mirage.

There is little disagreement on the core issue that constraints are important and need extra managerial attention and focus. With the simple chain analogy presented above, it is fairly obvious as to how the performance of the system can be optimized. In practice, it is harder for managers to see the forest for the trees because of the traditional management metrics they have to work with. In the following discussion, we will use the words bottleneck and constraint interchangeably.[3]

LOCAL OPTIMIZATION VERSUS GLOBAL OPTIMIZATION

The traditional management approach addresses the complex problem of optimizing system performance by breaking down the system into smaller, more manageable pieces. This approach became entrenched in the minds of decision makers in the heyday of the U.S. industry when it was convenient to run large businesses as a collection of autonomous operating divisions coordinated by a strong general office. The core objective for such an organizational and controlled structure was to design a system in which the people responsible for managing the smaller units could focus solely on their domain of authority. Units were treated as either cost centers or profit centers and assigned targets. Managers of these units would manage their domains to achieve and even beat these targets. The result was an organizational structure in which each unit was charged with and focused on improving its local performance. The logic was that if every unit improved then, *ipso facto*, the entire enterprise would improve. This system of operation was phenomenally successful in the sense that most post-World War II enterprises that were organized around this model grew their business significantly. Policies, procedures, performance metrics and all other elements that define organizational structure and function were based on this implied belief in local optima.

---

3. The TOC adherent would, however, differentiate between a bottleneck and a constraint. The former would be a resource or process whose capacity is less than the demand placed on it. A constraint is a resource or process that limits the performance of the system: It is the bottleneck with the lowest capacity.

Local optimization is geared towards improving isolated parts of the enterprise, and that usually does not help enterprise goals. To improve overall system performance, it is not enough to promote isolated efforts that focus on improving specific functions. Such an approach ignores the interactions between the various functions. Management must recognize and manage interdependence. As Deming[4] indicates,

> *"If economists understood the theory of a system, and the role of cooperation in optimization, they would no longer teach and preach salvation through adversarial competition. They would instead lead us into optimization of a system, in which everybody would come out ahead."*

Deming provides several examples of how lack of systems thinking and poor cooperation can be destructive to an enterprise. In one example, an increase in the cost of an engine of $30 would have decreased the cost of the transmission by $80. However, the center in charge of producing the engine was reluctant to accept the idea because it adversely affected that center's profits.

The lack of a systems perspective invariably leads to metrics, policies, and procedures that promote local optimization rather than global optimization. Local measures can, and often do, conflict with corporate goals, as the example provided by Deming illustrates. Most managers know intuitively that if they really want to grow the business, they must occasionally ignore traditional measures. Unfortunately, consistent reinforcement to work with local measures can, over time, obfuscate intuition. The goal of the manager should be to install measures that are truly global, i.e., measures that encourage actions consistent with the overall goals of the enterprise.

TOC presents a methodology that shows what must be done to promote the enterprise goal of making more money and presents a set of simple, global measures to achieve this goal. These measures are based on a *throughput world* perspective, an approach that focuses on meeting the goal through a growth strategy rather than just through cutting costs. To address the throughput world perspective, TOC provides two groups of techniques: a *Five-Step Focusing Process*, and a more generic problem solving approach

---

4. Ibid.

referred to as the *Thinking Process.*[5] We will present the throughput world perspective and the TOC measures shortly. However, we will first discuss the way decisions are made in traditional enterprises to underscore the simplicity and power of the TOC measures and the throughput world when we discuss them subsequently.

TRADITIONAL DECISION MAKING AND THE COST WORLD PERSPECTIVE

The traditional approach to managing an enterprise is, arguably, based on a *cost world* perspective, a perspective that focuses on minimizing costs and improving operational efficiencies. Cost control is a key factor that drives decision making in the cost world. The origins of the cost world can be traced to the start of the 20th century. As the U.S. industry grew in the 20th century, it generated demands on resources. When U.S. enterprises began to borrow money to pay for these resources, bankers and other lenders needed to know how these resources would perform and thus help the enterprise pay back the loans. For an enterprise that produced various products, determining product costs was important in deciding whether the product was profitable or not.

Products costs have three components: direct labor, direct material, and overhead costs. The first two were relatively easy to attribute directly to a specific product. Overhead costs, on the other hand, were difficult to trace to specific products. Hence, cost accounting systems were developed to track costs, with the primary goal of allocating overhead costs more precisely to specific products. The rise of the U.S. auto industry coincided with the rise of cost accounting as the primary decision-making tool in all industries. Cost accounting, more specifically, the issue of allocating overhead costs to determine product cost, was not a major problem during the days of Henry Ford because overhead costs were relatively low and typically only a few products were produced

---

5. The Thinking Process is a generic problem solving approach that is particularly valuable when dealing with policy constraints that are harder to pinpoint than physical constraints. It begins with the premise that to improve any system, three questions need to be answered: What should be changed? What should it be changed to? How can I cause this change to happen? To answer these questions, the Thinking Process uses a set of tools that identify the core problems constraining the system from reaching its full potential. For a detailed discussion on the Thinking Process, the reader is referred to the book by L. J. Scheinkopf, *Thinking For a Change: Putting the TOC Thinking Processes to Use*, St. Lucie Press, 1999.

by the enterprise. As enterprises began to diversify their product offerings, the question of how to allocate overhead costs accurately became increasingly important and *standard cost accounting* systems gained prominence.

STANDARD COST ACCOUNTING SYSTEMS

How does the Sales department decide whether to accept a new customer order? How does the Operations department decide what products to schedule and what batch size to run? How does the controller decide whether or not to approve purchase of new equipment? Such decisions are typically made using a standard set of guidelines and operating procedures referred to as the standard cost accounting system. This system was the driving force behind management control and decision-making processes in manufacturing enterprises during the 20th century. Managers of large, complex enterprises relied on this system to provide correct information to help them make critical operational decisions.

When it was first introduced, standard cost accounting was a powerful tool since it provided managers with the ability to make decisions that dramatically improved the performance of their areas and plants. However, as Lepore and Cohen point out, ". . . powerful solutions tend to make themselves obsolete . . . some of the basic assumptions of standard cost accounting became invalid in the 1940s, but as most companies were using the same concepts, the negative impact was not so noticeable."[6] There is now a growing awareness, even within the accounting profession, that the standard cost system has a number of fundamental flaws that often hinder, rather than help, decision making. Lepore and Cohen state that the Japanese did not, and still do not, use standard cost accounting methods to provide all the answers needed to make decisions.

In a foreword to a book that discusses TOC and its implications for Management Accounting,[7] Goldratt states that the accounting profession is fully aware of the problems with cost accounting systems currently in use. He suggests that one of the reasons why the accounting profession persists with such systems is because the conceptual difference between the cost world and the throughput

---

6. See page 29 in D. Lepore and O. Cohen (1999), *Deming and Goldratt: The Theory of Constraints and the System of Profound Knowledge*, North River Press, Great Barrington, MA.

7. E. Noreen, D. Smith and J. T. Mackey (1995), *The Theory of Constraints and its Implications for Management Accounting*, North River Press, Great Barrington, MA.

world is not well understood: The cost world directs the manager to think locally, but the throughput world forces the manager to think globally. We illustrate how cost accounting systems tend to promote local thinking that often runs counter to enterprise objectives using an example enterprise, National Pontoons, Inc., that makes steering wheels for pontoon boats.

CASE: NATIONAL PONTOONS, INC.

For simplicity we will initially assume that National Pontoons makes one product: black vinyl steering wheels. To make a finished product, National Pontoons procures raw material blanks from a local supplier at a cost of $10 per unit and uses two resources, Resource A and Resource B, to machine and fabricate the product, with each resource being run by a dedicated operator.

The product requires 6 minutes of processing time at resource A, and 9 minutes of processing time at resource B. National Pontoons runs two shifts, each 10 hours long, 25 days each month and employs four direct laborers across the two shifts to operate the resources. Each operator thus works for 25 x 10 = 250 hours a month. The direct laborers are paid $2,500 per month, so the direct labor rate is calculated as $10 per hour. The total wages paid to direct labor (four employees) is $10,000 per month or $120,000 per year. For the year 2003, the manufacturing overhead costs were $225,000, and Selling, General and Administrative (SG&A) expenses were $200,000. Table 6.1 abstracts the relevant data needed for computing product costs.

Table 6-1. Data for National Pontoons for Fiscal Year 2003

Raw Material Cost	$10 per unit
Processing time at Resource A	0.10 hours per unit
Processing time at Resource B	0.15 hours per unit
Labor Rate	$10 per hour
Direct Labor Wages Paid	$120,000
Manufacturing Overhead Costs	$225,000
SG&A Expenses	$200,000

The accounting system determines the standard cost for the product as the sum of the standard direct labor cost (the absorbed labor cost), plus the unit raw material cost, plus a unit overhead cost that accounts for the manufacturing overhead. Direct labor is often a relatively fixed cost that does not rise or fall as output varies because wages are typically paid, not based on units produced, but by the hour or even by the month as in this example. However, direct labor is typically tracked as a variable cost, and any difference between the standard labor cost and the actual labor cost incurred is reflected through labor efficiency and labor rate variances. The raw material cost is, arguably, the only variable cost, one that rises or falls in accordance with the output. Manufacturing overhead costs are generally separated into fixed and variable costs, but for simplicity, we assume that all manufacturing overhead costs are fixed costs in this example.

The direct labor cost at resource A is the hourly rate ($10) multiplied by the number of standard hours required to process one unit at the resource (0.10 hours), that is $10 x 0.10 = $1.00 per unit. Similarly, since 0.15 standard hours are required to process one unit at resource B, the direct labor cost at resource B is $10 x 0.15 = $1.50 per unit. The total direct labor cost (the *standard direct labor cost*) is thus $2.50 per unit.

Typically, sales of black vinyl steering wheels at National Pontoons had averaged about 40,000 in the past. Suppose, however, that in 2003, National Pontoons only produced and sold 30,000 units. At this level of production, the total (standard) direct labor cost is $2.50 x 30,000 = $75,000. The actual direct labor wages paid in 2003 was $120,000. The difference between the actual labor cost and the standard labor cost, $120,000 minus $75,000 = $45,000, is referred to as the *labor efficiency variance*. This is, no doubt, a relatively large number and we will discuss how National Pontoons can deal with this problem in a subsequent section in this chapter.

Continuing with the example, the overhead is allocated (absorbed) by arriving at an *overhead rate*. This rate is typically expressed in terms of direct labor hours or direct labor cost. In this example, we will express the overhead rate in terms of direct labor cost. The total standard direct labor cost is $75,000, and the total manufacturing overhead cost is $225,000. So, the overhead rate is $225,000/$75,000 = $3.00 per direct labor dollar. Since the total direct labor cost is $2.50, the overhead cost per unit is $3.00 x 2.50 = $7.50 per unit. The finished product cost is, therefore, $10 (direct material) + $2.50 (direct labor) + $7.50 (overhead) = $20 per unit. The same principles apply with multiple products, although the calculations are a little more involved as will be observed shortly. SG&A expenses have not figured so far in the product cost calculations. This is consistent with Generally

Accepted Accounting Principles (GAAP) calculations of inventory costs. To arrive at a selling price, enterprises often mark up product costs by an appropriate margin to cover the SG&A expenses.

Aside from arriving at product costs in this manner, the management control system would like to allocate the overhead to the different resources. One reason for allocating the overhead costs in this manner is to determine the cost of units in work-in-process (WIP) inventory at different stages in the process. In our example, after the raw material is processed by resource A, each unit of WIP is deemed to have more value. The added value is determined as the sum of the labor cost plus an allocation of the manufacturing overhead.

In the standard cost accounting system, the manufacturing overhead is typically allocated to the units processed by resources in proportion to the cost of direct labor for that operation. For the National Pontoons example, the overhead rate is $3.00 per direct labor dollar. Since the direct labor cost at resource A is $1.00 per unit, the allocation of the manufacturing overhead at this resource is simply $(3 x 1) = $3.00 per unit. Similarly, since the direct labor cost at resource B is $1.50 per unit, the allocation of the manufacturing overhead at resource B is $(3 x 1.50) = $4.50 per unit. This is consistent with our previous calculation which obtained the total overhead cost per unit as $7.50. Table 6.2 summarizes this information.

Table 6-2. Valuing Inventory Costs

COST CATEGORY	COST PER UNIT
Raw Material	$10.00
Direct Labor Cost at Resource A	$ 1.00
Manufacturing Overhead allocation at Resource A	$ 3.00
Direct Labor Cost at Resource B	$ 1.50
Manufacturing Overhead allocation at Resource B	$ 4.50
Total Cost	$20.00

The manufacturing process is shown in Figure 6.1, which also depicts the cost of a unit of inventory at the different stages in the process. The raw material inventory in front of resource A is valued at the raw material purchase price of $10 per unit. Since the sum of the direct labor cost plus the manufacturing overhead at resource A is $4, the WIP inventory present between resource A and resource B is valued at $10 + $4 = $14 per unit. The sum of the direct labor cost plus the manufacturing overhead at resource B is six dollars ($6). Hence, the finished goods inventory is valued at $14 + $6 = $20 per unit.

Figure 6-1. Inventory and its Valuation

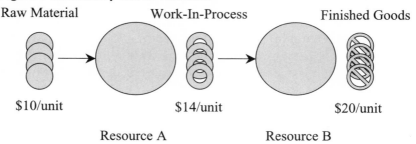

Raw Material   Work-In-Process   Finished Goods

$10/unit $14/unit $20/unit

Resource A   Resource B

The accounting method outlined above wants to capture the effort expended on the product in dollar terms, albeit in an approximate manner, since the allocation methodology is crude. We say that the allocation methodology is crude because it assumes that every manufacturing-related expense, including depreciation of equipment and facilities, indirect labor, and utilities is allocated to the product in proportion to the time it takes for processing at the individual resources. The allocation methodology becomes even cruder when (for internal management purposes) SG&A expenses are allocated across products in proportion to product costs, as it is typically done prior to determining the markup for the sales price.

Whether the allocation methodology is crude or not, *absorption costing* and variance reports are metrics typically used to measure performance on the shop floor. Such measurements often lead to behavior that runs counter to enterprise goals. For instance, since every item processed on a resource increases the value of the product, it provides an incentive for the shop supervisor to push products through the resources in his/her shop as quickly as possible. These products may not be needed downstream but that is not the supervisor's concern because he/she is measured based on overhead absorption and meeting targets. In the rush to meet these metrics, the output from the shop floor typically follows the well-known end-of-the-month syndrome, as shown in Figure 6.2. This behavioral pattern is sometimes referred to as the hockey-stick effect. Furthermore, because shop supervisors are evaluated based on how efficiently they utilize their resources, they are given incentives to create production schedules that operate the individual work centers work at close to 100 percent. The result is even higher levels of inventory when the output from the work centers is not consistent with the requirements downstream.

Figure 6-2. Inventory Valuation and the End-of-the-Month Syndrome

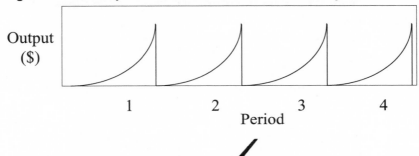

The local optimization mindset, combined with the cost world idea of adding value to the raw material cost as it progresses to become finished goods inventory, can lead to other bizarre outcomes. The following is an account derived from a real-world situation and described in the books, *The Haystack Syndrome*[8] and *Synchronous Management, Volume 1*.[9] (The name of the enterprise involved in this incident has been changed.)

CASE: VOLUNTEER MOTORS

Volunteer Motors was a well-known manufacturing enterprise that generated profits year after year until it reported a small loss one quarter in the early eighties. The principal shareholders, in a characteristic manner, fired the CEO and began to look for a replacement. One of the candidates, a self-proclaimed turnaround specialist, offered to come on board at a relatively low salary but indicated that if he was successful in returning Volunteer Motors to profitability, he would receive a sizeable bonus. The shareholders agreed and the new CEO took charge. He immediately announced that he was going to improve the bottom line through outsourcing

---

8. E. M. Goldratt (1990), *The Haystack Syndrome*, North River Press, Barrington, MA.
9. M. L. Srikanth and M. Umble (1997), *Synchronous Management, Volume 1*, The Spectrum Publishing Company, Guilford, CT.

where possible. He asked for a complete list of every component manufactured in the plant and instructed his Cost Accounting department to come up with accurate product costs for each component. At the same time, the CEO instructed his Purchase department to identify a supplier and a purchase cost for each of these components. The CEO next instructed an assistant to meticulously compare these product costs with their respective purchase costs. Whenever the product cost exceeded the purchase cost, the component was to be outsourced. Anyone who dragged his or her feet in complying with these requirements was unceremoniously shown the door. Even as components were outsourced, some of the direct laborers were laid off. At the end of four months, the CEO asked for a progress report and an updated list.

The new list revealed a number of new components that had not appeared in the previous lists. The components that had not been outsourced had to bear the overhead burden that the out-sourced components had previously shared. The CEO was puzzled, but explained this situation away as a residual effect of the previous administration. He asked his staff to repeat the outsourc-ing exercise again. At the same time, some more direct laborers were laid off. In time, the fourth quarter arrived and the financial statements presented a bleak picture. The CEO was still puzzled. He toured all the facilities in the enterprise and found lots of idle capacity. While the blue collar employees had been laid off, the buildings, equipment and infrastructure were still present, albeit without much work to do.

The CEO had to act fast. What could he do? We can only guess at his thought process at that time. Perhaps he may have realized how absorption accounting principles could help him because he made a quick assessment and realized that the major part of the enterprise's investment was in the final assembly plant. So, he obtained loans from more than 200 banks. He used this money to buy raw material, hired new operators, and ran his assembly plants round the clock. Finished goods inventory began to pile up in the delivery docks. The CEO persuaded the distributors who sold the products to accept shipments with the option to return unsold products. These shipments were then identified as sales on Volun-teer Motors' books.

Since finished goods inventory absorbs all the overhead costs, and since many of these products were booked as sales, the enter-prise showed a healthy profit at the end of the year. The CEO

informed the shareholders that he had achieved his goal of returning the enterprise to profitability and received a generous bonus.
However, he did not know how or where to proceed during future
quarters and resigned. This would probably have been a good
outcome for the enterprise except that when he resigned he left
the enterprise standing on a weak foundation. Within the next
quarter, dealers returned unsold products, and bank loans became
overdue. To survive, Volunteer Motors had to lay off tens of thousands of workers. It shrank to a one third of its original size and
totally restructured under a different name.

Decisions based on such measurement and control systems as
used by Volunteer Motors are incompatible with the application of
philosophies such as lean thinking and TOC. The biggest reason
for this incompatibility is that absorption costing and standard
variance reporting create incentives to produce excess inventories.
As noted by Noreen et al.

> *"Under absorption costing, building inventories tends to reduce the*
> *apparent average cost of goods sold. When production exceeds sales,*
> *fixed costs are spread across more units, and some of the fixed costs are*
> *reported on the balance sheet as part of additional inventories rather*
> *than on the income statement as part of cost of goods sold. Under*
> *standard cost variance reporting, a work center with a fixed labor force*
> *can improve its efficiency measure only by producing more output."*[10]

The idea of adding value to the product as it moves through the
production facility is well entrenched in the minds of many
managers. We saw this view puts pressure on management to create
more WIP and finished goods inventory, which become goods
nobody wants. Looking at this point a little differently, what is the
real value of an item sitting in the shop floor, as WIP or finished
goods inventory? One can argue that it is worth zero dollars. That
is, unless the item was produced in response to an order, all we
have done is taken a perfectly good unit of raw material and
destroyed it. We violated the RAP principle discussed in Chapter 2
(keep the material as raw-as-possible), and probably used a critical
resource to create inventory.

Although the standard cost accounting system is widely used, it
is increasingly being questioned. As early as 1984, Kaplan, one of
the originators of the Balanced Scorecard discussed in Chapter 4,
stated "Efforts to revitalize manufacturing industries cannot succeed if outdated accounting and control systems remain

---

10. E. Noreen, D. Smith and J. T. Mackey (1995), *The Theory of Constraints and its Implications
for Management Accounting*, North River Press, Great Barrington, MA.

unchanged."[11] The basic problem is how overhead is allocated, and financial and non-financial managers have sought ways of allocating overhead and indirect costs for many years. This explains the interest generated by Activity-Based Costing (ABC) systems. Although the basic elements of ABC had been in existence for decades, it was developed and presented in a structured manner only in the mid-to-late 1980s.[12]

ACTIVITY-BASED COSTING (ABC)

The standard cost accounting uses a simple formula to allocate indirect costs. In the example we presented, the overhead costs were allocated based on direct labor costs. That was a reasonable approach so long as labor was the biggest factor in production as was the case in the early 1900s. It made sense when the products were not too different as in the case of the Model T made by Henry Ford. Today, however, labor is rarely the biggest cost component. Furthermore, manufacturing enterprises do not make one product; typically, they produce many different types of products at the same facility. So, the old allocation formula is even further removed from identifying the true product cost. ABC provides an opportunity to obtain a better approximation of the true product cost.

The basic principle of the ABC system is "activities consume costs and products consume activities." The difference between standard cost accounting and ABC is that in standard cost accounting, products consume overhead costs, whereas the ABC system assumes costs are consumed by activities (that may or may not add value to the product). ABC is a methodology that identifies costs associated with activities and links those costs to products, services, and customers based on their consumption of those activities. Rather than allocate, for instance, the total cost of operating a resource directly to a range of products, ABC identifies the specific activities that go into making a specific product and attempts to figure the cost of those activities.

---

11. R. S. Kaplan (1984), "Yesterday's Accounting Undermines Production," *Harvard Business Review,* July-August 1984, pp. 95-101
12. A book by H. T. Johnson and R. S. Kaplan (1987), *Relevance Lost: The Rise and Fall of Management Accounting,* Harvard Business School Press, presented the framework for ABC. Subsequently, the paper by R. Cooper and R. S. Kaplan (1988), "Measure Costs Right: Make the Right Decisions," *Harvard Business Review,* September-October 1988, formally introduced the term Activity-Based Costing.

With ABC, the accountant first enumerates all overhead activities and their costs. ABC focuses on cost drivers that can guide the allocations with greater accuracy than is possible using a historical percentage allocation method. With the standard cost accounting system, we used direct labor cost as the cost driver. With ABC, cost drivers are allocated into one of four categories: unit-level, batch-level, product-level, and product-sustaining or facility-level.

Unit-level activities and their associated costs are probably the easiest to determine. Unit-level activities are activities performed for each product unit. Examples of unit-level costs are direct labor cost and direct material cost. (These are not overhead costs and are merely presented as examples.) Another example of a unit-level cost is the cost of a tool change-over when it is made after a fixed number of units produced at a machine because this cost can be directly translated to a per-unit product cost.

Batch-level activities are activities that are performed once for each batch of products. Batch-level costs are, however, independent of the number of units in a batch, so they are harder to allocate compared to unit-level costs. Examples of costs associated with batch-level activities are wages paid to production supervisors, machine setup costs not traceable to specific products, and material handling costs.

Product-level activities support the production of a product type or model. These costs do not vary with the number of batches produced. Examples of such costs are engineering support costs, and depreciation costs of equipment dedicated to a product line.

Finally, facility-level costs include the costs of operating the Accounting, HR, General Administration, Sales, and Plant Maintenance functions. Using different cost drivers to allocate costs reduces the overhead costs that are allocated arbitrarily.

We illustrate the ABC concept with a simple extension to the National Pontoons example. Suppose National Pontoons actually makes two products: the black vinyl wheels and wood-trim wheels. The sales of these two products in 2003 were 25,000 units and 5,000 units, respectively. For simplicity, we will assume that the raw material costs and direct labor costs are the same for both products. That is, these remain at $10.00 per unit for raw material and $2.50 per unit for direct labor (see Table 6.2) for the black vinyl wheels and the wood-trim wheels. The manufacturing overhead is $225,000, and for simplicity this overhead is assumed to be the sum of the salaries paid to the plant manager ($150,000), a quality control (QC) inspector ($63,000), and equipment depreciation ($12,000). In other words, we do not consider cost of utilities, etc., in this example.

The standard cost accounting approach would allocate the overhead costs based on the labor hours required by each product. Since the two products require the same amount of labor, the manufacturing overhead allocation for either product, obtained from the standard cost accounting approach, is $3.00 x 2.50 = $7.50 per unit just as before. The product costs obtained with this approach are summarized in Table 6.3.

Consider next, the product costs derived using ABC. Suppose that the QC inspector does not give any special treatment to either product. That is, he inspects the product at the same level of detail regardless of whether it is a vinyl wheel or a wood-trim wheel. This makes allocation of the QC inspector's salary ($63,000) a relatively easy task. The overhead allocation is simply $63,000/30,000 = $2.10 per unit regardless of the product type. This is an example of an allocation made at the unit-level. It is an allocation that uses the production volume as the cost driver. Similarly, since the two products require the same amount of time at either resource, depreciation can use production volume as the cost driver to arrive at an allocation of $12,000/30,000 = $0.40 per unit.

The allocation of the plant manager's salary requires more data. National Pontoons is interested in promoting its wood-trim wheels because it sees the demand for this product increasing over time. As a result, the plant manager spends more time planning and supervising the fabrication of this product. Suppose National Pontoons obtains data that suggest the plant manager spends 75% of her time on the wood-trim wheels. As a result, the plant manager's $150,000 salary is allocated as follows: 25% of the salary is allocated to vinyl wheels ($37,500) and 75% is allocated to wood-trim wheels ($112,500). Note that this is an example of an allocation made at the product level. The production volume for the vinyl wheel is 25,000 units, so the overhead allocation per unit is $37,500/25,000 = $1.50 for a vinyl wheel. Similarly, since the production volume for the wood-trim wheel is 5,000, the overhead allocation per unit is $112,500/5,000 = $22.50 for a wood-trim wheel. Table 6.3 presents the product costs that result from the ABC method of allocating overhead costs.

Table 6-3. Product Costs with Standard Cost Accounting and ABC

COST CATEGORY	STANDARD COSTING		ACTIVITY-BASED COSTING	
	Vinyl	Wood-Trim	Vinyl	Wood-Trim
Raw Material	$10.00	$10.00	$10.00	$10.00
Direct Labor	$ 2.50	$ 2.50	$ 2.50	$ 2.50
Depreciation	$ 0.40	$ 0.40	$ 0.40	$ 0.40
Mfg. O/H (QC Inspector)	$ 2.10	$ 2.10	$ 2.10	$ 2.10
Mfg. O/H (Plant Manager)	$ 5.00	$ 5.00	$ 1.50	$22.50
Product Cost	$20.00	$20.00	$16.50	$37.50

As Table 6.3 demonstrates, the differences in product costs that result from standard cost accounting and ABC can be dramatic. Because ABC forces the user to consider additional information, it usually provides product costs that more closely approximate the true product cost (assuming that management requires all these overhead costs to be allocated to products). In Table 6.3, we have not included the SG&A expenses. In this regard, it is possible to allocate some of the SG&A expenses to specific products as we allocated the plant manager's salary. (Such SG&A expense allocations would typically be carried out using cost drivers at either the product level or the facility level.)

The approach used to compute costs using ABC is conceptually simple. However, ABC requires a lot of information to be gathered, and that often makes it expensive to operate even with modern information systems. There are other problems with ABC. The choice of the cost drivers, for example, is somewhat arbitrary. As noted in *Synchronous Management, Volume 1*:

> *"Even the developers (Robin Cooper and Robert Kaplan) of the formal ABC concept admit that ABC systems are not capable of fully allocating all costs without significant distortions. They now suggest that when you have to make a totally arbitrary decision as to how to allocate a cost, you should not allocate that cost. In fact, as we will demonstrate, any system that allocates costs on a basis which might be considered arbitrary is fundamentally flawed. And since full-blown ABC systems are basically allocation systems that require many arbitrary decisions, it is questionable whether or not these systems can deliver valid information for making decisions."*[13]

---

13. M. L. Srikanth and M. Umble (1997), *Synchronous Management, Volume 1,* The Spectrum Publishing Company, Guilford, CT.

The choice of cost drivers has behavioral implications as well. Suppose that the Purchase department expenses are allocated to different functional units in proportion to the number of purchase orders these functional units generate. If the functional units generating these orders know that the ABC system is allocating costs based on the number of purchase orders, they will be motivated to place fewer purchase orders. Fewer purchase orders imply larger order quantities, which, in turn, imply higher average inventory levels. That is the exact opposite of what the enterprise would like to see. Instead, suppose that the expenses were allocated on the basis of the number of stock-keeping units. That would encourage the development of products that utilize common parts, which usually has a positive impact. So, cost drivers allocate cost or quantify some measure of past performance. However, *encouraging appropriate behavior is more important than measuring some aspect of past actions.* Indeed, one can seriously question the validity of, or the logic behind, trying to allocate sunk (fixed) costs across products.

For example, though ABC did help provide a way to allocate overhead costs among the products more equitably based on the activities involved, these costs may drive behavior that runs counter to enterprise goals. In the case of National Pontoons, ABC made the wood-trim wheels so much more expensive simply because the plant manager gave a lot of attention to the product to launch it successfully. If National Pontoons wishes to recover the resulting product cost (and the SG&A expenses), it will have to price the wood-trim wheel higher than $37.50. Yet, this is the product National Pontoons wants to promote: and at this price, the customer is less likely to buy it and may instead settle for the cheaper vinyl wheel or shop elsewhere for a wood-trim wheel.

To sum up the discussion on cost accounting systems, the problems they face with regard to determining product costs are as follows:

- The standard cost accounting system allocates all overhead costs to the products using a broad measure such as labor cost. That distorts the actual product cost.
- Attempts to ensure a more equitable allocation of overhead costs such as ABC systems can help approximate the product cost a little better. However, ABC systems still suffers from a certain amount of arbitrariness with regard to how the allocations are made. The choice of a cost driver is more difficult when costs are shared by more than one product. For example, no single cost driver can reflect all the relevant activities that take place in the Accounting department.

- The problem with ABC becomes worse when we consider some costs that are unrelated to a particular product or a particular customer. Examples of such costs include the CEO's salary and building and grounds maintenance. These are costs that cannot be allocated in any rational manner, leading one to conclude that, in general, there is no such thing as a true product cost. It is simply a result of a number of arbitrary assumptions.
- ABC systems can become difficult and expensive to maintain because the information requirements are significantly large.
- As we observed from the National Pontoons example, the allocation can sometimes make a product that the enterprise wishes to promote, prohibitively expensive to the customer, making it even harder to sell the product. So, though ABC has its uses in terms of determining where costs are incurred, its use for determining product costs, determining which products are truly profitable, and setting product selling prices become questionable.

Managers of enterprises that subscribe to lean thinking and TOC believe that cost accounting systems which try to absorb sunk costs provide product costs that often forces people to make incorrect decisions. Instead of absorption costing, forward-thinking managers use a variable costing approach in which only the variable costs are considered for product-mix decisions. This approach is otherwise known as throughput accounting.[14] We will discuss this approach in the context of the throughput world perspective, a global perspective that lets managers make more informed and meaningful decisions.

THE THEORY OF CONSTRAINTS AND THE THROUGHPUT WORLD PERSPECTIVE

As it applies to business systems, TOC is based on two premises: the goal of a business is to make more money now and in the future, and a system's constraints determine its output. A constraint is defined as anything that inhibits a system's performance toward its

---

14. The variable costing concept is not unique to TOC. Incidentally, when variable costing was originally conceived, direct labor was considered a variable cost because piece rates were common at that time. TOC acknowledges that absorption accounting was a reasonable approximation when direct labor was variable and little overhead existed. From a practical standpoint, and especially in the short-term, direct labor is almost as fixed as the other costs sunk into production facilities and equipment. Since the product mix can be adjusted without significantly impacting direct labor, throughput accounting classifies direct labor as a fixed operating expense. With TOC, the only variable cost is direct materials.

goals. As noted earlier, TOC encourages systems thinking: It takes a global perspective of decision making and emphasizes that decisions should be made for the good of the entire system. To simplify the decision-making process, TOC adopts the view that managers should focus on a system's constraints as a basis for making the right decisions because they cannot have a precise view of an entire complex system. To monitor performance, TOC prescribes three performance measures. All three measures are expressed in dollar terms:

- **Throughput** (T): The rate at which the system generates money through sales
- **Inventory** (I): All the money invested in purchasing things the system intends to sell
- **Operating expense** (OE): All the money the system spends, turning inventory (I) into throughput (T)

The T, I and OE measures do not consider any product-related costs. In that sense, these three measures are global measures, measures that are not distorted by the approximations used for determining product costs. We will make these terms more precise in the following discussion. As we continue to discuss these terms, the reader may find the model for relating these three measures, presented in Figure 6.3, useful.

The TOC definition of throughput differs from its conventional definition. In conventional usage, throughput is the rate at which the system produces products. The formula for throughput in the TOC world is sales revenue less totally variable costs, as shown in Figure 6.3. As noted earlier, with TOC, the only variable cost is direct materials. TOC views a business as a money-making machine. By using money through sales in the definition of throughput, TOC deliberately differentiates between a unit produced and a unit that is sold. If a unit is produced, but not sold, it remains on the books as finished goods inventory and not as throughput. In this manner, TOC creates a pull system, preventing the facility from continuing to produce products for which there is no demand.

It can be argued that the TOC definition of throughput is not novel. Even though TOC defines throughput as a rate, this definition is similar to the definition of contribution margin at a conceptual level. Throughput in TOC is revenue minus variable costs, and the general definition of contribution margin is revenue minus all variable costs. Similarly, at the conceptual level, it can be argued that there is no difference between the TOC approach to accounting, namely, throughput accounting, and variable costing.

Figure 6-3. A Model for Relating *T*, *I*, and *OE*

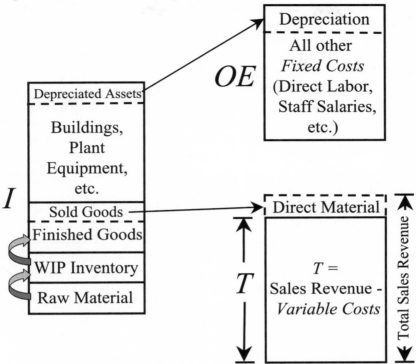

So, what is different about throughput accounting? The main difference relates to how direct labor is accounted for. In most of the TOC literature, throughput is defined as revenue minus direct materials. One implication of the simplified formula for throughput is that direct labor cost is fixed. Therefore, direct labor is typically not deducted when computing TOC throughput; and it is not absorbed into WIP inventory. Instead, it is included as part of operating expense. On the other hand, the typical approach with variable costing is to treat direct labor as a variable cost as observed earlier in footnote 14. This was a valid approach at the turn of the 20th century, the time when variable costing was originally conceived. At that time, the labor force was typically paid on a piece rate basis and management was able to adjust the labor workforce. It can be argued that in many enterprises today, direct labor is essentially a fixed cost.

The definition of inventory is a little different from its conventional interpretation. In addition to raw material, WIP and finished goods inventory, *I* (expressed in dollar terms) includes money invested in equipment because ultimately inventory is saleable, as is the entire facility. Any time the enterprise buys fixed assets or raw material (variable assets), the money invested in purchasing these assets goes into a bucket represented by I in Figure 6.3. As raw material is converted to WIP, and subsequently to finished goods, TOC does not use the value-added concept of cost-accounting systems. Instead, WIP and finished goods inventory are valued at the same price as raw material—see Figure 6.3.

Thus, the direct labor used to make the product, or the resource time used, is not taken into account when calculating the finished goods inventory value. This approach eliminates many undesirable practices. For example, with traditional costing methods, it is possible to move expenses from one period to another by attaching them to inventory (as an investment), thereby enhancing profit numbers when necessary.

TOC defines operating expense as the cost of turning inventory (I) into throughput (T). The definition of OE is simple and avoids making arbitrary distinctions. It includes all fixed costs and costs that do not vary directly with the output as shown in Figure 6.3. For example, salaries paid to managers would be classified under OE. No attempt is made to categorize the CEO's salary differently from the plant supervisors' salaries. TOC avoids these distinctions because allocating these indirect costs among the various products is difficult as we observed earlier. Other items that would go into the OE bucket include depreciation and SG&A expenses because these are fixed costs that typically do not vary with the production level.

A numerical example, using the National Pontoons example, may help clarify the preceding discussion. Suppose National Pontoons uses throughput accounting. It has compiled information on its asset base at the start of 2003 and its activities during the year:

Asset base as of January 1, 2003

Fixed Assets	$120,000
Raw Material Inventory (Units)	25,000
WIP Inventory (Units)	15,000
Finished Goods Inventory (Units)	20,000

Activity in 2003

Raw Material Purchases in 2003 (Units)	40,000
Number of Units Sold in 2003	30,000
Unit Selling Price	$30
Direct Labor Wages	$120,000

Plant Manager's Salary	$150,000
QC Inspector's Salary	$63,000
SG&A Expenses	$200,000
Capital Assets Acquired in 2003	$25,000
Depreciation in 2003	$12,000

The depreciation of $12,000 is calculated based on a straight-line depreciation of 10% per year on the asset base of 120,000 dollars. The implicit assumption is that assets acquired in 2003 will be depreciated over the next ten years. Based on this information, National Pontoons determines its asset base at the end of the year 2003, with its fixed assets calculated as follows: (Fixed Assets at start of 2003 + Capital Assets acquired in 2003 − Depreciation during 2003) = $120,000 + $25,000 − $12,000 = $133,000. Expecting to sell 40,000 units, National Pontoons had purchased 40,000 units of raw material. However, in 2003, it sold 30,000 units and Resources A and B produced 30,000 units. Hence, the raw material inventory at the end of 2003 increased by 10,000 units relative to the start of the year, leaving WIP and Finished Goods inventory unchanged. The asset base at the end of the year is as follows:

Asset base as of December 31, 2003

Fixed Assets	$133,000
Raw Material Inventory (Units)	35,000
WIP Inventory (Units)	15,000
Finished Goods Inventory (Units)	20,000

Based on the above information, the value of inventory (raw material + WIP + finished goods) at the start of 2003 is $600,000 [(25,000 + 15,000 + 20,000) x $10]. So, the value of I at the start of 2003 is $720,000 ($120,000 + $600,000). The value of OE during 2003 is the sum of wages paid to direct labor ($120,000), salaries paid to the plant manager and the QC inspector ($213,000), depreciation ($12,000), and SG&A expenses ($200,000) for a total of $545,000. The sales revenue from the sale of 30,000 units at $30 each is (30,000 x $30 = $900,000). The variable costs in the example only consist of direct material costs involved in the sale, which are valued at the raw material purchase price of $10 each (30,000 x $10 = $300,000). Thus, T = Sales Revenue − Direct Material = 600,000 dollars. At the end of 2003, there are 70,000 units of inventory in the system, as raw material or WIP or finished goods. All these units are valued at $10 each. Hence, the value of I at the end of 2003 is $833,000 ($133,000 + 70,000 x $10). The values of the three TOC measures are summarized below:

I (start of 2003)   = $720,000

T (in 2003)   = $600,000

OE (in 2003)   = $545,000

I (end of 2003)   = $833,000

The profit for National Pontoons is thus $T - OE = 55,000$ dollars. Even though National Pontoons bought 10,000 units of excess raw material in 2003, these excess units are not included in OE. Note that TOC defines OE as all the money that the system spends, turning I into T. Thus, until such time as these units are sold, they will only appear in I.

RELATING TOC MEASURES WITH TRADITIONAL FINANCIAL MEASURES

The financial measures of interest to an enterprise are net profit (an absolute measure), return on investment (ROI, a relative measure based on investment), and cash flow (a measure of survival). These three measures should be used together to be meaningful. For example, a net profit of $100 million would have no meaning unless one was told how much money was invested to realize this net profit. Cash flow is important because it is needed to pay the bills; an enterprise with a high profit and a high ROI might still find itself in trouble if it is short of cash to pay its suppliers because it has tied up all its money in inventory or in equipment.

Although the three TOC measures, T, I and OE, are quite different from traditional cost accounting measures, they can be equated with traditional financial measures as follows:

Net profit $=$ Throughput $-$ Operating Expense $=$ $T - OE$

$$\frac{\text{Return on}}{\text{Investment}} = \frac{Throughput - Operating\ Expense}{Inventory} = \frac{T - OE}{I}$$

$$\text{Inventory turns}\ =\ \frac{Throughput}{Inventory}\ =\ \frac{T}{I}$$

$$\text{Productivity}\ =\ \frac{Throughput}{Operating\ Expense}\ =\ \frac{T}{OE}$$

The financial measures calculated using the formulae above will have similar numerical values as would otherwise be obtained with a conventional analysis. For instance, the numerical value for ROI obtained using the TOC formula presented above would match the return on assets calculated with a traditional approach. The one significant difference would be with inventory turns. The TOC formula for inventory turns could be significantly less than the inventory turns obtained with a traditional approach because the inventory in the denominator of the TOC formula includes all capital assets that the enterprise has acquired. The traditional formula for inventory turns only includes the working capital inventory (namely, raw material inventory, WIP inventory, and finished goods inventory).

COST WORLD VERSUS THROUGHPUT WORLD

Ideally, we want to increase T and decrease I and OE. The cost world perspective, with its desire to optimize enterprise efficiency, would probably first do so by cutting costs. The cost world would, thus, emphasize reducing operating expense, with throughput and inventory receiving less importance. However, the rush to cut costs can arrest the competitiveness that cost-cutting efforts are meant to enhance.

The throughput world perspective, on the other hand, emphasizes T over I and OE. Throughput is the most important because it can theoretically be increased without limit. The other two measures can only go down to a certain minimum level. In other words, whereas the opportunities to make more money through reductions in inventory and operating expense are limited, the opportunities to make more money by increasing throughput are relatively unlimited. After throughput, TOC next emphasizes inventory reduction, placing *OE* as a distant third priority. The TOC ranking becomes a) *T*, b) *I*, and c) *OE*. Figure 6.4 compares the priority rankings for the cost world and the throughput world.

Figure 6-4. Priorities in the Cost and Throughput Worlds

Priority	Cost World	Throughput World
First	*OE*	*T*
Second	*T*	*I*
Third	*I*	

OE ← A distant third priority

In a sense, the cost world's focus on reducing *OE* mirrors the efforts enterprises take to improve their operational effectiveness. However, the problem with the cost world focus is that it does not aim at improving operational effectiveness per se, but instead tends to sacrifice long-term throughput increases for short-term gains. We will illustrate this point by revisiting the National Pontoons example.

LEVERAGING POWERS OF *T* AND *OE*: NATIONAL PONTOONS REVISITED

Recall that National Pontoons makes steering wheels for pontoon boats. It procures raw material for these steering wheels at a cost of $10 per unit. Its manufacturing overhead costs and SG&A expenses were $225,000 and $200,000 respectively. National Pontoons uses two resources, A and B, to produce the units. Each resource is operated by a direct labor employee. The time required to process the units is six minutes at resource A, and nine minutes at resource B. National Pontoons worked two shifts, had four direct laborers, and the total wages paid to these four operators was 120,000 dollars. In 2003, National Pontoons sold 30,000 steering wheels. The unit selling price was $30. Based on this data, the net profit for National Pontoons for 2003 is $55,000, as presented in Table 6.4.

The capacity for National Pontoons is estimated as follows. Resource B, which is the potential capacity constraint, requires nine minutes per unit. To produce 30,000 steering wheels, the time required from Resource B is 30,000 x (9/60) = 4,500 hours per year. Since National Pontoons works two shifts at twenty hours per day, 25 days each month, Resource B is available 500 hours each month, or 500 x 12 = 6,000 hours per year. Thus, National Pontoons only operated (in 2003) at 75% of its capacity. The unused labor capacity will show up as a significant labor efficiency variance on its books.

Table 6-4. Cost and Profit Data for National Pontoons

ITEM	DATA FOR 2003
Sales Revenue	$900,000
Raw Material Cost	$300,000
Direct Labor Cost	$120,000
Overhead Costs (including SG&A)	$425,000
Total Expenses	$845,000
Net Profit	$ 55,000

Suppose that National Pontoons focuses on becoming more profitable by reducing its expenses. Since it is only operating at 75% of its capacity, it reduces working hours in 2004 by 25% to 15 hours per day, and accordingly adjusts the wages paid to direct labor by 25 percent. The labor costs drop from $120,000 to $120,000 x 0.75 = 90,000 dollars. The other costs remain essentially unchanged. The resulting cost savings of $30,000 goes directly to the bottom line, so the net result is a sizeable increase in profits for National Pontoons, from $55,000 to 85,000 dollars. The leveraging power of *OE* is summarized in Table 6.5.

Table 6-5. Leveraging Power of OE for National Pontoons

ITEM	DATA FOR 2003	LEVERAGING POWER OF *OE*
Sales Revenue	$900,000	$900,000
Raw Material Cost	$300,000	$300,000
Direct Labor Cost	$120,000	$ 90,000
Overhead Costs (including SG&A)	$425,000	$425,000
Total Expenses	$845,000	$815,000
Net Profit	$ 55,000	$ 85,000

Suppose, instead, that National Pontoons focuses on using its installed capacity to improve its throughput in 2004. It embarks on a marketing campaign and at the same time drops its price by 5% across the board. That is, it drops its selling price from $30 to $28.50 (0.95 x $30 = $28.50). The marketing campaign costs an additional $10,000 for 2004. The combined effect of the campaign and the price drop boosts its sales to 40,000 units in 2004, that is, a 33.33% increase in sales, which results in a full capacity utilization of resource B. Thus, National Pontoons generates a revenue of (40,000) x ($28.50) = 1,140,000 dollars. The raw material cost for a sale of 40,000 units has now correspondingly increased by 33.33% to $400,000 and the overhead costs (including SG&A expenses) have increased by $10,000 to 435,000 dollars. Table 6.6 presents the data.

Table 6-6. Leveraging Power of *T* for National Pontoons

ITEM	DATA FOR 2003	LEVERAGING POWER OF *OE*	LEVERAGING POWER OF *T*
Sales Revenue	$900,000	$900,000	$1,140,000
Raw Material Cost	$300,000	$300,000	$ 400,000
Direct Labor Cost	$120,000	$ 90,000	$ 120,000
Overhead Costs (including SG&A)	$425,000	$425,000	$ 435,000
Total Expenses	$845,000	$815,000	$ 955,000
Net Profit	$ 55,000	$ 85,000	$ 185,000

This example suggests that the leveraging power of throughput can far exceed the leveraging power of operating expense. The reason why throughput has so much more leverage is fairly straightforward. First, for most manufacturing enterprises, the material cost is a large percentage of the total product cost. Second, it is relatively harder to get rid of fixed assets and infrastructure costs. So, enterprises that focus on reducing *OE* can only do so by trimming labor costs. However, labor cost is only a small fraction of the total cost of operating the enterprise and reducing it does not get you much leverage as this example demonstrates.

We can use the analogy we drew earlier between a set of processes and a chain to demonstrate how the cost world focus sacrifices long-term throughput increases for short-term gains. Taking the chain analogy one step further[15], suppose that instead of strengthening the weakest link (and improving *T*), we focus on improving the efficiency at the current level of performance (improving *OE*). Assume that the chain consists of ten links, where each link has a load carrying capacity of 100 pounds except for one

---

15. This analogy is attributed to Tony Rizzo, CEO, The Product Development Institute. See *http://www.pdinstitute.com/mailback/files/rightsizing.pdf.*

of them, which only has a load carrying capacity of 50 pounds. Management is unhappy with the cost of maintaining the nine strong links. So, it corrects (right-sizes) the chain by selling the nine heavy links, replacing them with nine links, each with a load carrying capacity of 50 pounds. On first glance, this is a truly efficient chain since every link is capable of carrying exactly the same load. What is the problem here?

The problem is the enterprise is locked into the current performance level. Before undertaking the cost-reduction program, there was one weak link that limited the load-carrying capacity of the chain to 50 pounds. Now, the enterprise has ten links, any one of which can break. If the enterprise desires to improve its performance in the future, it will have to work on *all* ten links in the chain. The same is true with enterprises that eliminate overcapacity. In addition to the vulnerable position it finds itself in when business picks up, it may find it harder to recruit employees fearful of getting axed in the next downsizing wave. We summarize this discussion with the next lean supply chain principle.

LEAN SUPPLY CHAIN PRINCIPLE 11

Decisions should promote a growth strategy. While enterprises should attempt to simultaneously increase throughput, decrease inventory, and decrease operating expenses, the focus must be on improving throughput.

How do we leverage the growth model advocated by the throughput world? For instance, what should we do when the enterprise finds it has excess capacity? In the National Pontoons example, we worked with a marketing effort that generated demand through a simultaneous cost-reduction program and a marketing campaign. In that example, the focus on *T* no doubt generated a much better return than did the cost world focus on *OE*. However, this is not the only approach one can pursue. Improving the bottom line is best done with a logical approach. The TOC presents a five-step focusing process for identifying the root cause of a problem and dealing with it effectively.

THE FIVE STEP FOCUSING PROCESS OF TOC

The five-step focusing process to improve system performance is based on the two simple premises of TOC: the goal of the enterprise is to make more money, now and in the future; and the system's constraints prevent it from making more money.

Step 1: Identify the System's Constraint(s)

The first step is to identify the constraint(s). TOC asserts that any enterprise has few real constraints, at most, a handful. The constraint can be a physical constraint, a market constraint, or a policy constraint. In turn, a policy constraint could arise due to the measures in place, the methods used, or the mindset that governs the strategic and tactical decisions of the enterprise.[16] We discuss each type of constraint.

- **Physical Constraints**: Physical constraints are the easiest to identify. Physical constraints can be machine capacity, staff availability, material availability, space availability, and so on. A machine capacity constraint is usually identified quite easily in a factory by identifying the resource where WIP inventories usually accumulate. If a constraint process has to shut down often for a lack of components, then the constraint is a materials constraint. Similarly, if output is not meeting customer demand because of operator availability, then there is a staff constraint.
- **Market Constraints**: Market constraints are a little harder to identify. In general, a market constraint exists if the demand for the enterprise's products and services is less than the enterprise's installed capacity or in some other way limits the bottomline performance of the enterprise. On the one hand, if the enterprise had excess capacity, that is a sure indication of a market constraint, one that is easily identified. However, sometimes, a market constraint can arise even when an enterprise produces various products and does not have enough capacity to satisfy all of the demand. In such a situation, there could be a limited demand for the product(s) that the enterprise would really prefer to sell.
- **Policy Constraints**: Policy constraints are, relatively speaking, the hardest to identify. In theory, there should be no policy constraints. However, it turns out that most constraints to system performance are policy constraints. For instance, the enterprise could create a methods constraint by never producing a batch of units below an economic order quantity. When resources are forced to produce in such quantities, there is a good chance of misallocating resource capacity to produce products for which there is no current demand. A measures constraint would arise if the measurement system drives behavior incongruous with enterprise goals. For instance, if the

---

16. M. L. Srikanth and M. Umble (1997), *Synchronous Management, Volume 1*, The Spectrum Publishing Company, Guilford, CT.

Purchasing department is measured on purchase price vari-ances, it would aggressively seek quantity discounts, leading to increased raw material inventory. A mindset constraint is when the shop supervisor has the attitude that all operators should be kept busy all the time. This attitude will, again, result in unnec-essary activities being performed.

Step 2: Decide How to Exploit the System's Constraint(s)

Exploiting the constraint means we use the constraint as profitably as possible. Although *exploit* has a negative connotation, this word has been chosen carefully. For instance, once we identify the constraint, it is tempting to consider a decision that simply does away with the constraint. Thus, if the constraint is a physical resource, one can consider acquiring additional resources. How-ever, the enterprise may not be in a position to acquire these resources immediately. Similarly, if there are policy constraints, that could take time to improve. What should the enterprise do in the meantime? Until the constraints are overcome by other means, the enterprise should work them as profitably (effectively) as possible; that is the real meaning of the word exploit.

For instance, if the constraint is a physical resource, the impli-cation is that every minute it is idle causes the enterprise to lose money. Exploit here means ensuring that the resource is never idle and waiting for parts, or that it never has to work on a defective component. On the other hand, if the market is the constraint, in the sense that we do not have enough demand for our products, we exploit it by making sure that not a single sale is lost as a result of our own actions or inaction. A market constraint implies that we have extra capacity, so we can grow market share by promising and delivering products more quickly to the customer. This is possible because the internal resources are not as congested, so products do not wait a long time before they are processed by the different resources. We can thus exploit the (market) constraint by guaran-teeing 100% on-time delivery to the customer. Alternately, we can exploit the constraint by producing the mix of products that maximizes profits as we will demonstrate shortly through an example.

Step 3: Subordinate Everything Else to that Decision

Once the decision is made as to how the constraint will be exploited, the third step in the five-step focusing process is to subordinate every aspect of system operation to this decision. In other words, we need to manage every part of the profit-generating system. How do we manage the vast majority of the enterprise's resources that, by definition, are not constraints? If we ignore them completely, they may stop functioning correctly, they may become constraints themselves, or they may function counter to enterprise goals. For instance, we may choose not to maintain non-bottleneck resources as diligently as we do the bottleneck resource. However, we do not want those non-bottleneck resources becoming bottlenecks because of our negligence.

In many instances, subordination deals with the process of scheduling. Typically, this means that the work must be started and sequenced in such a way that the constraint can always work or work smarter. For instance, in many manufacturing operations, heat treatment is typically a bottleneck. If the scheduler schedules a number of different products in one setup, it is possible to increase throughput without increasing the batch size. In Chapter 8, we will discuss a subordination technique known as the *drum-buffer-rope* (DBR). This technique, otherwise known as the *pull-from-the-bottleneck* model, is similar to the *kanban* system discussed in the previous chapter except that the input process in DBR is linked to the rate of production of the constraint in an attempt to utilize the constraint as effectively as possible.

Step 4: Elevate the System's Constraints

The fourth step tries to lift the restriction that is preventing the enterprise from making more money. Elevating the constraint means identifying ways in which the performance of the system can be improved, relative to its goals. For example, if you have a physical resource constraint, then you purchase another identical resource. In cases where the market is the constraint, we can elevate the constraint in various ways. The obvious approach is to advertise more effectively or advertise more. We can also try to find new markets for the products made by the enterprise.

However, as the five-step focusing process indicates, this step should only be performed after the exploit step. Many examples exist where the enterprise thinks it is necessary to elevate a perceived constraint and buys more equipment or subcontracts parts without properly exploiting the real constraint. So, before considering actions such as subcontracting, launching an advertising campaign, etc., one has to execute the second and third step. If the constraint still exists, or another constraint emerges, then it is time to execute the fourth step, unless it is a crystal-clear case where the constraint is out of proportion to everything else.

Step 5: If a Constraint Was Broken in a Previous Step, Go Back to Step 1

Can we stop with the fourth step? The answer is intuitively obvious. If we elevate the constraint, it probably will not remain a constraint. The performance will now be dictated by another element that has become the weakest link. To find the new weakest link, we must revisit all the steps once again. But this is not the entire fifth step. Goldratt adds a big warning: "Do not allow inertia to cause a system's constraints." For instance, the enterprise may have a policy of relocating workers to a constraint process. If this constraint is elevated, (for example, by replacing it with a faster process) and inertia causes the policy to remain in place, then workers will continue to get redirected to the old constraint even though they are no longer needed there. That may result in other resources needlessly becoming constraints. Step 5 is, therefore, a crucial step since it prevents inertia from derailing a continuous improvement process.

An Example of the Five-Step Focusing Process

We will consider an example to illustrate the Five-Step Focusing Process. Consider a small production system for manufacturing two products, P and Q, as shown in Figure 6.5. The goal of this system is to maximize profit. The weekly demands for P and Q are 110 units and 60 units, respectively. There are four resources used by the production system to meet demand: A, B, C, and D. These resources are shared among the various operations as shown in the figure. For instance, resource A takes 15 minutes to process one unit of raw material RM1 that is processed next by resource C for 10 minutes. Resource A is used to process raw material RM3 that is processed next by resource B. Resource D is an assembly operation that does the final operation for both products. For instance, it takes a unit or WIP from resource C and a different unit of WIP from resource B to produce a unit of Q, taking 5 minutes to perform this assembly operation. Note that when resource D assembles one unit of product P it requires a purchased part costing $5 to complete the assembly operation. Other pertinent data is presented in the figure. In particular, each resource operates independently for 2,400 minutes each week. The operating expenses, totaling $6,000, are incurred at the end of each week.

Figure 6-5. A Production System Manufacturing Two Products

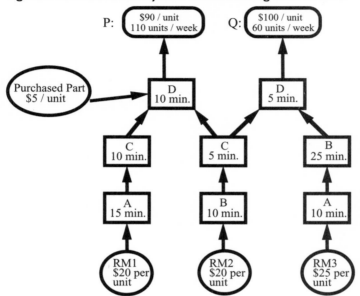

Time available at each work center: 2,400 minutes per week

Operating expenses per week: $6,000

The profit contribution for a product is the selling price less the price of materials used in the product. Thus, the contribution from product P is $90 – $5 – $20 – $20 = 45 dollars. Similarly, the contribution from product Q is $100 – $20 – $25 = 55 dollars. Step 1 is executed to determine if a constraint prevents us from meeting the market demand.

Step 1: Identify the system's constraints. If we do a capacity analysis of the production system, we find that Work Center B is overloaded as shown in Table 6.7:

Table 6-7. Capacity Analysis for the Production System

WORK CENTER	LOAD ON P (@110 UNITS)	LOAD ON Q (@ 60 UNITS)	TOTAL TIME REQUIRED	TIME AVAILABLE
A	1,650	600	2,250	2,400
B	1,100	2,100	3,200	2,400
C	1,650	300	1,950	2,400
D	1,100	300	1,400	2,400

Step 2: Decide how to exploit the system's constraints. Since we cannot meet the entire demand because of a capacity constraint at resource B, we might consider buying another identical resource. In the meantime, what should we do? We have to decide which product we want to give priority and produce it first. On first glance, since product Q has a higher profit margin ($55 per unit) than product P ($45 per unit), we may wish to use the constraint resource to produce as much as possible of Q, and then use the remaining capacity to produce P. Based on this approach, we will produce all 60 units of product Q that are demanded. That requires 2100 minutes from resource B, leaving 300 minutes that week; enough capacity to produce 30 units of product P. This product mix results in a net profit of $45(30) + $55(60) − $6,000 = − 1,350 dollars.

The above analysis was done in the cost world, where we worked with product costs and product profits. From a systems perspective (the throughput world), product costs do not have much meaning because we are primarily interested in system profits. To get the maximum profits, we want to exploit the constraint. That is, we need to get the maximum throughput (dollars per unit time) from the constraint. Analyzing the data, we find that when we run product Q through the constraint, resource B, it requires 35 minutes per unit, whereas product P only requires 10 minutes per unit from resource B. Each unit of Q brings in a profit margin of $55 which means that the rate at which the constraint generates profit is $55/35 = $1.57 per minute. Similarly, each unit of P brings in $45/10 = $4.50 per minute.

Thus, we prefer to produce as many units of P as the market would bear, and then use the remaining capacity available on the constraint to produce Q. To produce 110 units of P requires 110 x 10 = 1100 minutes of resource B. That leaves 2400 − 1100 = 1290 minutes available time on resource B each week to produce Q. So, with this available time, we can produce $1290/35 = 36$ units of Q which results in a total marginal profit of $45 x 110 + $55 x 36 = $6,930. After factoring out the operating expense of $6,000, we have a net profit of $930. Quite a difference from the cost world approach which resulted in a net loss of $1,350. This concludes step 2 of the five-step focusing process.

Step 3: Subordinate Everything Else to This Decision. In this example, what this means is we should keep resource B fed all the time. So, we can first allocate B to work on raw material RM2, and while B is processing these units, get resource A to process 36 units of raw material RM3 each week to produce product Q. (Any more units A produces beyond these 36 units would accumulate in front of resource B.)

Step 4: Elevate the Constraint. We have exploited the bottleneck. Now we can elevate it. At this stage, we recognize that in addition to the fact that resource B is a bottleneck, there is another bottleneck. What is it? It is the demand mix. Ideally, we would like to have more demand for product P because it results in more throughput (dollars per unit time) on the bottleneck. So, we have two choices to make: generate more demand for product P or buy another resource B. Either of these choices could elevate the constraint. If we choose the latter option, B will no longer be a bottleneck since it will have plenty of capacity to produce the entire demand per week. In that case, we next have to generate more demand. If there is adequate external demand, the internal constraint will no longer be resource B, but in all likelihood it would be resource A since that has the next highest workload. In any case, since we have elevated the constraint, we now have to execute steps 1 through 5 again. This is what is known as the process of ongoing improvement.

CONCLUSIONS

This chapter presented a number of key concepts and principles.

- Systems are analogous to chains. Every system has a weakest link, the constraint, which ultimately limits the success of the entire system.

- Cost accounting systems can provide valuable information for identifying where costs are being incurred. However, care should be taken when using accounting systems that allocate fixed costs to products. TOC avoids making such allocations and instead presents a set of three measures to gauge the financial impact of any decision.

- Many enterprises improve performance by improving all their processes at the same time. While it is a good idea to remove waste in any form, a potential downside is that the enterprise's focus may become diffused. Besides, time saved at non-constraint resources can be a mirage. Strengthening links other than the weakest link does not improve the strength of the chain.

- At the same time, many enterprises reduce costs and trim resources so the capacity of these resources matches the capacity of the weakest link. Enterprises following this approach are adopting a cost world perspective. The cost world perspective promotes local thinking and encourages behavior that runs counter to enterprise goals.

- The focus should be on growth or improving throughput. TOC prescribes a throughput world perspective. Enterprises that adopt the throughput world perspective have an immediate competitive advantage because most of the competition is still stuck in the cost world.

- The five-step focusing process provides a systematic way to identify bottlenecks and to exploit/elevate them. The focusing process works particularly well with physical constraints.

7

Success Stories in Applying Lean Thinking and Theory of Constraints

"We all have ability. The difference is how we use it."
Stevie Wonder

Many amongst us are familiar with the work of Stevie Wonder. This musical legend has won multiple Grammy Awards and a Grammy Lifetime Achievement Award. He was one of the first inductees to the Rock and Roll Hall of Fame. The above quote is reflective of the fact that Wonder overcame many obstacles in his career, capitalizing on them instead of being overwhelmed by them. For instance, as a premature infant he was placed in an incubator and accidentally given too much oxygen, resulting in his blindness. The ever-optimistic Wonder said his blindness allowed him to concentrate on his sense of hearing. He, thus, found a way to use his abilities most effectively!

While enterprises have to contend with multiple obstacles, the real challenge is to view these obstacles as opportunities for improvement. As Lee Iaccocca, the former CEO of Chrysler Corporation, once said, "We are continuously faced by great opportunities brilliantly disguised as insoluble problems." These problems are not unique to the enterprise and are, in all probability, the same problems faced by its competitors. In Chapter 4, we discussed how some enterprises are able to gain a significant edge over their competitors who are making the same products. These enterprises have developed an ability to adapt management tools and techniques such as lean thinking and the Theory of Constraints (TOC) in their own setting and to deploy them successfully. This chapter discusses two success stories in the application of lean thinking and TOC. These case studies are of particular interest because they also demonstrate that the language of lean thinking and TOC is universal. That is, lean thinking and TOC do not apply only to enterprises that build repetitive products and enjoy a well-developed infrastructure. These management philosophies apply in various situations and settings that, at first glance, may appear to present significant barriers to their application.

The first case discusses an enterprise in a developing economy that has successfully applied lean thinking to squeeze out waste in its supply chain and to grow its business. This is Sundaram Brake Linings, Ltd. (SBL), an enterprise in Chennai, India, involved in the manufacture of brake linings, clutch facings, and disk brake pads for original equipment manufacturers (OEMs) and for the after-market: domestic and export. The case shows how this enterprise has successfully deployed lean thinking across its supply chain to grow its business even though the logistics infrastructure in India is not yet fully developed. The case also discusses some additional lean terms such as *heijunka, pacemaker,* and *water spiders* that were not discussed in the chapter on lean thinking.

The second case shows how the TOC and lean thinking can be applied in the Maintenance, Repair and Overhaul (MRO) industry. Though almost every industry involved in the production and delivery of goods and services has to deal with unpredictable demand, the MRO industry is probably unique in this regard. In this industry, predicting when the demand from the customer will take place is very difficult. Furthermore, the quantum of work associated with that demand varies greatly. This case study shows how TOC was applied to improve the throughput at the Marine Corps Logistics Base in Albany, Georgia, an enterprise that maintains and overhauls a wide variety of equipment. This case discusses some additional concepts such as the critical chain and the simplified drum-buffer-rope technique, topics not covered in the chapter on TOC.

LEAN THINKING AT SUNDARAM BRAKE LININGS, LTD., CHENNAI, INDIA

The TVS Group is the largest manufacturer of automotive components in India. The group produces electrical systems, diesel fuel injection systems, braking systems, automotive wheels and axle fasteners, powder metal components, radiator caps, two wheelers and computer peripherals. With annual revenue of over $1 billion, the group has the largest distribution network for automotive products in India. Within the TVS Group, Sundaram Brake Linings (SBL) is an enterprise involved in manufacturing brake linings, disk brake pads, and woven clutch facings. SBL is located in Chennai, a city with a well-established supplier base for the automotive industry in India. Incorporated in 1974 as a joint venture with Abex Corporation, a U.S. enterprise, SBL commenced operations in 1976 and became a 100% Indian-owned enterprise in 1995.

SBL is a relatively small enterprise in the TVS Group, with an annual revenue of less than $30 million. However, it is an enterprise with a difference in its business philosophy and in its commitment to quality. Starting in the late 1980s, SBL introduced many changes in its manufacturing process, cut layers of hierarchy, lowered inventory levels, and modernized its plant at Chennai. In the process of making these changes, it has improved its operational efficiency and made substantial cost savings without firing its operators or cutting wages. SBL has practiced lean thinking and Total Quality Management (TQM) as an integral part of its business for a number of years. In 2001, it won the prestigious Deming Application Award. In the world of manufacturing and quality management, winning this award is like winning a Grammy Lifetime Achievement Award in the music industry, or an Oscar in the movie industry. The chairman and managing director of SBL, K. Mahesh, a passionate advocate of lean thinking, was recently singled out for praise by James P. Womack, co-author of *Lean Thinking*.

When I visited SBL in February 2004, the focus on quality, total productive maintenance, and waste elimination was evident. SBL views lean as an ongoing journey that never stops and is committed to the pursuit of perfection. It pursues perfection through *kaizen* (continuous improvement) events to take out waste and non value-added activities. Periodically, it also engages in *kaikaku* (breakthrough) events aimed at achieving radical improvements in performance and growth. This case study presents the ongoing implementation of lean thinking in its truck brake lining cell.

SBL is a second-tier supplier of truck brake linings to Brakes India, Kalyani Brakes, and Automotive Axles. These enterprises, in turn, supply truck brake assemblies to leading OEMs: Tata Motors, Ashok Leyland, Mahindra & Mahindra, and Bajaj Tempo. SBL is a major supplier of brake linings for heavy commercial vehicles manufactured by Tata Motors and Ashok Leyland. The OEM market has a fairly stable demand. SBL supplies products to the after-market, a market that has a much more volatile demand. The raw material for brake linings is procured from various suppliers, many of them located in close proximity to SBL. To highlight this enterprise's lean journey, we first present the value stream map for truck brake linings as it existed in April 2000.

The Value Stream Map—April 2000

Figure 7.1 presents a value stream map for the truck brake lining family of products, as of April 2000. At that time, the truck brake lining cell was producing 4,560 brake linings a day. The value stream map shows that the major production processes within SBL are the following: Blending, Compounding, Pre-forming, Pre-curing, Press-curing and Finishing. SBL has generally been able to obtain a relatively firm monthly delivery schedule from its major customers. It routes the customer demand to the production department. In April 2000, the production department used to generate a bi-weekly schedule that was relayed to the Press-curing operation. This schedule drove all the operations for the manufacture of truck brake linings within SBL.

Figure 7-1. Value Stream Map—April 2000

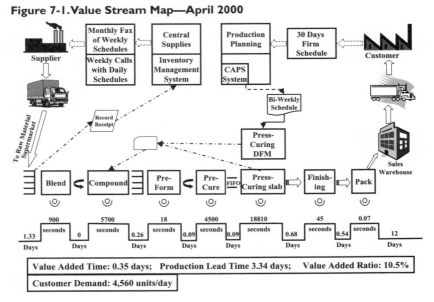

Value Added Time: 0.35 days; Production Lead Time 3.34 days; Value Added Ratio: 10.5%

Customer Demand: 4,560 units/day

Figure 7.1 shows that as of April 2000, SBL had already set in place many lean thinking concepts. For instance, most of the operations were driven through pull signals. Raw material required to meet the bi-weekly schedules were relayed through *kanban* pull signals to the Compounding process that, in turn, resulted in pull signals to the upstream process. The Compounding process pulled raw material from a *supermarket,* and this raw material withdrawal was updated in the inventory management system. The Purchase department (shown as Central Supplies in Figure 7.1) determined its monthly requirements using the inventory management system and faxed these requirements to its key suppliers. The Purchase department subsequently updated the monthly requirements with weekly schedules that were communicated to suppliers by telephone. As of April 2000, the products flowing out of the Press-curing operation were pushed to the Finishing operation from where they were packed and shipped to the sales warehouse for onward dispatch to the customer.

In April 2000, management had estimated its *value-added ratio* (VAR)[1] to be 10.5%, obtained as follows. The total value-added time was approximately 29,973 seconds. Assuming a total of 86,400 seconds in a day (24-hour operation), that equated to a value-added time of 0.35 days. The total elapsed time, from the moment that raw material was received from suppliers until the finished brake lining was delivered to the sales warehouse, was 3.34 days. This number included the 0.35 days of actual value-added time and an average of 2.99 days that the material spent waiting to be pulled (or pushed) between the various processes, before it ended up at the warehouse. Note that SBL is estimating the lead time based on the time the product spends within the four factory walls. The time the raw material waits in the warehouse before it is drawn into the shop floor and the time the product spends waiting in the sales warehouse (12 days as of April 2000) were not included in the VAR calculation. However, a VAR of 10.5%, based on the time raw material is drawn until the time product is delivered to the sales warehouse, is still impressive.

The Value Stream Map—November 2003

Not content with a VAR of 10.5%, the management at SBL continued to drive down the non-value-added time in the supply chain. First, a number of *kaizen* events were conducted at the Finishing process and at the processes upstream of the Finishing process. SBL next implemented *heijunka* (load leveling) and

---

1. The Value-Added Ratio is the ratio of the actual value-added work expressed in time units divided by the elapsed time for the process to complete.

mixed-model scheduling at the Finishing process to smooth production. Lean thinking was then leveraged beyond its factory walls to improve its raw material procurement, at the same time reducing the amount of raw material kept in inventory. Next, SBL implemented pull signals from its sales warehouse to initiate production in its shop floor, and also worked on demand smoothing. These efforts helped in reducing the number of days that the finished product spent in the sales warehouse, from 12 days to 6 days. Figure 7.2 presents the value stream map that resulted in November 2003 as a result of all these improvements.

Figure 7-2. Value Stream Map—November 2003

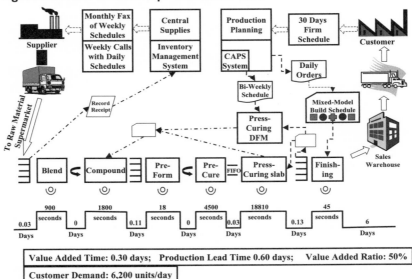

As Figure 7.2 indicates, these changes resulted in a dramatic reduction in non-value-added activities and increased the VAR to 50 percent. As noted in Figure 7.2, concurrent with these improvements, SBL grew its business from 4,560 units to 6,200 units per day. The following sections discuss, in more detail, how the various *kaizen* events were put through.

Creating Flow at the Finishing Process

The Finishing process receives material from the Press-curing process in the form of a long *slab* which is separated into individual brake linings by a sawing operation (the *slabsaw* operation). This is followed by some grinding operations and drilling operations. SBL had already put through a number of improvements in the Finishing process prior to April 2000. For instance, in 1997, the finishing line had seven operators as shown in the load chart in Figure 7.3a.

Figure 7-3. Load Chart for a Finishing Cell

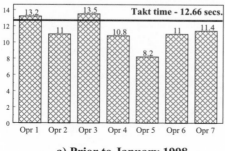

a) Prior to January 1998

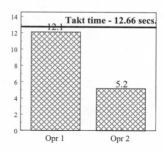

b) After May 2001

As shown in Figure 7.3a, the *takt* time at the Finishing cell was 12.66 seconds. The figure shows the operators were not level-loaded. In fact, some of the operators were loaded beyond the *takt* time. SBL worked on level-loading the operators and on *kaizen* events to reduce some of the wasteful activities the operators were performing. The *kaizen* events included automation of some drilling, grinding and the slabsaw operation, modification of existing layouts, redistribution of work elements, and introduction of *poka yoke* (mistake-proofing). With these improvements, SBL was able to reduce the number of operators in its finishing cell from seven to two by May 2001, as shown by the load chart in Figure 7.3b. With the increased demand of 6,200 units per day, the reduced *takt* time will require a redistribution of work among the operators.

Allocating work to the operators based on *takt* time implicitly assumes that the resources are completely reliable. SBL, like many other enterprises in the TVS Group, gives significant attention to Total Productive Maintenance (TPM) and equipment reliability issues. SBL recognizes the need to adhere to TPM practices to increase its productive capacity and decrease process variation. So, it has provided detailed charts and figures at each machine denoting the safety checks that should be made by the operators at the start and the end of each shift. The metal panels in some of the machines have been replaced by transparent plastic shields so that operators can observe whether the machine is receiving proper lubrication. The results of its efforts at TPM practice have been exemplary. As shown in Figure 7.4, there was a significant reduction in downtime from 2,100 minutes in April 2000, to 90 minutes in January 2004.

Figure 7-4. Reduction in Equipment DownTime

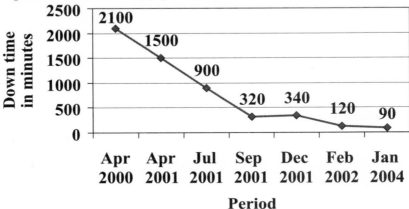

SBL worked on a number of other *kaizen* events at processes upstream of the Finishing process. Some of its improvement initiatives led to reduced setup times at the Pre-forming presses and drilling machines, and allowed some operations at other machines to be combined or integrated. Specifically, the *kaizen* events implemented were as follows:

- Creating flow in the pacemaker (Finishing process)
- Setup time reduction in Pre-forming presses
- Eliminating one Pre-forming press
- Slab cooling arrangement
- Establishing a supermarket
- Setup time reduction in drilling machine
- Integration of the chamfering operation
- On-line printing/packing
- Combining two drilling operations and eliminating one drilling machine

By effecting on-line printing and packing, SBL was able to integrate the Packing process with the Finishing process thereby eliminating the delay of 0.54 days between the Finishing and the Packing process steps. SBL next implemented a pull system from the Finishing process to trigger production at the upstream Press-curing process, and established a supermarket between the

Press-curing and Finishing process to supply material to the Finishing process as needed. SBL began to provide a daily mixed-model build schedule to the Finishing process that essentially pulled all processes in the facility. With these enhancements, the delay between the Press-curing and the Finishing process was reduced by 0.55 days (from 0.68 days down to 0.13 days). In sum, the amount of non-value-added activity eliminated totaled 0.54 + 0.55 = 1.09 days.

We will next discuss how SBL implemented the daily mixed-model build sequence. To do that, we first need to discuss a few concepts, specifically, *heijunka*, pacemaker, and the Spiderman.

Heijunka, the Pacemaker, and the Spiderman

One way to respond to customer demand without building a finished goods inventory is to use a load-leveling technique called *heijunka*. In a multi-product environment, this technique absorbs customer demand variation by dynamically managing the model-mix and production batch sizes. The concept is simple: Given the number of products to be produced in any given period, the goal is to produce them in suitably sized batches so that the variation on the workload at different resources is kept low. A *heijunka* application results in a repetitive production sequence for that scheduling period, which dictates the model-mix. It results in minimal inventories since the production system only produces items in response to customer demand during that period.

The *heijunka* technique is typically used to generate a mixed-model schedule at one operation along the production process, an operation referred to as the *pacemaker*. The pacemaker drives the entire production process. Because the pacemaker requires a high level of reliability, it is carefully maintained and managed. To ensure close adherence to *takt* time, the pacemaker should ideally have short changeover times to allow for frequent model changes to support a mixed-model production schedule. All the upstream processes are linked to the pacemaker through pull signals using *kanban* cards and supermarkets. All processing downstream of the pacemaker usually proceeds in a continuous flow. In essence, the rest of the processes fall in step with the pacemaker.

By releasing small amounts of work to the pacemaker at frequent intervals, we can create a sensitive indicator that signals whether there are production problems anywhere along the production process. This amount of work released is usually a multiple of *takt* time, referred to as the *pitch increment,* and this is typically linked to the basic unit of shipment. For instance, if the *takt* time is one minute and products are shipped to the customer in pallets of fifteen units each, then the pitch increment is fifteen minutes.

In practice, the pacemaker is driven by a *heijunka* box similar to that shown in Figure 7.5. The *heijunka* box is loaded by the production planning department according to the mixed-model build schedule. The example shown in Figure 7.5 only goes out to 10:00 a.m. but would generally cover the entire day. In this figure, the pitch increment is fifteen minutes. This is the frequency with which a *water spider* will come to the box, take whatever card or cards are in that time slot, withdraw the product type and the quantity specified on the *kanban* card in the box, and signal the appropriate process.

Figure 7-5. The Load-Leveling (*Heijunka*) Box

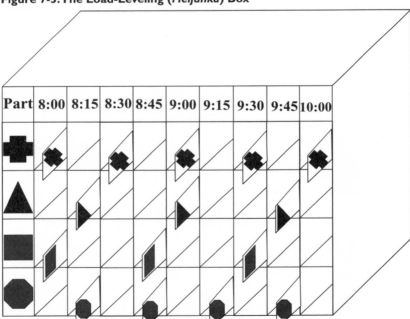

Water spiders are workers who service work locations with parts or materials. They replenish materials at point of use and deliver finished products to their destination. The water spiders enable the operators to focus their attention on operations that add value. Water spiders are assigned value-added and non-value-added (but necessary) tasks to provide the required support. The water spider is usually a jack-of-all-trades who stocks the line, fills in for an operator who needs to use the bathroom, or just helps out if an operator gets behind. Scheduling the pacemaker using the *heijunka* box may appear to be cumbersome since the *heijunka* box might be the size of a wall to allow for all the products needed; this could be one of the water spider's tasks. In SBL, the water spider is (humorously) referred to as the Spiderman. The Spiderman plays a key role in SBL's manufacturing process. SBL uses the Spiderman to stock the line and withdraw finished parts.

Implementing *Heijunka* at SBL

When SBL adopted *heijunka* to schedule its truck brake line in April 2000, it chose the Finishing process to be the pacemaker. The pacemaker was provided a mixed-model build sequence on a daily basis by the production department. SBL uses a Spiderman to deliver materials to the various processes as required and to help maintain the schedule cards. Figure 7.6 shows a Spiderman operating the *heijunka* box.

Figure 7-6. Load Leveling (*Heijunka*) Using the Spiderman

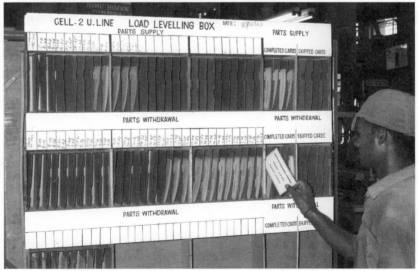

In SBL, the *heijunka* box paces the Finishing process, telling it when to change over to another product. It highlights non-adherence to each pitch increment. As shown in Figure 7.7, the Finishing operation is fed by the upstream Press-curing process through a supermarket, with the help of a Spiderman. The Spiderman issues parts at regular intervals, withdraws finished parts at regular intervals, raises an alarm if there is a shortfall, and helps with any course correction if needed.

Figure 7-7. Parts Supply and Withdrawal Using the Spiderman

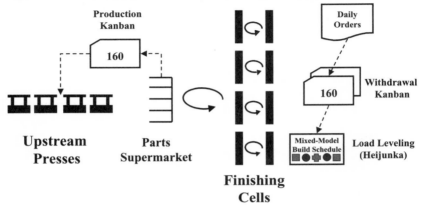

Improvements in Compounding and Raw Material Procurement

Just as the pull from Finishing triggers production at Press-curing, a pull from the Press-curing process triggers production at the Compounding process. A Spiderman assists with the Compounding process as well. At the Compounding process, a series of *kaizen* events were conducted which led to the following improvements:

- Layout improvements to eliminate operator walking
- Raw material bag weight reduction
- Raw material bag weight optimization to suit mix batch size
- Mix batch size modification to match raw material bag quantity
- Skids replaced by mobile trolleys to eliminate re-handling of bags.
- Bag weight decreased for four materials to reduce handling and fatigue of Spiderman.
- Visual control system introduced for raw material issue by the Spiderman.
- Side wall opened for easy transfer of recycled materials.

With the help of the Spiderman, the delay in transferring material between the Compounding and Pre-forming processes was reduced from 0.26 days down to 0.11 days. Additional enhancements subsequently reduced the non-value-added time at the Compounding process from 5,700 seconds down to 1,800 seconds. The use of the Spiderman allowed for more frequent issues of raw material to the Blending and Compounding processes, with the frequency increasing from once a day to once every 45 minutes. Combined with some layout modifications, the above events resulted in a significant reduction in raw material and work-in-process (WIP) inventory. The time the raw material spent, waiting to be picked up for blending and mixing, dropped from 1.33 days to 0.10 days. Figure 7.8 highlights the dramatic reduction in inventory in the mixing section.

Figure 7-8. Reduction in Inventory in Mixing Section

Before 2003   November 2003

The raw material inventory reduction is facilitated by an efficient milk run operation that delivers raw material from the suppliers to SBL every day. Figure 7.9 shows the daily milk run. Suppliers are contacted by telephone each day and advised what to supply the following day. By November 2003, SBL had improved its VAR from 10.5% to 50% within its factory walls and was in a better position to accommodate the increased demand of 6,200 brake linings per day.

Increased Responsiveness to Customer Demand

SBL next worked on improving responsiveness to customer demands. It identified the following steps for improving responsiveness:

- Agreeing on what customer really wants
- Understanding the customer ordering process
- Providing smooth flow
- Shifting from Push to Pull
- Continuing to reduce inventory

Figure 7-9. Daily Milk Run for Raw Material Requirements

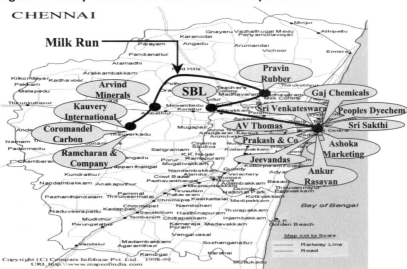

The shift from push to pull was effected at the sales warehouse where *kanban* cards are used to generate pull signals on the pacemaker process, as shown in Figure 7.10.

Figure 7-10. Introducing *Kanban* Cards at Sales Warehouse

a) Before (October 2002)   b) After (August 2003)

SBL is continuing to make efforts to understand the customer ordering process and to match actual end-user demand while at the same time maintaining low inventories. SBL is particularly interested in improving its market share in the after-market products, a market with high margins. The supply chain for the after-market products is long: SBL supplies products to the wholesaler who, in turn, supplies to dealers. The dealer sells the product to the end-user. Thus, whereas the OEM market demand is fairly stable, the orders for after-market products display the classic bullwhip effect. SBL continues to work on reducing non-value-added time in the post-production processes. These efforts are paying off. The time that products spend in the sales warehouse has now dropped from 12 days down to 6 days, as shown in Figure 7.2.

THEORY OF CONSTRAINTS AND LEAN THINKING AT THE MARINE CORPS MAINTENANCE CENTER, ALBANY, GEORGIA

The Maintenance Center at the Marine Corps Logistics Base, Albany, Georgia, is responsible for the regeneration and reconstitution of the equipment required by the Marine Corps for combat readiness. The Center undertakes complex maintenance operations that include rebuilding equipment to original manufacturer's specifications. It repairs and overhauls a wide variety of products that include small arms, amphibious vehicles, light armored vehicles, fuel tankers, trucks, earthmoving equipment, and logistics vehicle systems.

In 2001, the Maintenance Center was struggling to complete equipment repairs on time and was coping with an increasing backlog of work. Asking for "plus-ups" or additional time to complete the work, had become a normal way of doing business. For instance, on the MK-48 program, entailing overhaul of a heavy-duty hauler for the Marine Corps, the Center was only producing five units a month against a demand of ten per month. Customers were threatening to divert their orders to the private sector in search for better service.

At that time, scheduling of maintenance operations was based on a Manufacturing Resource Planning (MRP-II) system. This was a push system that loaded the resources at the Center based on anticipated customer demand. This was resulting in frequent rescheduling and expediting of critical items. The Center's management team reviewed alternate approaches to schedule production, and picked one that drew on principles prescribed by TOC. It contracted with Vector Strategies[2] to implement a *Critical Chain*[3] pilot project on the MK-48 vehicle. The Critical Chain is an application of TOC principles specifically tailored for managing complex projects like programs for the overhaul of several major pieces of equipment. The pilot project proved successful and the

2. *http://www.vectorstrategies.com*
3. E. M. Goldratt (1997), *Critical Chain*, North River Press, Great Barrington, MA.

Maintenance Center began implementation of the Critical Chain methodology plant-wide in April 2002. Used in conjunction with concepts drawn from lean thinking, this implementation has generated dramatic improvement in the Maintenance Center's performance.

The Critical Chain

In 1997, Goldratt introduced the Critical Chain methodology to apply TOC concepts to manage large projects. Program Evaluation and Review Technique (PERT) is probably the single most popular project management tool and it has been in use for decades. PERT provides the means for identifying the critical path, which is the major determinant of the project completion date since the critical path is the single longest chain of linked events embedded in the overall project. The Critical Chain methodology expands on the notion of a critical path and helps determine where buffers should be placed to prevent unplanned disruptions from delaying project completion.

Figure 7.11 illustrates the Critical Chain methodology. This figure represents a project that has four sets of activities that must be completed before a synchronization operation, represented by C4 in the figure, can be completed. The synchronization operation could be one of various operations. For instance, in a manufacturing setting it could be an assembly operation, and in a project management setting it could represent the commissioning operation.

The analyst uses historical data to obtain an estimate of the average time for each activity. These estimates are summed to obtain the average time it takes each series of activities that must be completed before the assembly operation can begin. Suppose an analysis reveals that the series of activities with the longest average time is C1-C2-C3. This determines the critical chain[4] that must be monitored the most closely since any slippage of these items will cause slippage of the overall project. The activities along the critical chain, namely, C1, C2, C3, and C4 are termed critical activities. Activities not on the critical chain are not critical items: They can slip some and not have the overall project slip because their completion takes less time than the completion of the critical chain.

---

4. We will use the lower case ("critical chain") to identify the set of activities that must be most closely monitored, and the upper case ("Critical Chain") to identify the methodology.

Figure 7-11. The Critical Chain Concept

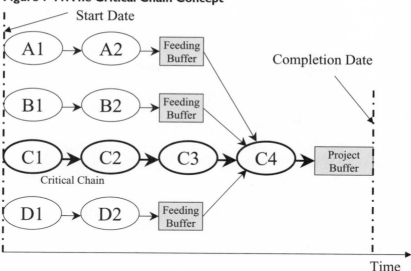

Time

Project Buffers, Feeding Buffers and Capacity Buffers

The estimate for the project duration (the lead time) is obtained as the sum of the average activity times for the critical activities plus a safety time, termed the Project Buffer. This buffers against any variation in the completion times of activities times along the critical chain. The Project Buffer is based on the variance of the total activity time. An overall measure of this variance is obtained simply by summing up the variance (the square of the standard deviation) for each activity.

In addition, for each non-critical activity that feeds a critical activity, a Feeding Buffer is placed between the non-critical activity and the critical activity, as illustrated in Figure 7.11. The Feeding Buffers are determined in a manner similar to the way the Project Buffer is calculated. It must be noted that the Project Buffer and the Feeding Buffers are *time buffers* and not inventory buffers. In essence, the time buffer increases the planning lead time from the absolute minimum value required to process the products to one which can accommodate disruptions that are likely to occur. With properly sized buffers, the activity along the critical chain that requires inputs from non-critical chain activities has a better chance of being able to start as soon as its predecessor task on the critical chain is complete. This means average throughput time should be reduced, and so less inventory is tied up in the system of activities overall.

Implementing the Critical Chain at the Maintenance Center

The overhaul process at the Center starts with the disassembly of each vehicle to determine its work scope, which is the amount and nature of the work to be done on that product. The work scope also indicates which parts can be repaired and which parts need to be replaced. Parts that require repair are routed through a series of support shops that include cleaning, blasting, painting, machining, body work, weapons work, and so on. Parts that need replacement are either replaced from existing spare-parts in stock or ordered from an external source. Some of these parts are difficult to procure if they are not in stock for various reasons, including obsolescence.

The MRP II Scheduling System

At the time the pilot project began, scheduling was based on an MRP II push system. Products were introduced into the shops without regard to the status of the resources dedicated to the repair activities. This led to false starts and delays, increased inventories, and lowered throughput. Another problem that the MRP II scheduling practice created was that it resulted in multitasking. Multitasking here refers to some projects (repair jobs) possibly needing activities that require a common resource (employee or machine). When these resources are required to attend to more than one project, the resources are moved between projects even before they complete all the processing on a given project and hand it over to the next activity in the sequence. As a result, each one of the projects involved tends to take more time than if they were completed one at a time from start to finish. The problem of multitasking at the Maintenance Center arose as follows: Given the perception that many units had to be disassembled to get parts for units in assembly, it was believed that disassembled parts should be sent immediately to the support shops to have as much time as possible to move through the repair cycle. Consequently, many of the resources were subject to multitasking. This is a problem that the Critical Chain is designed to address.

As a first step toward applying TOC, the Maintenance Center's management sought input from throughout the organization on where bottlenecks were believed to be a serious problem limiting output. Opinions varied as to what were and were not bottleneck activities, but every major activity in the Maintenance Center was believed to be an important bottleneck by at least someone in the facility.

In applying TOC to address the Mainteance Center's problems, the main shop where the main products were first disassembled and subsequently reassembled, and the support shops (e.g., cleaning, repair), were modeled as the Critical Chain. The Critical Chain analysis of the data collected revealed that, contrary to everyone's opinion, the facility had more than enough of capacity to carry out the activities required to meet the demand for repair and overhaul of ten MK-48s per month. The root cause of the consistent shortfalls and high inventory levels seemed to be the scheduling system in place that was pushing products out to the shop floor without regard for the status of the resources.

The bottleneck was, thus, not a physical resource constraint. Rather, it was a policy constraint introduced by the scheduling process. In fact, when it was analyzed in greater detail, this policy constraint was really a methods constraint; one based on scheduling using the MRP II system. If the material releases were properly timed, it was observed that the Center had ample capacity—the constraint was really *the market*. This discovery allowed Vector Strategies to use a *Simplified Drum-Buffer-Rope* (S-DBR) technique to model and schedule the activities in the shops that processed components removed from the main products.

The Simplified Drum-Buffer-Rope (S-DBR) Technique

The standard DBR model is a technique used to schedule all the resources based on the pace of the bottleneck, and we will discuss this technique in more detail in Chapter 8. For the moment, we simply observe that the standard DBR technique requires specialized software to implement it. However, when the enterprise has an MRP or an MRP II system in place and it is not constrained by any internal resource, an alternate technique known as the Simplified Drum-Buffer-Rope (S-DBR) model can be used. This was exactly the situation at the Maintenance Center. As observed earlier, they had discovered that the constraint was not an internal resource. Rather, the constraint was the market.

The S-DBR model has some advantages. It does not require any specialized software and this can be a significant benefit for enterprises that might be unwilling or unable to invest in specialized DBR software[5].

Results from the Implementation of Critical Chain and S-DBR

The Maintenance Center was able to use an S-DBR approach to scheduling in conjunction with the existing MRP II business system. Only the Critical Chain portion of their solution required additional software. The MRP II system facilitated the S-DBR schedules since the MRP II database already had stored data on lead times for items supplied by vendors.

Table 7.1 presents the results of implementing the Critical Chain on the MK-48 and the LAV-25. The LAV-25 was the second product on which the methodology was implemented. Table 7.1 presents the "Before" and "After" values for two key metrics measured at the Center: the repair cycle time (in days) and the ratio of WIP to monthly demand. The table also shows the ideal (minimum) values for these metrics based on a mathematical analysis using TOC and the Critical Chain. The ideal value for each metric is presented as "TOC/CC" in Table 7-1.

Table 7-1. Results on the MK-48 and LAV-25 Lines

	REPAIR CYCLE TIME (DAYS)			UNITS IN WIP/MONTHLY DEMAND		
Line	Before	TOC/CC	After	Before	TOC/CC	After
MK48	167	52	58	5.5	1.75	1.4
LAV-25	212	99	119	4.3	3.2	3.1

As Table 7.1 indicates, repair cycle times for the MK-48 were reduced by a factor of three, from an average of 167 days to an average of 58 days. For the LAV-25, the corresponding figures were 212 days and 119 days, before and after. The WIP levels (relative to demand) were reduced significantly, as shown in the table. Other products showed similar reductions in cycle times and WIP.

---

5. E. Schragenheim and H. W. Dettmer (2000), *Manufacturing at Warp Speed: Optimizing Supply Chain Financial Performance*, CRC Press, Boca Raton, FL.

The cost to repair products went down by 25 to 30% mainly because the reduction in delays resulted in more throughput without any increase in the cost of repair. All the product lines were 99% on schedule to customer requirements. Figure 7.12 shows the increase in output realized on the MK-48 line. The capacity for the MK-48 line was now more flexible and could work with a rate of anywhere between ten units per month to as high as 23 units per month, as indicated by the figure.

Figure 7-12. MK-48 Monthly Output

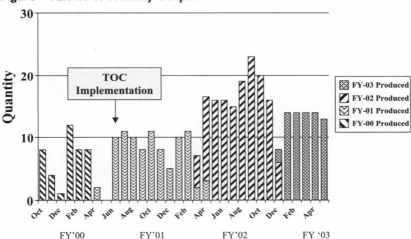

Combining Lean Thinking and TOC at the Maintenance Center

At the Maintenance Center, a corporate plan was developed for implementation of lean thinking and a lean team was set up. Some of the results of the lean efforts resulted in the Maintenance Center being subject to a *6S* activity (many enterprises add a sixth S for Safety) and a reengineering of the supply warehouse. The *6S* activity resulted in a significant increase in available shop floor space. Hundreds of man-hours associated with the testing and repair of cables on the AAV and LAV family of vehicles were saved. Tools in excess of $200,000 were turned in for redistribution and future use. The process flows in production work centers were streamlined. Another major benefit from the convergence of lean thinking and TOC was that it resulted in increased morale for the employees of the Maintenance Center. The workplace is cleaner, less cluttered, and safer. The Maintenance Center has become more flexible and better positioned to meet its responsibilities for regeneration and reconstitution of critical supplies.

Managing an MRO facility is a more challenging task than managing most manufacturing facilities because of the high degree of uncertainty that prevails in repair operations. Unlike a typical flow shop manufacturing setting where the enterprise knows the sequence of operations required to complete the finished product, the MRO facility is much like a pure job shop facility. In the MRO facility, the work scope of a product that arrives at the facility is not known unless the product is disassembled and inspected. The work scope varies greatly even for the same product, such as the MK-48. It is difficult to predict the percentage of parts that must be replaced and the percentage of parts that should be repaired. To add to the complexity, the original manufacturer may no longer produce the parts that have to be replaced.

The magnitude of culture change was greatest in the support shops through which disassembled parts were routed for repair. Holding disassembled parts for release caused great fear among the workforce, and resistance was substantial. This aspect of the implementation was the last part of the culture change accepted and accomplished by the Maintenance Center. But as they saw significant improvement with every other aspect of the implementation, they gained the courage to move forward.

The work carried out to date has made the Maintenance Center a showcase of world-class overhaul and repair performance. Weekly tours are conducted, hosting officers and executives from government and private overhaul and repair operations. The Maintenance Center's web site and monthly reports prominently features TOC and lean applications.

Managing the Lean
Supply Chain

8

Creating Flow through the Supply Chain

"Just let go, let it flow, let it flow, let it flow, Everything's gonna work out right ya know"
– Toni Braxton

Have you ever visited a facility where a manager enthusiastically shows you a lean cell, a cell that puts out products at an extremely rapid pace, with minimal delays between operations? At the same time, you may have observed that the products flowing out of the cell create a pocket of work-in-process (WIP) or finished goods inventory that waits for a long time before it moves downstream. By creating a lean cell, the manager has eliminated some waste from the system. However, his actions have not created a smooth flow of products across the enterprise. Unless the products are delivered to the customer at the same rate at which the cell operates, all that the manager has done is create an island of excellence that, at best, serves as a showcase for visitors.

In a larger context, the situation portrayed above is similar to a situation where one of the enterprises in the supply chain is extremely efficient, processing products with minimal delays. However, if these products end up as finished goods that wait for a long time before the customer picks them up or they end up at the customer's facility as raw material that the customer does not intend to use right away, then the enterprise has only created inventory in the supply chain.

We have emphasized repeatedly that the focus in the supply chain should be on reducing lead times. The lead time is directly affected by the rate at which the product flows through the supply chain. Long lead times are symptomatic of poor flow and, conversely, the lack of flow results in long lead times. Reduced lead times and improved flow go hand in hand, creating a virtuous cycle. Therefore, the supply chain managers should focus on reducing lead times and improving flow. That will allow the supply chain to have higher throughput with lower inventories and allow it to respond flexibly to changing customer preferences.

This chapter develops some principles for improving flow through the supply chain. We will build on some of the concepts and principles presented in the previous three chapters. We will show how lean thinking and the Theory of Constraints (TOC) can work together to create flow. Following that, we present a simple example of a clinic that treats patients. We use this example to develop three lean supply chain principles that relate to creating flow in the system, especially in the presence of variation. For clarity, the principles developed in this chapter are obtained through an example presented at the enterprise level, rather than at the supply chain level. However, these principles apply directly to the management of supply chains.

TOC AND LEAN THINKING CAN WORK TOGETHER TO CREATE FLOW

The chapter on lean thinking presented tools and techniques that enterprises can use to create flow by removing waste and reducing lead times. The chapter on Systems Thinking and the Theory of Constraints developed a systematic methodology that identified the system constraints that inhibit flow and/or prevent the system from generating more profit and then prescribed steps for managing these constraints. We begin by comparing lean thinking and TOC to show how they complement each other. Next, we discuss how we can exploit the synergy between these two philosophies to help create flow across the lean supply chain.

Comparing TOC and Lean Thinking Philosophies

Lean thinking and TOC have the goal of reducing the lead time from the instant an order is received until it is shipped to the customer (and payment is received). Both philosophies address the need for enterprises and supply chains to remain competitive through a process of ongoing improvement, albeit in different ways. Lean thinking emphasizes continuous improvement and the pursuit of perfection to create and maintain flow across the enterprise or supply chain, while TOC presents a five-step focusing process to enhance the throughput objective of the supply chain.

Both philosophies promote the notion of continuous flow, and they attack the batch-and-queue method of production. Both work on surfacing hidden capacity and minimizing all types of inventory, especially WIP and finished goods inventory. To that end, both philosophies emphasize pull production although the exact manner of implementing pull may differ. Lean thinking would emphasize *kanban* pull signals whereas TOC would probably emphasize a model that reacts to pull signals from the bottleneck (a "pull-from-the-bottleneck" model). However, this is a relatively minor difference, one that would matter only to the diehard lean thinking proponent or the diehard TOC proponent.

There are some differences in the philosophies. A key difference in perspective relates to how *muda* (waste) is eliminated. The lean thinking purist would attempt to remove all forms of waste. The TOC purist would argue that such efforts might dilute or diffuse the efforts of the enterprise. That is, while eliminating *muda* is fine, the supply chain should focus its efforts on removing any wasteful activities only at the bottlenecks.

The TOC purist's arguments have some validity. In the effort to remove *muda* everywhere in the system, there is a danger that a cost world bias may dictate some decisions. For example, if an enterprise attempts to build a balanced production line, one in which all the resources are loaded close to the *takt* time, any excess capacity may be considered waste and could be a candidate for elimination. We will shortly use a simple example to show that focusing on balancing the capacities of all resources will limit the potential of the system when variation is present. The focus should instead be on balancing flow, not capacity. Thus, the TOC purist may not even attempt to remove excess capacity at non-bottleneck resources since these resources currently have some protective capacity; removing excess capacity would make them capacity constraints as well. In other words, the purist would argue that TOC and lean are in direct conflict here because what lean considers as *muda* would be considered as something TOC would deem important to maintain.

On the other hand, the argument that the focus should only be on removing waste at bottleneck resources could result in missed opportunities. As explicated by Parkinson's Law, "Work expands to fill the time available for its completion."[1] Over time, the amount of *muda* that builds up at non-bottleneck resources may easily go

---

1. C. N. Parkinson (1987), *Parkinson's Law*, Ballantine Books; Reissue edition, New York, NY (April 12, 1987).

unrecognized unless it is periodically monitored. A lean effort may thus free up resources from non-bottleneck operations that could well be redeployed to assist the bottleneck operations and, thereby, generate more throughput.

Many lean practitioners have recognized that the bottleneck resource is the first candidate to be considered for improvement. These practitioners are recognizing that attempts to reduce process time variation should first be directed at the bottleneck resource, followed by attempts to reduce process time variation at non-bottleneck resources (that have the least protective capacity). In other words, they are subscribing to the principle of balancing flow and not capacity. Even as many lean practitioners are following this principle, likewise, more TOC practitioners are starting to use many of the lean tools for improvement efforts that, at first glance, only have a local impact.

While both philosophies advocate reducing the variation that causes inventories to exist, another major difference between the two philosophies is that the TOC purist will leave inventory buffers in place until the variability is removed or reduced. On the other hand, the diehard lean proponent would first remove the inventory so it exposes the problems that cause such variation and then would attack these problems.

Exploiting the Synergy between TOC and Lean Thinking to Create Flow

Moore and Scheinkopf[2] suggest that it is possible to exploit the synergy between TOC and Lean to create flow, capturing the best of both worlds by adopting a framework based on the Five-Step Focusing Process covered in Chapter 6, as follows:

- **Adopt a throughput world perspective.** It is much easier to promote a growth model than a model that has the goal of cost cutting. The latter goal will encounter considerable resistance from employees fearful about losing their jobs.
- **Define the system (to be improved), its purpose, and the measures to be used.** Start with the system that is within your control – gain internal control before trying to change or control customers and/or suppliers. By gaining control within the enterprise, credibility needed to influence customers and suppliers is gained.

---

2. R. Moore and L. Scheinkopf (1998), "Theory of Constraints and Lean Manufacturing: Friends or Foes?" Chesapeake Consulting, Inc.

- **Identify the system's constraint.** Map the value stream as suggested by lean thinking. The current process flow map will reveal *muda* that can be quickly eliminated; the intent here is not to reduce cost but rather to reduce the number of dependencies quickly and increase protective capacity. A *kaikaku* approach, as suggested by lean thinking, can be applied at this stage.
- **Decide how to exploit the system's constraint.** This step is an ideal step for applying lean techniques. The system's constraint is a resource that limits the output of the entire system. Identify the root cause for why the constraint is limiting throughput and look for ways to implement *kaizen* and/or *kaikaku* events that will free up capacity at the constraint or remove variability at the constraint. Is there *muda* associated with setups? Is there *muda* associated with skilled laborers being diverted to performing tasks that an unskilled worker could perform? It is often useful to establish a throughput per hour value for constraint operations. Is the constraint being used to generate the best throughput possible or should it be deployed on other products? Would employing another employee help improve throughput, even if this employee is underutilized?
- **Subordinate to the system's constraint.** The concept of subordination applies to lean and TOC. In TOC, the drum-buffer-rope (DBR) system limits the release of material into the system, just as the *kanban* system in lean does. A number of support activities should be subordinated to the constraint operation as well. For instance, if the constraint goes down, then plant maintenance should immediately attend to the constraint even if it means setting aside unfinished work on a non-constraint. The quality control personnel should focus on inspecting any item before it is worked upon by the constraint because the constraint should never have to work on an item that is defective. Engineering design should focus their efforts on improving tooling and fixtures at the constraint, and so on.
- **Elevate the constraint.** This step should, as prescribed by the Five-Step Focusing Process, be undertaken only after the exploit step. The exploit step is often sufficient to remove internal constraints and avoids having to buy additional equipment or employing additional resources. Quite often, the exploit and subordinate steps increase the capacity of the constraint by a significant amount. Like TOC, lean also emphasizes capital avoidance. Even if additional capital resources are needed, the equipment does not have to be new.
- **Avoid inertia. Identify the next constraint if a constraint is broken.** Enterprises always have at least one physical constraint or a market constraint (not to mention policy constraints). As

soon as one constraint is broken, another one will surface somewhere in the enterprise. Awareness of this fact will help maintain the process of improvement as an ongoing effort.

CREATING FLOW: THE IMPACT OF VARIABILITY AND DEPENDENCY

Two factors that significantly affect flow are variability and dependency. Variability seriously affects flow, yet this is an often neglected or overlooked factor in the design of product delivery systems. Many enterprises design their work flow assuming a deterministic scenario. That is, they design their processes assuming that everything will function according to plan. As we all know, processes do not function that way for a number of reasons. Customer orders get cancelled; operators are absent; machines break down; tools required to perform a specific operation are not available when needed; the logistics provider is delayed by a traffic backup; the supplier's deliveries are affected by a strike, etc. If the enterprises run these resources at high levels of utilization, the presence of variation will lead to large queues that build up in front of these resources.

Dependent events, too, are pervasive. For instance, Sales cannot provide a quote to the customer until Engineering has reviewed the desired specifications; the customer order cannot be placed unless a quote is presented; the product and process must be developed by Engineering before it can be handed over to Operations; funds must be available before supplies can be ordered; Operations cannot begin work on the product unless the suppliers have delivered raw material; the order cannot be shipped till the logistics provider arrives and so on. Although dependencies are pervasive, they are typically assumed away during the system design phase, and the various activities, events and processes involved in the delivery of the product are often designed and developed in isolation. Complex tasks are broken down into a large number of simpler tasks and managers focus on optimizing these simpler tasks adopting the classical local optimization stance. With no variability in the system such an approach could possibly achieve the global optimum. However, in the presence of variation, efforts to optimize dependent activities in isolation typically fail to produce desired results.

The Youngsville Clinic

To motivate the discussion, we consider a health care enterprise that has leased a clinic in Youngsville, NY, to test patients for cardiac care. The clinic specializes in a test that determines the flow of blood through the heart muscles. The test involves three steps: preparing the patient by administering a small dose of a nuclear medicine (Prep), a stress test involving a treadmill exercise (Test), and a monitoring of the patient after the stress test during which a series of pictures of the heart are taken (Monitor). The Test activity takes an average of 60 minutes per patient and this activity must be administered by a physician. The Test activity should begin no later than one hour after the Prep activity is completed otherwise the effects of the nuclear medicine will wear off and render the test useless. Similarly, the Monitor activity should begin no later than one hour after the Test activity is completed.

The enterprise has hired the services of a physician to work 8 hours a day from 8:00 a.m. to 4:00 p.m., at a rate of $750 per hour. The physician is willing to work one extra hour each day on overtime if necessary, at a rate of $1,500 per hour. The Prep and Monitor activities each average 28 minutes per patient. The enterprise has hired two lab technicians for these activities, paying each of them at a rate of $120 per hour. The overtime rate for a lab technician is $240 per hour if the technician works more than 8 hours on a given a day. Figure 8.1 represents this process graphically. The lease on the clinic costs the enterprise $2,000 per day, including the cost of equipment, utilities, etc. The cost of supplies is $200 per day.

Figure 8-1. A Clinical Process with Three Activities

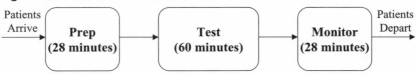

The enterprise charges $2,500 for each patient treated. For simplicity, we assume a big demand exists for the services provided by this clinic. So, the more patients that the clinic can serve, the more revenue it will generate. We will assume that patients in

Youngsville arrive at the scheduled time and that the Prep activity can be started on a patient immediately upon arrival. How many patients can the clinic service every day, and what is the resulting profit?

To answer this question, let us first assume all activity times are constant. The physician is the bottleneck that determines the throughput. The physician is required to test each patient for 60 minutes, whereas each lab technician works with a patient for 28 minutes. Since the physician works for 8 hours a day and the Test activity takes 1 hour, the Youngsville clinic should be able to service up to eight patients every day. However, there are some scheduling issues to consider. The three activities, Prep, Test, and Monitor, are dependent activities: a specific sequence of steps are required to complete the process. So, the approach would be to schedule patient arrivals and the work for the lab technicians in such a way that the physician never has to wait to test the next patient. The following lean supply chain principle articulates this approach.

LEAN SUPPLY CHAIN PRINCIPLE 12

Focus on bottleneck resources because they control the flow. Synchronize flow by first scheduling the bottleneck resources on the most productive products; then schedule non-bottleneck resources to support the bottleneck resources.

This principle is in line with steps 2 and 3 of the Five-Step Focusing Process covered in Chapter 6, which asks us to exploit the constraint and then subordinate everything else to this decision. If we follow this principle, we can schedule eight patients per day. We will schedule the lab technician who performs the Prep activity to start work at 7:30 a.m. That will allow the physician to see the first patient at 8 a.m. Thereafter, the physician can test patients exactly every hour, with the last test starting at 3:00 p.m. For ease of presentation, we will assume the physician and lab technicians can take short bio breaks as well as a lunch break while the patient is being treated. Table 8.1 presents the schedule for the deterministic scenario.

With this schedule, the lab technician who performs the Prep activity works from 7:30 a.m. to 3:00 p.m. for a total of 7.5 hours a day. The lab technician performing the Monitor activity also works for 7.5 hours, from 9:00 a.m. to 4:30 p.m. every day. The total daily expense of operating the clinic is $10,000 and this includes the physician's charge of $6,000 ($750 per hour for 8 hours), the $1,800 in wages paid to the two lab technicians (two technicians at

$120 per hour for 7.5 hours), the lease charge of $2,000, and the cost of supplies of $200. The revenue from treating eight patients is $2,500 x 8 = $20,000. The net profit is $10,000 per day.

Table 8-1. Schedule of Visits to the Clinic: Constant Activity Times

PATIENT	ARRIVAL TIME	"PREP"		"TEST"		"MONITOR"	
		Start	Finish	Start	Finish	Start	Finish
I	7:30	7:30	7:58	8:00	9:00	9:00	9:28
2	8:30	8:30	8:58	9:00	10:00	10:00	10:28
3	9:30	9:30	9:58	10:00	11:00	11:00	11:28
4	10:30	10:30	10:58	11:00	12:00	12:00	12:28
5	11:30	11:30	11:58	12:00	1:00	1:00	1:28
6	12:30	12:30	12:58	1:00	2:00	2:00	2:28
7	1:30	1:30	1:58	2:00	3:00	3:00	3:28
8	2:30	2:30	2:58	3:00	4:00	4:00	4:28

The workload, though, is highly unbalanced. The lab technicians are only utilized 28 minutes in a 60-minute cycle, whereas the physician is utilized 100% from 8:00 a.m. to 4 p.m. Suppose management wants to cut costs (improve profits) and decides to work with just one lab technician. By working with one lab technician, the workload is more balanced since the one remaining lab technician is now occupied for 56 minutes in a 60-minute cycle.

The only apparent challenge is to schedule the lab technician so this person can carry out the Prep and Monitor activities without delaying the physician. In our example, the scheduling is easily accomplished as follows. Instead of having the lab technician complete the Prep and Monitor on patient 1 before starting the Prep on patient 2, the technician completes the Prep on patients 1 and 2 before beginning the Monitor activity on patient 1. Thereafter, the lab technician always performs the Prep activity on patient $n+1$ before performing the Monitor activity on patient n. As seen from Table 8.1, this simple trick allows the clinic to work with one lab technician without any problem, when activity times are deterministic.

The lab technician now works for nine hours a day from 7:30 a.m. to 4:30 p.m. He is paid $1,200 per day (8 hours worked on regular time at $120 per hour plus $240 for an hour worked on overtime). Since the clinic was formerly paying the two lab technicians a total of $1,800 per day, it is now saving $600 every day. The other expenses remain the same so the total expense drops from $10,000 to $9,400 per day. Hence, the profit for the Youngsville clinic increases from $10,000 per day to $10,600 per day.

The Impact of Variation

As you are reading this, you are probably thinking that such a deterministic situation is highly unlikely even with scheduled patient arrivals because there will be some variation in the activity times. Let us consider a more realistic situation with variation in the activity times. To keep it simple, we will continue to assume that the patients arrive at their scheduled times. In other words, we assume that arrival times are still deterministic, with a patient arriving every 60 minutes, starting at 7:30 a.m. Assume that the Prep and Monitor activities each take 20 minutes for 50% of the patients, and 36 minutes for 50% of the patients. (The average Prep and Monitor activity times are still 28 minutes.) Assume, too, that the Test activity takes 50 minutes or 70 minutes, each with probability 0.50. Figure 8.2 shows the distribution of these activity times.

Figure 8-2. Distribution of Activity Times for the Clinic

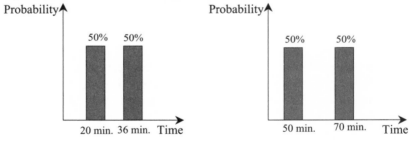

Distribution of Activity Times
for Prep and Monitor

Distribution of Activity Time
for Test

While the physician and the lab technician still have sufficient capacity to complete their activities in isolation, the dependency between the activities in the presence of variation makes scheduling much harder than in the deterministic case. Table 8.2 presents the actual realization of activity times for eight patients scheduled on a given day. How can we effectively schedule the physician and the lab technician? And can the physician still complete eight patients a day by 4 p.m.?

Table 8-2. Actual Realization of Activity Times on a Given Day

PATIENT	"PREP"	"TEST"	"MONITOR"
1	36 minutes	70 minutes	36 minutes
2	36 minutes	50 minutes	36 minutes
3	36 minutes	70 minutes	36 minutes
4	36 minutes	50 minutes	36 minutes
5	20 minutes	70 minutes	20 minutes
6	20 minutes	50 minutes	20 minutes
7	20 minutes	70 minutes	20 minutes
8	20 minutes	50 minutes	20 minutes

As before, the physician is the bottleneck and the more expensive resource. So, the clinic wishes to schedule the lab technician so it keeps the physician utilized as much as possible. Table 8.3 presents a schedule that keeps the physician occupied as much as possible and schedules the activities of the lab technician accordingly. At the same time, the developed schedule ensures that the elapsed time between the completion of one activity and the start of the next activity on a patient never exceeds one hour as stipulated. This schedule is based on full knowledge of activity times for all patients and that helps us generate a good schedule. Of course, we usually do not know the activity times in advance, so the schedule that would have unfolded in practice would have been much worse than that presented in Table 8.3.

Table 8-3. Schedule for Variable Activity Times—One Lab Technician

PATIENT	ARRIVAL TIME	"PREP"		"TEST"		"MONITOR"	
		Start	Finish	Start	Finish	Start	Finish
1	7:30	7:30	8:06	8:06	9:16	9:16	9:52
2	8:30	8:30	9:06	9:16	10:06	11:06	11:42
3	9:30	9:52	10:28	10:28	11:38	12:02	12:38
4	10:30	10:30	11:06	11:38	12:28	12:58	1:34
5	11:30	11:42	12:02	12:28	1:38	1:38	1:58
6	12:30	12:38	12:58	1:38	2:28	2:28	2:48
7	1:30	1:54	2:14	2:28	3:38	3:38	3:58
8	2:30	2:48	3:08	3:38	4:28	4:28	4:48

With this schedule, the physician and the lab technician are forced to work overtime. The physician works overtime for 28 minutes and the lab technician works overtime for 78 minutes (since he came in at 7:30 a.m., he completes 8 hours of work at 3:30 p.m.). The total wages paid to the physician is $6,700 (for 8 hours at $750 per hour on regular time plus 28 minutes on overtime at $1,500 per hour). The total wages paid to the lab technician is $1,272 (for 8 hours at $120 per hour on regular time plus 78 minutes on overtime at $240 per hour). The lease charge is $2,000 and the cost of supplies is $200. The total expense incurred by the Youngsville clinic this day is $10,172. The revenue is $20,000 (eight patients at a charge of $2,500 per patient), so the net profit for this day is 9,828 dollars.

The schedule provided by Table 8.3 raises a number of issues for discussion. It shows that variability and dependency can cause significant degradation of performance. The degradation was observed even with no variation in the demand because patient arrivals were assumed to be completely deterministic. While the first patient did not have to wait for any time between activities, the second patient waited a total of 70 minutes (10 minutes between Prep and Test; 60 minutes between Test and Monitor), the third patient waited 66 minutes, and so on. The combined waiting time, across all eight patients was 336 minutes resulting in an average waiting time of 42 minutes per patient. Furthermore, the flow of patients through the system was quite uneven. Even though patients arrived every 60 minutes, nearly two hours elapsed between the time the first patient left the clinic and the time the second patient left the clinic. The elapsed time between the departure of the fourth and fifth patients was only 24 minutes. Why was there uneven flow (and large lead times)? Was it due to factors beyond management control?

The variation in the activity times caused lead times to increase. However, the main reason for the uneven flow is because management decided to operate in the cost world and attempted to balance the capacities of the two resources involved in delivering health care: the physician and the lab technician(s). By so doing, they had loaded both resources close to 100%.

This situation is similar to one we discussed in Chapter 6, where we drew an analogy between a set of processes and a chain. Suppose that a chain consists of ten links and one of them is the weak link (the bottleneck). The ability of the chain to pull or lift objects is limited by the weakest link. The throughput world will focus on strengthening the link. Suppose, instead, that management is working in the cost world: It is unhappy with the cost of maintaining nine strong links, and "right-sizes" the chain by selling the nine heavy links and replacing them with nine links that have the same capacity as the weakest link. On first glance, this is an efficient chain since every link is capable of carrying the same load. What is the problem here? The problem is that there are now ten weak links, any one of which can break.

As a result of the action we undertook with a cost world perspective in our hospital clinic example, not only is the physician a bottleneck but the lab technician is close to becoming a bottleneck. The result is that there is no wiggle room to accommodate any variation or schedule disruptions.

Yes, the goal is to ensure all resources work at the same pace and, no doubt, that pace is dictated by the bottleneck resource, which is the physician in this example. However, we want the products (the patients in this example) to flow as smoothly as possible.

Let us assume that we are unable to eliminate the variation. What would improve flow in this example? Suppose we had stayed with two lab technicians. In that case, scheduling would have been simpler and the experience for the customer would have been much better. Table 8.4 presents the schedule that would have developed if we had, instead, stayed with two lab technicians.

Table 8-4. Schedule for Variable Activity Times—Two Lab Technicians

PATIENT	ARRIVAL TIME	"PREP"		"TEST"		"MONITOR"	
		Start	Finish	Start	Finish	Start	Finish
1	7:30	7:30	8:06	8:06	9:16	9:16	9:52
2	8:30	8:30	9:06	9:16	10:06	10:06	10:42
3	9:30	9:30	10:06	10:06	11:16	11:16	11:52
4	10:30	10:30	11:06	11:16	12:06	12:06	12:42
5	11:30	11:30	11:50	12:06	1:16	1:16	1:36
6	12:30	12:30	12:50	1:16	2:06	2:06	2:26
7	1:30	1:30	1:50	2:06	3:16	3:16	3:36
8	2:30	2:30	2:50	3:16	4:06	4:06	4:26

With this schedule, the physician works overtime only for 6 minutes. The lab technicians each work at most 7.5 hours without incurring overtime. The total wages paid to the physician is $6,150 (for 8 hours at $750 per hour on regular time plus 6 minutes on overtime at $1,500 per hour). The total wages paid to the two lab technicians is $1,800 (two people for 7.5 hours at $120 per hour on regular time). The lease charge is $2,000 and the cost of supplies is

200 dollars. The total expense for this day is 10,150 dollars. Since the revenue is $20,000, the Youngsville clinic makes a net profit of $9,850 for the day. Thus the profit increases when the clinic re-employs the second lab technician. In addition, with two lab technicians the average waiting time per patient drops from 42 minutes down to 13 minutes. Furthermore, there is a steady flow of patients departing from the clinic. In summary, instead of working in the cost world to balance capacities, by hiring an additional lab technician and focusing on throughput, the clinic was able to do the following:

- Create a smooth flow of patients through the system
- Reduce the waiting time for patients
- Increase profits in this example (albeit by a small amount).

The next lean supply chain principle summarizes the learning from the clinic example:

LEAN SUPPLY CHAIN PRINCIPLE 13

Do not focus on balancing capacities. Focus on synchronizing the flow.

The objective is not one of balancing capacities or improving the utilization of all equipment and human resources. The objective is to synchronize flow so we move products (or customers) through the enterprise as smoothly and quickly as possible. By operating in the cost world, the clinic no doubt saved on the salary paid to one lab technician. However, it created a scheduling nightmare for the clinic, resulted in unhappy customers, and worked the physician and the lab technician overtime. In general, with a set of dependent activities and more than one of the resources operating close to 100%, we can experience serious interference and congestion in the system, especially if processing times are variable.

Even for this small example with two resources, we saw the disruptive effect of variation in the system. A number of important measures of system performance, such as lead time, WIP, and flow are affected by variation. In Chapter 2, we said that Taiichi Ohno is believed to have stated that "Inventory is the root of all evil." A more precise statement is "Variation is the root of all evil" since variation causes inventory buildup. Our last lean supply chain principle summarizes the effects of variation.

LEAN SUPPLY CHAIN PRINCIPLE 14

Reduce variation in the system. Reduced variation allows the supply chain to generate higher throughput with lower inventory and lower operating expense.

The clinic example shows us how lean thinking and TOC can work in concert to obtain better flow and increased throughput velocity. With its systems perspective, the TOC Five-Step Focusing Process can first be applied to leverage/exploit the bottleneck. For instance, the questions one may ask are: Can the average Test activity time be reduced through improved technology/equipment? Can the physician offload some of the activity time to a technician? Can we address the variability in test times using lean thinking (perhaps in conjunction with techniques such as Six Sigma)? Lean thinking can also address the variability in the Prep and Monitor activities and work on removing any wasteful activities performed by the physician and the lab technician(s).

What are some steps enterprises can take to minimize the impact of variation? In the following sections, we will discuss two specific ways enterprises can reduce variability in the system and improve flow. As we observed in Chapter 2, when products are produced and shipped in large batches it produces a bullwhip effect, which increases variation in the supply chain and significantly impedes flow. So, we first consider setup time and batch size tradeoffs. Next, we discuss how to reduce variation and enhance flow through pull systems, and present several methods for implementing pull. We present a simulation called the Dice Game that shows how you can manage a production line much more effectively using pull systems. We conclude the chapter with a discussion on why pull systems have an inherent ability to reduce system variation.

THE IMPACT OF BATCH SIZE ON FLOW

Until now, we have not considered the impact of set-up times on the smooth flow of products through the enterprise. It is difficult to overestimate the importance of set-up times because they affect batch sizes. No doubt lean thinking aims at reducing set-up times. However, in many cases set-ups simply cannot be eliminated. When set-up times become significant, they usually drive many enterprises to make wrong batch-sizing decisions. For instance, the manager is driven to consider building products using a variant of the economic order quantity (EOQ) formula.

The rationale behind the EOQ formula is one of local optimization. When batch sizes are large, we have few setups and incur less set-up cost. However, with fewer setups we end up carrying a lot of inventory, resulting in high inventory holding costs. Conversely, when we produce in small batch sizes, we incur more set-up costs but incur less inventory holding costs. The EOQ formula is used to compute a batch size that optimizes the sum of the set-up costs plus the inventory holding costs.

Too often, rules such as those prescribed by the EOQ formula only divert our attention from the enterprise objective of creating flow. They tend to force managers to work around the problem rather than work through the problem. For instance, the EOQ formula assumes the set-up costs are given. The manager may blindly accept the set-up times or costs as given and not consider the fact that setups could be reduced, perhaps by significant amounts. The EOQ formula can thus result in inventory decisions that almost always err on the high side; that is, it usually results in batch sizes that are larger than necessary. As a consequence, the inventory levels are higher as are lead times and operating expenses.

Cost-based batch-sizing decisions result in local optima that may be suboptimal for the enterprise as a whole. Producing in large batch sizes increases the variation in the system, exacerbating the bullwhip effect as we pointed out earlier. Even within the enterprise, large batch sizes create unnecessary work stops and starts as products move through the enterprise in large batches. Batch-sizing decisions must therefore be made in the context of what is best for the performance of the enterprise or the supply chain as a whole. These decisions must consider the synchronous flow of the products through the enterprise or supply chain. That raises a potential problem. In many situations, there may be some compelling reasons for producing products in relatively large batches. What can the enterprise or supply chain do to work with such constraints? To answer this question, it is necessary to distinguish two types of batches, the process batch and the transfer batch.

Process Batch versus Transfer Batch

In a dedicated assembly line that produces a single product, what is the batch size? The process batch size is the size of the entire production run, which is a large number. However, to keep the product flowing, we will probably not wait till the assembly line finishes all the parts in the process batch. Rather we will move the products forward as soon as they leave the assembly line. From the product's perspective, each unit processed is moved individually, so that the batch size appears to be just one. This is the *transfer batch* size. We introduced the notion of a transfer batch in Chapter 5 when we discussed one-piece flow. By definition, one-piece flow relates to moving products one at a time between workstations. In other words, it relates to a transfer batch of size one. (*One* could even refer to one pallet.) Formally, the definition of process batch and transfer batch are as follows:

- Process batch is the quantity of a product processed at a resource before the resource is set up to make another product.
- Transfer batch is the number of units moved at a time, from one resource to the next.

Differentiating between the process batch and the transfer batch makes it convenient to promote flow even when the resources are forced to produce in large batch sizes. Ideally, the process batch at non-bottleneck resources should be kept as small as possible to keep the flow of materials smooth and balanced. However, when there are set-up times involved at the non-bottleneck resources, we should take care that the setups at these non-bottlenecks do not cause them to become constraints. At bottleneck resources that have significant set-up times, the process batch will generally be larger. In such cases, it is still possible to have a smooth flow with small transfer batches.

However, instances will occur where a transfer batch of size one is not possible or is impractical. For instance, as we discussed in Chapter 5, if the upstream process is a heat-treatment operation that has to produce a batch at a time, moving these parts one at a time once they come out of the furnace may not be meaningful since the parts are removed from the furnace all at once. Similarly, if the downstream operation requires a setup each time it begins work on a new product, then moving parts to this operation with a transfer batch of size one may be pointless. In such situations, it may be appropriate to reduce the process batch size to the extent possible. In Chapter 9, we will discuss how it may still be possible to achieve small lot production in the presence of significant set-up times.

The flow of products through the enterprise is affected by the manner in which raw material is released into the production line and by the manner in which the various resources are scheduled.

We will consider a series of dependent processes and examine different approaches to manage them using push and pull mechanisms. By doing so, we provide further insight on why a system that works with pull signals to control job releases into the system is able to work more effectively than push systems.

CONTROLLING FLOW THROUGH THE SYSTEM[1]

We compare and contrast different methods for releasing raw material and scheduling the resources using a simple serial production process that operates on a single product. More specifically, we will compare the traditional method of scheduling production using a Materials Requirement Planning-based (MRP-based) push system with techniques that respond to pull signals. Examples of systems that respond to pull signals include the *kanban* system that we covered in Chapter 5. The MRP system is not discussed in this chapter. It is, however, worth noting that whereas MRP can be a very useful planning tool, it is deployed as a scheduling tool, resulting in a push system.

A Serial Production System

The serial production process we consider consists of a number of resources, denoted by R1 through R6 as shown in Figure 8.3. Raw material is received and processed by resource R1, after which it is processed by resources R2 through R6. When the unit completes processing at resource R6 it becomes a finished product. Each resource has a different average processing capacity. The resource with the lowest average processing capacity is resource R3. Though the average processing capacity for a resource is constant over time, the processing capacity at any given instant may vary due to several factors, such as breakdowns, changeovers, and so on.

Figure 8-3. A Serial Production Process with Six Resources

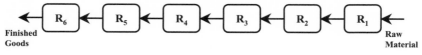

Finished Goods ← R$_6$ ← R$_5$ ← R$_4$ ← R$_3$ ← R$_2$ ← R$_1$ ← Raw Material

1. The material in this section is inspired by E. M. Goldratt and R. Fox (1986), *The Race*, North River Press, Great Barrington, MA.

To contrast the differences in scheduling production using a push system and various pull systems, we replace the six-resource production line with an analogous model consisting of a fleet of six operators. This fleet of operators could represent a set of material handlers moving packages, a fleet of truck drivers moving cargo, or a convoy of troops. Figure 8.4 presents the model. In this figure, the rightmost operator (operator 1) models resource R1 while the leftmost operator (operator 6) models resource R6 and each operator moves from left to right. The height of the operator models the average processing capacity of the resource: the shorter the operator, the lower the average processing speed. Thus, the shortest operator models the bottleneck resource. In Figure 8.4, the bottleneck is operator three. Processing times are allowed to be variable. That is, the speed at which an operator walks is not necessarily constant.

Figure 8-4. A Fleet Analogy

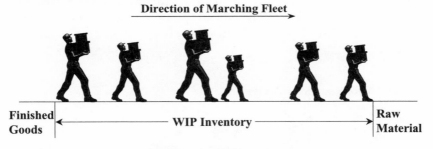

To see how this model works, consider, for instance, operator one. Each time this operator takes a step forward (moves to the right), he increases the distance between himself and operator 2 (assuming operator 2 has not moved at the same time) by one step. The analogy is that each time operator 1 moves forward by one step, he processes one unit of raw material and puts it behind him in his output buffer (which is the input buffer for operator 2). In other words, he creates one additional unit of WIP that now has to be processed by operator two. Thus, when the leftmost operator (operator 6) takes a step forward, he creates one unit of finished goods inventory.

Suppose one unit of WIP is between each operator. If all the operators moved forward at the same pace, then one unit of WIP will be between each operator at all times. However, since the six operators walk at different (variable) rates, the number of units of WIP between each operator will vary over time. Even though the pace of an operator varies over time, his average speed is constant. Thus, a taller operator immediately to the left of a shorter operator is generally close on the heels of his colleague, often having to wait for his colleague to make a move.

Over time, the gap between operator 2 and the bottleneck operator 3 will continue to widen. (This corresponds to an increase in inventory between resources 2 and 3.) When the fleet of operators spreads out, it corresponds to an increase in inventory in the system. The task of the scheduler is to contain inventory, namely, ensure that the fleet remains as close together as possible. How can the scheduler achieve that?

In *The Goal*,[2] Goldratt and Cox use a similar analogy, except that in place of a fleet of operators, they use a troop of boy scouts. The slowest Boy Scout in *The Goal* is Herbie, and the troop leader, Alex Rogo, wishes to keep the troop as closely packed as possible. So, Alex Rogo asks Herbie to move to the front of the line and rearranges the troop so that they are in increasing order of height following Herbie. Figure 8.5 shows such a rearrangement of the fleet in our example.

Figure 8-5. Rearranging the Fleet

While such a rearrangement works for a troop of boy scouts and may work with a fleet of operators in general, it is unlikely to work well if the fleet of operators models a production shop. It is generally not possible to rearrange equipment to have the capacity constraints at the front of the shop and the equipment with the highest processing capacity performing the last operation. That is because precedence constraints in a manufacturing operation might specify that operation 2 must be completed before operation 3, and so on. Even if the sequence of operations could

---

2. E. M. Goldratt and J. Cox (1992), *The Goal: A Process of Ongoing Improvement*, North River Press Publishing Company, Great Barrington, MA.

be rearranged, it may not be possible to move all the equipment so they are lined up in that same sequence. For instance, moving heat treatment furnaces is usually not possible. So, we look for alternate ways of keeping the fleet close together.

Using a Push System to Address Flow

One option is to have a drummer set the beat that all operators will follow. To further ensure that everyone keeps pace, we could employ a conductor who will urge everyone to stay at the same pace. Such an arrangement is depicted in Figure 8.6.

Figure 8-6. Trying to Close the Gap: A Push System

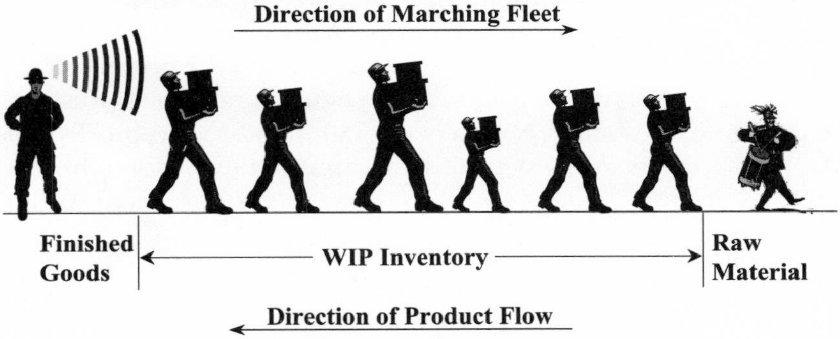

Direction of Marching Fleet

| Finished Goods | WIP Inventory | Raw Material |

Direction of Product Flow

As Goldratt and Fox point out,[5] such an arrangement is merely the MRP system in disguise. The conductor is the expeditor who is constantly moving around, wanting to ensure every resource is functioning as per plan, and the drummer is the materials management system, assisted by a computer, that pushes raw material onto the shop floor and lets each operator operate more or less independently as long as work is to be done. The MRP system does not tell each operator when to stop. As long as material is in front of the resource, the resource typically continues to operate. As a result, not all the operators operate according to the drumbeat, and typically, the gap between the operators will continue to widen if left unchecked. Typically, the MRP system closes the gap by running overtime, moving operators around, etc.

A number of signaling mechanisms can be employed so the pace of the operators is controlled and no one steps too far out of line. These signaling mechanisms are basically pull signals and are

---

5. E. M. Goldratt and R. Fox (1986), *The Race*, North River Press, Great Barrington, MA.

broadly referred to as the *kanban*, the Constant Work-in-Process (ConWIP), and the DBR mechanisms. We examine each one of these signaling mechanisms in the context of our fleet analogy.

Controlling Flow Using *Kanbans*

One way to prevent the fleet from spreading is to tie a rope between each pair of operators. To accommodate variation in the pace of the operators and to prevent them from bumping against each other, we provide some slack in the rope. The amount of slack allowed determines the maximum number of steps that the upstream operator can advance ahead of his downstream colleague. We make sure that the fleet of operators do not march independent of the customer demand. So, we tie a rope between the last (most downstream) operator and the customer. The length of this rope has a similar interpretation. Figure 8.7 presents such an arrangement. As the caption in the figure states this represents, in principle, the *kanban* system of operation. More specifically, it is the in-process *kanban* system that we discussed in Chapter 5.

Figure 8-7. Closing the Gap: The *Kanban* System

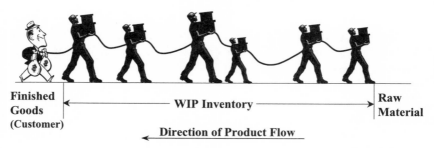

In this figure, if a downstream operator starts to fall behind, then the rope between this operator and the neighboring upstream operator becomes tight, forcing the upstream operator to stop. In the same manner, with a *kanban* system, the length of the rope represents the maximum inventory allowed to accumulate between two resources. If this maximum amount is reached, then the upstream resource will stop operating until the downstream resource consumes some of the WIP inventory. Continuing with the analogy, the customer can represent the finished goods inventory buffer and the length of the rope between the most downstream operator and the finished goods inventory buffer represents the maximum finished goods inventory that can accumulate in the system.

The slack in the rope between operators 1 and 2 determines the release of jobs into this system. As long as the rope is slack, the pace of operator 1 corresponds to the rate at which jobs are released into the system. If the rope is tight, then operator 1 stops, which corresponds to a temporary stoppage of jobs released into the system.

What is the effective pace of this system? If the system is capable of producing parts at a faster rate than the customer is demanding them, we have an external bottleneck (the customer). In that case, the rope tying the last operator to the customer will become tight, eventually stopping further processing by the operators. On the other hand, if the customer is demanding products faster than the system can produce them because of an internal bottleneck, then the rope tying the last operator to the customer will remain slack because the customer picks up finished goods almost as soon as the last operator puts them out. So, the flow in this system is ultimately dictated by the customer.

How much inventory will this system accumulate? The maximum distance between the first and last fleet operator (the maximum amount of WIP inventory in the system) will be the sum of the lengths of the ropes between each pair of operators. Thus, we place a cap on WIP, and that drives all the benefits of pull systems.[6] As Little's Law, presented in Chapter 2, indicates, the lead time is directly proportional to the inventory in the system. Thus, placing a cap on WIP in turn places a cap on lead times.

By tying a rope between each pair of operators, each operator is pulled by his upstream operator. By doing so, however, we have constrained the system too severely. If any one of the operators becomes disabled, the rest of the fleet will quickly come to a halt. All the ropes upstream (to the right) of this operator will become tight and all the operators downstream of this operator will catch up with their upstream partner and not be able to move forward.

---

6. W. Hopp and M. Spearman (2001), *Factory Physics*, 2nd Edition, Irwin McGraw-Hill, Boston, MA. Chapter 10. Hopp and Spearman indicate that the magic of a pull system is simply because it places a cap on WIP.

Controlling Flow Using ConWIP

The method we next discuss is not as restrictive. This method ties a rope between operators 1 and six. There is also a rope tied between operator 6 and the customer (the finished goods inventory buffer). In essence, when the rope between operator 6 and operator 1 becomes tight, it forces operator 1 to stop. This rope can become tight in two ways: Operator 6 can be constrained from moving forward because the rope between operator 6 and the customer has become tight, or operator 1 can move too far ahead of operator 6. In any case, operator 1 can now resume moving forward only when operator 6 makes a move. This mechanism, where the last operator signals the first operator is usually called the ConWIP protocol. The ConWIP protocol takes its name from the WIP inventory level in the system being usually constant, determined by the lengths of the ropes between the first and last operator, and the last operator and customer. Figure 8.8 presents the fleet analogy for this protocol.

Figure 8-8. Closing the Gap: The ConWIP Protocol

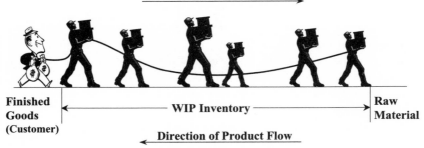

As with the *kanban* system, the drumbeat is set by the customer. If there was no rope tying the last operator to the customer, the drumbeat would have been set by the last operator. In fact, the reader may have observed that instead of having two ropes, we could have as well used a single rope from the first operator to the customer without violating the ConWIP protocol. However, that will result in a less disciplined system as we discuss below.

Unlike the *kanban* system of operation, the other operators proceed in a less restricted manner since they are not constrained by a rope tied to them. They stop only if they bump up against their upstream operator. The ConWIP protocol is generally self-balancing. Each operator, except the first, essentially works at his own pace so long as a gap is between him and the upstream operator. In other words, the only pull signal is from the last operator (or the customer) to the first operator, with the rest of the operators working in a push mode. The ConWIP protocol is a hybrid of push and pull. However, we have again placed a cap on WIP. Therefore, the ConWIP protocol should generally perform as well as the *kanban* system, and in many instances even better than the *kanban* system since the ConWIP protocol does not restrict the activity of the operators as much as the *kanban* system does.

The danger with the ConWIP protocol is that, when many operators are in the fleet, we do not have as much discipline as with a *kanban* implementation. Unlike the *kanban* implementation where there is a rope tying each pair of operators, with the ConWIP implementation there is only one between the first and last operators. Because there is a rope between each operator pair, ropes are likely to get taut more quickly with the *kanban* system relative to the ConWIP protocol. That focuses attention on removing variability from the process faster than would otherwise happen if the process used the ConWIP protocol.

Controlling Flow by Pulling from the Bottleneck

The DBR model ties the rope from the first operator to the bottleneck (this bottleneck could be the customer). Thus, the slowest operator sets the pace for the entire system. However, an adequate amount of slack is provided in the rope. The reason for providing this slack is as follows: While we do not want the operators upstream of the bottleneck to work at a faster rate, at the same time we never want to stop the bottleneck. In other words, this mechanism would like to maintain a buffer in front of the bottleneck operator. The rationale is that it is likely that one of the upstream operators might be temporarily disabled. When that happens, the bottleneck operator should be allowed to continue moving. As we noted earlier, time lost at a bottleneck resource translates to possible lost revenue. Figure 8.9 presents the fleet analogy for this model. In this figure, we assume a resource constraint exists, so the rope is tied to the resource constraint. When the market is the constraint, a specialized version of the DBR model will be in effect as we will discuss shortly.

In Figure 8.9, the pace at which the operators can move is set by the bottleneck operator. This model is a hybrid system in that it has elements of push and pull, just as with the ConWIP protocol.

Figure 8-9. Closing the Gap: The Drum-Buffer-Rope (DBR) Model

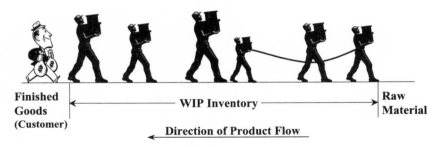

Though there is a pull from the bottleneck operator to the first operator, the remaining operators in the system are not similarly constrained. This model is a pull-from-the-bottleneck model. Note, though, that we have labeled the figure as the DBR model. We will explain why this model is often referred to as the DBR model.

The Drum-Buffer-Rope (DBR) Model

Three critical ingredients are required for a good, workable production plan. First, there must be up-to-date information on the actual customer demand. Second, sufficient raw material must be available to support the production plan. Finally, the proposed plan should not overload the constraint resource(s). In the DBR model, the drum is the detailed master production schedule that matches the customer demand with the system's constraints. Figure 8.10 presents the DBR model for the case of an internal constraint.

Figure 8-10. The Drum-Buffer-Rope (DBR) Model

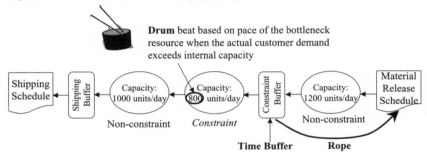

Since any system has to account for disruptions and variability in the manufacturing process, we need to provide a protective cushion or buffer to keep the product flowing. The buffer in the DBR model is a *time buffer* rather than an inventory buffer.

The term, time buffer, was mentioned in Chapter 7 in the context of the Critical Chain implementation at the Maintenance Center of the Marine Corps Logistics Base, but it has a different interpretation when used in the context of Critical Chains. In the DBR model, the time buffer refers to a protection provided by having extra units of material in front of the bottleneck so it is never starved for work. However, the amount of protection is measured in terms of *time*, not in terms of number of units. That is, if the amount of inventory in front of operator 2 is six units, and if the processing rate for operator 2 is ten minutes per unit, then the six units represents a time buffer of one hour. If a problem occurs somewhere upstream of operator 2 and disrupts the flow of material, then this operator can continue to work uninterrupted for one hour.

The advantage of using time to represent the protection provided to the bottleneck is best understood in the context of a process that operates on multiple products. In that case, quantifying the protection given to the constraint in terms of units of inventory becomes difficult especially when the processing times for different items could be quite different. For example, consider a simple case where the bottleneck processes two types of products, one requiring 5 minutes per job and the other requiring 30 minutes per job. If we consider maintaining an inventory buffer, then we need to be careful about specifying how many jobs of each type we need to maintain in front of the constraint. However, if the goal is to ensure that the constraint is always occupied productively, it is enough to specify that there should be, say, 60 minutes of work buffered in front of the constraint. This could be some appropriate combination of units of job types one and two.

Thus, time is a common denominator that identifies the amount of protection desired. The time buffer is added to the sum of the setup and run times to arrive at a planned lead time that is quoted to the customer. In essence, the time buffer increases the planning lead time from the absolute minimum value required to process the products to one which can accommodate disruptions that are likely to occur.

The rope in the DBR model refers to the mechanism that releases work into the production process. The rope is essentially a communication device to ensure that raw material is not introduced into the shop floor at a rate faster than the constraint can handle. If the constraint is not an internal bottleneck but is the market demand, then the rope ensures that the raw material is not introduced onto the shop floor at a rate faster than the customer demand rate. Often, another buffer, called the Shipping Buffer, is used to protect situations where the customer's order might be delayed due to some disruptions that take place after the products are processed at the constraint(s). This buffer is, again, expressed as a time buffer for the reason noted above.

In a serial production process, the constraint buffer and the Shipping Buffer provide adequate protection from unplanned disruptions. In more complex flows, there will be additional time buffers at other locations in addition to the two defined in Figure 8.10. In essence, the DBR model can be summarized as follows:

- Develop a master production schedule consistent with system constraints (Drum).
- Protect system throughput from inevitable disruptions by placing time buffers at a relatively few critical points in the system (Buffer).
- Tie production at each resource to the drum, i.e., the production schedule (Rope).

The book, *Synchronous Management*, presents a comprehensive treatment of the DBR model.[7] We next consider a special case of the DBR model that applies when the constraint is not an internal constraint but an external (market) constraint. This is the Simplified Drum-Buffer-Rope (S-DBR) model

The Simplified Drum-Buffer-Rope (S-DBR) Model

The standard DBR model is used to schedule all the resources based on the pace of the bottleneck. However, when the bottleneck is external (the market) and the enterprise has a MRP or a MRP II system in place, an alternate technique known as the S-DBR model can be used. The drumbeat in S-DBR comes from the market and is based on firm orders. As orders come in, a quick check is made on the total workload at the most heavily loaded

---

7. M. L. Srikanth and M. Umble (1995), *Synchronous Management*, The Spectrum Publishing Company, Wallingford, CT.

internal constraint. This is the capacity constrained resource (CCR). If the CCR is not too heavily loaded, the order is accepted and released into the shop floor for processing. No buffer is in front of the CCR. The only buffer maintained is the Shipping Buffer. The rope is no longer tied to the CCR. Instead, the rope is tied to the market (the Shipping Buffer); in other words, the material release schedule is directly generated by firm orders received. (See Figure 8.11.) Notice the similarity between the S-DBR model and the ConWIP model.

Figure 8-11. The Simplified Drum-Buffer-Rope Model

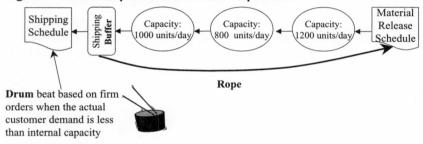

The S-DBR model has some advantages. It does not require any specialized software and this can be a significant benefit for enterprises that might be unwilling or unable to invest in specialized DBR software.[8] The S-DBR approach needs just one buffer: the Shipping Buffer. Finally, the S-DBR approach is more focused on market demand and ties the organization to its customers more directly.

We next present a simulation often used to explain the phenomena of variability and dependency. This simulation is known as the Dice Game. The simulation is easy to set up and run. In addition to underscoring the impact of variability on the performance of the system, the simulation draws out the performance differences between push and pull systems more explicitly. In particular, it shows that a system which uses a pull signal to control job releases is more stable (less variable) compared to an equivalent system which schedules job releases based on forecasts (a push system).

---

8. E. Schragenheim and H. W. Dettmer (2000), *Manufacturing at Warp Speed: Optimizing Supply Chain Financial Performance*, CRC Press, Boca Raton, FL.

THE DICE GAME

The Dice Game was originally used in the context of a manufacturing operation but has since found widespread use to demonstrate the effects of dependencies and variability in a number of other contexts, notably in logistics and supply chain operations. The manufacturing process has six to eight sequential operations that process material as shown in Figure 8.12. This process is simulated with a team of six to eight players. Typically, a number of teams simultaneously play the game, providing a spirit of friendly competition among the teams. We will discuss the setup for one team.

Figure 8-12. The Layout for the Dice Game

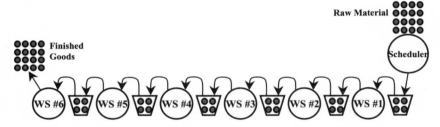

The first operation is the scheduling operation denoted in the figure as Scheduler. The scheduler schedules work into the system and has an unlimited amount of raw material available. Each workstation has four units of WIP inventory in its input buffer. The raw material and WIP inventory can be simulated using Lego pieces, poker chips, etc. The configuration shown in Figure 8.12 has one scheduler and six operators for a total of seven players.

Each player is given a single die. The Dice Game is run for twenty days. At the start of each day the scheduler rolls his/her die to determine how many jobs need to be scheduled that day (an excellent forecasting system). At the same time, each operator rolls a die to determine the production capability of the operator's workstation. The workstations are, thus, modeled as unreliable resources with high variability. The production capability on a given day is anywhere from one to six jobs per day. So, a high roll of the die means the workstation will have few problems that day.

Each operator determines the number of jobs that can be processed that day at his/her workstation and moved downstream (to the next higher-numbered workstation) at the end of the day. This number is the smaller of the number of jobs in the operator's input buffer and the roll of the die. The scheduler will always schedule the number provided by the roll of his/her die since it is assumed that an ample supply of raw material is available to the scheduler. Each player moves these jobs downstream to his/her output buffer. The scheduler moves the jobs to the input buffer of workstation 1, operators at workstations 1 through 5 move their jobs into the input buffer of their immediate downstream workstation, and the operator at workstation 6 moves jobs to the finished goods buffer. The transfer to the downstream process always takes place at the end of the day. Operators are not allowed to steal jobs from their upstream operation. In other words, the pieces processed at workstation n on any given day cannot be used by the operator at workstation $n+1$ on that same day.

At the start of the simulation, each workstation has four units of WIP inventory in its input buffer, as indicated earlier. With six workstations, the WIP inventory is 24 at the beginning of the game. The system-wide WIP inventory and the system throughput are monitored using a scoring sheet as shown in Table 8.5 below. Typically, the player from each team who is operating the last workstation is asked to keep score. In Table 8.5, the initial WIP of 24 units is identified as the WIP at the end of Day 0 (zero). This makes it convenient for players to calculate WIP. The WIP at the end of each day is calculated as follows:

WIP at the end of day = WIP at end of previous day + Jobs Released – Jobs Completed

Table 8-5. Dice Game Score Sheet: *Push* Simulation

DAY	JOBS RELEASED	JOBS COMPLETED	WIP AT THE END OF THE DAY
0	---	---	24
1			
2			
.			
.			
20			

The number of jobs released each day is the face value of the die rolled by the scheduler, since the scheduler has ample raw material. The number of jobs completed each day is the actual number sent to finished goods. This number is the smaller of the number of jobs in the last operator's input buffer and the roll of his/her die.

The throughput of this system is obtained by adding up the jobs completed column over the 20 days. What do you think this throughput would be? Over a large number of rolls, the average daily capacity of each workstation should be 3.5 (since each number between 1 and 6 is equally likely), so it is tempting to conjecture that the system will produce seventy units on average over the 20 days. However, on some days the workstation may have a production capacity (a roll of the die) greater than the WIP inventory in the workstation's input buffer, representing lost production capacity. Therefore, the total number of jobs shipped at the end of 20 days of simulation will typically be lower than seventy. You will find the ending WIP inventory is usually higher than the WIP inventory at the beginning of the game.

The game, as described above, simulates a push system since the scheduler pushes jobs into the system based on a forecast (namely, the roll of a die). The results from the Dice Game generally validate Lean Supply Chain Principle 13. The results show that a balanced system will not produce a smooth flow of products if products are pushed through the system, in the presence of variation. The flow is uneven and WIP inventory accumulates at different points in the production line at different times. Furthermore, when the game is run with multiple teams, the throughput and the amount of inventory accumulation at the different tables will significantly differ. In sum the Dice Game will show that push systems are neither stable nor predictable.

Variations on the Dice Game

A number of variants of the Dice Game bring about other learning points. One such variant is to introduce a bottleneck workstation; This may be implemented by giving one of the players, say, a four-sided die. (A four-sided die is available in most hobby shops.) Alternately, the capacity can be increased by giving the players die with eight, ten, or twelve sides. It is possible to incorporate overtime as well by allowing one or more players an additional roll of the die. Another variant is to simulate a reduced variation production line as follows. With a die roll of a one, two, or a three, the production capability is assumed to be three. With a dice roll of a four, five, or a six, the production capability is assumed to be four. These assumptions simulate a reduced variation setup where each resource has a capability of three or four jobs every day. The impact of reduced variation on throughput and flow will be dramatic, validating Lean Supply Chain Principle 14 (see above).

Simulating the ConWIP Protocol

The Dice Game can bring about a number of additional learning points when it is used to simulate the ConWIP protocol. As with the standard version of the Dice Game, the simulation is initialized with four units of WIP inventory in front of each operator. However, while all the operators roll their individual die on each day, the scheduler does not roll a die. Instead, on the first day of simulation, the scheduler releases 4 jobs into the system. After that, he/she releases the number of jobs that were completed by the system at the end of the previous day. This essentially keeps the WIP level fairly constant at around 24 units each day. The WIP level will not be exactly 24 units at the end of each day since there is a one-day lag in the information transferred from the last station back to the scheduler.

Table 8.6 presents the score sheet for this simulation. This score sheet is the same as before except that the number of jobs released on day 1 is set equal to four.

Table 8-6. Dice Game Score Sheet: *ConWIP* Simulation

DAY	JOBS RELEASED	JOBS COMPLETED	WIP AT THE END OF THE DAY
0	---	---	24
1	4		
2			
.			
.			
20			

The results from the Dice Game with the ConWIP protocol are quite revealing. The results will no doubt differ slightly from one game to the next because of the variability in the rolls of the die. However, the participants will realize that the variation in the system has dropped. The throughput numbers as well as the WIP levels across the different teams will be fairly close to one another. The simulation will reveal that even if the processes in the system have considerable process variation, yet *pull systems are more stable and predictable* compared to push systems.

PULL SYSTEMS ARE MORE STABLE AND PREDICTABLE THAN PUSH SYSTEMS[9]

Pull systems are more stable and predictable than push systems because a pull system inherently has less variation. In general, two types of variation exist in any production system: process variation and system variation. In the Dice Game, the process variation is simulated by the roll of the die. So each workstation has a variation in production capability from one day to the next; this variation is the same whether the system is operated in a pull mode or a push mode. The other type of variation, the system variation, is not as apparent; and it is higher for the push system compared to the pull system, as we explain below.

Comparing Pull and Push Systems for Variability

Intuitively, since the ConWIP system keeps the WIP level fairly constant, the variation in WIP levels will be higher for the push system, compared to the ConWIP (i.e., the pull) system. Hopp and Spearman[10] demonstrate that the pull system has less variation in lead time than a comparable push system. The explanation for the reduced lead time variation stems from the fact that the ConWIP system holds the WIP level fairly steady. Fixing the WIP level introduces a *negative correlation* between the WIP levels at the different workstations.

For example, suppose we fix the WIP level in the system at 20 jobs. With the variation in processing times at the different stations in the system, the number of jobs present at the workstations at different points in time will vary. Suppose at a given instant we find that all 20 jobs are present at workstation 1 (presumably because there was a breakdown at station 1 that caused the pile up). Then we know with certainty that there are no jobs at any of the other stations. Thus, knowledge of the WIP level at workstation 1 provides

---

9. For a more detailed discussion on this topic, see W. Hopp and M. Spearman (2001), *Factory Physics*, 2nd Edition, Chapter 10. Boston, Irwin McGraw-Hill.
10. W. Hopp and M. Spearman (2001), *Factory Physics*, 2nd Edition, Chapter 10. Boston, Irwin McGraw-Hill.

information about the WIP level at the other workstations: the knowledge that there were 10 jobs at workstation 1 would tell us there are ten jobs distributed across the other workstations. So, when the number of jobs at a workstation, or a set of workstations, is high, then that has to be offset by a correspondingly smaller number of jobs at the other workstations. Such a negative correlation between the WIP levels tends to dampen the variation in lead times.

In contrast, with a push system, the WIP levels at individual workstations are more or less independent of one another. In other words, when the WIP level at, say, station 1 is high, it will give us no information on whether the WIP level at station 4 is high or low. The WIP levels at several stations could be high (or low) simultaneously. In other words, the variation in WIP levels is typically higher in push systems. Since WIP levels are proportional to the lead times (as per Little's Law), the result is that lead times are more variable in a push system than in an equivalent pull system.

Comparing Pull and Push Systems for Efficiency

In general, a pull system uses the system resources more effectively than a push system implying that it is preferable to operate a system using pull signals wherever possible. Using fairly rigorous analysis, it can be shown that, for the same level of throughput, the push system will have more WIP than a comparable pull system would. Similarly, for a given level of throughput, the push system will have longer average lead times than a comparable pull system would. We state these results below without proof.[11]

> **The ConWIP Efficiency Law**: *For a given level of throughput, a push system will have more WIP than an equivalent ConWIP system.*

> **Corollary to the ConWIP Efficiency Law**: *For a given level of throughput, a push system will have longer average lead times than an equivalent ConWIP system.*

---

11. For a more detailed discussion on this topic, see W. Hopp and M. Spearman (2001), *Factory Physics*, 2nd Edition, Chapter 10. Boston, Irwin McGraw-Hill, Boston, MA.

CONCLUSIONS

The concept of flow is central to managing the lean supply chain. It is useful to consider a river analogy when considering how to flow the products through the supply chain. You want the river to flow smoothly, all the way from the mountain to the river, without having it collect in dams along the way. Dams are analogous to pockets of inventory; they impede the smooth flow of the product through the value stream, decrease throughput velocity, and increase lead times. All of these factors inhibit competitiveness. From a systems perspective, you therefore want to do the following:

- Focus on the bottleneck resources because they control the flow. You want to synchronize flow by first scheduling (focusing on) the bottleneck resource so that it works on the most productive product family. The non-bottleneck resources can then be scheduled to march in step with the bottlenecks.
- Care should be exercised in scheduling resources especially in the presence of variation. In particular, if all resources end up having similar workloads, variation can wreak havoc and significantly increase lead times. Therefore, you must work on reducing variation in the supply chain. In the presence of variation, the focus should be on synchronizing (balancing) the flow, not on balancing capacities.
- Large batch sizes impede flow. They also result in increased variation. If large batch sizes are deemed necessary, then use process batch sizes and transfer batch sizes judiciously to move the product through the supply chain. The process batch size can be large at the bottleneck in order to minimize the setups. However, in that case, the transfer batch size should be made as small as possible. In any case, the batch size for non-constraints can be small since they have additional capacity by definition.
- Use pull methods to execute wherever possible. Pull systems have inherently less variation than a comparable push system. As a consequence, for a given level of throughput, a push system will have more WIP and higher lead times than a comparable pull system.

9

Rate-Based Planning: Planning and Scheduling the Drumbeat[1]

"Can you hear the drum beat? Hakuna Matata."[2]
Boney M.

A central concept of pull is that one operation will serve as the drumbeat for the internal upstream processes and the external suppliers. In the short term, the drumbeat process (referred to as the pacemaker process in Chapter 7) maintains a constant production rate and constant product mix. This creates a flat demand pattern for the upstream processes and the suppliers. A finished goods inventory buffer or an order queue uncouples the drumbeat process from the short-term variation in customer demand. (As we discussed in Chapters 2 and 3, the lean supply chain is not about zero inventories but about strategic use of inventories.)

The production and delivery of materials to the drumbeat process from the upstream processes (internal or external) is driven entirely by pull signals that transmit data on the actual usage of parts. No centralized schedule is used to coordinate production. Scheduling is done only at the drumbeat process and all the other upstream processes respond to pull signals from the process immediately downstream.

However, there must be a plan. Over the longer term the level of demand will change and, therefore, the rate of the drumbeat

---

1. Dr. Thomas G. Greenwood, Founder of the Lean Enterprise Systems Design Institute of the University of Tennessee and President of Lean Works, Inc., has done extensive work in the development of rate-based planning methods. He has taught and implemented these methods in numerous enterprises. We are grateful for his many contributions to our understanding of these methods.
2. Hakuna Matata is a Swahili term that literally means, "There are no problems."

and the mix will change. The internal and external suppliers must prepare to respond to changes in the rate of the drumbeat. To respond appropriately, they need a forecast, which is the production plan for future periods.

Traditional Materials Requirement Planning (MRP) systems are not well suited for planning the rate of the drumbeat. When the MRP schedule is frozen for several weeks into the future, it does not allow for a quick enough response to the variation in customer demand. On the other hand, when the MRP schedule is not frozen, it often results in schedule nervousness, namely, a production schedule constantly in flux.

This chapter introduces a tool for planning the rate of the drumbeat called rate-based planning. Rate-based planning provides the means for setting the rate of the drumbeat in future periods; at the same time, it provides a certain amount of flexibility to accommodate rate changes.

THE GOALS OF RATE-BASED PLANNING

To understand the rationale for rate-based planning, you must first understand the three primary planning and scheduling goals. These objectives can be articulated from a functional perspective:

- Operations would like a production rate that never changes.
- Marketing would like instantaneous changes in the production rate in response to changes in demand, to avoid late deliveries, stock-outs, and overstocks.
- Purchasing and the external suppliers would like a firm long-term commitment to future production rates to plan and schedule future material needs.

Although it is impossible to maintain a production rate that never changes, the first goal is to translate the possibly varying customer demands into a smoother production plan that insulates the production processes and the suppliers from the short-term variation in demand. For example, suppose the points plotted in Figure 9.1 show the weekly demand for a manufacturer of transmissions for trucks and buses. This figure shows the aggregate or total demand across the different types of transmissions produced. The dotted line shows the underlying trend in demand.

It would be difficult for the drumbeat to change in response to the week-to-week fluctuations around this trend. For example, the demand in week seven is about 750 and the demand in week eight is about 1250. Setting the drumbeat at 750 in one week and

Figure 9-1. One Year of Weekly Demand and the Underlying Trend

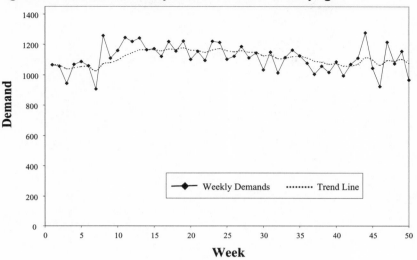

changing it to 1250 the following week would be unrealistic. Instead, adhering to the first goal to the extent possible (a production rate that never changes) would be preferable by setting the rate of the drumbeat to track the underlying trend in the demand.

The second goal is to respond quickly to true changes in the demand level. A slow reaction time (lead time) creates high variation in the inventory, which in turn results in stock-outs and overstocks. Figure 9.2 shows the effect of a 4-week lead time on the production and inventory levels that will result from a schedule generated by the MRP system.[3]

---

3. The production and inventory levels in Figure 9.2 were generated using standard infinite loading MRP computations as follows. In each week t, the inventory was computed as the previous week's ending inventory plus the current week's production minus the current week's demand: Inventory(t) = Inventory(t-1) + Production(t) – Demand(t)

The forecast of the weekly rate of demand was based on an exponential smoothing formula that was fit to the data. The forecast is a weighted average of the previous weeks forecast and the most recent demand: Forecast(t) = 0.8 x Forecast(t-1) + 0.2 x Demand (t)

Since the lead time was four weeks, the production level for week t+4 was computed and frozen in week t. This production level was computed as the difference between the target inventory and the current inventory plus forecasted demand over the 4-week lead time minus the production orders that were already outstanding: Production(t+4) = Target Inventory – Inventory(t) + 4 x Forecast(t) – P(t+1) – P(t+2) – P(t+3).

The target inventory represents the target safety stock. This was set at 679 units.

Figure 9-2. Bullwhip Effect Created by MRP with a 4-Week Lead Time

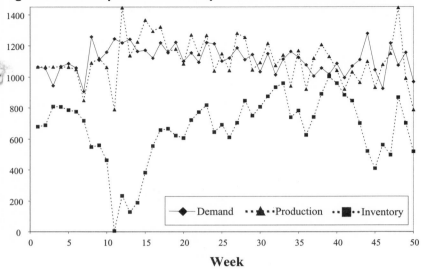

Week

As Figure 9.2 indicates, the variation in the inventory level is much larger than the variation in demand. In addition, each change in demand is followed by a much larger change in production 4 weeks later. This is just the bullwhip effect discussed in Chapter 2. The reaction time causes the variation in production to be much larger than the variation in demand. Since a 4-week delay occurs in reacting to demand variation, the change in the production level must cover the variation in the current week's demand and the change in the forecasted level of demand over the next 4 weeks.

Since no production process could economically accommodate such large swings in the production rate, most of the variation created by the lead time will be absorbed by the inventory. Thus, the variation in the inventory will actually be much larger than shown in Figure 9.2 and will result in some combination of late shipments, lost sales, overstocks, and other failures.

The third goal is to reduce the uncertainty for Operations, Purchasing, and the upstream suppliers in planning future capacity and materials requirements. This goal would suggest the weekly rates of the drumbeat should be determined and fixed (frozen) for several weeks into the future. However this goal conflicts with the first and second goals. The period of the freeze in the schedule represents a delay in responding to changes in the level of demand, i.e., lead time. The slow response time will create large swings in the inventory resulting in stock-outs and overstocks. And although the freeze will make production levels predictable in the short-term, it will result in a large variation subsequently. Any change in the level of demand accumulates over the entire period of the freeze and must be absorbed in future levels of production.

THE FLEXIBILITY REQUIREMENTS PROFILE

Rate-based planning does not use a frozen schedule. Rather, it produces a plan but permits deviations, within specified ranges, from that plan. This compromise gives Operations and the suppliers a forecast of future production, with a guaranteed level of accuracy (goal one), while retaining some flexibility to respond quickly to changes in the demand level (goal two). Since the amount of change from the plan is constrained, rate-based planning has a smoothing effect on production (goal three).

Rate-based planning begins with a predetermined weekly profile of flexibility that has been agreed upon by Operations and the suppliers. This is the flexibility requirements profile that gives the amount by which the actual drumbeat can deviate above or below the current plan for future weeks (this amount is usually expressed as a percentage of the planned drumbeat).

The concept of a predetermined amount of flexibility was introduced by Constanza[4] in his linear planning methodology. He refers to the weekly profile of flexibility as the planning flex fence.

Typically, smaller deviations from the plan will be permitted for weeks in the near future than for weeks in the more distant future. For example, the flexibility requirements profile may require that the drumbeat for the first 4 weeks should not deviate above or below the plan by more than 5 percent. For weeks 5 through 8, the allowable deviation may be 10 percent, and for weeks 9 through 12, the allowable deviation may be 15 percent. An example profile is shown in Figure 9.3. Although the profile in this example is symmetric, this need not be the case in general. That is, the allowable upward and downward deviations could be different during a given week.

To the supplier, the lower bound on the flexibility requirements profile represents a commitment from the buyer, guaranteeing the minimum quantity of materials that will be bought in

---

4. J. R. Costanza (1996), *Quantum Leap*, John Costanza Institute of Technology (3rd Edition).

Figure 9-3. A Flexibility Requirements Profile

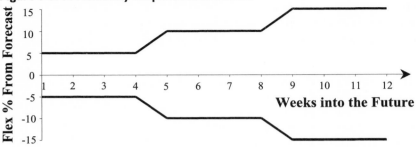

the future weeks. The upper bound represents a commitment from the supplier to the customer (buyer) guaranteeing the ability to ramp up beyond the plan by the specified amount.

The rules for using the flexibility requirements profile is as follows. Every week that the production plan is updated, the updated production plan should respect the constraint that the planned rate of the drumbeat must stay within the bounds that have previously been established (i.e., committed to). In addition, new bounds are computed only at the flex fences, that is, the weeks at which the bounds change. In the example of Figure 9.3, weeks 4, 8 and 12 indicate the flex fence positions. The bounds for a particular week are recomputed at each flex fence but remain unchanged in the intervening weeks. In the example of Figure 9.3, the bounds on the production of a particular week will first be established 12 weeks into the future. The bound would be recomputed when the week is 8 weeks into the future and again when it is 4 weeks into the future.

COMPUTING THE AGGREGATE RATE-BASED PLAN

Rate-based planning begins at the aggregate level. The aggregate plan is then translated into plans for the individual end items. Table 9.1 shows an example aggregate rate-based plan. This plan, based on the demand data given in Figure 9.1, is for the total number of transmissions of all types to be produced. (It is for the week of March 17; This was week 11 in Figure 9.1.) The actual demand of 1246 for this week represents orders received in the 7 days prior to the beginning of the week. These orders must be shipped during the week. During the week of March 17, the production of 1050 is the number of transmissions to be produced. The ending inventory of 660 represents transmissions that will be in inventory at the end of this week if the 1050 units are produced as per schedule.

Table 9-1. The Rate-Based Plan for the Week of March 17

Current Week's Schedule

Forecast of Future 12 Weeks

11	Current	5%	5%	5%	5%	10%	10%	10%	10%	15%	15%	15%	15%
Week	17-Mar	24-Mar	31-Mar	7-Apr	14-Apr	21-Apr	28-Apr	5-May	12-May	19-May	26-May	2-Jun	9-Jun
Demand	1246	1125	1125	1125	1125	1125	1125	1125	1125	1125	1125	1125	1125
Production	1050	1150	1150	1150	1150	1200	1200	1200	1140	1125	1125	1125	1125
Lower Bound		1050	1050	1100	1100	950	950	1000	1050	900	900	950	950
Upper Bound		1150	1150	1150	1150	1200	1200	1200	1200	1250	1250	1250	1300
Inventory	660	685	710	735	760	835	910	985	1000	1000	1000	1000	1000

The March 17 plan shows the forecasted demand, production, and inventory for March 24 through June 9 (12 weeks). These values are all planned values based on the information that is available on March 17th. That is, they are all based on a demand forecast of 1,125 units per week for each of the next 12 weeks, a beginning inventory of 660 (at the start of the week of March 24) and a target inventory of 1000 (at the end of the week of June 9). The target inventory of 1000 is the desired buffer against variation in customer demand.

The production levels represent the most likely levels of production. These production levels are required to bring the inventory to the target level of 1,000 as soon as possible, given the current forecast, the current inventory level, and the bounds on the production level. These bounds were established over the 12 weeks using the flexibility requirements profile and the information that was available that the time. The planned production level in any week cannot violate the upper and lower bounds established for that week.

In our discussions, we will use the term *schedule* to denote a fixed production quantity to be executed. In Table 9.1, the production of 1050 in the Week of March 17 represents the schedule. We will use the term *plan* to denote the forecasted future production values. In the table, the production values for the weeks of March 24 through June 9 are the plan. These values will change within the prescribed bounds in future weeks.

The week of June 9 will be used to illustrate how the planned production and the bounds are computed and updated. This week will be tracked from the time it first enters the 12-week planning horizon until it becomes the current week. We will show the plans that develop each week from March 17 (when the week of June 9 first entered the planning horizon) until June 9th.

On March 17, the week of June 9 is 12 weeks into the future. First the planned production for that week will be computed. The net requirement for the week of June 9 is computed using the formula:

Net requirement = Forecasted Demand + Target Ending Inventory – Ending Inventory of the Prior Week

The forecasted demand is 1,125, the target inventory is 1000, and 1000 is the planned June 2 ending inventory. Thus the net requirement is $1125 + 1000 - 1000 = 1125$. The planned production for June 9 is set to this net requirement.

Assume that the flexibility requirements profile shown above in Figure 9.3 is being used. June 9 is 12 weeks into the future and the flex requirements for this week are fifteen percent. Thus the upper bound is computed as the planned production plus fifteen percent or $1.15 \times 1125 = 1300$ (rounded to the nearest 50) and the lower bound is planned production minus fifteen percent or $0.85 \times 1125 = 950$ (also rounded). Thus, on March 17, a commitment is made between the buyer and the supplier that the actual drumbeat will be between 950 and 1300 for the week of June 9.

Updating the Rate-Based Plan

As indicated in Table 9.2, Week 12 represents the rate-based plan established for the week of March 24. Below that is the plan for the week of March 31 (presented as Week 13), and the third set of figures repeat the plan for the week of April 7th. The updating of the planned production for the week of June 9 will be illustrated as it progresses through these three weeks (these are 11, 10, and then 9 weeks into the future). The bounds will remain unchanged during these three weeks.

Table 9-2. The Rate-Based Plans for the Weeks of March 24, March 31 and April 7

12	Current	5%	5%	5%	5%	10%	10%	10%	10%	15%	15%	15%	15%
Week	24-Mar	31-Mar	7-Apr	14-Apr	21-Apr	28-Apr	5-May	12-May	19-May	26-May	2-Jun	**9-Jun**	16-Jun
Demand	1219	1144	1144	1144	1144	1144	1144	1144	1144	1144	1144	**1144**	1144
Production	1150	1150	1150	1150	1200	1200	1200	1200	1250	1205	1144	**1144**	1144
Lower Bound		1050	1100	1100	1150	950	1000	1050	1150	900	950	**950**	950
Upper Bound		1150	1150	1150	1200	1200	1200	1200	1250	1250	1250	**1300**	1300
Inventory	591	597	603	609	665	721	777	833	939	1000	1000	**1000**	1000

13	Current	5%	5%	5%	5%	10%	10%	10%	10%	15%	15%	15%	15%
Week	31-Mar	7-Apr	14-Apr	21-Apr	28-Apr	5-May	12-May	19-May	26-May	2-Jun	**9-Jun**	16-Jun	23-Jun
Demand	1242	1164	1164	1164	1164	1164	1164	1164	1164	1164	**1164**	1164	1164
Production	1150	1150	1150	1200	1200	1200	1200	1250	1250	1250	**1291**	1164	1164
Lower Bound		1100	1100	1150	1150	1000	1050	1150	1150	950	**950**	950	1000
Upper Bound		1150	1150	1200	1200	1200	1200	1250	1250	1250	**1300**	1300	1350
Inventory	499	485	471	507	543	579	615	701	787	873	**1000**	1000	1000

14	Current	5%	5%	5%	5%	10%	10%	10%	10%	15%	15%	15%	15%
Week	7-Apr	14-Apr	21-Apr	28-Apr	5-May	12-May	19-May	26-May	2-Jun	**9-Jun**	16-Jun	23-Jun	30-Jun
Demand	1164	1164	1164	1164	1164	1164	1164	1164	1164	**1164**	1164	1164	1164
Production	1150	1150	1200	1200	1200	1200	1250	1250	1250	**1291**	1164	1164	1164
Lower Bound		1100	1150	1150	1150	1050	1150	1150	1150	**950**	950	1000	1000
Upper Bound		1150	1200	1200	1200	1200	1250	1250	1250	**1300**	1300	1350	1350
Inventory	485	471	507	543	579	615	701	787	873	**1000**	1000	1000	1000

In this example, the forecast weekly rate of customer demand was updated weekly using the following formula:

New Forecast = 0.8 x Old Forecast + 0.2 x Current Demand.

For example, the forecasted rate of demand made in the week of March 17 was 1125 per week (Table 9.1). The actual demand in the week of March 24 was 1219 (Table 9.2). Therefore, the forecasted rate of demand made in the week of March 24 is the following:

New Forecast = 0.8 x 1125 + 0.2 x 1219 = 1144

The forecasting model is an exponential smoothing model that was fitted to the data. However, rate-based planning can be used with whatever forecast method is applicable to the data.

Over the 3 weeks shown in Table 9.2, the lower and upper bound for the week of June 9 do not change. However the planned production changes within these bounds. These computations are summarized below.

March 24 computation of the June 9 planned production:

Planned production = Net requirement
                   = 1144 + 1000 − 1000 = 1144

March 31 computation of the June 9 planned production:

Planned production = Net requirement
$$= 1164 + 1000 - 873 = 1291$$

April 7 computation of the June 9 planned production:

Planned production = Net requirement
$$= 1164 + 1000 - 873 = 1291$$

None of these net requirements fell outside the previously established bounds for June 9th. If a net requirement had been smaller than the lower bound of 950, the planned production would have been set to this lower bound. If the net requirement had exceeded the upper bound of 1300, the planned production would have been set to this upper bound. (There was no change in the planned production between the weeks of March 31 and April 7 because the actual demand for the week of April 7 was equal to the prior weeks forecast. When this unlikely event occurs the plan does not change.)

When the week of April 14 begins, the week of June 9 is 8 weeks into the future. It will pass through a flex fence and the bound will be tightened to be within 10% of the plan. The resulting plan created at the start of the week of April 14 is shown at the top of Table 9.3. First the net requirement for the week of June 9 is computed as follows:

Net requirement = 1166 + 1000 - 851 = 1315

The net requirement exceeds the previously established upper bound of 1300. Thus, the planned production is set to the upper bound.

Planned production = 1300.

The computed upper bound (plan + 10%) would be 1.1 x 1300 = 1430. However this exceeds the previously set upper bound of 1300. So, the upper bound stays at 1300. The lower bound (plan − 10%) is 0.90 x 1300 = 1170 and that rounds down to 1150.

The bounds for the week of June 9 remain unchanged in the rate-based plans of April 21, April 28, and May 5 as shown in Table 9.3. The planned production for the week of June 9 varies within these bounds taking on values of 1206, 1300, and 1300 on of April 21, April 28, and May 5 respectively.

Table 9-3. The Rate-Based Plans for the Weeks of April 14 through May 5

15	Current	5%	5%	5%	5%	10%	10%	10%	10%	15%	15%	15%	15%
Week	14-Apr	21-Apr	28-Apr	5-May	12-May	19-May	26-May	2-Jun	**9-Jun**	16-Jun	23-Jun	30-Jun	7-Jul
Demand	1172	1166	1166	1166	1166	1166	1166	1166	**1166**	1166	1166	1166	1166
Production	1150	1200	1200	1200	1200	1250	1250	1250	**1300**	1181	1166	1166	1166
Lower Bound		1150	1150	1150	1150	1150	1150	1150	**1150**	950	1000	1000	1000
Upper Bound		1200	1200	1200	1200	1250	1250	1250	**1300**	1300	1350	1350	1350
Inventory	463	497	531	565	599	683	767	851	**985**	1000	1000	1000	1000

16	Current	5%	5%	5%	5%	10%	10%	10%	10%	15%	15%	15%	15%
Week	21-Apr	28-Apr	5-May	12-May	19-May	26-May	2-Jun	**9-Jun**	16-Jun	23-Jun	30-Jun	7-Jul	14-Jul
Demand	1120	1157	1157	1157	1157	1157	1157	**1157**	1157	1157	1157	1157	1157
Production	1200	1200	1200	1200	1250	1250	1250	**1206**	1157	1157	1157	1157	1157
Lower Bound		1150	1150	1150	1200	1150	1150	**1150**	1050	1000	1000	1000	1000
Upper Bound		1200	1200	1200	1250	1250	1250	**1300**	1250	1350	1350	1350	1350
Inventory	543	586	629	672	765	858	951	**1000**	1000	1000	1000	1000	1000

17	Current	5%	5%	5%	5%	10%	10%	10%	10%	15%	15%	15%	15%
Week	28-Apr	5-May	12-May	19-May	26-May	2-Jun	**9-Jun**	16-Jun	23-Jun	30-Jun	7-Jul	14-Jul	21-Jul
Demand	1219	1169	1169	1169	1169	1169	**1169**	1169	1169	1169	1169	1169	1169
Production	1200	1200	1200	1250	1250	1250	**1300**	1209	1169	1169	1169	1169	1169
Lower Bound		1150	1150	1200	1200	1150	**1150**	1050	1050	1000	1000	1000	1000
Upper Bound		1200	1200	1250	1250	1250	**1300**	1250	1300	1350	1350	1350	1350
Inventory	524	555	586	667	748	829	**960**	1000	1000	1000	1000	1000	1000

18	Current	5%	5%	5%	5%	10%	10%	10%	10%	15%	15%	15%	15%
Week	5-May	12-May	19-May	26-May	2-Jun	**9-Jun**	16-Jun	23-Jun	30-Jun	7-Jul	14-Jul	21-Jul	28-Jul
Demand	1156	1166	1166	1166	1166	**1166**	1166	1166	1166	1166	1166	1166	1166
Production	1200	1200	1250	1250	1250	**1300**	1178	1166	1166	1166	1166	1166	1166
Lower Bound		1150	1200	1200	1200	**1150**	1050	1050	1050	1000	1000	1000	1000
Upper Bound		1200	1250	1250	1250	**1300**	1250	1300	1300	1350	1350	1350	1350
Inventory	568	602	686	770	854	**988**	1000	1000	1000	1000	1000	1000	1000

When the week of May 12 begins, the week of June 9 is four weeks into the future. It will pass through another flex fence and the bound will be tightened to be within 5% of the plan. The resulting plan created at the beginning of the week of May 12 is shown at the top of Table 9.4. The planned production for the week of June 9 is computed as 1300. Thus, the upper bound stays at 1300, and the lower bound (plan − 5%) rounds to 1250. These bounds for the week of June 9 remain unchanged in the rate-based plans created at the beginning of the next three weeks, as shown in Table 9.4. During these 3 weeks, the planned production varies within the bounds taking on values of 1291, 1282, and 1250.

Table 9.5 shows the plan for the week of June 9; Table 9.4 shows that the week of June 2 ended with 946 in inventory. The actual demand of 1221 shown for the week of June 9 (Table 9.5) represents the new orders that had been received by the beginning of that week. The actual production for the week of June 9 is 1300. (The determination of the quantity and mix of this actual production is described in a later section.) The ending inventory for the week of June 9 is 1025.

Table 9-4. The Rate-Based Plans for the Weeks of May 12 through June 2

19	Current	5%	5%	5%	5%	10%	10%	10%	10%	15%	15%	15%	15%
Week	12-May	19-May	26-May	2-Jun	9-Jun	16-Jun	23-Jun	30-Jun	7-Jul	14-Jul	21-Jul	28-Jul	4-Aug
Demand	1222	1177	1177	1177	1177	1177	1177	1177	1177	1177	1177	1177	1177
Production	1200	1250	1250	1250	1300	1250	1216	1177	1177	1177	1177	1177	1177
Lower Bound		1200	1200	1200	1250	1050	1050	1050	1050	1000	1000	1000	1000
Upper Bound		1250	1250	1250	1300	1250	1300	1300	1300	1350	1350	1350	1350
Inventory	546	619	692	765	888	961	1000	1000	1000	1000	1000	1000	1000

20	Current	5%	5%	5%	5%	10%	10%	10%	10%	15%	15%	15%	15%
Week	19-May	26-May	2-Jun	9-Jun	16-Jun	23-Jun	30-Jun	7-Jul	14-Jul	21-Jul	28-Jul	4-Aug	11-Aug
Demand	1101	1162	1162	1162	1162	1162	1162	1162	1162	1162	1162	1162	1162
Production	1250	1250	1250	1291	1162	1162	1162	1162	1162	1162	1162	1162	1162
Lower Bound		1200	1200	1250	1100	1050	1050	1050	1050	1000	1000	1000	1000
Upper Bound		1250	1250	1300	1200	1300	1300	1300	1300	1350	1350	1350	1350
Inventory	695	783	871	1000	1000	1000	1000	1000	1000	1000	1000	1000	1000

21	Current	5%	5%	5%	5%	10%	10%	10%	10%	15%	15%	15%	15%
Week	26-May	2-Jun	9-Jun	16-Jun	23-Jun	30-Jun	7-Jul	14-Jul	21-Jul	28-Jul	4-Aug	11-Aug	18-Aug
Demand	1155	1161	1161	1161	1161	1161	1161	1161	1161	1161	1161	1161	1161
Production	1250	1250	1282	1161	1161	1161	1161	1161	1161	1161	1161	1161	1161
Lower Bound		1200	1250	1100	1100	1050	1050	1050	1050	1000	1000	1000	1000
Upper Bound		1250	1300	1200	1200	1300	1300	1300	1300	1350	1350	1350	1350
Inventory	790	879	1000	1000	1000	1000	1000	1000	1000	1000	1000	1000	1000

22	Current	5%	5%	5%	5%	10%	10%	10%	10%	15%	15%	15%	15%
Week	2-Jun	9-Jun	16-Jun	23-Jun	30-Jun	7-Jul	14-Jul	21-Jul	28-Jul	4-Aug	11-Aug	18-Aug	25-Aug
Demand	1094	1148	1148	1148	1148	1148	1148	1148	1148	1148	1148	1148	1148
Production	1250	1250	1100	1148	1148	1148	1148	1148	1148	1148	1148	1148	1148
Lower Bound		1250	1100	1100	1100	1050	1050	1050	1050	1000	1000	1000	1000
Upper Bound		1300	1200	1200	1200	1300	1300	1300	1250	1350	1350	1350	1300
Inventory	946	1048	1000	1000	1000	1000	1000	1000	1000	1000	1000	1000	1000

Table 9-5. The Rate-Based Plan for the Week of June 9

23	Current	5%	5%	5%	5%	10%	10%	10%	10%	15%	15%	15%	15%
Week	9-Jun	16-Jun	23-Jun	30-Jun	7-Jul	14-Jul	21-Jul	28-Jul	4-Aug	11-Aug	18-Aug	25-Aug	1-Sep
Demand	1221	1163	1163	1163	1163	1163	1163	1163	1163	1163	1163	1163	1163
Production	1300	1138	1163	1163	1163	1163	1163	1163	1163	1163	1163	1163	1163
Lower Bound		1100	1100	1100	1100	1050	1050	1050	1050	1000	1000	1000	1000
Upper Bound		1200	1200	1200	1200	1300	1300	1250	1300	1350	1350	1300	1350
Inventory	1025	1000	1000	1000	1000	1000	1000	1000	1000	1000	1000	1000	1000

Figure 9.4 illustrates that, in this example, rate-based planning provides a good compromise among schedule smoothness, responsiveness, and accuracy of production rate forecasts. The figure shows the weekly production and inventory levels generated by the rate-based planning computations. Although the production levels are not totally smooth, they are certainly less variable than the weekly demand shown in Figure 9.1 and much smoother than the production levels generated by an MRP algorithm (with the 4-week lead time in Figure 9.2).

The largest week-to-week change in the rate of production is 100, or about 10%, which is the distance between the upper and lower bounds for the initial 4 weeks of the flex capacity requirements profile. However, these changes in production rates were anticipated. By definition, these production rates are within 5% of the forecasts given 4 weeks earlier, within 10% of the forecasts given 8 weeks earlier, and within 15% of the forecasts given 12 weeks earlier.

Figure 9-4. Production and Inventory Levels from Rate-Based Planning

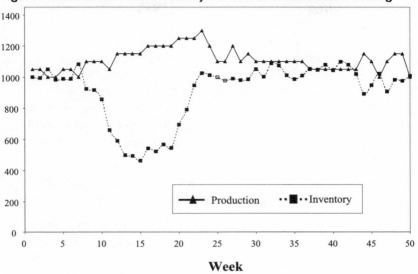

Week

The inventory levels show that the rate-based plan reacted more quickly to changes in customer demand than did the MRP schedule. The variation in inventory is about half of that created by the MRP schedule with the 4-week lead time presented in Figure 9.2.

DEFINING THE FLEXIBILITY REQUIREMENTS PROFILE

The flexibility requirements profile defines the permissible ranges of variation from the planned drumbeat rates. These ranges represent a negotiated agreement between an enterprise and its critical suppliers. The ranges reflect the capability of the supply chain to ramp up from the plan and the willingness of the customer (the buyer) to commit to future purchases when demand falls short of the plan.

From a purely mathematical perspective, the flexibility requirements profile should permit sufficient deviation from the plan to permit timely reaction to shifts in the level of demand. They should restrict deviation sufficiently to have a smoothing effect on the rate of the drumbeat. The ranges that give the smoothest production schedule should be estimated on simulations with historical data.

In the above example, suppose the flexibility requirements profile restricted the range of deviation from the plan to only one percent for the first 4 weeks. Permitting only such a small amount of deviation effectively amounts to a 4-week freeze. The lack of responsiveness would cause huge variation in inventories similar to those created by an MRP with a fixed 4-week lead time as shown in Figure 9.2. Thus, a bullwhip effect on production would occur similar to that shown in Figure 9.2. On the other hand, suppose the range of deviation from the plan was permitted to be ±20% for the first 4 weeks. The resulting schedule will have large swings (perhaps as large as 40%) between consecutive weeks. A flexibility requirements profile that is too loose will have little smoothing effect on the week-to-week variation in the drumbeat.

RATE-BASED PLANNING AND THE THEORY OF CONSTRAINTS

Viewed from a Theory of Constraints (TOC) perspective, rate-based planning integrates two types of constraints into the planning and scheduling process:

- The external market constraint
- The internal constraints on capacity and material supply.

The market constraint is unique because it is the most unpredictable.

As a planning tool, rate-based planning identifies which type of constraint is expected to become the bottleneck in the future, i.e., the constraint to be elevated. As a scheduling tool, it sets the drumbeat according to the bottleneck constraint whether it is the internal constraint on production capacity and/or material supply or external market constraint.

For example, in the plan presented in Table 9.1, the planned production levels are at their upper bounds for the next 7 weeks. This is a statement that the current bottleneck is internal, i.e., the market exceeds the available capacity and/or material supply. It is a forecast that the bottleneck is expected to be internal in future weeks. On the other hand, had the planned levels been at the lower bounds, this would have indicated that the market is the bottleneck and is expected to be the bottleneck in future weeks.

The market constraint can quickly change from a bottleneck to a non-bottleneck or vice versa. Therefore, rate-based planning gives it special focus. Without this focus, the natural tendency is to become internally focused during periods of growing demand when the bottleneck is internal. The internally focused company is vulnerable when the market becomes the bottleneck. This was the case in the computer hardware industry, which experienced a drop in sales in the first quarter of 2001, after a decade of growth. Some chip manufacturers ended up with a year's supply of inventory.

The market constraint is unique in another way. It is subject to short-term variability that cannot be eliminated. Thus, it must be buffered by a finished goods inventory (or an order queue) to prevent its capacity from being reduced by stock-outs and to protect the internal constraints from this variability.

DEFINING THE DRUMBEAT OPERATION

The rate-based plan defines the rate of aggregate production. However the selection of the process to serve as the drumbeat process and the positioning of the buffer inventories requires some careful thought. The drumbeat process and the processes upstream from the drumbeat process will be buffered from the variation in customer demand by inventory. This will not be the case for the processes downstream from the drumbeat process.

For example, in an assemble-to-order process there would be a buffer inventory of components. The drumbeat of the rate-based plan would control the processes that build these components. The production rate in final assembly would, by design, vary in response to variation in customer demand.

The raw-as-possible (RAP) principle indicates that the inventory can be minimized by having the smallest amount of product differentiation prior to the drumbeat process. This minimizes the amount of inventory needed to buffer the process against variation in demand. However, the processes downstream from the drumbeat must:

- be capable of absorbing the variation in customers demand and
- have short enough flow times to be able to turn around customer orders quickly.

The transmission example used here is a configure-to-order process. Only three basic transmissions are configured: a five-speed, a six-speed and a heavy-duty six-speed transmission. However dozens of different final configurations can occur. The bell housing, the shift linkage, the mounting brackets, and electronic controls will differ depending whether the transmission is to be used in a truck, a bus, a van, or motor home. The transmission will differ depending on the engine (diesel or gasoline) and the chassis (front engine, cab over engine, or a rear engine layout) with which the transmission is to be used.

The inventory buffer consists of the three basic undifferentiated transmissions. The addition of the external features is done after the customer's orders are received. The process that does this differentiation is not insulated from the variation in customer demand.

TRANSLATING THE AGGREGATE RATE-BASED PLAN INTO PLANS FOR END ITEMS

The rate-based plan is developed for the total or aggregate demand. It is a plan for optimally accommodating the inevitable changes in demand volume while staying within the capabilities of the manufacturing processes and the suppliers.

However, the demand mix and the aggregate demand volume will vary. To be useful, the aggregate plan must be translated into plans for individual end items. This section illustrates how the aggregate rate-based plan is portioned into plans for the different end items. The following section will discuss how this plan is used each week to compute a schedule for end items. Then, the translation of the aggregate plan into a *plan for materials* will be discussed. Following that, we will discuss the integration of the material plan into the scheduling process.

The rate-based plan can be considered as series of weekly *file drawers* of future capacity (illustrated in Figure 9.5). Each weekly file drawer is partitioned into capacity reserved for each of the three end items: the five-speed transmission T5, the six-speed transmission T6 and the heavy duty six-speed transmission TH6. The total size of the weekly file drawers can be expanded or shrunk within the ranges given by the lower and upper bounds of the aggregate rate-based plan. In addition, the partitions can be moved. For example, when the demand for T5 is lower than the forecast, but the demand for T6 is higher, then some of the capacity reserved to T5 can be reallocated to T6.

We use a simple two-product example to illustrate how the aggregate plan is apportioned into plans for individual items. Suppose with two products A and B, A is forecasted to comprise 64% of the demand and B is forecasted to comprise 36% of the

Figure 9-5. Allocation of Planned Aggregate Capacity to End Items

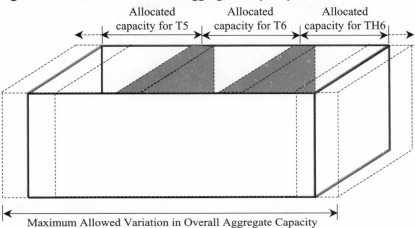

demand. Let $P_A = 0.64$ denote the proportion of the forecasted demand that is for product A, and $P_B = 0.36$ denote the proportion of forecasted demand that is for product B.

Suppose that the aggregate plan for a given future week is 2500, with a lower bound of 2000 and an upper bound of 3000.

To compute the planned rate of production for an end item for future weeks, it is only necessary to multiply the proportions times the aggregate plan.

$$\text{Plan}_A = P_A \times \text{aggregate plan} = 0.64 \times 2500 = 1600$$

$$\text{Plan}_B = P_B \times \text{aggregate plan} = 0.36 \times 2500 = 900$$

However, the lower and upper bounds for the two end items should not be strictly proportional to the aggregate lower and upper bounds. This is because, percentage-wise, the demand for end items will be more variable than the aggregate demand and because opportunities exist to gain additional flexibility for these end items by reallocating capacity between the two end items (i.e., moving the partitions within the file drawer).

Thus, the flexibility range used in computing the lower and upper bounds is proportional to the square root of P, times the corresponding range in the aggregate rate-based plan: [5]

Upper bound = P x aggregate plan + $\sqrt{P}$ x (aggregate upper bound – aggregate plan)

Lower bound = P x aggregate plan – $\sqrt{P}$ x (aggregate plan – aggregate lower bound)

Upper Bound$_A$ = 0.64 x 2500 + $\sqrt{0.64}$ x (3000 – 2500) = 2000

Lower Bound$_A$ = 0.64 x 2500 – $\sqrt{0.64}$ x (2500 – 2000) = 1200

Upper Bound$_B$ = 0.36 x 2500 + $\sqrt{0.36}$ x (3000 – 2500) = 1200

Lower Bound$_B$ = 0.36 x 2500 - $\sqrt{0.36}$ x (2500 – 2000) = 600

Percentage-wise, the bounds for A and B are wider than those for the aggregate plan. (For the aggregate plan, the range is ±20%; for A it is ±25% and for B it is ±33%. The bounds on A and B do not add to the corresponding aggregate bounds. For example, the sum of the upper bounds for A and B is 2000 + 1200 = 3200, while the aggregate upper bound is 3000. These apparent inconsistencies only reflect that constraints occur on the individual production levels of A and B as do different constraints on the total production. The production of A could be as high 2000, and the production of B could be as high 1200 but *not simultaneously*. The total production of A and B must satisfy the upper bound of 3000 on aggregate production.

Suppose with our earlier transmission example, the proportions of the total demand comprised by T5, T6, and TH6 transmissions respectively are P_{T5} = 0.42, P_{T6} = 0.33, and P_{TH6} = 0.25. Table 9.6 below illustrates the use of these formulas to translate the aggregate plan into rate-based plans for the end items. The plan is for the week of June 2 and gives the forecast of the next 12 weeks for each of the three end items.

---

5. There is empirical data that shows that many demand processes exhibit the property that the standard deviation of demand (a measure of variability) is proportional to the square root of the average demand. The theory of Poisson processes predicts that this should be the case under certain assumptions.

Table 9-6. The Rate-Based Plan for the End Items, Computed during the Week of June 2

Week	Aggregate Plan	Lower Bound	Upper Bound	T5 (p=.42) Plan	Lower Bound	Upper Bound	T6 (p=.33) Plan	Lower Bound	Upper Bound	TH6 (p=.25) plan	Lower Bound	Upper Bound
9-Jun	1250	1250	1300	525	525	557	413	413	442	313	313	338
16-Jun	1100	1100	1200	462	462	527	363	363	420	275	275	325
23-Jun	1148	1100	1200	482	451	516	379	351	409	287	263	313
30-Jun	1148	1100	1200	482	451	516	379	351	409	287	263	313
7-Jul	1148	1050	1300	482	418	581	379	323	466	287	238	363
14-Jul	1148	1050	1300	482	418	581	379	323	466	287	238	363
21-Jul	1148	1050	1300	482	418	581	379	323	466	287	238	363
28-Jul	1148	1050	1250	482	418	548	379	323	438	287	238	338
4-Aug	1148	1000	1350	482	386	613	379	294	495	287	213	388
11-Aug	1148	1000	1350	482	386	613	379	294	495	287	213	388
18-Aug	1148	1000	1350	482	386	613	379	294	495	287	213	388
25-Aug	1148	1000	1300	482	386	581	379	294	466	287	213	363

DETERMINING THE ACTUAL SCHEDULES FOR THE END ITEMS

Eventually the rate-based plan must be converted into a schedule for actual production for end items. This is the week in which the schedule becomes frozen. In the transmission example, the freeze occurs at the start of the week of actual production. Ideally, this would be the case, but in other instances, the schedule may become frozen 1 week, 2 weeks, or more into the future. This freeze would be due to the limitations of the manufacturing processes and the external suppliers to respond quickly. (However, inability to make small changes in the plan implies the necessity of making much larger changes later.) The flexibility requirements profile would reflect this period of freeze by having 0% flexibility during the future weeks in which the plan becomes frozen into a schedule.

In converting the plan into a frozen schedule, separate schedules are computed for each of the end items. If the total production violates an aggregate bound, then the end item plans must be adjusted to satisfy the aggregate bound. The computations will be illustrated by using the plan for the transmissions in Table 9.6. When the week of June 9 becomes the current week, this plan will be used to compute the schedule.

Step 1. Compute the net requirements for each end item:

Net Requirement = Current week's Demand
+ Target Inventory – Current Inventory

Suppose the June 9 net requirement for T5, T6, and TH6 are 600, 450, and 300 respectively.

Step 2. Compare these net requirements to the respective bounds for the end items and make the necessary adjustments. The net requirement for T5 exceeds the upper bound of 557, so the target production for T5 is set to 557. The net requirement for T6 exceeds the upper bound of 442, so the target production for T6 is set to 442. The net requirement for TH6 is below the lower bound of 313, so the target production for T5 is set to 313.

Step 3. Compare the sum of the target production levels to the bounds on aggregate production. If the sum of the target production levels fall within the bounds for aggregate production, then these target production levels become the actual schedule. If the sum of the target production levels fall outside the aggregate upper bounds or lower bound, they are scaled proportionally to meet the aggregate bound. In the example, the sum of the target production levels is $557 + 442 + 313 = 1312$. This exceeds the upper bound of 1300 on aggregate production, so the production levels of the end items will have to be reduced to meet this upper bound. The target level of TH6 is at its lower bound so it cannot be reduced. The total production of T5 and T6 ($557 + 442 = 999$) will be reduced by 12 units or about 1.2 percent. The target production of T5 and T6 will each be reduced by 1.2% giving production rates of 550 for T5 and 437 for T6. The production rate for TH6 will be 313 for a total of 1300 units.

TRANSLATING THE AGGREGATE PLAN INTO PLANS FOR MATERIALS: THE PLANNING BILL OF MATERIALS

A planning bill of materials (BOM) gives, for the forecasted product mix, the average usage of individual parts as a fraction of the aggregate production. A generic template for the planning BOM for the transmissions is given below in Figure 9.6. There are some parts common to all three transmissions. Some are unique to a particular transmission. Some parts are shared by two of the transmissions.

This planning BOM shows, for example, that for parts used only in T5 transmissions, the planned usage rate will have $P = .42$, which indicates the usage rate will be 42% of the rate of the aggregate plan. Similarly for parts used only in T6, the planned usage rate will be 33% of the rate of the aggregate plan. Parts that are used in both transmissions, T5 and T6, will have a planned usage rate that is 75% of the rate of the aggregate plan.

Figure 9-6. The Planning Bill of Materials

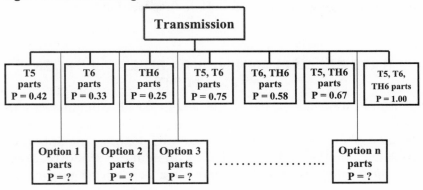

These usage rates can be used to translate the aggregate rate-based plan into a rate-based plan for any specific part, to be shared with the supplier of that part. The computations in computing this plan are the same as those illustrated in the previous section in computing plans for the end items.

$$\text{Planned part usage} = P \times \text{aggregate plan}$$

$$\text{Upper bound on part usage} = P \times \text{aggregate plan} + \sqrt{P} \times (\text{aggregate upper bound} - \text{aggregate plan})$$

$$\text{Lower bound on part usage} = P \times \text{aggregate plan} - \sqrt{P} \times (\text{aggregate plan} - \text{aggregate lower bound})$$

In developing the actual schedule, the constraints on the availability of parts must be taken into account. The production of each end item must observe the bounds for that end item, and the aggregate production must satisfy the bounds of the aggregate rate-based plan. *In addition* the total production of subsets of end items sharing common parts cannot exceed the upper bound on the usage of the common part. For example, the total production of T5 and T6 cannot exceed the upper bound established for the parts common to these two transmissions.

The calculation of the upper and lower bounds for individual parts illustrates the importance of *parts commonality*. Parts commonality buffers operations from variation in the mix of customer demand. For example, percentage-wise, a part that is common to all end items requires only half of the flex capability of a part that is used in only 25% of the end items.

RATE-BASED PLANNING IN A BUILD TO ORDER ENVIRONMENT

In a build to order environment, a backlog of orders is used to buffer operations against the short-term variations in customer demand. The computations for developing the rate-based plan are the same as in the build to stock environment except the planned drumbeat rate is computed to maintain a target order queue:

$$\text{Planned Production} = \text{Forecasted demand} - \text{Target order} \\ \text{queue} + \text{Previous weeks ending} \\ \text{order queue}$$

If the computed planned production exceeds the upper bound, it is set equal to the upper bound. If it falls below the lower bound it is set equal to the lower bound. An example is shown in Table 9.7 below. In this example, the target order queue is set to 1000, which is about 1 week's demand. For the current week (April 7), 1515 is the ending order queue. To get this order queue back to the target level, the following weeks show the planned production at the upper bound, ramping up from the current level of 1150 to 1200 in 2 weeks (April 21) and to 1250 in 6 weeks (May 19).

Table 9-7. The Rate-Based Plan for a Build-to-Order Environment

14	Current	5%	5%	5%	5%	10%	10%	10%	10%	15%	15%	15%	15%
Week	7-Apr	14-Apr	21-Apr	28-Apr	5-May	12-May	19-May	26-May	2-Jun	9-Jun	16-Jun	23-Jun	30-Jun
Demand	1164	1164	1164	1164	1164	1164	1164	1164	1164	1164	1164	1164	1164
Production	1150	1150	1200	1200	1200	1200	1250	1250	1250	1291	1164	1164	1164
Lower Bound		1100	1150	1150	1150	1050	1150	1150	1150	950	950	1000	1000
Upper Bound		1150	1200	1200	1200	1200	1250	1250	1250	1300	1300	1350	1350
Order Queue	1515	1529	1493	1457	1421	1385	1299	1213	1127	1000	1000	1000	1000

The rate-based plan for the end items is shown in Table 9.8 below. This plan will be used for order promising, as is explained in the following section.

Table 9-8. Rate-Based Plans for End Items in a Build-to-Order Environment

Week	Aggregate Plan	Lower Bound	Upper Bound	T5 (p=.42) Plan	Lower Bound	Upper Bound	T6 (p=.33) Plan	Lower Bound	Upper Bound	TH6 (p=.25) plan	Lower Bound	Upper Bound
14-Apr	1150	1100	1150	483	451	483	380	351	380	288	263	288
21-Apr	1200	1150	1200	504	472	504	396	367	396	300	275	300
28-Apr	1200	1150	1200	504	472	504	396	367	396	300	275	300
5-May	1200	1150	1200	504	472	504	396	367	396	300	275	300
12-May	1200	1050	1200	504	407	504	396	310	396	300	225	300
19-May	1250	1150	1250	525	460	525	413	356	413	313	263	313
26-May	1250	1150	1250	525	460	525	413	356	413	313	263	313
2-Jun	1250	1150	1250	525	460	525	413	356	413	313	263	313
9-Jun	1291	950	1300	542	321	548	426	230	431	323	153	328
16-Jun	1164	950	1300	489	350	577	384	261	462	291	184	359
23-Jun	1164	1000	1350	489	383	610	384	290	491	291	209	384
30-Jun	1164	1000	1350	489	383	610	384	290	491	291	209	384

ORDER PROMISING IN A RATE-BASED PLANNING ENVIRONMENT

With rate-based planning, orders are promised against available capacity. Table 9.9 shows an example. The table gives, for each week, the number of items promised, the available to promise (ATP) amount, and the upper bound on capacity. The items promised represent orders that have been taken for items to be produced in that week. The ATP amount tells how many more items can be promised for that week without violating an upper bound. This information is provided for aggregate production as well as the individual end items. The week of April 7 is the current week. The table gives the order promising information for the next 12 weeks.

The earliest promise date of production for each of the end items is the earliest week in which the available to promise is nonzero. For T5, this is the week of April 14, for T6, it is the week of April 21 and for TH6, it is the week of April 28th.

The aggregate ATP amount is computed as follows:

Aggregate ATP = Aggregate Upper Bound – Aggregate Promised

The ATP amount for each item cannot exceed the aggregate ATP amount:

ATP amount for end item = Minimum(aggregate ATP amount, end item upper bound – end item promised)

In the example, the aggregate ATP for the week of April 14 is 182, but the ATP amount for T6 and TH6 is 0. This is because the promised quantities for T6 and TH6 are equal to their respective upper bounds. In other instances, it would be possible for an end

Table 9-9: Order Promising with Rate-Based Planning

Week	Aggregate Promised	ATP	Upper Bound	T5 (p=.42) Promised	ATP	Upper Bound	T6 (p=.33) Promised	ATP	Upper Bound	TH6 (p=.25) Promised	ATP	Upper Bound
14-Apr	968	182	1150	300	182	483	380	0	380	288	0	288
21-Apr	450	750	1200	0	504	504	150	246	396	300	0	300
28-Apr	97	1103	1200	0	504	504	0	396	396	97	203	300
5-May	0	1200	1200	0	504	504	0	396	396	0	300	300
12-May	0	1200	1200	0	504	504	0	396	396	0	300	300
19-May	0	1250	1250	0	525	525	0	413	413	0	313	313
26-May	0	1250	1250	0	525	525	0	413	413	0	313	313
2-Jun	0	1250	1250	0	525	525	0	413	413	0	313	313
9-Jun	0	1300	1300	0	548	548	0	431	431	0	328	328
16-Jun	0	1300	1300	0	577	577	0	462	462	0	359	359
23-Jun	0	1350	1350	0	610	610	0	491	491	0	384	384
30-Jun	0	1350	1350	0	610	610	0	491	491	0	384	384

item (for which the promised is not equal to its upper bound) to have no ATP because the aggregate ATP is zero. This would imply that all of the available aggregate capacity had been promised to fill orders for other end items.

Although it is not shown in this example, the computations of the ATP amount should take into account the rate-based plans for critical shared parts. For example, the total amount promised of T5 and T6 in any week should not exceed the upper bound on parts shared by these two transmissions. Similarly, the promising of transmissions with options should not violate the upper bound on the availability of these options. To give an example, Dell, Inc., accepts an order for a computer and promises delivery only if all of the parts required to build the computer will be available. If the parts will not be available, the Dell order-management process steers the customer to an attractively priced alternate choice. (This is known as *up-selling* as noted in Chapter 1.)

EXPLOITING DIFFERING CUSTOMER RESPONSE TIME REQUIREMENTS

In many manufacturing environments, the customers may have differing response time requirements. For example, the transmission manufacturer may sell replacement transmissions to the after-market. These after-market customers need shipment within a week and are willing to pay a premium price. Another group of customers may be OEMs who are using the transmissions to build trucks and bus chassis. These customers will place orders a month prior to expected shipment. Other customers may be military parts depots that order spares in large quantities and expect the shipments to be shipped over the next 3 months.

Suppose that each of these customers account for one third of the current demand. To meet the demand of the 1-week lead time customers, it is necessary to reserve one third of the capacity until the week before actual production. This allows the orders with a 1-week lead time to be placed in the schedule for the following week. Another one third of the capacity will be reserved until a month before the actual production.

Table 9.10 below shows an example of the order promising spreadsheet (with the current week as April 7). Orders with a 1-week lead time received during the current week can be promised against the available capacity of 96 for April 14th. (If the number of these short lead time orders falls short of 96, orders from future weeks may be pulled in to complete the plan.) Similarly, orders received during the current week with a 1-month lead time can be promised against the 190 units of available capacity in the weeks of April 28 and May 5th. Orders with lead times of more than one month will be promised against the available capacity of the week of May 12 and beyond.

Table 9-10. Using Reserved Capacity to Satisfy Customers with Short Lead Time Requirements

Week	TH6 (p=.25) Promised	Reserved	ATP	Upper Bound
14-Apr	192	0	96	288
21-Apr	200	100	0	300
28-Apr	110	100	90	300
5-May	100	100	100	300
12-May	83	200	17	300
19-May	0	209	104	313
26-May	0	209	104	313
2-Jun	0	209	104	313
9-Jun	0	219	109	328
16-Jun	0	239	120	359
23-Jun	0	256	128	384
30-Jun	0	256	128	384

For future weeks 5 through 12 (May 12 to June 30), two thirds of the available capacity is reserved. For weeks 2 through 4 (April 21 to May 5), the reserved capacity is reduced to one third of the available capacity. For week 1 (April 7), all remaining capacity has been made available for order promising.

PRESERVING THE DRUMBEAT: SCHEDULING BATCH PROCESSES

This section deals with the planning and scheduling of batch processes, i.e., processes with setups that prevent mixed-model production. The proper management of batch processes is critical to the functioning of pull systems. The functioning of pull system requires that:

- a steady drumbeat produces smooth demand signals for all upstream processes and
- the response time of the upstream processes to these signals is short and predictable.

However, if a batch process produces in batches that are too large, infrequent, or unpredictable, then the processes upstream from the batch process will experience highly variable demand, and the processes downstream from the process will experience long and highly variable response times.

The objectives in scheduling batch operations are the following:

- Produce each item as frequently as possible, subject to the limitations imposed by the time available for setups.
- Maintain a periodic production plan, i.e., a production sequence that is of fixed time duration and is repetitive.
- Optimize, within this periodic plan, the frequency of production of items according to volume. (For example, high volume products might be produced every shift, while medium volume products may be produced every other shift and low volume products produced every third shift.)
- Produce in quantities dictated by the drumbeat of the downstream process. When an item is produced, the production quantity will be determined by the *kanban* pull signals from the downstream processes, not by some predetermined lot size.
- Maintain some flex capacity as a buffer against process variation and variation in the pull signals.

Building the Periodic Production Plan

We will use an example to illustrate our method for building the period production plan. Consider a machining cell that makes six different items. The weekly demand (shown in Table 9.11) is the usage rate at the current drumbeat. The table shows the cycle times in seconds for these six different items, i.e., the production times in seconds per unit. The table also shows the weekly amount of run time required to meet the demand for these six items.

Table 9-11. Weekly Demand, Cell Cycle Time and Run Times

Product	Weekly Demand D	Cell Cycle Time (sec.)	Run Time hrs/week
A	2000	24	13.33
B	1000	30	8.33
C	2750	21	16.04
D	1450	31	12.49
E	850	23	5.43
F	1240	27	9.30
		Total:	65

For example, the current usage for part A is 2000 pieces per week. The cell is capable of producing one piece every 24 seconds. The run time to meet a weeks demand for part A is (2000 pieces) x (24 pieces/second) = 48000 seconds or 13.33 hours. The total run times for all six products is approximately 65 hours.

Other information:

- The cell is in operation for two 8-hour shifts, 5 days per week. The total time available is 80 hours per week.
- The setup for each item requires 10 minutes.

Step 1. Allocating flex capacity. There will be variation in the daily usage and variation in process execution. Thus, without some flex capability to respond to this variation, it would be impossible to keep up with the drumbeat. For this particular example, 10% of the available 80 hours will be reserved as flex capacity, leaving 72 hours available for the 65 hours of run time and setups. This leaves

$72 - 65 = 7$ hours available for setups. (It would be reasonable to reserve 10% of the available time as flex capacity in a machine cell. When the time is not needed, it can be used for maintenance and other activities. Another option would be to reserve less flex capacity and use overtime when additional flex capacity is needed.)

Step 2: Determining the maximum number of setups that can be done in the available time. The TOC model of Throughput, Inventory, and Operating Expense shows that the optimal number of setups is the maximum number that can be done in the available idle time. Performing more setups allows a reduction in batch sizes and, therefore, a reduction in inventory. And as long as the time devoted to setups does not exceed the available idle time, this inventory reduction does not reduce throughput or increase costs. In the example, there are 7 hours per week available for changeovers. Each changeover requires 10 minutes:

Maximum number of setups = (7 hours/week x 60 minutes/ hour)/10 minutes/setup = 42 setups/week.

Step 3: Allocating the Setups among Products. To minimize the total *kanban* inventory of the products, the fraction of the available setups allocated to a particular product is proportional to the square root of the usage rate for that product:

$$\text{Fraction of setups allocated to product i} = \frac{\sqrt{D_i}}{\sum_{j=1}^{N} \sqrt{Dj}}$$

This fraction is referred to as the Square Root Ratio (SRR). The formula assumes that the setups for each of the products require the same amount of time. When the setup times are different the formula is the following:

$$\text{Fraction of setups allocated to product i} = \frac{\sqrt{D_i / S_i}}{\sum_{j=1}^{N} \sqrt{D_j / S_j}}$$

Where S_i is the setup time for product i.

Table 9.12 shows the computation of the optimal allocation of the 42 setups per week among the products in the example. Column 3 gives the square root of the weekly demands for each product. The sum of these square roots is 231.22. Column 4 gives the square root ratios. For example, the ratio for product A is

44.72/231.22 = 0.19. This says that 19% of the 42 available setups should be allocated to product A. Column 5 gives the number of setups to be allocated to each product, computed as the SRR times the total number of setups. For product A, this number is 0.19 x 42 = 8.5.

Table 9-12. Computing Number of Setups Allocated to Each Product

| 1 | 2 Weekly Demand | 3 | 4 Square Root | 5 | 6 | 7 |
Product	D	Sqrt(D)	Ratio (SRR)	SRR*42	Rounded	Rounded
A	2000	44.72	0.19	8.0	10.0	10.0
B	1000	31.62	0.14	5.9	3.0	5.0
C	2750	52.44	0.23	9.7	10.0	10.0
D	1450	38.08	0.16	6.7	5.0	5.0
E	850	29.15	0.13	5.5	3.0	5.0
F	1240	35.21	0.15	6.3	3.0	5.0
	Sum	231.22				

The week has ten shifts, so an arbitrary choice is made to round the number of setups to the nearest multiple of five. This rounding is done to fit the setups into a periodic schedule. In general, it is desired that some products be made every shift, some every other shift, and perhaps some every third or fourth shift. Column 6 gives the number of setups rounded to the nearest multiple of five. Product A and C will be made ten times per week or every shift and the other products will be made five times per week or every other shift.

Step 4: Building the Periodic Production Plan: The periodic production plan sequences the batches into specific shifts. To do this, the average batch sizes and the average time required for each batch must be determined. Table 9.13 gives these computations for the example. For example, product A with a weekly demand of 2000 is produced ten times per week thus the average batch size is 200. Product A has a 24-second cycle time per piece. The average batch run time is 200 pieces/batch x 24 seconds/piece = 4800 seconds/batch = 80 minutes/batch. To this run time, the 10-minute set-up time is added, giving a total of 90 minutes required for each batch of product A. The computations for the other batches are similar.

Table 9-13. Computing Time Requirements for each Product

1 Product	2 Weekly Demand D	3 Batches per Week	4 Average Batch Size	5 Cell Cycle Time secs	6 Avg. Batch Run Time Minutes	7 Run Time plus Setup Time
A	2000	10	200	24	80	90
B	1000	5	200	30	100	110
C	2750	10	275	21	96	106
D	1450	5	290	31	150	160
E	850	5	170	23	65	75
F	1240	5	248	27	112	122

Table 9.14 shows the periodic production plan for producing these products across the two daily shifts. In building this plan, the products to be made every shift (A and C) were first put into each shift. Then the products that are to be made in only one shift were scheduled in descending order of hours per shift. Each product was allocated to the shift that currently had the least total amount of work assigned.

After products A and C were assigned to both shifts, the sequence in which the remaining products were assigned was: D to shift 1, F to shift 2, B to shift 2 and E to shift one. By assigning the products in descending order of time requirements to the shift having the most remaining time available, it was possible to create a schedule that balanced the workload across the shifts. In this example, the total average time assigned to the first shift was 431 minutes or 7 hours and 11 minutes. Shift 2 was assigned 428 minutes or 7 hours and 8 minutes.

Table 9-14. The Periodic Production Plan

1st shift	Product	C	A	D	E	Total
	Mins./batch	106	90	160	75	431

2nd shift	Product	C	A	F	B	Total
	Mins./batch	106	90	122	110	428

The resulting periodic production plan is shift 1 (CADE) and shift 2 (CAFB). Therefore, the interval between consecutive batches is fixed at 8 or 16 work hours. The quantity produced in each batch will be determined by the pull signals.

The number of periods (in this case, the number of shifts) involved in building the periodic production plan is the smallest number that is a multiple of all individual product cycles. For example, if some products are to be made every shift, some every two shifts, and some every three shifts, the periodic production plan would involve a period of six shifts. Some of the products that are made every two shifts would be scheduled in shifts 1, 3, and 5 and some would be scheduled in shifts 2, 4, and 6. Some of the products that are made every three shifts would be scheduled in shifts 1 and 4, some in shifts 2 and 5, and some in shifts 3 and 6. The products would be added to the schedule in descending order of time requirements, to the shift having the most remaining time available.

If the set-up times are sequence dependent, the order could be rearranged within the shift to optimize the set-up sequence. For example, if it requires less time to set up for product E when it follows product A, then the plan for shift 1 could be changed to CAED. However, the equal time intervals between runs of a product must be preserved. For example, a schedule with shift 1 (ADEC) and shift 2 (CAFB) would defeat the purpose of the period production plan, because product C would made at the end of shift 1 and again at the beginning of shift 2.

From a process improvement perspective the goal is to reduce setup times. For example, if the setup time can be halved, this allows twice as many setups in the period production plan. This halves the response time and the WIP, and also smoothes the pull signal to upstream processes.

CONCLUSIONS

- In pull execution, one process serves as the drumbeat for all upstream processes.
- A finished goods inventory or an order queue will be used to buffer the drumbeat process from short-term variation in customer demand.
- In the short term, the drumbeat process will have a constant rate of production and a fixed product mix.
- The upstream processes are driven by pull signals from the drumbeat processes, rather than a centralized schedule.
- The size of the buffer inventory can be reduced by postponing the differentiation of the product to processes downstream from the drumbeat process. However, the processes that do the differentiation must have flow times shorter than the customers

expected lead time and must be capable of flexing in response to short-term variation in customer demand.

- From a TOC perspective, rate-based planning integrates the vitally important market constraint into the planning process. It is a tool for identifying which constraint (market or production capacity) is expected to be the bottleneck in the future.
- As a planning and scheduling tool, rate-based planning establishes the drumbeat according to the constraint. When the constraint is internal, the drumbeat is at the upper bound. When the market is the constraint, the drumbeat is at its lower bound.
- The purpose of rate-based planning is to plan and schedule the rate of the drumbeat, while ensuring three characteristics:
  a. The actual schedule will be within a specified range of the long-term plan.
  b. Adequate flexibility exists to respond quickly to changes in the volume and mix of customer demand.
  c. The short-term variations in scheduled volume and mix are small.
- Rate-based planning is done at an aggregate level. The aggregate plan is then portioned into plans and schedules for specific end items.
- Percentage-wise, there will be more flexibility in the plan for specific end items than in the aggregate plan because:
  a. The demand for specific items will be more variable than the aggregate demand.
  b. When some items are produced at a rate smaller than the plan, the capacity can be allocated to other items.
- The scheduled drumbeat must stay within the bounds on the individual end items and the bounds on aggregate production.
- The planning bill of materials gives the average usage rates for individual parts in the forecasted product mix. It can be used to translate the aggregate rate-based plan into a plan for individual parts. Percentage-wise, the range of variation for individual parts will be larger than that of the aggregate rate-based plan.
- In a build to order environment, order promising should be linked to the rate-based plan. The promised orders should observe the constraints on available capacity in the aggregate rate-based plans, the available capacity in the rate base plans for the individual end items and the availability of critical parts.
- When customers have differing lead time requirements, reserved capacity is built into the plan. This capacity is freed up later for the short lead time customers.

- Integrating batch processes into a pull system requires that these processes give short predictable response times to pull signals from downstream processes. The batch processes must generate smooth demand for the upstream processes. These goals are achieved by implementing the periodic production plan.
- The periodic production plan does the following:
  a. Provides a fixed repetitive cycle of production among the items produced by a batch process.
  b. Gives a fixed time interval between successive batches of any given item.
  c. Schedules more frequent batches of higher demand items and less frequent batches of lower demand items.
  d. Reserves some flex capacity.
  e. Performs as many setups as possible in the available time in excess of run times and flex capacity.
  f. Allows the actual quantity in each batch to be determined by downstream pull signals.

This chapter was contributed by Kenneth C. Gilbert.

10

Effective Deployment of Information Technology

"Technology is so much fun but we can drown in our technology. The fog of information can drive out knowledge."
– Daniel J. Boorstin (1914-2004)

During the Mass Production Age (circa 1880 to 1980), the ability to manage a growing enterprise was a major competitive advantage that defined which enterprises survived and which did not. This was a period in which people perceived a need for strong cost controls, based on detailed information from various departments and business units, to manage business enterprises more effectively. As enterprises grew, so did the task of collecting and analyzing the vast amounts of information needed for controlling costs. This was a period in which demand often exceeded production capacity, and the information needs for managing businesses developed accordingly.

On the other hand, the current stage of supply chain evolution (which we referred to as the Consumer Age in Chapter 1) is characterized by a volatile and competitive environment. The information required to manage complex supply chains in this competitive business environment is different from the information needs of the Mass Production Age for many reasons. Supply chains are larger and more complex than ever before. The old rules that applied in a world where demand outstripped production capacity, and where cost control was the primary focus, are no longer relevant in a consumer-centric world where capacity exceeds demand. Moreover, as we discussed in Chapter 6, the cost world leads to decisions that are often counter to enterprise objectives. Proper application of Information Technology (IT)[1] will provide a critical competitive weapon during the current stage of the supply chain evolution.

The corporate world knows of the need for better information to manage complex supply chains in a competitive business climate. Private and public enterprises, worldwide, have made enormous investments in IT. For example, in 1999 alone, U.S. enterprises invested $373 billion on IT. This investment represented more than 30% of all non-residential fixed assets in the country.[2] Some estimates indicate that until the slump in IT investments that followed the dot-com implosion at the turn of the 21st century, half of all capital investment was related to IT. According to Nicholas G. Carr,[3] even with the recent sluggishness in technology spending, businesses around the world continue to spend well over $2 trillion a year on IT.

IT AND ITS IMPACT

The widely held belief is that IT has the power to initiate a new phase in the management of supply chains. However, overall, the report card on IT adoption to date (selection, installation, and usage) has been disappointing in how the projects have unfolded and in the results delivered. Almost all major IT projects undertaken by enterprises have turned out to be far more expensive than estimated and taken significantly longer to reach their conclusion. Often, the conclusion was a project termination, far short of original plans, simply because time, money, and patience had run out. A recent report by Foster[4] states that about 23% of all IT projects are canceled before completion, and about half of the projects fail in terms of meeting budget, functionality, and schedule. The report states that in terms of the overall success rate in meeting budget, functionality and schedule, only 28% of the projects make the grade.

---

1. We use the term, Information Technology, to collectively denote the tools used for the proper selection, collection, and analysis of key data for decision-making. The tools include both the technology (hardware) that facilitates the collection and exchange of data, as well as software such as Enterprise Resource Planning and Supply Chain Management Systems that use the data.

2. D. W. Jorgensen and K. J. Stroh (2000), "Raising the Speed Limit: U.S. Economic growth in the information age," *Brookings Papers on Economic Activity*, 2000.

3. N. G. Carr (2003), "IT Doesn't Matter," *Harvard Business Review*, June 2003.

4. T. A. Foster (2003), "Making the ROI Case for IT Investment," *http://www.supplychainbrain.com*, May 2003.

The findings in Foster's report echoes those of numerous studies by researchers all over the world, covering public and private enterprises. These studies claim no clear link exists between IT investments and the financial benefits resulting from these investments. The studies found no positive correlation[5] or they found that investment in IT did not bring about productivity growth or yielded only a very low increase in productivity,[6] at least until the mid-1990s.

The "IT Productivity Paradox"

The apparent contradiction, speedier computing and communications along with slower productivity growth, is referred to by economists as the IT productivity paradox. The IT productivity paradox is attributed to Nobel Laureate, Robert Solow, who stated in 1987 that "The computer age can be seen everywhere, except in productivity statistics."[7] Interestingly enough, a *New York Times* report[8] published in March 2000 reported that Solow subsequently retracted his statement in an interview, indicating that "You can now see computers in the productivity statistics."[9] Many proponents of IT point to this interview as proof that Solow's famous IT productivity paradox is dead. Proponents of IT point to technological advances, such as e-mail, eBay, the Internet, and the cell phone, as proof that IT has affected the economy only in a positive way. There continues to be a debate on the IT productivity paradox, with some claiming that it never existed at all.

It is not our intent to adopt either position on this ongoing debate. Regardless of whether the IT productivity paradox remains valid for the U.S. economy as a whole, a noticeable gap remains between the expectations from IT implementations and results delivered for Supply Chain Management (SCM). As far as

5. A. Barua, C. Kriebel, and T. Mukhopadhyay (1995), "Information Technologies and Business Value: An Analytic and Empirical Investigation," *Information Systems Research*, vol 6, pp. 3-23

6. E. Oz (2002), "The 'Vanishing' IT Productivity: A Simple Theory," *Proceedings of the 36th Hawaii International Conference on Systems Sciences*, Hawaii 2002. Also, see, for instance, P. Strassman, "Computers Have Yet to Make Companies More Productive," *Computerworld*, September 15, 1997, and P. Strassman, *The Business Value of Computers*, Information Economics Press, New Canaan.

7. R. Solow (1987), "We'd Better Watch Out," *New York Times Book Review*, July 12, 1987.

8. Solow, quoted in the article by L. Uchitelle, "Productivity Finally Shows the Impact of Computers," *New York Times*, New York, March 12, 2000.

9. Indeed, the productivity figures for 1995- 2003 did show a significant improvement over 1973-1995, although the multifactor productivity figure was still well below the corresponding figure to 1948-1973.

we are concerned, the IT productivity paradox appears to exist in the context of SCM. Thus, when we discuss IT and its impact on productivity, we are concerned with its affect on SCM rather than on the economy.

There is no lack of explanations for the failure of IT projects in delivering promised results. The list of pitfalls offered as explanation for the failures is long and varied:

- There has not been enough time for computers to affect productivity.
- There is no paradox since computer investments over the last 20 years have amounted to a small percentage of GDP.
- The failure of IT projects is the result of our focus on the wrong metrics.
- There is a lack of executive commitment (apparently from the same executives who approved, and are paying, large sums of money to implement IT projects).
- The enterprise was at fault because it did not implement the IT project correctly.
- There is a lack of attention to the cultural/organizational issues necessary to support full-scale implementation.

Other explanations include failure to re-engineer the process, lack of training, lack of discipline, and so on. As with all lists, some truth is in each item in the list but none of them satisfactorily explains why failures have continued after these causes were identified.

So, why is there such a big gap between expectation and reality? People expected that IT was going to deliver breakthrough results and it simply has not. This raises an interesting pair of questions:

- Why have executives continued to invest heavily in IT?
- If IT does help, then why has it been so difficult to see the evidence in productivity?

The first question has a plausible explanation. Executives known for their intelligence and business savvy would not have made the kind of major investments we have seen in the past decade if they did not expect major returns. The only possible explanation is that these executives see a potential in IT that far exceeds the reality of the results delivered thus far. A corollary to this is that something has blocked full capitalization on IT services. What possible factors are inhibiting the maximization of IT?

In his paper on re-engineering, Hammer[10] made the observation that most IT applications were still being used for automation of existing methods of work. It should come as no surprise that the initial design and use of computer systems was to automate and improve the manual systems already in use. Computers were used to do the same tasks that were being done before, but they could do them faster and with fewer errors. However, the continued focus on automating existing practices explains why the productivity paradox has persisted because it has masked the true power of the computer and IT in general.

To use an analogy, if automobiles had been used exactly as horse-drawn carriages were, namely, if they had continued to operate exactly as before, using the same dirt routes, then nothing much would have changed. That is, people would have predetermined you can only travel 50 miles a day and would have planned on doing no more. Perhaps they would have traveled a bit faster and had more time at their rest stops, but otherwise everything would have remained more or less as it was. To take full advantage of the new technology (the automobile), the infrastructure changed. Roads and highways were constructed and support systems such as gas stations were set up. Most importantly, the new technology and the resulting infrastructure gave rise to new applications that would otherwise not have been feasible. For example, the concept of overnight delivery would not have been possible without the infrastructure that grew to support the automobile.

The majority of ERP software system implementations were failed attempts to reengineer the business. Inevitably, these attempts resulted in simply automating existing processes. All of the existing planning, reporting and control procedures were incorporated into the existing system. One of the major contributors to the long and complex nature of IT projects was that each project required an inordinate amount of time to modify the procured software to enable the enterprise's unique policies (or, more appropriately, characteristic policies that were purely an accident of that enterprise's history).

That consulting organizations were eager to charge for all the man-hours required to customize each implementation added more incentive to maintain existing and outdated policies and practices. A sinister side-effect, pointed out by Goldratt, et al., in

---

10. M. Hammer (1990), "Reengineering Work: Don't Automate, Obliterate," *Harvard Business Review*, July-August 1990, pp. 104-112

the book, *Necessary but not Sufficient*,[11] is that such a practice tended to make software packages more complex. Today, ERP systems are so complex that replacing an existing version with a newer version can be as intensive an undertaking as the original implementation.

ERP SOFTWARE SYSTEMS

The initial use of computers in business enterprises was for administrative functions such as accounting. The computers automated the work done by clerks and made it possible to perform financial analyses easily and quickly. The subsequent evolution of IT took two distinct forms: the capability to organize and retrieve information and the capability to perform complex calculations rapidly. ERP systems are the direct result of the first development while SCM software systems were the result of the second development. Consider first ERP systems.

ERP was the poster child for the IT age and the emergence of the fully integrated and fully synchronized enterprise. The value of ERP systems lies in the data they organize and make available to everyone in the enterprise. The ERP system evolved from its predecessors, the Materials Requirement Planning and Manufacturing Resources Planning (MRP and MRP II) systems that we briefly discussed in Chapter 8. MRP and MRP II systems were primarily and incorrectly(as indicated in Chapter 8) used for scheduling manufacturing activities. They were not linked to the company's financial systems and not linked to the company's sales and order management system. ERP systems evolved from a need to provide a more fully integrated system that linked all of these major systems together. ERP is defined in the American Production & Inventory Control Society (APICS) dictionary in two ways:[12]

- An accounting-oriented information system for identifying and planning the enterprise-wide resources needed to take, make, ship, and account for customer orders. An ERP system differs from the typical MRP II system in technical requirements such as the graphical user interface (GUIs), relational database, use of fourth generation language, and computer-aided software engineering tools in development, client/server architecture, and open system portability.

---

11. E. M. Goldratt, E. Schragenheim and C. A. Patak. *Necessary But Not Sufficient: A theory Of Constraints Novel*, North River Press, 2000.
12. APICS Dictionary, 8th and 10th editions.

- More generally, a method for the effective planning and control of all resources needed to take, make, ship and account for customer orders in a manufacturing, distribution, or service company.

Several factors about these definitions are noteworthy. First, the focus of the information was on the Finance function and not the Operations function. These systems were primarily sold to CFOs and CIOs as a tool for automating and integrating cost and other financial information that was dispersed previously, in a redundant and error-prone fashion, across a myriad of different electronic and manual systems. They were sold as a way to reduce the total investment in IT by eliminating costs involved in maintaining and integrating different systems. Furthermore, the widespread fear of an impeding Y2K disaster with older legacy systems contributed to the quick adoption of ERP systems in the 1990s by many large and small enterprises.

The second noteworthy factor in the APICS definitions is the reference to an enterprise-wide scope of the ERP system. A goal of ERP systems is to integrate the information needs of all departments and functions into a single database that can serve the different departments' particular needs. The objective is that when a salesperson enters a customer order (or the customer does so via the Internet), all parties involved in the take, make, ship, and account functions can see this order. They can make complementary plans to ensure this order can be fulfilled profitably.

The third element is the reliance on technology to enable the system and to make the use of the system easier. Though GUIs and relational databases have made the systems user friendly, the sheer scope and objectives of ERP systems made them complex. ERP aims at streamlining the data needs of different departments, each with their own unique data and system needs, by combining their programs and data requirements into a single, integrated database. The intent is to allow the various departments to share information and communicate with each other easily. Building a single database that serves the needs of people in finance as well as people in manufacturing, procurement, and human resources is, however, a major undertaking. Figure 10.1 captures the vast increase in scope from the MRP system to the ERP system.

Figure 10-1.The Explosive Growth in Scope from MRP to ERP Systems

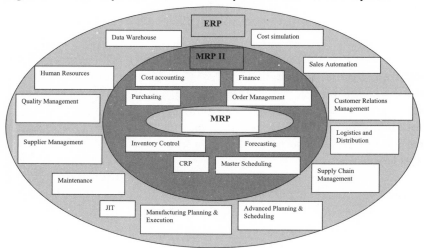

Failure rates of ERP systems run as high as 70%. That is, 70% of ERP implementations have failed to deliver the expected payoff at the individual level, the department level, or the enterprise level. The failure of ERP to deliver significant bottom-line value to enterprises can be attributed to the following:

- ERP systems share the limitations of MRP systems in that they are not capable of modeling the complex flows that characterize enterprises, much less, supply chains. Although they have the ability to capture all of the cost components, they are rudimentary in terms of their ability to model the actual flow and the complex characteristics of these flows.
- While the intent of ERP was to integrate the system so all departments and functions work together optimally, the implementations typically automated existing processes and systems. These processes and systems were, however, designed to help each of the departments/functions manage their local areas efficiently, in accordance with traditional performance metrics.
- The amount of effort required to build, run and maintain a system that captures all of the relevant data was high.

The core reason for the stark failure of ERP systems has been the failure of all segments of the business management community (managers, consultants, and academics) to understand or exploit the true capability of these systems and then ask how organizational processes should be designed to take advantage of the new capabilities. ERP failed to deliver real value because nobody effectively allowed it to deliver real value. All that ERP systems have been used for is consolidation of data and automation of clerical tasks to eliminate redundant work (like re-entering information) and thereby avoiding errors rather than using it to integrate systems. Computers were used to do the same tasks that were being done before, but they could do them faster and with fewer errors. However, the volume of data required to make simple computations was quite large. Moreover, no sophisticated method existed for capturing and maintaining data accurately, so the integrity of the data maintained by these systems began to be questioned. For instance, data accuracy remains a major obstacle in MRP systems and is one of the reasons most often cited for the dismal track record of MRP systems. The same holds true for ERP system implementations in general.

Move from ERP to SCM software systems

Another major weakness of MRP/ERP systems was their inability to assess the impact of any disruption. By design, they were planning systems, not execution systems. If a supplier was late, these systems could only show you a list of the customer orders that were affected. The system could not make any assessment when the order was likely to be shipped, thereby allowing the manufacturer to make alternative arrangements to meet customer demand. For example, perhaps materials could be reallocated from less critical orders to more important ones. Or, the products on order could be replaced with an upgraded model with a negotiated price discount to appease all parties. The MRP/ERP system could not report the effect of the disruption upstream so accommodations could be made and that created additional problems in the production line. SCM software systems arose as a direct result of some of the shortcomings of ERP systems.

SCM SOFTWARE SYSTEMS

Unlike ERP systems, which are transaction systems that do planning, SCM software systems include planning and execution systems. These systems aim at harnessing the computational power of modern computers, particularly their ability to perform complex calculations rapidly. The reasoning was that such computational power would allow for better coordination of supply chain activities.

SCM execution systems are designed to create precise schedules for managing a single factory. The volume of data elements involved, however, makes scheduling a complex task. Even a medium-sized factory involves hundreds, and often thousands, of different parts that are processed across hundreds of machines. Moreover, the routings of these parts can be quite different and the load on the machines different. The problem is further complicated by two additional factors:

- The individual tasks are subject to a high degree of variability. Everything from customer orders to receipt of material from suppliers and processing times at work centers is subject to variability. Any plan created with one set of initial data is quickly made obsolete by these variations. This has resulted in a need to constantly re-plan to accommodate the new conditions. The speed with which systems can create schedules becomes a factor for this endeavor and has been a focus of SCM software systems.

- Characteristics of equipment and processes are often extremely complex and have to be modeled, perhaps crudely, to create a feasible schedule, let alone an optimal one. To use a simple example, consider the process of managing a heat treatment furnace, a fairly common piece of factory equipment. First, the processing time does not change linearly with the number of units. Most furnaces are batch processing resources. That is, a batch is put in and the door is closed for a set amount of time. Furthermore, the furnace has to be set up differently for different parts. The difference may manifest itself as a change in temperature and/or a change in the environment in which the heat treatment takes place. Finally, the time to change the furnace from one setting to another depends on its prior setting. For instance, if the temperature setting changes from 1600°F to 1800°F, it may only take 20 minutes to increase the temperature; but if it changes from 2400°F to 1600°F, you need a much longer cooling time. Thus, the scheduling process for even a simple furnace can create multiple complexities depending on the level of detail desired.

Systems that attempted to create optimal (or even feasible) schedules had to have the logical capability to consider all of the scheduling complexities (due dates for end products requiring these parts, product and component availability, and process characteristics) and had to optimize the plant performance by balancing delivery dates, costs, and inventories. In addition, execution systems had to have the ability to handle unplanned disruptions. Consider, for instance, the reporting and handling of a disruption in the normal operation of a process. The high degree of interactions present in a supply chain, or even within a single factory, means that the impact of disruptions propagates through the entire network. For example, if a machine has a serious breakdown, it will delay the ability to ship customers' orders. What is not so obvious is that it affects the machines that supply parts to it from the upstream stations. These resources do not have to spend valuable time to rush parts that end up waiting for the downstream machine to be restored to working condition.

Issues of data availability and quality, as well as problems of integration with legacy or established ERP systems, have plagued SCM software systems. Data issues fall into two categories: Is the data available? and is the available data of sufficient quality? Since ERP systems have primarily been accounting systems, the data elements that they focus on are different from that needed for effective supply chain planning. For example, the total direct labor time involved in processing a part is of importance to accounting but not the specific machine on which the part is processed nor on the setup times involved at different machines. These two items of information are, however, extremely important for good scheduling. Similarly, for the furnace example discussed above, to generate proper schedules, detailed information has to be maintained on set-up times for different parts, the difference in changeover times for different temperatures, and so on. Such information is rarely available in any computer system.

To summarize the discussion we have had so far, a significant amount of effort has been made towards harnessing the power of IT for better managing supply chains. At the same time, despite the promised benefits of IT, the results have not been commensurate with the trillions of dollars invested. Though a number of reasons have been forwarded to explain the failures, probably the most compelling reason is that the true power of IT has not harnessed because most IT applications that were developed simply sought to automate existing methods of work.

THE TRUE POWER OF IT

For the economy to feel the impact of IT, significant benefits from IT investments have to occur. By significant benefits, we mean breakthrough levels of results and not just incremental results. What, then, are the proper processes to follow so that business enterprises can unleash the true power of IT?

To answer this question, we need to question whether IT is or can be a breakthrough technology. Let us first understand the difference between breakthrough technology and productivity technology. Productivity technology helps people do the tasks they currently do faster and better, i.e., it improves their productivity. The impact of such technology on the enterprise is a function of how many tasks are impacted, and is typically measured in single digit percentages. In contrast, breakthrough technology enables people to do things they could not do before, and it has a dramatic impact on productivity (provided the breakthrough is in the mainstream of the business). Improvements are measured in orders of magnitude. A clear distinction between the two can be seen by an analogy drawn from two everyday applications of technology: The television was breakthrough technology, but the television remote control was productivity technology.

If IT is a breakthrough technology then it should enable enterprises to do things they could not do before and should not simply automate current operations. What is the new capability that IT provides? To answer this question, it is helpful to look at what key business executives felt intuitively about the power of IT. Jack Welch, CEO of General Electric from 1980 to 2001 and ranked among the top business leaders of the 20th century, commented that he wanted to "get the soul of a small company into this sometimes muscle-bound large company body."[13] The power of IT lies in its ability to enable this transformation. Properly used, IT has the power to provide large enterprises the ability to react quickly to market and demand changes, and communicate decisions clearly and quickly to every employee affected by the decision.

Large Company Body and Small Company Soul

To understand the true capability of IT and the impact that it can have, let us examine the phrases *a small company soul* and *large company body*. Small companies (by implication, entrepreneurial enterprises) have several desirable characteristics:

- Ability to react to market and demand changes.
- Decision making is fast. This is characteristic of entrepreneur intuition and simple organization structures.

---

13. J. Welch (1999), "Letter to Shareholders," in GE-Annual Report 1999.

- Decisions are made with awareness of their impact on the enterprise. This is a clear advantage with smaller enterprises.
- Decisions are made with everyone's input and can be communicated quickly throughout the enterprise.
- Prudent risks are taken routinely. This is the characteristic most associated with entrepreneurial spirit and is also a characteristic of size since it is simpler for a small company to evaluate risks as well as to bring everyone on board.

In this context, small company soul means to be able to grasp the full picture, assess alternatives, and take quick action. Large companies (that is, bureaucratic enterprises) also have several desirable characteristics:

- They enjoy economies of scale in production and in distribution/sales. Large enterprises clearly have the cost advantages afforded to large volume production/procurement.
- They have a large pool of resources, capital and labor, at their disposal. These resources can be freed of current tasks or committed to new initiatives.
- They can afford a greater level of risk than small enterprises. What may appear to be an impossible level of investment risk for a small enterprise may well be a small percentage of a large enterprise's investment. This is not to mean that the total percentage of their capital that can be put at risk is different. Rather, it means that the same capital represents vastly different percentages of available capital to these two enterprises.

In a large enterprise, procedures and policies are put in place to ensure that information from different parts of the enterprise is evaluated in the context of the entire enterprise and that the right decisions are taken and communicated to all parties concerned for appropriate action. In creating this bureaucracy, speed was knowingly sacrificed.

An unintended consequence of bureaucracies was that adherence to the procedures and policies became the *de facto* modus operandi. Ineffective policies continued to rule and creativity was stifled. Absent such a bureaucracy, it is possible that a large company could have all its advantages yet still have a small company soul. The singular capability that IT provides is to eliminate the requirements for a bureaucracy that is slow and tenaciously dependent on the procedures it created. IT can make the necessary information available to all managers in the enterprise, to help them assess the full picture. The computational and simulation capabilities of IT can help managers evaluate consequences of different options available and choose the best alternative for the enterprise. IT can quickly communicate to each employee what he or she needs to do to support the new decision. The employees, in turn, can see the information that necessitated this change and its impact on the entire enterprise. Effectively deployed and used, IT can enable a large enterprise to have a small company soul.

But here lies the catch: Effective usage and deployment are not easy tasks. The post-World War II era witnessed the emergence of organizational structures that managed large complex enterprises by breaking them into smaller units that were further divided into sub-units. Policies, procedures, and performance metrics were devised on the belief that optimizing these sub-units, in isolation, would result in global optimization. It came as no surprise that enterprises developed functional silos, as the champions of reengineering[14] pointed out. But this was as it was supposed to be: The alternative of maintaining a global, enterprise-level perspective as the enterprise grew larger would have been seemingly impossible in those days without the ability that IT provides.

To illustrate the enormity of attempting to maintain a global perspective, consider a simple production decision on the shop floor: what job to process next at a given work center. The correct decision, based on enterprise-level impact, would require that we understand the relationship between jobs at this work-center and customer orders. Moreover, relationships between the jobs at this work-center and other components that are required to fill customer orders would have to be evaluated. The impact on purchasing and on other customer orders that may require this resource (or other shared resources) or on the production of components used for these orders would have to be evaluated. All of these evaluations would have to be made even as customer orders continue to arrive.

The collection of all this data, let alone the integration and interpretation required to make a decision, would have been inconceivable prior to the emergence of IT. Therefore, enterprises focused on the local information that could be easily gathered and focused on using it to make the best local decision possible. However, now that IT is available to enterprises, the issue shifts from whether it is possible to maintain a global perspective to how to best maintain a global perspective.

---

14. M. Hammer and J. Champy (1994), *Reengineering The Corporation*, Harperbusiness, 1994.

HOW TO EXPLOIT IT FOR SUPPLY CHAIN MANAGEMENT

How can IT help enterprises achieve a small company soul? A small company soul effectively means the capability to take decisions from a global (enterprise-level) perspective and do it quickly. This capability requires two elements:

- Availability and access to all relevant data/information
- A clear understanding of how the decisions will affect the global optimum

Both capabilities are present in small enterprises as a direct result of their size and the intuition of the managers. The intuition is a result of their ability to see and experience the impact of decisions on the enterprise, again as a result of the smaller size. An obvious capability that computer systems can provide is making the data, once created, available to everyone instantaneously. This has been the benefit under which most systems have been sold and implemented. However, mere access to information is not enough. In the rush to achieve this capability, an important question was never addressed; What are the rules by which we can achieve global optimization?

The understanding of how to achieve global (enterprise-level) optimization will determine the type of information to be collected. In the first wave of ERP/SCM software applications, it was assumed that the computer would solve the problem if it was fed all available data. The core problem with this assumption was that the understanding of the rules to achieve global optimum, as well as the data deemed relevant for this purpose, was based on the local optimization mindset of the pre-computer era.

One reason for the IT productivity paradox is that enterprises did not redesign their policies and practices to take full advantage of the new capabilities afforded by IT. For instance, with the capabilities afforded by IT, we can track many of the costs, formerly assigned as general overhead according to standard cost accounting, to specific products. Since direct labor has become a steadily decreasing percentage of the total cost while other overhead costs have grown in importance, this improved understanding of costs could be critical. This was the argument made by Johnson and

Kaplan[15] when they introduced the concept of Activity-Based Costing (ABC). As we discussed in Chapter 6, ABC is an allocation methodology and has the same limitations as standard cost accounting in this regard. Yet, Johnson and Kaplan deserve credit for the observation that new capabilities made possible by IT require us to re-examine the basic assumptions of current accounting systems (even management control systems). Understanding the problems inherent in these assumptions allow the use of these new capabilities to design systems free of prior constraints.

Goldratt, et al.,[16] presents an approach to take full advantage of breakthrough technology. The authors suggest that the following questions be answered:

- What is the new capability provided/enabled by this technology?
- What current limitations does this new technology remove?
- What are the new rules needed for full exploitation of this new capability?

While the answers to these questions may appear axiomatic, correctly answering each of them is difficult. Nevertheless, these answers are a necessary condition to realizing the potential of breakthrough technologies and to avoid letting technologies become subservient to current practice and policy. Our job as managers is to rewrite policies and practices to enable the enterprise to flourish rather than enslave new technologies and capabilities to current practice and policy. At the same time, we have to be careful not to let the technology drive the application. We want IT to evolve according to a demand pull philosophy, and not let it evolve based on a technology push approach. We now present a set of answers to the above questions from an IT perspective.

What New Capabilities does IT Provide?

The way IT has been applied to date, especially through SCM software systems, reflects an emphasis on its ability to handle the inherent dynamics of real-world business through constant re-computations rather than deciding on a given course of action and staying the course. In other words, the implicit assumption is that if the computer has all the information, then it can respond to

---

15. T. H. Johnson and R. S. Kaplan, *Relevance Lost: The rise and fall of cost accounting.* Harvard Business School Press, 1987.

16. E. M. Goldratt, E. Schragenheim and C. A. Patak. *Necessary But Not Sufficient: A theory Of Constraints Novel,* North River Press, 2000.

every change in the environment to keep plans current and optimal with an instantaneous adjustment to change. There are two problems with this approach. To date, no one has succeeded in making all of the data (or even the vast majority of the data) available or accurate. Of far greater significance is that continuous re-optimization is the same as no optimization at all.

Optimal performance requires that the created plan has the robustness to accommodate deviations (dynamic changes in the environment are known to occur) and that these plans are then executed and not continuously re-formulated. To use a simple analogy from sports, teams win by disciplined execution of a well-conceived game plan to handle different play strategies of the opposing team (meaning the plan recognizes the opponents and range of plays they can execute). Rarely do teams win by winging it, or by constantly adjusting to minor feints by the opposing team. IT has the capability to provide a better visibility on customer plans, allowing the enterprise to adjust to changing demand patterns if necessary. In turn, the enterprise can communicate its own production plans to upstream suppliers who can plan their schedules accordingly.

What Current Limitations does IT Remove?

Some of us are probably familiar with variations of the following phrase: "The only actions possible are local, but the only results that count are global." When the capability of IT is seen as the ability to help make local decisions in concert with the global good, it is easy to see the current limitation that it removes. IT can help maintain the connection between local actions and enterprise-level results. It can make available, to every person in the enterprise, all the information they need and in a format that will allow these persons to complete their job. In other words, IT can help every person identify what to do and then assist in effective task execution.

Consider, for instance, order management. In today's complex supply networks, an order placed with one supplier may require products from multiple suppliers to be consolidated and shipped to the customer. A desktop computer system ordered from Dell will require the computer from Dell, the monitor from Sony, and an audio system from Harman Kardon, and the printer to be shipped to arrive at the customer's door as a single delivery.[17] IT

17. Dell is increasingly consolidating the delivery of these different items by having its suppliers co-located near its assembly plants.

allows consolidated and distributed order management and provides visible order tracking across complicated distribution networks. IT systems can improve visibility and leverage event management and analysis tools for increased effectiveness.

Within the enterprise, as orders are received, IT provides customer service representatives (who receive orders) the ability to provide delivery dates for each order. With proper application of IT, the customer service representatives have visibility on inventory levels and on the production plans and internal delivery schedules. Therefore, IT assists due-date promises that can be met more reliably and cost effectively without having to resort to overtime or having to carry large just-in-case inventory.

What are the New Rules Needed for Full Exploitation of IT Capability?

In answering this critical question, keep the following points in mind:

- A current set of rules and procedures exists. Any rule or procedure that can undermine the capabilities of IT will continue to be in effect if left untouched.
- The term *rule* is used in the broad context of management control systems. It is not limited to the detailed procedures for planning and control. Of particular importance is the metrics used to evaluate the performance of an enterprise's sub-units. Often, these metrics serve to evaluate the performance of individual managers. As a result, they have a profound impact on the managers' decision-making processes. These metrics, anchored as they are in the locally centric cost accounting system, must be replaced with a better alternative. Otherwise, these old metrics will make it impossible to implement new rules and procedures. Indirectly, the old metrics will block the realization of significant benefits.

We illustrate the meaning and ramification of these points with a single application. We have chosen use demand management/ forecasting as an example because it is widely used in industrial enterprises and is one of the most widely implemented modules of SCM software systems. The traditional view of IT is that the computer can use sophisticated forecasting algorithms and improve forecasting accuracy. The simple reality is that computers can merely perform a vast number of computations quickly. Table 10.1 contrasts the traditional manner in which this application has been designed and applied with the manner in which it ought to be designed and applied.

Table 10-1. Traditional and Proposed Rules for IT in Demand Forecasting

TRADITIONAL RULE	PROPOSED RULE
Forecasting can be done precisely to be used as a reliable predictor of demand. Use the daily/weekly forecast numbers generated by the computer as the new demand and regenerate the entire operations plan. Production, procurement, etc., should all be continuously adjusted to new forecast demand. The effectiveness of the forecasting system is measured by evaluating the forecast accuracy.	Some amount of uncertainty is associated with every forecast. Build operations plans robust to this degree of uncertainty. Use the computer to evaluate any sales of item(s) drifting beyond these limits and to identify any trends in these changes. In other words, do not change anything until a trend is spotted and agreed to by all involved functions. Do not react to change until you know that the change is a reflection of a trend and not part of anticipated variation. *Stable plans that are adjusted only slightly can handle most fluctuations in demand.*

To illustrate the differences in approach between the traditional and proposed rules for demand forecasting, we consider a hypothetical application to a sport such as (American) football. In the context of this sport, forecasting is the ability to predict what offensive plays are most likely to be called by the opposing team in a given situation. If a team operated under the traditional mindset outlined above, then the forecast information would be used to identify the predicted play (based on an algorithmic analysis of all prior plays called in similar situations by this team) and then arrive at the highest probability defensive play that would be effective against the predicted play. The analysis might, for instance, suggest that it will be a simple out pattern with the quarterback throwing to the inside receiver on the right side of the formation, a distance of exactly 8.5 yards from the line of scrimmage and 2.5 yards inside the field of play. Under the traditional mindset, the defense (our team) would commit to this play.

A person familiar with the game of football would immediately see the folly of committing the entire defense to a specific play. Instead, the correct approach, the one that is usually followed would have the defense plan on defending a medium pass play out to the right. The positioning of the players in the defense and how they begin to respond would allow for a certain degree of flexibility, where they only commit after they see how the play begins to develop.

Similarly, the new rules for demand management allow an enterprise to plan its production better in conformance with demand forecasts. With the new approach, we do not commit all our production resources to react to a single point estimate of the demand forecast. As many of us are well aware, the probability that the actual demand would exactly match the demand forecast is practically zero. Instead, we should first obtain a range of values for the demand forecast. If we can discern no upward or downward trend from the previous demands, we do not have to make any significant changes to our production plans. Instead, we wait for the actual demands to materialize and work toward fulfilling that demand using available flex capacity if necessary. At the same time, we will broadcast the range of demand forecasts upstream to our suppliers so they can cope with the possible variation in our customer's demand. If, on the other hand, demand forecasts show a noticeable trend over the long term, we will accordingly take action to ramp up or ramp down the production levels, communicating such actions to our suppliers.

In Chapter 9, we numerically demonstrated how the proposed rules allow us to derive production plans and communicate these plans to our suppliers using the concept of flex fences. With this understanding of rules governing the proper usage of IT, we will discuss the current SCM software systems used to manage industrial enterprises and supply chains.

As observed earlier, the earliest SCM systems were rudimentary Factory Planning systems. From these simple beginnings, SCM software systems evolved rapidly as they sought to apply their core capability (modeling and optimizing complex interconnected networks) to more segments of the industrial enterprise. The first step was to expand Factory Planning systems to include multiple factories: the first supply chain application. When the same part can be processed by a plant in Michigan and another in Mexico (both belonging to the same enterprise), the decision on where to make parts for a specific customer becomes more complex. In addition to capabilities and capacity considerations, transportation costs and production costs will have to be factored. This task taxes the computational capability of computers.

Since Factory Planning systems had first developed this capability, it was natural for these systems to be expanded to cover these internal supply chain issues. However, solution suites offered by SCM software system providers cover an ever-increasing scope of activities. These solution suites cover network design and optimization, order fulfillment management, Vendor Managed Inventory (VMI), Collaborative Planning, Forecasting, and Replenishment (CPFR), logistics management, demand management and order management, in addition to the basic manufacturing planning and scheduling solutions. Specifically, these systems are designed to help users as follows:

Supply Chain Network Design: These systems allow the user to design the most cost-effective manufacturing, transportation, and distribution network. Typically based on some underlying mathematical optimization algorithms, these systems can factor global transportation and distribution costs as well as production costs and sourcing costs.

Demand Management: These systems were initially based on some simple forecasting algorithms. Since then, they have evolved, beyond using historical data, to accommodate events such as promotions. They can adaptively manage volatile demand, help steer demand among products, and can optimize price lists and customer quotes to maximize margins and/or gain market share.

Order Management: In today's complex supply networks, an order placed with one supplier may require products from multiple suppliers to be consolidated and shipped to the customer. For example, as discussed earlier, a desktop computer system ordered from Dell will require the computer from Dell, the monitor from Sony, and an audio system from a different supplier. All must arrive at the customer's site as a single delivery. These systems allow consolidated and distributed order management and provide visible order tracking across complicated distribution networks. Such systems can improve visibility and leverage event management and analysis tools for increased effectiveness.

Demand Fulfillment: Demand fulfillment systems account for activities that relate to delivering the product/service once the customer order has been received. These systems help enterprises provide more accurate estimates of delivery dates to customers while maintaining lower inventories, and help the user make due-date promises that can be profitably met. They identify the level of inventories required at different locations to minimize costs and even allow enterprises to offer customers alternative products or options when the originally requested product is not available.

VMI and CPFR: These techniques exploit the Internet to allow for suppliers to proactively engage prime customers in developing forecasts and in confirming short-term production and delivery commitments. They also allow the supplier to take full control of replenishing inventory.

Global Logistics Management: In a global supply network, logistics and transportation play a vital role. Complexities include choosing modes of transportation, paying duties and taxes, optimizing the loading of trucks or containers, choosing specific routes, and so on. Information about the material's location and its arrival date at the customer's location is critical and web services are used extensively to enable real-time intelligent information sharing.

The logical next step was to expand the scope of SCM software systems to manage true supply chains, namely all of the different enterprises that were involved in the activities that designed, sold, created, delivered, and serviced the products and services purchased by the end consumer. In addition to the technical challenges of how systems from different enterprises could be linked together, many strategic and tactical issues had to be resolved. (Many of them have not yet been addressed.) The measured expansion into the multi-enterprise supply chain system was propelled forward by the explosive growth of the Internet towards the late 1990s.

THE INTERNET AND THE FUTURE OF SCM SOFTWARE SYSTEMS

The Internet boom in the late 1990s distorted the normal methodical growth of business management systems. The use of the Internet was growing at a phenomenal rate and technology enterprises saw a tremendous opportunity with a small time window. Many software enterprises jumped in amidst a barrage of hype, the likes of which had not been seen before. The promises made by these enterprises, and the customer expectations created, were so far ahead of actual system capabilities, that the products were nicknamed Vaporware (as opposed to software). Equally caught up in the hype were the customers for these products.

Though no one could clearly articulate how the Internet could be used to create a new business model, many enterprises were evolving and investing in e-business strategies. Staggering amounts of money were spent on e-business models. Of course, with the burst of the dot-com bubble in the year 2000 came the harsh realization that reality was far different from the exaggerated expectations. The reality was that the technology was in its early stages of development. Furthermore, the new business model had not recognized another reality: that the goal of a business was to make money and that meant acquiring and servicing customers while keeping investments and costs under control.

Even though the dot-com implosion disrupted the progress of SCM software systems, such disruptions have occurred before at different times. From the steam engine to the automobile, every technological revolution has gone through downturns. However, such downturns do not spell doom. They inevitably set the stage for long periods of growth.

Today, a few years removed from the Internet hysteria, there is a better comprehension of the true capabilities of the Internet and how it can help businesses operate more effectively. Internet technology is new and to get the most out of it, we need to answer the same technology application questions discussed earlier. For instance, we had drawn on an analogy between IT and the automobile to highlight that if technology is used merely to extend existing practices, then nothing would have changed.

To draw another analogy with the automobile, as the price of the automobile plummeted from $1,000 down to $260 following the innovations of Henry Ford, the number of automobiles sold tripled during the period from 1919 to 1929. The Great Depression that followed the crash of 1929 set back the automobile industry, but the setback was short. Continuing low prices pushed sales of automobiles up well before the Great Depression was over. And, as we noted in Chapter 5, during the golden era of U.S. industry following World War II until the 1960s, sales of automobiles rose even more, propelled by manufacturing efficiencies and plenty of cheap oil. Similarly, the setback to the growth of SCM software systems will be short. Robert Hof observes that "tech still has its equivalent of cheap oil: the relentless march of greater chip density at lower costs, plus even faster jumps in storage capacity and the accelerating spread of fast Net access."[18]

---

18. R. D. Hof (2003), "Why Tech Will Bloom Again," *Business Week*, August 25, 2003.

The tech industry has the ability to recharge the economy. IT contributes up to 10% of the gross domestic product and accounts for nearly 50% of all capital spending.[19] Many opportunities for IT continue to open up. According to Michael Dell, there is no shortage of new ideas and new technology applications; and technology is showing no signs of maturing whatsoever. However, at the same time, to take advantage of these opportunities, the enterprises involved in IT need to reinvent themselves rapidly. Specifically, as far as SCM software systems are concerned, they must harness the power of IT to enable Jack Welch's vision of a large company body with a small company soul. That is a tough challenge.

The Challenges and Opportunities for IT

Even as SCM software systems become increasingly sophisticated and more in step with the needs of the lean supply chain, the enterprises that use these systems face another kind of challenge. To paraphrase the words of Bill Gates, given that everybody has always had access to the same technology, is it possible for an enterprise to gain any competitive advantage through effective deployment of IT for managing supply chains? This is a similar question to one we posed in Chapter 4, where we discussed how an enterprise can increase its competitive advantage over another enterprise that is making the same products. Robert Benson, Professor of Information Management at Washington University in St. Louis states, "It's what the organization does to use information and reach out to customers that matters. The purpose of IT is to change the behavior of its users to better achieve their business objectives."[20]

Enterprises like Dell, Inc., and Wal-Mart have successfully exploited IT to better leverage their competitive position in the marketplace. Enterprises have also effectively deployed IT to gain a competitive advantage. However, ensuring that the resulting software system does not automate existing practices is a challenging task. This is a challenge made more complex because many of these enterprises have to contend with legacy systems (a problem that Dell did not have to contend with).

---

19. Ibid.
20. B. Violino (1997), "ROI," *Information Week,* June 30, 1997.

Many enterprises have spent large amounts of money installing ERP systems. Though ERP systems may find many proponents who argue that these systems have helped enterprises manage supply chains more effectively, they may have, in fact, hindered the successful adoption of effective supply chain practices in the past. ERP systems were originally intended to integrate different software systems and present a unified database to the enterprise. Just as with MRP systems, ERP systems are more geared for planning and reporting functions. (As with MRP, the P in ERP stands for Planning.) By themselves, they do not have the ability to model and optimize complex interconnected networks, but instead rely on bolt-on SCM applications for that purpose. Integrating such bolt-on applications is difficult unless the same ERP vendor is providing the bolt-ons; and even there the integration to existing legacy systems may not be successful. There is also the challenge of a lack of commitment (from the same executives who approved, and paid out, large sums of money for ERP installations).

Interestingly enough, the big ERP vendors, including SAP, PeopleSoft (with J.D. Edwards) and Oracle are promoting SCM software systems. This is an encouraging trend because these vendors are in a better position to provide the correct bolt-on SCM applications to ERP. That ERP vendors have moved into SCM appears to have legitimized the market.[21] Another encouraging development is that, whereas planning systems enjoyed more attention in the past, the trend is to focus more on execution systems rather than planning systems.[22]

Exploiting New Technologies

Perhaps the most newsworthy technology trend is the proliferation of wireless supply chain technologies, notably Radio Frequency Identification (RFID) systems. RFID has the potential to revolutionize the management of supply chains. We discussed this technology briefly in Chapter 3, and identified a number of potential applications for RFID in SCM. RFID is still in its infancy and has not really been proven to work successfully in this arena. Therefore, we can only make an educated guess at its potential use for applications other than product tracking. Indeed, at present most of the RFID initiatives in SCM focus on tracking, namely,

---

21.   D. Navas, reporting on an interview with L. Lapide, Vice-President of Supply Chain Management, AMR Research, in "Supply Chain Software Stands Tough," *Supply Chain Systems Magazine*, December 2003.

22.   D. Navas, *Supply Chain Systems Magazine*, December 2003, *http://www.scs-mag.com/*.

affixing RFID tags to pallets and cartons exchanged between business entities so that the pallets and cartons can be tracked more accurately. In particular, the application for RFID that immediately comes to mind is one that simply replaces the UPC bar code.

However, applications such as product tracking are just the tip of the iceberg. To revisit an analogy presented earlier, we had portrayed the situation where the automobile replaced the horse carriage as a means of transportation. At that time, no one could have predicted the infrastructure that would grow to support the automobile, and the different industries it would spawn. Although originally conceived for transporting people, the automobile industry has, in fact, generated a number of new industries and businesses such as trucking, overnight delivery, gas stations, and so on.

Similarly, RFID has the potential to completely change current logistics and SCM practices. The future of SCM depends greatly on how enterprises manage information on the movement, storage and delivery of goods and services. Large enterprises have attempted to manage this information by investing in new information systems, typically ERP systems. As discussed earlier, these systems often fail to live up to expectations. One of the reasons for their poor performance is because the quantity and location information for products is not captured (because it requires sophisticated tracking software) or the information is captured and stored in incompatible systems at different enterprises in the supply chain. Hence, when products are transferred from one enterprise in the supply chain to another, the accompanying information is not easily captured.

RFID technology, on the other hand, facilitates easy data capture at the source. Furthermore, since all the product data and product history can be stored on the chip, the issue of interfacing or transferring information between incompatible systems does not arise. A properly designed RFID system has the potential to solve many of the problems in tracking and managing information that are now typically handled using cumbersome, less manageable ERP systems.

This is just one example of the many possible enhancements that RFID can bring to logistics and SCM. Other potential RFID applications were briefly discussed in Chapter 3. Needless to say, a full exploitation of RFID would mean that enterprises would have to redesign their policies and practices to take full advantage of this technology.

Supply Chains and Third-Party Information Logistics[23]

Managing information is a difficult task. In fact, it is becoming increasingly difficult to process information from the sea of data that we have at our disposal. However, as supply chains become more competitive, information management could well become a competitive weapon. Michael Dell stated the success of Dell, Inc., is due to its ability to "substitute information for inventory." So, as supply chains continue to become leaner, the larger enterprises orchestrating the supply chain will demand that the suppliers build a significant amount of IT content around their products to support optimal planning and scheduling processes. No longer will IT be a "good to have" capability for suppliers. Rather, IT will become a "must have" capability that suppliers should possess, to compete for their customer's approval.

The growing demand on IT places the suppliers in an awkward situation where their survival depends on their IT capabilities, but they find themselves unequal to this task. These developments may force a supplier to invest in IT on a regular basis and maintain a highly skilled IT workforce, a requirement that small and medium-sized enterprises will find difficult. This is a proverbial double-edged sword: in order to survive these suppliers must invest in IT, but they do not have the capital to invest in IT. What is a supplier to do?

This is a situation similar to one that suppliers faced in the 1980s and 1990s. As the environment became more competitive, there was tremendous pressure on suppliers to deliver products faster, cheaper, and in smaller lot sizes. Many small and medium-sized enterprises were unable to cope with these pressures because they did not have the resources to invest in a logistics infrastructure. Their main focus was on manufacturing a product. The burden of coordinating the logistics activities thus fell on the willing shoulders of third-party logistics providers (3PLs), resulting in a tremendous growth in demand for 3PL services. A survey of CEOs of Fortune 500 enterprises, conducted in 2002 by Accenture and Northeastern University, revealed that over 90% of the respondents are using the services of one or more 3PL providers.[24]

---

23. The material in this section is based on a paper by M. Singh and M.M. Srinivasan (2004), "Suppliers and the Information Technology Challenge: Is Third Party Information Logistics the Solution?" submitted for publication.

24. R. Lieb and M. Hickey, "The Use of Third Party Logistics by Large American Manufacturers, the 2002 Survey," *http://www.accenture.com/*.

As a part of the 2002 survey, respondents were asked to comment on utilizing the services of 3PL enterprises to help with other functions, specifically, IT-related tasks. Although some respondents indicated interest in using 3PLs for some IT-related services, there was a general lack of faith in the 3PL's abilities to handle these services. The desired IT-related capabilities were fourfold: 1) the ability to operate the enterprise's IT system, 2) the ability to integrate the enterprise's system with systems of other suppliers, 3) the ability to design systems for the enterprise, and 4) the ability to implement new systems.

These IT requirements cannot be readily met by 3PLs. If 3PLs choose to undertake the task of supporting IT demands, then they will have to manage multiple objectives and shift their focus from their core competency, namely, logistics. The management of IT and logistics differ in nature and require completely different workforce skill sets. Furthermore, the complexity of the IT solution, which would require the 3PLs to support different supply networks with various execution and planning software, and process workflows, is truly daunting. One only needs to recall the well-documented struggles of industry leaders in implementing and maintaining ERP systems to realize the challenges that 3PLs will face addressing these needs.

Enter the information logistics service provider, more precisely, the third-party information logistics (3PIL) provider. As we envision it, the 3PIL will be an enterprise focused on building sophisticated IT skills that can be subcontracted by suppliers to meet any supply chain's information needs quickly, without significant investment on the part of the suppliers. This proposed approach closely mirrors the use of 3PLs to manage logistics. Information Logistics will, instead, deal with the management of "moving" data and information, providing "the right *information* at the right time and right place."

In the future, 3PILs can meet a significant need of both suppliers and buyers. From the suppliers' point of view the most desirable scenario would be the availability of a 3PIL service provider that will link their planning systems and databases to various buyers quickly and effectively without any significant changes to their systems and with minimal maintenance. Such a service will allow the suppliers to maintain their focus on manufacturing and invest in IT capabilities at their own pace. At the same time, the buyers would like a similar ability to select a supplier and instruct the 3PIL service provider to ensure a smooth information flow that will meet their planning and procurement requirements quickly and easily.

No doubt, these requirements translate into an extensive set of business process and technical requirements for the 3PIL service provider. To be able to hook up to any software system seamlessly in a short amount of time is a challenging task. The 3PIL service provider must have a very reliable and robust system that can connect with a variety of software and hardware, and be able to support diverse workflows. In addition, the systems will be subject to constant upgrades. The 3PIL service provider must therefore have skills in the area of process, hardware, and software management, implementation, and maintenance. A new type of business enterprise will be required – *a pure information play.*

CONCLUSIONS

Despite the dot-com implosion that took place at the turn of the 21st century, enterprises recognize the power of the Internet to capture and distribute information, as well as to facilitate demand management, procurement, manufacturing and sales. Fundamentally, the growth of the Internet essentially enables very close connectivity between enterprises. In effect, all enterprises that make up the supply chain can have access to all required information as if they were a single enterprise. Whether we are exploiting the computer as a source of information or we are exploiting the computer as a sophisticated decision tool, the entire supply chain can be treated as an integrated and interdependent entity. IT provides the ability to *compress time, eliminate errors and synchronize decisions across the supply chain by an order of magnitude.*

Just as systems thinking has been the most important enabler of SCM systems from a philosophical/conceptual point of view, so too has the Internet become the most important enabler from a technology-related point of view, since it opens up radically new ways to operate supply chains. Many people think that IT will usher in a new era of SCM.

- Effectively deployed and used, IT has the power to allow a large enterprise to have a "small company soul." It can enable quick decision making, decisions that are made with a better awareness of their global affect on the supply chain.

- However, to date, the true power of IT has not been effectively exploited. The true power of IT is that it can help maintain the connection between local actions and enterprise level results. IT has the capability to provide the enterprise with a better visibility on customer plans, allowing the enterprise to better adjust to changing demand patterns *if necessary.*
- To exploit the true power of IT, enterprises have to redesign their policies and practices to take full advantage of the new capabilities afforded by IT. For instance, enterprises like Dell and Wal-Mart have successfully exploited IT to better leverage their position in the marketplace.
- The challenge is to ensure that IT is not used to merely automate existing practices.
- We must also take care not to let technology drive the process. We do not want to get into a technology-push situation. Rather, we need to exploit the true power of IT through a demand-pull.

GLOSSARY

3PL Third-Party Logistics Provider. A third party logistics provider provides a number of logistics services such as warehousing, order management, distribution and transport services to its customer, using its own assets and resources.

4PL Fourth-Party Logistics Provider. The fourth-party logistics provider is a logistics integrator that manages the 3PLs in addition to a set of other supply chain-related activities such as IT management. It is an additional service layer between the 3PL and its customer (the enterprise) that tries to manages these activities without necessarily carrying any assets.

5-S A term used to denote a systematic process for organizing the workplace based on five simple, yet powerful, activities: *Seiri* (tidiness), *Seiton* (organization), *Seiso* (cleanliness), *Seiketsu* (neatness), and *Shitsuke* (discipline).

ABC Activity-Based Costing is a management accounting system that assigns costs to products based on the amount of resources used to produce a product.

Arm's-Length Relationship A relationship that is developed when the enterprise out-sources non-core activities to "specialist" suppliers. With this arrangement, the buyer shops for the best prices, each time he/she needs to procure parts or raw materials.

ATP Available To Promise. ATP is the uncommitted portion of an enterprise's inventory or planned production. It is a tool used to promise a delivery schedule to the customer.

Balanced Scorecard A management tool used to translate an enterprise's vision into a set of performance indicators based on four perspectives: Financial, Customer, Internal Business, and Innovation & Learning.

BTO Build-To-Order. The term, Build-To-Order, is used to denote a process that produces custom products to meet a customer's specific needs. Contrast with Build-To-Stock.

BTS Build-To-Stock. The term used to denote a process that builds products in anticipation of future demand.

Bullwhip Effect A term used to denote a phenomenon wherein minor fluctuations in demand at the end-user or the retail level results in huge variation in demand at upstream enterprises in the supply chain.

Business Ecosystem The business ecosystem for an enterprise comprises of the enterprise itself, its customers and suppliers, as well as the competitors, the owners/stakeholders, government agencies, and other regulatory bodies that impact the operations of the enterprise. This definition essentially enlarges the domain of a supply chain, to include the competitors, stakeholders, regulators and the complementors. See related definition for **Complementors**.

Complementors Complementors are business entities that facilitate the development and growth of the enterprise's supply chain even though they do not directly participate in the product that the supply chain deals in. For example, an enterprise that makes sneakers is a complementor to an enterprise making golf clubs.

ConWIP Constant Work-In-Process. A scheduling methodology that controls the release of work into the system. ConWIP is so called because it maintains the work-in-process inventory in the system at a constant level. It is a pull system in the sense that when a job exits the system, a pull signal is sent by the last operation to trigger the release of a new job into the system.

CPFR Collaborative Forecasting, Purchasing and Replenishment. This is a business practice aimed at reducing inventory costs while improving product availability across the supply chain. It is a way to synchronize the demand forecasts that the buyer and the supplier have for the product, to arrive at a single consensus forecast.

Cross Docking A process by which products are moved from one enterprise to another enterprise through an intermediate warehouse, without storing the products in the warehouse for more than a few hours.

DBR Drum-Buffer-Rope. DBR is a scheduling methodology that controls the release of work into the system. It is a pull system in the sense that when a job is completed by the constraint resource, it sends a pull signal to trigger the release of a new job into the system.

DPI Design Process Integration. This is a term we use to refer to the set of activities and processes that integrate Design with Marketing and Operations

EDI Electronic Data Interchange. EDI refers to the transmission of information between computers using highly standardized electronic versions of common business documents.

EOQ Economic Order Quantity. EOQ is the order quantity that minimizes the sum of the ordering cost and the cost of holding inventory.

ERP Enterprise Resource Planning. ERP grew out of **MRP** and **MRP II** systems to integrate quality, human resources, Information Technology (IT) and payroll systems within the MRP framework (see related definitions for **MRP** and **MRP II**). It is thus an information system that integrates all manufacturing and related applications for the enterprise.

GAAP Generally Accepted Accounting Principles. GAAP refers to a widely accepted set of rules, conventions, standards, and procedures for reporting financial information, as established by the Financial Accounting Standards Board

Heijunka *Heijunka* is a term used to denote the distribution of the production of different product types evenly over the course of an hour, day, week, or month. *Heijunka* is used to avoid excessive batching of product types and volume fluctuations, especially at the operation that drives the entire production process. (This is the **pacemaker** process – see related definition for **pacemaker** process.)

Heijunka **box** The *Heijunka* box is a visual scheduling mechanism that enables the *heijunka* technique by dividing up the scheduled production into discrete time intervals. Within each time interval, the work is allocated using a **mixed-model schedule** (see related definition for **mixed-model schedule**) to level the production as much as possible.

I The abbreviation used by the Theory of Constraints for its definition of Inventory. The Theory of Constraints definition for Inventory includes capital assets in addition to raw material, work-in-process and finished goods inventory.

IT Information Technology. We use the term, Information Technology, to collectively denote the tools used for the proper selection, collection, and analysis of key data for decision-making. The tools include both the technology (hardware) that facilitates the collection and exchange of data, as well as software such as **Enterprise Resource Planning and Supply Chain Management (Software) Systems** that use the data.

JIT Just-In-Time. JIT is based on the production methods employed by the Japanese automakers to make quality products in the quantity needed, when asked for. It also relates to the concept of reducing inventories by working closely with suppliers to co-ordinate delivery of materials just before their use in the manufacturing or supply process.

Kaikaku *Kaikaku* refers to the radical redesign of processes and methods geared for achieving breakthroughs in performance and growth. Some enterprises refer to this as a *kaizen* blitz.

Kaizen Taken from the Japanese words *kai* (change) and *zen* (good), it is used to denote the philosophy of promoting continual improvement across all areas of the enterprise.

Kanban A *kanban* is usually a printed card that is used to control production or supply of parts. It contains specific information such as a part name, description and quantity to be produced or supplied. It facilitates an orderly flow of material through the entire supply, production, and distribution processes.

Lead time The lead time is defined as the elapsed time from the moment an order is received until the time the order is executed and delivered correctly to the customer.

LTL Less-Than-Truckload. LTL refers to a shipment that would not, by itself, fill the truck to capacity by weight or by volume.

Mixed-Model Scheduling Mixed-model scheduling is an approach used to level-load the operators and manage them much more effectively. The goal is to produce every product as quickly as possible, at the same rate at which customer demands are made. The Japanese manufacturers otherwise refer to this concept as *heijunka* .

MRO Maintenance, Repair & Overhaul.

MRP Materials Requirement Planning. The MRP system is a computer-based information system that is used as a scheduling tool to determine a) when to order material, and b) how much material to order. MRP is deployed as a push system that computes schedules, based on demand forecasts, for what should be started (pushed) into the line. With these production schedules, the MRP system is also used to determine when the orders for raw materials and component parts must be released based on the procurement lead times.

MRP II Manufacturing Resources Planning. MRPII is a method for the effective planning of all the resources within a manufacturing enterprise. In addition to the outputs produced by MRP systems, MRP II is designed to support capacity requirements planning, cash flow planning and manpower planning. It also has a simulation capability to answer "what-if" questions.

Muda *Muda* is the Japanese word for "wastefulness," namely, any activity that consumes resources but creates no value for the customer. The elimination of *muda* is central to lean thinking.

NPD New Product Development. NPD refers to the various steps involved in creating new products for the enterprise to either grow its business, or to replace those among its products that are in the final ("decline") stage of their life-cycle. The NPD process steps include concept generation, product and marketing plan creation/evaluation, and the eventual commercialization of the new product.

OE The abbreviation used by the Theory of Constraints for its definition of Operating Expense. The Theory of Constraints definition for Operating Expense includes all non-variable expenses that are incurred regardless of the level of output.

OEM Original Equipment Manufacturer.

One-Piece Flow One-piece flow refers to the concept of moving products one unit at a time between workstations. This is in contrast to the other extreme where we might process an entire batch of parts at a workstation before moving the batch to the next downstream workstation. The goal of one-piece flow is to reduce the lead time or equivalently reduce work-in-process inventory in the system.

OPT Optimized Production Technology. OPT is a computer-based management system used for production planning and scheduling to maximize revenue. It is based on identifying the bottleneck, scheduling the bottleneck resources so that they are utilized as productively as possible, and then scheduling other non-bottleneck resources to support the bottleneck.

Order Qualifier Order qualifiers are attributes that a product must have for the customer to even consider purchasing it from you. Order qualifiers and order winners determine the competitive priorities your enterprise or supply chain should focus on.

Order Winner Order winners are the attributes the product must possess if you want to get the customer's order. Order qualifiers and order winners determine the competitive priorities your enterprise or supply chain should focus on.

Pacemaker A basic concept of lean manufacturing is to schedule operations at only one point in the overall process. This point is referred to as the pacemaker because it drives the work for all the other operations in the process. It smoothes the flow of products through the process by pulling work from upstream operations and flowing product to the customer through the subsequent operations.

Poka yoke Literally meaning "fool-proof," *poka yoke* or mistake-proofing is aimed at developing techniques to prevent defects from being passed on to the next process.

POS Point-Of-Sale.

Productivity Frontier The productivity frontier represents, at any given time, the sum of all existing best practices. It represents the maximum value that an enterprise can create in the delivery of a product or service, using the best available technologies, skills, and management techniques.

RAP Raw As Possible. A very important principle that should drive the design of new products and services. It provides a very convenient way to meet customer demand quickly, without storing a lot of finished goods inventory. At the same time, it delays committing raw material, labor, and fixed assets to make products based on forecasts, in anticipation of future demand. We want to work with a relatively small number of standard products ("modules") internally in semi-finished or finished form to configure a large variety of end products.

Rate-Based Planning A central concept of pull is that there should be one operation (the **pacemaker**) that serves as the drumbeat for the upstream processes and the external suppliers. Rate-based planning provides the means for setting the rate of the drumbeat in future periods; at the same time, it provides a certain amount of flexibility to accommodate rate changes. In the short term the drumbeat process maintains a constant production rate and constant product mix. This creates a flat demand pattern for the internal upstream processes and the external suppliers.

RFID Systems Radio Frequency Identification Systems.

S-DBR Simplified Drum-Buffer-Rope.

SG&A expenses Selling General & Administrative expenses. SG&A expenses consist of the combined payroll costs (salaries, commissions, and travel expenses of employees other than those directly involved in manufacturing), and advertising expenses incurred by the enterprise.

Spaghetti Diagram This relates to a map of the path taken by a product as it travels in the system. It is so named because the product's route in a traditionally managed system usually resembles a bowl of spaghetti.

Standard Work Standard work relates to a clear specification how tasks should be performed. The specification includes the *takt* time, the precise sequence in which the tasks should be executed, and the standard amount of work-in-process that needs to be maintained to perform the tasks.

Strategic Flexibility Strategic flexibility is the ability of an enterprise to periodically reinvent its existing processes and systems to respond to changing customer preferences. Strategic flexibility also allows the enterprise to reposition itself when the competitive environment changes.

T The abbreviation used by the Theory of Constraints (TOC) for its definition of Throughput. TOC defines Throughput as the rate at which the system generates money through sales. This definition is different from the standard definition of throughput (units per hour) in two ways. The TOC definition translates the units sold into monetary terms so that the sale of all the different types of products can be represented with a single number. Second, the TOC definition only considers the products that have been actually sold (and paid for by the customer), not items produced.

Takt time This is a measure of customer demand, and is the drumbeat of a lean production system. *Takt* time is determined by dividing the available time by the number of units demanded by the customer in that same time interval. It is used to size the production facility's capacity appropriately so as to meet the customer demand.

TPM Total Productive Maintenance. TPM is a term used to denote the systematic execution of maintenance by all employees. The goal of a TPM program is to significantly increase productive capacity and decrease process variation while, at the same time, increasing employee morale and job satisfaction.

TQM Total Quality Management. TQM is a management approach to long-term success through customer satisfaction. It is based on the participation of all members of an enterprise to improve the processes, products and the culture in their workplace.

UPC Universal Product Code. The Universal Product Code is a bar code found on almost any package sold. It is a 12-digit numeric code used to uniquely identify many different suppliers of many different items that travel through the supply chain.

Vertical Integration A term used to denote the situation where the enterprise produces the required inputs to the process in-house and maintains control over the buying and sourcing units.

Virtual Integration A virtually integrated system seeks to link the core competencies of individual enterprises through various mechanisms such as cost-sharing and risk-sharing agreements so that these enterprises can act as a larger, single entity.

VMI Vendor Managed Inventory; a process in which the supplier is responsible for replenishing the customer's shelves.

Water Spider Water spiders are workers who service work locations with parts or materials. They replenish materials at point of use and deliver finished products to their destination. The water spiders enable the operators to focus their attention on operations that "add value."

WIP Work-In-Process.

INDEX